For
Mike + L
+ ?
# 22 ?

Thank you for ~~being~~
being my Friend.
Walk With God.

With
Love
Charlie
1-28-98

A WAR STILL RAGING

One Man's Struggle for Life in Vietnam and Beyond

Charles D. Matherson

(with C. Stephen Byrum)

Milton Publishing Company, Inc.
Post Office Box 6
Lookout Mountain, Tennessee 37350

ISBN 1-879908-01-8

Acknowledgements

It is difficult to say "Thank You" and to express appreciation adequately in words. I am the kind of person who likes to **show** others how I feel. Nevertheless, this book has become an important part of my life, and like most parts of my life, it would not have been possible without the help and support of other people who mean a great deal to me.

My deepest appreciation must go to my family. I want this book to be dedicated to my wife and closest friend for twenty-two years, Sandy. This dedication extends to our four sons, Doug, Brad, Justin, and Joshua; and, without doubt, to my Mother.

Sandy's strength, love, faith, and friendship have carried me through many painful, confusing, and depressed days. Her comfort and love have helped make me the man I am today. Without Sandy I do not think that I could have continued in this life.

She lived her marriage vows when others would have run away. I realize there were days, weeks, and months when I put her through a world of worry and hurt. For this I am truly sorry. I love Sandy and thank God for blessing me with a wife and friend as loyal as she has been.

Doug, Brad, Justin, and Josh have seen more than any young persons should ever see. The pain of war, the deformed and devastated men and women in the VA facilities where they visited me, are just small pieces of the actual face of war that have been forced on their young lives. I pray that they and others like them will never see battle. I know I have not been a perfect father. I thank my sons for loving me as I went through the pain of my battle injuries, my depression and unpredictable mood swings. The get-well cards they made pulled me through many rough days. Their love gave me strength to fight away the depression and pain. I love each of them in a very special way.

My Mother's love, faith, strength, determination, and courage have been the most loving gift a Mother could give to her child. My Mother gave me all this and more. For the days, weeks, and months she spent caring for me at Walter Reed, for all of her prayers, I will always love her.

I wish to extend a special thanks to my friend Steve Byrum. Without his help, it would have been impossible for me to tell this story. His writing skill and knowledge of human life have made my dream of writing this book a reality. The following people took time to read the original manuscript. Their encouragement and feedback was a great help.

Mrs. Kay Amantea	Mrs. Becky Hansard
Mrs. Patricia Borkoski	Frank Martin
Dr. John Trimpey	Mr. and Mrs. Steve Hedrick
Richard Lockery	Mr. and Mrs. Bill Whittaker
Mrs. Juanita Ward	Mrs. Judy Boles
Mrs. Paula Gardner	Melody Martin
Dennis Stitely	Mr. and Mrs. Bill Spencer

To those other wives, children, families, and friends of Vietnam-era veterans, and to those who have loved and helped veterans of all of our nation's wars, I thank you for supporting your loved ones, especially during those times in which their wars have still raged into your lives. And I thank those doctors and nurses who worked with me and others like me, and who had such a large part in saving our lives.

Above all, I thank God that my life has been spared. Each day is a gift to me, an opportunity to live, a chance to yet put Vietnam and all that followed one more day behind me and to get on to making something that is much better.

Chattanooga, Tennessee   Charles D. Matherson
Summer, 1991   "Chuck"

To Sandy

A War Still Raging
(One Man's Struggle for Life in Vietnam and Beyond)

Soldiers usually don't go off to war. Rather, it is young men in the flower of youth who leave homes and families and enter fields of conflict having little idea of what they may meet there. If they are lucky enough to come home, they return as soldiers—members of a unique brotherhood that stretches across the ages among those who have looked death squarely in the face, have the physical and mental scars to prove it, and yet have survived.

These young men always take something of their homes and families with them to the battlefield. The uniqueness of their backgrounds colors everything they think, everything they feel, everything they do. And, inevitably, they bring something of the battlefield back with them when they return. The experience there follows them—marks the very fabric of their being—for the rest of their existence. It is always there—like a shadow demanding that some light of insight or explanation be thrown on it, yet somehow it is aloof and even immune to that light. It is always there—like a relentless, confusing puzzle demanding sorting, yet with each level that is resolved another deeper level is unveiled. It is always there—like a vague demon who speaks a foreign tongue, yet a demon that cries out for clarification, articulation, exorcism.

In chronicles of war the battlefield is the centerpiece. But, like a staged performance, there is both a background and a future for the actors. Beyond the parameters of the curtain's rise and fall on the events of that centerpiece, there are moments of preparation and aftermath. These moments give the centerpiece its keenest focus.

To chronicle a man's life in the midst of battle in Vietnam is not enough. It is all a half-truth without exploring what he brought there, what he took away with him, and what remains long after the jungle has absorbed the sounds of conflict and the smell of dying.

I met Chuck Matherson in the early fall of 1987. He was a large man in his early forties—like myself—but there was still the distinct carriage of youth. Our ages and our mutually distinctive accents betrayed a common heritage; we were both of that group sometimes called "sons of the South." Somehow or other I have come to make it a practice of catching people's eyes and letting my judgments about them begin from that point. It's hard to let go of Chuck Matherson's eyes. Part of it is the color; beyond that there is a look of some old pain and probably some pain that is pretty new, a look of someone who is searching partly for a place to hide but even more simply for a place, and some odd mixture of both fear and determination. All of this was couched in a tentative smile, but a real smile that had long since lost any implication of pretext or pretense. Later, I would see that smile broaden in an uproar of laughter and become warped in the devastation of the deepest grief and unpurged guilt.

Some of my colleagues had sent Chuck to me. They had gotten to know him, had heard his story, and felt that it needed to be told. One was a veteran Navy pilot and the other a veteran of another sort—a 60s war protester and objector of the most outspoken type. In their own ways, each was still trying to work his way through the "Vietnam experience." They were both convinced that Chuck's story could speak to the divergent spectrum marked by their personal lives and containing, in their strong opinion, most of the young adults in the United States today. I was something of the "campus writer;" maybe I could give Chuck some advice.

What they didn't know was that across the past decade I had been caught up in my own sorting process as it related to Vietnam. I had not gone; my high marks in college and graduate school had insured a certain and comfortable II-S deferment. My academic setting had continuously reinforced what I still think were very justifiable anti-war feelings. A couple of times I had marched in protest. I liked Eugene McCarthy. I voted for George McGovern. I want to make one disclaimer: even in those times of protest and engagement with what I thought was a negative system, I clearly drew a hard line between "anti-war" and "anti-soldier"—I always had best friends who were in Vietnam and in no way were my negative feelings ever directed at them.

Vietnam always haunted me. My friend Leo Smith had been one of three men to walk out of a firefight where most of an entire company had been overrun and destroyed; he was given most of the medals for heroism that the army bestowed. My friend Bobby Cagle had to kick a North Vietnamese soldier to death to keep from being killed himself; he was a prisoner for a while and then came home with malaria. My friend Freddy Sherlin was killed; his mother has his medals and a neatly folded flag that fills only a fraction of an empty space that is still in her home.

Somehow, though I knew on an intellectual level that the war was "wrong," and I was glad that I did not go, there was a part of me that felt that if Leo and Bobby and Freddy—and many others—went that I should have as well. I learned later of "survivor's guilt" and wondered if there was some kind of "never went guilt." I read the Vietnam stories and saw the Vietnam movies, but still there was an unsatisfied lack of completion.

When Chuck Matherson showed up in my office, my first thought was not about helping this guy—who seemed totally serious about the project of telling his story—but how the telling of his story, and my writing it down, might help me. Maybe this could be my part in the sorting out of Vietnam. Maybe this could be some way to work off some of the debt that I felt to the Freddy Sherlins who had given their lives in a vainglorious cause that should not have been allowed to detract in any way from their own valor and glory.

To be honest, I didn't have a great deal of optimism about much coming of Chuck Matherson's initial visit. There had been countless times in which people had come to me about writing a book, only to be quickly dulled in their enthusiasms by the hard discipline that writing becomes. I spoke discouragingly about the time that would be involved in the kind of project which he was envisioning; that we would be working hours on end over a year or more just to get everything down. I set up a time for us to meet again, and basically felt that I had probably seen the last of this warrior, this "vet" from that continuously familiar group that time insists on not passing by.

Nothing could have been further from the case. Not only was he right there at the appointed time the next week, but across the succeeding ten months we spent up to six or eight hours together every week. It was gut wrenching at times for him. It played on every emotion he had and touched most of mine. If it was a cleansing and purging time for him, it was for me as well. We may have been coming from opposite ends of a spectrum about Vietnam, but the result was the same. Those who have seen Chuck's story have also sensed a similar cleansing, purging, and sorting out of this dogged "Vietnam experience."

The result of our months of work is a story which, to me, gives a striking and even startling insight into human existence. It is not just a war story, a slice of dramatic gore from a Hollywoodish battlefield. Nor is it the drug-crazed and foul-mouthed stereotype and caricature of a person shoved off by war into a mentally deficient post-war existence. Rather, this is a story of a boy-become-man, a coming-of-age story lived out in the rage of a war that still goes on for Chuck Matherson and many others like him.

We had one working principle as Chuck's story was put into writing: there would be absolutely no "poetic license," no sensationalizing for effect, and no composite events or characters. Everything in this story, for better and for worse, is exactly as it happened to the most obsessively careful degree that is possible. There is the beautiful and the ugly—there is the real.

This story works because of Chuck's telling and not because of my writing. I have written Chuck's story because he simply did not see himself as a "writer" when we started this project. It is amazing how much his writing skills have improved in his two years of college. It is a great benefit, however, of this story that Chuck's educated, cognitive powers are only now beginning to develop. He brought to the project a superb memory for even the smallest details. His memories are like a photograph that has feeling, sight, sound, and smell. Had Chuck been more strongly writing oriented, I believe that a great deal of this moving story would have been lost.

Because of this story, I am able to see the soldier of Vietnam as a real human being. I understand more than I ever have about what it means to go to war—and—to come back. Our two years of work have not simply been a passive engagement with a random collection of remembrances from a man's life. This story has caused me to touch base with the deepest levels of my own existence; I am better because Chuck Matherson has told his story. I'm sure that he feels that he is as well.

As long as Vietnam hangs back there somewhere like a skeleton in our cultural closet, Chuck Matherson's story will be valuable. It will make a difference for everyone who needs to read it. This is not a hope; it is an absolute certainty.

C. Stephen Byrum
Chattanooga, Tennessee
Summer, 1991

Glimpses

It's all glimpses. Random photographs fallen out of life's box on a rough, uneven floor. No organizing principle. Pieces of some kind of puzzle, and I'm looking for the corners that can start me on the way to building some kind of frame. I've tried for twenty years, but I can't put it down and walk away.

CAN THO (The Mekong Delta) 1968—They almost overran us. Tet. They got to the edge of the runway. I don't know what happened to the people in the outer bunkers. Artillery hit them first, then the rush of screaming shadow men like ants running through a fire. There were flares and noise everywhere, all night.

By daylight, it had all calmed down. They were still out there in the smoke and undergrowth, but someone had gotten a couple of gunships airborne and they were cutting the tree lines to shreds. The smoke was so dense that the copter blades looked like beaters stirring through the thick batter of one of Momma's Christmas cakes. The heat, the smell, the smoke—everything just stuck to you like a goulish shield. We saw it on each other and in our fear looked away. This was no day for eye contact.

Straight out in front of where this other guy and I—I never knew him—had established a makeshift bunker in the panic were fifteen or twenty Vietcong bodies. We crept out there in the smoke. Most of them were dead from the head wounds inflicted by the grazing fire of our M-60. All of them had been wounded and bandaged from sometime before their death, but they had kept coming. Black shorts, barefooted, no shirts. Their skin was like elephant hide.

In most of their clinched hands were American hand grenades with the detonating pins still in place. Within seconds, they would have been close enough to hurl them at us. The mud slime had dried on their stiff, dead remains and turned everything a dense, pale blue. It was like they were packaged, dressed in an envelope, but with no forwarding address—no place to go.

We took the bodies and rammed them head first into the mud in front of us. They sunk into the ground, chest deep and, after a while, we had a human fence. If their friends came again, maybe they would run into this and turn to the side or turn back; maybe they wouldn't get to us.

I looked out at all we had created, a nightmare somehow conceived to save life. I remembered all the ways, sunk into the marrow of my bones, I had been taught to respect the dead. But now, all of that had to be pushed into the background. What else went with it? Now all that mattered was maybe—just maybe—getting the enemy to pause for a second. Let them stop long enough to look at what we had done to their brothers and friends. In that moment, we might gain the advantage that would save our lives. But what if they didn't think about brothers and friends?

MY CANH 2 (The Highlands) 1966—It wasn't a high hill, just enough so you could look down where we had been, where the trap had been, where Rick had died and all the others. As I had made it back through all the death, I knew if anyone was left they would try to get to that hill. Some sergeant took the three Vietnamese civilians I had found out there—and saved—and told me to take the M-60 and protect that spot on the side of the hill against anything that came. He left. Except for believing that there were other Americans out there with me in the dark, I was by myself. More by myself than I guess I ever had been in all of my life.

The walls of napalm came and it was quiet for a while. Then, the moaning and crying started. All night long. I heard them dying, crying for their mothers, crying for God. It crossed my mind that here was the most macho fighting force in the entire United States Army, and these men-of-men were crying for their mothers. But that was what I wanted to do. I didn't want to die. I wanted my mother—not like a baby does, but like a boy who is afraid does. There was a total feeling of helplessness.

I stayed like the sergeant said. There was nothing else to do. That was "the valley of the shadow of death" the country preachers had talked about back in the Carolinas of my childhood. I don't know what happened to Rick—to any of them. I had hidden his dead body in a bomb crater. Maybe it's still there.

MURFREESBORO, TENNESSEE (VA Hospital) 1989—This used to be a military mental hospital; now anyone can come. Maybe they've quit being able to determine if we're sick or hurt or just crazy. On the other hand, it's gotten to where it's hard for me to tell much difference between the patients, who are supposed to be sick, and the ones who are supposed to be well and here to help.

I've been in and out of places like this for two decades now. They all look about the same, but this one is bigger. Some of the corridors must go on for miles.

When I got to feeling better, I wanted to walk. I got a wheelchair, just in case I got tired, and started pushing it along the corridor, all shiney and clean and smelling like an overdose of Lysol. After a while I got off into what must have been the psych ward area. Suddenly, the staggering approach of a gigantic black man, eyes glaring, zombie faced, reminded me it was two in the morning and no one was around. Maybe if I didn't make eye contact he would pass on by. Maybe I should act as crazy as he was acting, or maybe if we were both acting crazy it really wasn't an act. While I tried to decide, he evaporated into the dark and was gone.

Then, here came another one—right out of a Stephen King novel—this time white, but still a giant and still with the zombie look on his face and in his walk. I couldn't be lucky two times in a row, and I wasn't. He walked straight to me, taking up more of the hallway in front of me all of the time. Then a voice that echoed with loud uncertainty: "I can't find the fishing hole. Do you know where the fishing hole is?" On nothing more than gut impulse, I stammered back: "Hell, man, I can't even find my helicopter!" He walked away, satisfied that there was no help here.

The guy down the hall has a tiger in his room. He doesn't want to go in. He's already beaten up pretty well on one orderly who has tried to convince him to go on to bed. Finally, they had to strap him down, but someone didn't check his clenched hand. He hid his cigarette lighter and now he has set his bed on fire. The orderly he beat up has run in and pulled him out—saved his life. I'll try to sleep while they put out the fire.

COOPER CITY, FLORIDA 1982—Those damned Seminoles got crazy when they were drunk. We had been out in the Everglades together enough by now that I was accepted. I told them I had always wanted a bleached out alligator skull, not a live gator for God's sake. Maybe they wanted to see me kill it and skin it; we had done about everything else back in the swamps.

They might have been a little out of place in our thoroughly upper-middle class subdivision, but over the past several months as things had come apart, Sandy had gotten accustomed to all kinds of people knocking at our door and looking for me. She hadn't gotten accustomed to four drunk Indians carrying a live alligator and wanting to know if Chuck wanted it in his garage.

Sandy had learned how to shoot a gun, and I had even talked to her about checking out the AR-15 I had bought. My Seminole friends were probably lucky on that day that we hadn't gotten around to that little exercise. By the time she got through telling them what all they could do with that alligator, I expect they didn't think I was the only one crazy in my family. I expect they weren't nearly as drunk any longer either. You could sober up in a hurry if a woman, wild-eyed with fear, stuck an AR-15 in your face and told you to either get out of her yard with your very live alligator or you and the alligator both would be dead and hanging in Chuck's garage.

TUY WAH (The Highlands) 1966—The rice harvest was over now, and it should have been a time for local celebrations and festivals. Instead, the farmers were scared. The North Vietnamese were coming to get food so the war could continue. We were coming to destroy that food supply before it got into enemy hands. For the farmers, it was only a matter of who would come first. This time, we did.

We started burning the rice, and it wasn't long until their houses—it was easier to burn them if we thought of them as "hooches"—were all on fire, too. The rice popped like popcorn when the heat was just right. We stood around and ate it; tasted pretty good.

The people stood around as well and just looked. They made eye contact; in fact, they were unrelenting. Sometimes a guy would throw his rice down and just turn away and walk off. It was like the look they gave was too much! It helped to call them "Gooks," although the "Gooks" were who we were supposed to be fighting. We were supposed to be helping these people. How were we helping if all we did was burn their rice?

Mostly, they didn't look mad. Maybe they were afraid, too. They looked puzzled. I knew what it was like to work in a field all day. I knew what it was like to take great pride in a good harvest, to just look at it and feel a sense of accomplishment in all of the work that had been done. I came to help. This didn't help. I never touched these people, but I was hurting them all the same. They didn't understand. I didn't either.

SOC TRANG (The Delta) 1967— We took the South Vietnamese in on our choppers (helicopters) in the morning. Then we would go back to a distant landing area and wait. We would sleep and play with kids, the same kids whose fathers we had taken off to war. We didn't know much of their language, but the games we played didn't need words. Laughter is universal.

Later in the afternoon the call would come, and we would go back out to bring them home. Sometimes we brought them back alive; at other times, bodies were stacked in the bay of the chopper like firewood. I had learned to treat dead bodies with the greatest respect. It hurt to simply throw these men in on top of each other. It was all undignified, but there was little time for dignity when you had become the target in a field of fire. It wasn't enough for the Vietcong and North Vietnamese to simply kill their southern brothers. They knew we would come for the bodies. It was our "dignified" thing to do. They would try to kill us as well. No time for dignity.

We would land, and there would be the same kids, their mothers, and some odd lot of old people. We lay the bodies out in a neat row beside the roadway and left. As we pulled away, we could see the women and children starting to sort through the dead, looking for people they loved. Finally, if they were unlucky, a husband or father or son would be found. They would howl toward an empty heaven—except for our aircraft—and beat at themselves. Perhaps, they were trying to beat away reality. Then, they would beat at the dead soldiers, as if to give them new life. After a while, they would sink to the ground and lie there with them, exhausted, while some officer stood at a distance and took a body count.

SAIGON (The First Time) 1965—The deuce-and-a-half transport trucks we were being transported across the city in were different from anything I had seen stateside. Along the sides where our backs rested, they had been reinforced with steel plates.

I asked a sergeant who was riding with us why this was the case. He answered, nonchalantly, that the steel helped knock off hand grenades or sniper bullets. I answered: "Wasn't this Saigon? Wasn't this a long way from a war zone? Weren't these our allies?" He just looked off like I was stupid; he had answered this question all that he was going to.

SAIGON (The Second Time) 1967—I had gone up from the Delta to have some stomach pains checked into. Things were slow, so maybe a few days off wouldn't be a bad idea anyway. I slept soundly in the quiet hospital ward; the first real safe sleep and real quiet that I could remember in a long time.

Maybe I was dreaming. Maybe they had given me some strange drug. I was waking to a vision: a beautiful army nurse—an officer—leaning over at the end of my bed, rolling those huge round eyes all over me, sucking on my big toe. I had seen too much to be startled. What was I going to do about this? I didn't know much more about women than I did war. It wasn't a dream.

SOC TRANG (The Delta) 1967—You took care of your equipment first. I took the M-60 off its mount on the side of the chopper and soaked it in the barrel of jet fuel that cleaned the guns so well. After supper, the pieces would be so clean you only had to wipe them dry. I went ahead and reloaded the chopper with ammunition. It had been so "hot" out there on this day that we were nearly out, and I wouldn't have been surprised to have been called back at any time. First things first; taking care of details was part of my reputation and pride.

I went ahead and had supper and went over to the base club. We sat around and swapped war stories and waited for the ground reports to come in. I felt really good about this day. A group of South Vietnamese were being overrun when we got there. We dropped in and out with our gunship and routed the enemy. We chewed at treelines, boats on the shoreline of a small river, and even caught them in open fields as they tried to escape. Great shooting! And while we did our work, there was no telling how many from the outpost had been able to escape into the transport choppers. We had saved lives today. I wanted to be a "savior" more than anything else.

After a while the ground troops came on in. You could tell in a moment something was weighing in the air, something was wrong. One of the guys said, "You know that sanpan your gunships blew the hell out of." The next few words were garbled or my heart was suddenly racing so hard I didn't hear them. Then I heard ". . . nuns and children . . ." I didn't hear anything else. I knew. It was **my** gunship. It was **me**! I walked out into the dark. There has never been dark like that. Its shadow is still there.

****

How the hell can I make sense out of all this? And if I can't, how can my country—how can my own kids? But we've all got to make some kind of sense out of it. We can't let it happen again.

Where do you start?

Maybe at the beginning.

Chapter I

A large part of what I carried with me to Vietnam took shape in the southeast corner of North Carolina, about an hour's driving time north of the South Carolina border, and maybe a little more than that to the Altantic coast. When I look at that section of the world on a map, it seems about as insignificant and unessential as a place can be—almost as unimportant as Southeast Asia. It would be a long time before I would ever hear of Vietnam. People along the Carolina coast didn't know anything much about that part of the world. We were concerned about crops and weather, and later, about pretty girls and fast cars.

I lived in three crossroad towns—Bladenboro, Laurinburg, and Whiteville. Although the towns took up different spaces, they were about alike; to speak of one of them was to describe them all. They were farming communities and mill towns. The first settlers had moved in from the coast and brought with them the genteel manners of their English forebears. They knew farming and how to use the creeks and rivers that flowed toward the coast to power mill wheels. When cotton came to the South they were perfectly situated for the small textile operations that developed across the region.

Some people got rich. They owned large tracts of land or built the mills. In most cases they also operated the general stores and had rental or tenant housing. Most of the people were far from rich. They were workers. Generations within a family might work the same farm or be employed at the same mill. A son would follow a father who had followed his own father. Especially when World War II came and afterwards, there was a lot of work for women. My people were workers. Genteel manners and big-house ways had been lost back along the way.

It would be wrong, however, to paint all of this in bleak and somber images. Too many stereotyped stories of the South have shown the world of my youth to be harsh and terrifying. It just isn't so. Most of the time we were basically happy. Since no one had much, we didn't have a lot to make comparisons. Even those in the wealthy families weren't that wealthy, and my circle of friends always included kids from every level of the community. We didn't think much about rich and poor, and we didn't "judge"

1

people in terms of what they had. It got hot along the border between the Carolinas and everybody had to work hard to make ends meet, but we had more good times than not.

Thinking back about it, I'm sure we must have been a little isolated from the outside world; not any more than ten thousand other little rural hamlets spread out across the heartland of American, but isolated all the same. News leaked in from Washington, New York, and beyond, but we were mostly concerned about who was winning local ballgames, television, and the price of tobacco. We were not what some people wanted to call "backward," but for better and for worse our world-view did not extend much beyond our own county lines and city limits. Our necks were red, but we weren't "rednecks."

That isolation began to end with the "Big" war. The troop trains stopped right in the middle of Bladenboro to take on coal and water. They were carrying troops from Fort Jackson in South Carolina and Fort Gordon in Georgia to Wilmington where they would be shipped out for Europe. The young men would drop sheets of paper with their names and addresses on them, hoping to get letters from home even if those letters were from strangers.

I was born in September of 1945, so I can't remember this. I've heard it told so many times that it feels like I saw it. My mother did, and she still recalls the sad looks of homesickness and loneliness on the faces of the boys on the trains. Two decades later she could easily have seen the same looks on the faces of two of her own sons.

I can remember after the war how the string of cars filled with young veterans brought their families to Myrtle Beach for the new American phenomenon of vacations. We counted cars, watched for license plates from other states, and wondered some about what a real "vacation" would be like. Faces stared out at us as we played and worked along the roadsides. Faces, dulled by hours of staring at one small hamlet and then another, dulled by hours of road dust long before the convenience of air-conditioning, seemed to ask "Who are you?," "Do you have a story?," "What's special about your world?," "Will we ever meet again?" Our stares back asked the same questions of these beach-bound interlopers.

Maybe my world and my story were not unique in any special way, but it has all become unique to me, like other people's worlds have become unique to them. In Vietnam, when I asked what all of the fighting and dying was about, it was images of this place and these people that always came back as the only acceptable explanation for why I was there. It wasn't so much God, it wasn't so much country—that's all too abstract to die for—it was this place and these people.

What was unique was being the sixth of seven children and the complexity of family interactions that were always being generated. What was unique was orienting a large part of life to Bridgers' Trading Company at the corner of Highway 211 and Railroad Street. The Bridgers owned the mill, a lot of land, and operated the main general merchandise store. They issued tokens called "Maggie's Gold"—for Maggie Bridgers—which their employees could use at their store instead of money and were generous in the lines of credit which were extended when money and tokens ran out. Some might have felt that this was a system of control where people ended up "owing their souls to the company store"; for most, it was a set of informal arrangements that allowed life to work more easily most of the time.

On one occasion I slipped off from home with my sister Kay, very much against the instructions of my mother, to get a Coke at Bridgers. I felt very grown up as I marched into the store, surveyed the possibilities of what my token would buy, and then paid for the cool delicacy that had been fished from a red and white container filled with bottles and ice. Out the door I went, confident that I could return as undetected as I had left, only to find my way home blocked by a large, stubborn goat that was roaming loose in the town. The goat wouldn't move and I was afraid, too. It was stymied at this impasse that my mother found me and made me painfully aware that she was to be "minded" without question.

Events like this flesh out time and space. There is no need to compare events of childhood with those of another person to see whose was the best or whose was the most important on some opinionated scale of value. Events like this, and ten thousand others like it, make us unique and make us feel that somehow our space and time must have been among the most special of all. Here are the roots of our valor and honor. Here is what the flag that we follow symbolizes.

This all sounds idyllic. It wasn't. I won't sell the day-to-day happiness of those earliest times short for anything, but it wasn't idyllic. We knew about happiness, but we knew about struggle as well. We knew plenty about struggle, and that's part of the uniqueness, too.

My father died before I was three years old. I have searched my memory for him, but nothing is there except what I have been told. He was a skilled electrician and had gotten probably the best job he had ever had at Laurinburg working for the Laurinburg Oil Company. They processed cottonseed, peanut, and soybean oil, and somehow there has stuck in my mind the savory smell of cured hams, an aroma that surrounded the company plant. It's strange how you could recall an odor but not someone's face.

In a short period of time, my dad was promoted to Night Supervisor and was in charge of all of the plant maintenance during the night shift. There was some sort of breakdown in the equipment that required a large electrical line to be spliced. Knowing as much about electricity as he did, Dad made sure that all the current had been turned off the line. He began the splicing work when suddenly power came back on the line. The force of the voltage tearing through his body blew his shoes off. Some men knocked him loose from the live line with a wooden ladder, but it was too late. There was a sense of mystery that surrounded the accident, but it was never made clear. There was nothing to do to bring him back anyway. He was 36 and my mother with her seven children ranging in age from seven months to twelve years was barely 34.

There is absolutely no way to put into words the strength of character, the stark stamina, the determination, and the power of love that allowed my mother to keep our family in tact. Maybe she just did what she had to do to survive, but plenty of people would have given up, compromised, or simply been crushed under the burden She didn't, and sometimes the only way that I can explain why I didn't die in Vietnam—and beyond—is because something of her blood is flowing through my veins. Maybe even deeper than blood was the daily example of her life that must have formed my character on some vitally necessary level more than anything else in all of my existence.

When word came that my father was dead, she was living in a rental, tract house with nothing more than a few pieces of furniture, the family's clothing, and random personal items. There was no obvious place to turn. Advice was abundant to "give the kids up for adoption," but nothing could have been more offensive to everything she was about as a mother. That advice may have lighted a fire in her that drove her on when life was at its darkest. All that my father left was an insurance policy—it was worth $526.00.

One of the local ministers came to our aid. Although this was well before the time of industrial compensation for job-related accidents in the South, he felt certain that the Laurinburg company would help in some way if my mother asserted herself. She did this with some degree of success. The company provided the finances for the purchase of a $2500 house in Whiteville which had two bedrooms, a dining room, living room, and kitchen. The toilet was outside. Not much for eight people, but at least it was a start. Momma had to repay the company at $50.00 per month. We moved in sometime during August of 1948.

The people from the local churches were always good to my mother and our family. Men of the church picked us up and took us to all of the services. At Christmas time there were always packages of food and small gifts left on our doorstep. Momma made sure that all of us were in church every Sunday. In spite of all that would happen, something of my mother's faith and the faith of the people at that little First Presbyterian Church was always hidden away somewhere deep in my life.

Momma took whatever work was available. Usually this meant seasonal farm labor. She picked strawberries and harvested corn. She spent hours on end working in the tobacco harvests. A typical day started at six in the morning and lasted until nine at night. She would take us younger kids with her, lay us out on a burlap sack near where she worked, and we would sleep and play. The highlight of our day was the food she would fix. She could take a sausage biscuit, fried chicken, or deviled eggs and spread them out like a picnic for a king. Our black playmates were always bargaining for bites of our food; everything except the deviled eggs which somehow they had gotten the impression had come from the devil himself.

My oldest brother, Russell, helped out all that he could. He went to work in the movie theaters in Whiteville when he was 14. At first he cleaned up, but soon was "promoted" to sales at the refreshment counter. Finally, he was responsible for running the movie projector itself. It was no small mark of pride to know that it was your brother who was doing something so important. He was able to bring in $7.00 a week.

Patsy and Ellen, my older sisters, took care of all of the various responsibilities of the home while Momma was working. Their "play" as children ended up being the babysitting that they did for their younger siblings. Soon, they too, would help in the tobacco, handing it to the stringers and helping hang it in the barns to dry. Later, they would have to work themselves while they were in school to help make ends meet. Patsy and Ellen were fun to be around and great protectors as well. They covered up for me and my antics more times than I can ever remember, and on more than one occasion took spankings that were mine. I don't remember as much about Bobby as the others since he had been taken to Virginia to live with my Aunt Margaret and Uncle Herman.

As soon as I was old enough I started doing my part. Somehow, we had the clear idea that in this family everyone had to contribute. It wasn't so much a chore. Mostly it was a deep feeling that you were part of a unit—a special group—in which everyone depended on everyone else. I grew up wanting to pull my part of the load, not being a "slacker" that someone else had to take care of. The first real money I brought home came from selling bags of boiled peanuts. The peanuts were boiled in salted water and then sold for ten cents a bag, three bags for a quarter. As a reward for our efforts, we could eat all of the "pops"—the imperfect, second grade nuts—that we wanted. I still would rather have the "pops" than the regular nuts. Our financial profit was two cents on each bag.

That feeling of "family" would come to follow me in many phases of my life. When my own family was established, it was stronger than ever and there was no limit to what I would do for my wife and children. It would extend into my work experiences and the sense of duty that I felt for the people I worked for. In a powerful sense, "family" penetrated through that group of soldiers that I would fight beside. We would become more than friends or companions caught up in a trying circumstance; we would become "brothers."

In 1953 Momma moved us six miles outside of Whiteville into the country where we became tenant workers on a large farm. Our house was simply too small and the house provided on the farm was at least a little larger. Momma kept the house in town and rented it out. There was a whole new world to experience in the country. I liked to play in the woods, make sassafras tea, and try to catch small rabbits. We would tease large snapping turtles—"cooters"—with sticks and see just how big of limbs that they could snap in two with their powerful jaws. Occasionally, someone would get a toe or finger caught and painful cries of terror would rise from the woods. No turtle ever caught me. We didn't have toys like the kids in town, but a "June Bug" tied to a tobacco string made a suitable substitute.

We helped dig holes in the ground and line them with straw. Then, we would carefully fill the holes with potatoes. These "tater banks" would help provide food throughout the winter. We helped raise pigs to the point that they were little more than tame pets. Then, from a safe distance, we would watch on frosty cold mornings while the adults came with their guns and knives. We knew what was going to happen, were afraid to watch, but couldn't help but watch. The hogs were shot in the heads, their throats were cut, and they were strung up with ropes while all of their blood drained out. Later, they were dipped into boiling water, their hair cleaned from their skin, and the butchering process begun. Little did I know that the deep emotions stirred by death and slaughter would rise in other powerful ways before my life was long removed from these simple moments of childhood.

The best cuts of the meat were hung in a smokehouse to cure in air filled with sweet, salty smells. The lesser pieces were ground and stuffed into casings made from intestines as sausage. We got a good bit of this. Large buckets of lard were divided around among the workers, and whatever was left—parts that I didn't like to even think about—were taken away by the black workers as chitterlings (chittlins). All of this process was like a kind of haunting bad dream that was carefully hidden in some back corner of the mind until someone wanting a last piece of sausage or bacon at a family meal would offer the reminder that we were eating last spring's pet. The strategy usually worked and left me with a strange feeling in the pit of my stomach over the food that I had just eaten.

The blacks who worked on the farms had children who were my playmates. For a very long time we were colorblind. Finally, I learned the word "nigger" and made the mistake of using it in my mother's presence. I will never forget her response. She sent me out of the house immediately to find and bring back a switch.

There was always the warning that "it had better be a good switch." When I returned with the sharp, wiry piece of leafy new growth from a backyard tree, she stripped off the leaf buds and striped the backs of my legs. The shrill of my cry matched the singing of the switch as it cut through the air. I was never to use that term again. Color didn't matter. People were people. You judged people by the kind of job they did, not by their color or where they had to sit in the movie theaters. Other people had feelings just like we did. It was a lesson that I never forgot; it was a lesson that would make a great difference in Vietnam.

My best friend was Buster Carter. His family owned a large construction company, but social distinctions did not make much difference in our part of the world. People respected others for character and effort, so my mother and, in turn, her family may have been short on money but were still respectable people. The Carters treated me like I was one of their own. One year, when scouting had become the major activity for young boys in the community, they bought me scout shoes so that I would not feel out of place in the local troop. I watched television for the first time at the Carters' house.

There was very little that Buster and I wouldn't do. We were experts at knocking down wasp nests. Hornet nests posed a larger challenge, but one that was never avoided. We got into serious trouble when one hornets' nest was brought down too close to a community baseball game. People were getting stung all over the place. I remember that it was the time of flattop haircuts and I must have had a pound of butch wax holding mine straight up. The hornets would buzz around my head, strike at it with their stingers, but never quite be able to get through the wax.

My brother Russell was old enough to drive and managed to get a job as a route man for Pepsi Cola. We were proud to have the large, colorful truck parked at our house in the evenings and over the weekends. We didn't have a car and there were too many of us for relatives to come and take for a drive very often. To ride in a vehicle was a grand adventure. On those occasions when Russell let us ride in his truck, we felt as big as anyone in the whole countryside. But, there was a price to pay. On cold nights when it seemed like the chilling wind was blowing right through our house, we would have to get up, take extra blankets outside, and wrap them around the truck. Any bottles that froze and broke would come out of Russell's pay. Russell never forgot us and the way that we all helped. When he eventually got married and went on to a better job, he and his new wife, Grace, surprised Joe and me with brand new, bright green bicycles for Christmas. They were the most beautiful bicycles I had ever seen.

In 1954 hurricane Hazel bombarded the Carolina coast. We were close enough to the coastal area that the huge storm surrounded where we lived. The winds heaved and roared at the house to the point that I was sure that it would blow away. Huge oak trees big enough that it would take three men to reach around them were uprooted in our front yard. I had never known fear like this. It was the first disruption I had ever felt that Momma couldn't take care of. I cried out for her but the storm raged right on without ceasing. Years later I would hear others cry out for their mothers while a different kind of storm raged around their lives.

In the Fall of 1955 we moved back to Whiteville. Momma had gotten a job at a small loan company, and rental money made it possible for her to enlarge our old house a little. We now had a toilet indoors and there were two more bedrooms.

There was still plenty of mischief for boys to explore in town. My friends and I would make regular raids on Memory's Market. Our raids usually produced a pack or two of cigarettes which we would race to the woods to smoke in their entirety until we were thoroughly sick. One of our friends figured out how to make a low grade of moonshine liquor and again we were thoroughly sick. It is no small wonder that we did not poison ourselves. We continued in scouting, although there were times when the scout oath was altered to say "on my honor I will do my best to take what you give me and steal all the rest." It wasn't meant to be mean. We were basically good kids out having fun. We never hurt anyone, and miraculously as it seems thinking back, none of us ever got hurt.

In grammar school, I didn't do all that well. I was beginning to understand that a lot of other kids had more than I did. They didn't try to make me feel any less, but I felt that way. I compensated by trying to be the class clown. One day I bravely put baby snakes in the teacher's desk. To my surprise even more than the teacher's, they turned out to be baby rattlesnakes. On another occasion, a friend and I fashioned a chocolate candy bar out of Ex-

Lax and presented it to the class bully, our arch enemy, in exchange for his "protection" on that day. A couple of hours after he had dashed down the "candy bar," and right in the middle of class, the bully "exploded" in a moment of embarrassment that he has still probably not lived down. He either never figured out what we had done or was too weak to do anything about it.

Most of my fun-filled innocence of childhood ended when I was in the seventh grade. I took a job at a small drive-in restaurant waiting on cars. I would walk and hitchhike back and forth to work, and when I got there had to dress in a little white jacket. I felt degraded having to serve people that I knew and expected, whether it was true or not, that my appearance was making me the butt of all sorts of unkind jokes. I was beginning to feel that I was missing something.   Noticing the distinction in what I had compared to others was finally becoming a big deal. There was too much that was second-hand, too many "hand-me-downs," nothing new, and somehow I started losing sight of the fact that honorable effort, facing up to the struggles of life, was a lot more important than what a person had. I never quit. With all that was at stake for the family—and with all of the strength of character sunk deep into my bones from my mother's example—quitting was simply never an option. There were days when I would like to have left or changed lives with one of my friends, but those weren't options either. There was one option—work.

Chapter II

An older teenage boy and girl pulled into the Starlight Drive-In. I knew them pretty well. They were from over near Tabor City and were regular customers. Every time they came in, they called for me to take their order. They liked me just like most of the regulars did; we kidded around a lot, and they had even nicknamed me "Bat," making a play on words between my last name, Matherson, and the famous television character of that time who recreated the western legend Bat Masterson.

When I brought the tray of food to the car and hooked it on the window, the boy was in a strange kind of rage, looking at me in a hateful way that I had never seen on his face before. The girl was pushed back on the far side of the front seat where I couldn't see her face at all. She usually sat about as close to him as she could get. He started yelling and cursing at me, and I was too stunned to move or respond.

Suddenly he pulled out a small pistol and aimed it at my stomach. He shouted: "I'm gonna shoot your ass for all of this bad service!" In one quick movement, he cocked the hammer on the gun and shot it point blank into my side.

Burning pain and fear streaked throughout my body and mind. "I'm shot! I'm shot!," I seemed to be yelling to myself inside my head more than to anyone that might be nearby. All the while I could see a look of stark terror rising in the face of the boy with the gun, and he yelled, "It's a blank! A blank!" The girl was somewhere screaming in the background.

It was a blank pistol, but it had been fired at such close range that the fire of the gunpowder and the force of the explosion had burned a hole about the size of a baseball in my white server's jacket, the brand new white shirt that Momma had bought me and that I was wearing for the first time that day, and into my side. My side was scorching in pain from the fire and the specks of powder that filled the wound.

I raced for the bathroom and began to splash water all over the front of my clothes and stomach. The boy raced in behind me halfway crying and apologizing. In the confusion I still had not understood that it was a prank that didn't turn out right; I still thought he was trying to kill me. We struggled and yelled back and

11

forth with the bathroom door surging and slapping to and fro between us until he finally got me calmed down enough to convince me that he had meant no harm.

He started trying to help. All I could say was, "Momma's goin' whip my ass for ruining this shirt." A new shirt didn't come easily in those days. He quickly produced more than enough money to buy a new shirt and crammed it into my pocket. That took care of one pain, but then there was the pain in my side.

The boy started mumbling to himself and halfway to me, something about gun powder and blood poisoning. We had to put something on the wound. We looked around the bathroom and finding nothing headed back toward his car while he yelled over his shoulder, "I've got it. Wait a minute." In a moment he was back with a new bottle of English Leather after shave lotion. With the prospect of blood poisoning echoing back and forth in my mind, anything beat nothing. The strong, sweet smell of the after shave lotion, that I could never have afforded for myself, offset little of the new burning pain that it sent through my side when he poured it on. What an odd smell the fear and gunpowder mixed with English Leather made as it soaked into my skin and rose in the late-night humidity that surrounded us.

By now it was nearly closing time, two o'clock in the morning. I walked home filled with fear that death might claim me while I slept. Morning came and since I wasn't dead, I went on to school. Of all things, in science class the conversation turned to blood poisoning and I couldn't contain one question after another about being shot. Finally, it became clear that there was a problem, and I was sent to the school nurse who heightened my fears by sending me quickly on to the town doctor, Dr. Hoskins. With the highest of humor, he examined my burn and gave me every assurance he was positive I would live.

I went away from the doctor's office that day almost overwhelmed with the feeling that there was more about life that I didn't know than maybe I could ever know. I didn't know the word naive, and I didn't have anyone who could explain to me that every kid in a situation like mine was naive. I knew I wasn't stupid or dumb, but I felt stupid and dumb. Somewhere deep within myself I had a huge curiosity about life. But it wasn't just an ordinary curiosity. Somehow I felt, although I could never have explained it at the time, that if you could ever understand something then you wouldn't have to be afraid of it anymore. If you could understand, you wouldn't be afraid.

Maybe it's just natural for a young teenager to think that he is dumb, to somehow realize that there is a world of things out there that he doesn't know anything about. Maybe it is the time in a person's life when there are a heck of a lot more questions than answers. Maybe that's one reason teenagers feel so clumsy and awkward. I know I did. And I know that I especially felt that way about death and dying. Maybe you just start thinking about death for the first time, and you are afraid of it and curious about it all at the same time. There were a lot of things that were making me curious and afraid—and wanting to understand—about death. Death had confused me when it came for my father. It startled me, inside out, when that gunfire blasted into my side at the drive-in parking lot. I honestly felt like I was going to die, and I knew— more than anything else—I didn't want to die!

When we had lived at Laurinburg, everybody knew what they had in the glass case at the funeral home. Laws wouldn't allow anything like it today, but in rural North Carolina thirty years ago it was a fascination. A circus had come through the region and one of its clowns, a little Italian man, had been killed in a fight. There were no family or no funds for burial. The funeral home had embalmed and mummified the clown and placed him in a standing position in a glass case. It was eerie to stand there and look at him, to summon up the courage to study his face, and to feel—like a kid would—that he was somehow looking back at you.

This whole air of curiosity and fear was heightened by the presence near our hometown of what had become the pretty famous "Maco Light." Legend told of a train that had broken down on the tracks between Wilmington and Atmedelco. The conductor had stood in thick fog on the back of the train waving his lantern as a warning signal to any oncoming trains on the same track. A train had come but did not see the light soon enough to stop. It had struck the conductor and severed his head from his body. The body was found but neither the head nor the lantern had ever been discovered. Obviously, in the legend, a strange light could be seen on some foggy nights moving along near the old rail line; it was the conductor with his lantern looking for his head!

Of course, this story or some variation of it became the ghost story to tell on camping trips or when children gathered around older people on the cool front porches of a summer evening. The only problem was that there were always people coming in from the larger cities nearby, sometimes even from the colleges, who were seriously searching for ghosts and felt that there was some substance to this particular story. Every family had at least one person who had seen the light.

My brother Bobby made friends one summer with a boy who was studying to be a preacher and was financing his education by selling Bible dictionaries in our area while he was out of school. On one particular night which I will never forget, they had been out drinking a little and saw "the light." They parked their car in the woods near the track—something they would have had to be drinking a little to do in the first place—and headed out down the old train tracks looking for the headless conductor. They finally made it out onto one of the many trestled bridges in that particular swampy area when "the light" suddenly became a train bearing down on them. Suddenly sobered by the oncoming train, they raced back across the bridge and had to hurl themselves into the swamp to keep from being run over by the train. Their brush with reality did little to discount in my mind the possibility of the ancient conductor out there somewhere in the swamp looking for his head. Death, fear, and curiosity again were all mixed around in my mind.

Finally, I had my own close call with death, death of the worst sort—drowning. The Carter family had a boat and sometimes we would go fishing up on Lake Waccamaw. In the old Indian stories, Lake Waccamaw had been created by the gods for a beautiful Indian princess. It was dark, clear and cold, spring fed, and was filled with deep holes. Almost every summer word would come that someone had drowned there.

I wasn't a good swimmer, but nobody knew. It was not the kind of secret that a thirteen year old admitted. Sometimes Buster's neighbor would drive the boat out into the lake and we would jump off the side and dog-paddle around; it wasn't exactly swimming but the boat was always close enough to grab hold of just in case you needed it.

On this particular day, Buster and I jumped off the boat into the cold water. No sooner had we surfaced with the shaking yelling brought on by the sudden chill of the water than the neighbor hit the gas on the boat and took off in a swell of laughter across the lake. He had no idea about my lack of swimming ability.

Immediately I panicked and began to yell—well outside of any possibility of his hearing—that I couldn't swim, that I was drowning! I began to thrash with all of my power at the water, but it did no good. I prayed for a bottom to touch but it wasn't there. Buster tried to help but I pulled him under, too. I was gagging, crying, and screaming all at the same time. This was it! It was terrifying!

For some reason the neighbor just happened to look back. Even from a distance he could size up what was happening. He raced the boat back and drug us out of the water just in time. I sank back into the floor of the boat too exhausted and overwhelmed to do anything but tremble. I awakened in the night in panicked nightmares for weeks. I would never completely get over the fear of water that came that day. The swamps of Vietnam and the wide expanse of ocean that we flew over to get there brought back that chilling tremble time and again. I had looked death in the face. We half-laughed to each other about all this the next day, but all three of us knew without question that this had been a "close one."

Not long after this an interesting turn of events took place. I was always looking around for a job. Sure, there was the drive-in, but anything else that could be worked in would help out just that much more. Peacock's Funeral Home in Whiteville got me to start washing their cars. Between the dust of the back-county, North Carolina roads and Peacock's desire to have their clients ride in more luxury than most of them would ever experience under any normal conditions, I stayed pretty busy. After a while, there were other odd jobs that were added on. I would clean up inside the building. Eventually, the cleaning extended to the prep room and its strange array of embalming instruments. The funeral home owners were extremely discrete about bodies, so I was always in the room either just before or just after a body was there.

Here was finally an unsurpassed opportunity for curiosity to be vented. The most I ever did though was to slip a random peek inside the embalming room; I was afraid of being caught. It would not be the last time I would be in this environment. Yet, one very real change did occur as my curiosity was satisfied, as I understood death in a way that accepted it as another part of life; the fears that had been stimulated in me—all the way back to the pistol rammed at my side at the drive-in—seemed to go away. Death was there, as real as the corpses on the table in the prep room, but it wasn't terrifying anymore. It was simply another fact of life.

It seemed always to be important to people who talked to me about Vietnam, from fellow soldiers to Army doctors, to try to understand why I would volunteer to go back for a second tour of duty when I didn't have to. Sometimes people would suggest or even explain that I must have had some sort of death wish. It sounded crazy, or made me think that they thought that I was crazy. I didn't feel crazy. Somehow I simply felt, again maybe in a way that I couldn't exactly explain, that I had sorted death out. I didn't want to die, I could even admit to fearing the pain that might come in death, but there had been a distinct passage that had occurred—from curiosity to understanding to a loss of crippling fear. Maybe I went back, maybe I was able to function in the situations that I fell into, because the obstacle of that handicapping and jeopardizing fear simply was not there—it had been left somewhere among the mummified remains of an Italian clown, the wound of a blank pistol, what was probably swamp gas, and the deep cold of an Indian lake back in North Carolina.

Chapter III

Work interfered with everything. There were, however, simply no other options for me at that time. It was not a matter to be discussed or debated. Momma wasn't being cruel, and we didn't have to have any heartfelt talk about its necessity. It didn't cross my mind to complain. It simply had to be done. Russell had worked, and even Bobby was sending most of his Army money from Korea back home to keep the home going. He sent enough so that my older sister, Kay, could go to business college in Wilmington. He sent Joe and me a beautiful army jacket with bright insignias that even the richer boys envied; I would wear it for now—it would be handed down to Joe later. Russell did his part, Bobby did his, Patsy and Ellen worked at the local drugstore—and now it was my turn—there was just no question about it.

I loved junior varsity football. "Buck" Jolley was our coach. He had been an outstanding player at Wake Forest and was a strict disciplinarian. His philosophy was to be in better shape than your opponents so you could outlast them; for us that meant run, run some more, and run some more. He didn't care to jerk us around on the ballfield or in the school hallway if that was what it took to bring us into line. His toughness and directness appealed to me. It was honest and straightforward. I might not always like it, but I could live with tough anytime if it was honest. I think about what it might have been like to go on in sports, but there just wasn't time.

Across the summer following the ninth grade I had learned to drive behind the wheel of tractors and farm trucks. I had also started noticing girls, and the prospect of dating loomed strongly on the horizon of my life. Every conversation that I seemed to be hearing, from other boys and the men that I worked around, had to do with women. To compare the exploits and adventures that they claimed to be having with what I was experiencing was like comparing day and night. Sure, I smiled and laughed and nodded my head in agreement at all the right places, letting them assume that I was well beyond being a rank amateur when it came to women, but all the time I was painfully aware that I hadn't really even had a date. It never entered my mind that most of what I was hearing was exaggeration and downright lies; I simply felt even more left out and passed over. But, what was there to do?

I was so naive about this whole part of life that my cousin, Ann, before she would arrange what small amount of dating—if you wanted to call it that—that took place over that summer, had to explain the basics of using deodorant. That may seem funny now, but at that time it was part of the most serious and intimidating movement into a new world imaginable.

All of Ann's efforts didn't make much difference in the long run anyway. Again, there just wasn't time. By the time tenth grade started, I was driving but it wasn't a car on a date with a girl. It was a school bus loaded with children. The local school principal "helped us out" by making this new job available.

I was lost in school. First they had held me back. Then they moved me up. I was moved into levels where I didn't know what was going on. The more lost I became, the less interest I had. Sometimes I tried but it didn't do any good. Even being something of the school clown was starting to get old. I didn't get in any more trouble than most kids. Someone had convinced me that the biology teacher, Mr. Powell, couldn't hear very well, especially if you lifted both feet off the ground when you talked. One day he called me down in class for loudly carrying on a conversation in the back of the room; I was totally surprised—my feet were carefully lifted at least a foot off the floor. Maybe he had heard the nickname that we had christened him with—"Herman Hogshit." All in all, I am not painting a portrait of a troubled, badly adjusted youth, simply one who had become isolated in work and didn't know a great deal about either school work or the world I was a part of. Nor was I dumb; I simply hadn't had time to become smart.

Mostly I was tired. And who wouldn't be. Getting up early enough to do a bus route in the morning, carrying the kids home when school was over, having only the short part of what remained of the afternoon to catch a little odd work here and there; and then it was off to the Starlight where midnight-till-two-in-the morning closings were typical. The walk home and falling half-dressed across the bed to sleep all became a blur.

Life was work, school was a necessary interlude between jobs. To top it all, I picked up another job at the local Esso station and commenced that time-honored rite of passage for many boys in the

South, working at a "filling" station. This allowed me to cut back on the number of jobs as the station compensated for what I was doing at the funeral home and the drive-in.

Here, it seemed that the world came and went in random cycles of sameness and enlightenment. There were always things going on that hadn't changed in decades; there were always things happening that were new. Above all, there was an odd collection of mentors ready to usher yet another gullible kid toward adulthood.

The men that hung out around the service station seemed to know more about life than all the preachers and teachers that I had ever known. Their stories were endless and told with an animation that would make any stage actor proud. They might be backward and on some lower rung of society as far as the general community was concerned, but the greasy, ill-kept environment of the station was their stage. They were experts on politics, religion, athletics, and—above all—women. I learned about cars but a whole lot more about all the rest. I learned, above all, how much I had left to experience in this world.

I remember the weekend chicken bogs—a combination of chicken and rice in a large, black cast iron pot—that they would cook. It was spicy, hot and had a smell that set your taste buds to aching. There were more "oohs" and "aahs" over these old boys' cooking than any compliments that I had heard at a church social. There were also the discreet trips to the back of the station where someone had stashed an ample supply of moonshine liquor. I never remember anyone getting drunk or mean, but by the time the bottom of the pot was being scraped for the last bites, there was a warm, bright glow on most of the faces in the crowd.

I remember one woman in particular who bought her gas there. These were "full-service" times when gas was pumped, oil checked, air put in tires, and—most certainly—windows washed. The woman knew what she was doing, too. She would come in wearing a low cut dress that showed more than enough for the imagination of any sixteen-year-old and would pull the dress high up her thighs exposing more than enough but not quite enough. Maybe lots of boys who have worked around stations experienced this, but it was a first for me.

Every time her car pulled in, men would begin to race to see who would clean the windows. After a while, I was always sent; I think that they got more fun out of watching me do that front windshield than they did catching the woman's act. I know that there must have been times when I worked on that windshield for fifteen minutes. I would say, "Wait a minute, there's a little more over here. This place sure is stubborn, but don't worry I'll get it. Oh, here's another place. Let me get it." On and on I would go, carrying on a conversation more with myself than with her. She knew exactly what I was doing, but as long as she didn't mind I didn't either.

I often wondered what my own father would have been like, the kinds of places he would have gone, where he would have fit in. Somehow, I think that he would have been liked, respected, in this place. It was the special kind of place with the kind of people that give you roots. You hate to leave a place like this and never get so far away that you don't feel something of a drawing, a tugging of the string that it has tied to your life.

About the time that ninth grade started, Momma went to Florida to see her brother and his wife who lived in Hollywood. At that time Hollywood was a small town on the main road between Fort Lauderdale and Miami; a lot of people had migrated out of the Carolinas into South Florida after World War II and during the 1950s. Her brother had done pretty well for himself with the wrecker and auto repair business that he owned.

More than anything else, Momma needed to "get away from it all" for awhile. Besides the full responsibility of a family, she worked as physically hard everyday as anyone. In addition, she seemed to be the person in our extended family that everyone leaned on when there was any kind of problem. She carried the emotional burdens of a lot of people. Her own mother had even had a severely handicapping stroke, and Momma was having to take care of her. As the wear and tear mounted, she began to experience some health problems. Her doctor felt the Florida weather might be good for her.

She came home after a couple of weeks strong again and filled with all kinds of enthusiasm for Florida. The weather was better, Uncle Herman and Aunt Margaret had really done well, and there were a lot better job opportunities for all of us. Since Kay would be finishing school by the first of the year and there were no jobs for her in Whiteville, it would be a good time to move. Momma didn't worry long over decisions; while she had been in

Hollywood on her visit, she had signed a contract to buy a house in her brother's neighborhood.

Plans immediately began to be made. Kay would finish school. The house in Whiteville would be rented out. Joe could go on in school in Florida as soon as we got there. I would leave immediately, live with my Uncle and Aunt, start getting the new house ready to be lived in, and find work.

It is important to know how matter-of-fact all of this was. It was all part of a larger scheme of survival. School and the other aspects of being a teenager were not part of the consideration. Again, it was not cruel; it was simply necessary. It was my turn to do my part.

I cannot stress enough how strong the imperative "my turn to do my part" was there. There may have been a mixture of feelings of being scared and being excited about something new that was about to happen, there may have been some sadness at leaving friends and patterns that were familiar, but there was no feeling of resistance to what had to be done. You simply did what you had to do—no negative fatalism about it at all—and took your turn.

There is no question in my mind that this whole approach that had sunk into the deepest marrow of my life had a great influence on all that took place in Vietnam. It, too, had to be done; it, too, was my turn. There is nothing really complicated or deep here— you simply did what you had to do. It was not a matter of glory, but a matter of fact. You either faced it and handled it the best you could, or you ran from it. Nothing about my entire existence conditioned me to do anything but face it.

Chapter IV

Getting to Florida was no easy task. With the family not having a car and funds anything but spectacular, a bus or train ticket was completely out of the question; there was the need to "catch a ride." I guess that I would have hitchhiked, something that I had plenty of experience with, but Momma made arrangements with an uncle in Bladenboro, who thought that he could get me with a truck driver, who would be making a run all the way into South Florida.

While I was waiting at my uncle's house for the final arrangements to be made, I felt for the first time that I was on my own. Momma had taught me those larger lessons about life that shape a person's character. She ingrained into me the importance of trust and that a person's word was about the most significant possession possible. She believed that maybe you could risk too much and go out on a limb for other people too far sometimes, but still I understood that almost everyone was worth a chance. Above all, she had always pulled for those people who were underdogs: the Blacks, the half-breed Indians, and those folks who were noticeably poorer than we were. Now, Momma would not be there. She had left her mark, and it would be up to me to show how deeply those marks had gone.

I felt thrown into the world, caught up in a great whirlpool of situations that were new and unfamiliar. I had the right background but I didn't know the ropes. Suddenly, I could empathize better than ever with those half-breed underdogs. It was like the world knew exactly where it was going, that it was not interested in slowing down to let me jump on, and if I was going to find a place and make one for my family, I was going to have to do it myself. To feel alone is one of the most desperate feelings there is. Throw in awesome responsibility, and suddenly you are not a boy anymore.

Finally, my uncle got me a ride with a trucker heading for Lake Okeechobee, in the middle of South Florida, to pick up a load of fresh produce. As nightfall approached, I climbed into the cab of a long-nosed Peterbilt carrying everything I had in the world in a small bag. There wasn't much talking. I was tired but I couldn't go to sleep. I was intrigued by all that I was seeing. As I have said earlier, my world was pretty limited and travel had seldom been possible. There was a huge world out there, and the high cab of the Peterbilt provided a vantage points the likes of which I had never seen.

Suddenly it dawned on me that I had no idea whatsoever about where I was going. I had a name, "West Hollywood, Florida," and a telephone number but that was all. I hadn't even thought about looking at a map, didn't know if the trip was ten hours or ten days, and could not have imagined what lay along the road between North Carolina and Florida. Buster Carter had been there on vacation, but all he could talk about was the way all of the boys looked bigger because they swam and worked out all of the time. It was like venturing into a land of giants.

Trust or no trust, if that truck driver was man enough not to sleep, I wasn't sleeping. I was almost like Hanzel and Gretel going into the deep woods; if I could keep track of signs, different turns, and unusual land formations, I could find my way back if I had to. As the headlights of the truck penetrated one segment of new land and then another, I was enveloped in a silence bracketed by the guttural roar of the truck's engine and the random sweeping swish of cars as they passed, making their own journeys back toward where I had come from. My mind could not help but wish that I was in one of those cars—going home.

We worked our way across Florida throughout the next day. This was right before the Interstate systems were completed in most of the South so there were crowded two-lane roads, small towns to go through every ten or fifteen miles, and all kinds of construction. We finally ended up into the night at a produce warehouse near Okeechobee. It was the end of the line for my uncle's friend. He would rest while his truck was loaded and head back north as soon as possible. He had promised to find me a ride on further south. I still had not slept.

I hung around a truck stop restaurant and watched the odd collection of people that meandered in and out. Some were loners who stayed off to themselves, while others seemed to be carrying on a party that had only been interrupted by intervals of travel halfway across the country. The more I overheard, the more I realized what a tiny part of this world I had experienced. I kept telling myself that Momma would not have sent me out if I hadn't been ready. I kept telling myself that Momma knew best and right then I couldn't remember her ever being wrong about anything important. At the same time, I'm not sure I felt very ready.

Right before he pushed off, my uncle's friend came in with another man. He called me over and introduced us. This man was going right through West Hollywood and could drop me off. It was all pretty matter of fact, like these men made these kinds of transfers as easily as the mindless shifting of gears that filled every minute of their working hours. He wished me "Good Luck" with no more hint of a smile than was possible to indicate clearly that, in fact, I would need a lot of good luck.

I pulled out in a smaller truck with an equally untalkative driver. You got the idea that their minds had to be somewhere else or they couldn't stand the monotony of their jobs. The roads were all straight and flat now, the scenery all looked the same—flat, low ground and sky, and I drifted off into sleep.

After what seemed like only a moment or two, I jerked awake in a daze. The first thing that I saw was the edge of a sign we were passing by that read "West Hollywood, Florida." All I could think was "Which way am I going? Am I north, south, east, or where? I've missed where I was supposed to be!" It was almost as if, were I to have missed my destination—which, in fact, I hadn't—I could never get there. I began to yell for the driver to stop and let me off. Startled by my sudden frenzy, he jerked the truck off to the edge of the road, and I jumped out into the rising cloud of sandy dust and heat that the truck created as it skidded to a halt.

As the dust settled and the truck pulled away, it felt like I was on a whirling, blurring circus ride. The ride had been disengaged from its engine and was coasting to a stop. The blur had settled down and objects were beginning to come into focus. Only an unbalanced dizziness remained that made you uncertain of your step. There were colors everywhere and more traffic and people than I think that I had ever seen.

Stretching out down one side of the road was the "Seminole Indian Reservation." What was actually a bustling tourist trap gave me the immediate impression of being put down into an alien world. There were people in strange colored garments, row upon row of Indian teepees, big signs and statues of alligators, and palm trees. I had never seen a palm tree.

My eyes raced through the entire environment for something familiar that I could lock onto. Across from the "Reservation" was the Oasis Truck Stop and across the main highway a Phillips 66 service station. This brand of gasoline was not common in North Carolina at the time, but I had heard the name. At least, I knew my way around gas stations. I crossed the main highway to the station. My feet were communicating to my brain the strangeness of walking on the sandy ground for the first time.

I was suddenly very thirsty. The station had a water cooler and I helped myself. My mouth filled with a taste like the bitterness of a pecan hull. Never had I tasted water like this before! What a strange land this was with ground that moved like mounds of salt under your feet and water that tasted like the dregs of an old well; what a stranger I was in this strange land!

While the phone rang, I almost held my breath in hopes that a friendly voice would come on the other end. If it hadn't, I'm not exactly sure what I would have done next. I knew I'd do something, but it would just be a lot simpler if someone answered. My Aunt Margaret came on the line and God must have somehow been watching over me that day; I was only a few minutes from where Uncle Herman worked.

He took me to his house and fed me. There is no telling what his first thoughts must have been about the grinning, pitiful, anxious man-child that he saw standing in that sandy parking lot waiting to be picked up. He probably didn't know whether to laugh or cry. Given the same choice, I would probably have cried. But that was not even a choice—you didn't cry.

After a quick visit, Uncle Herman drove me around to the house nearby that Momma had bought. You could hardly see the house for the weeds. They were four or five feet high in most places. The place looked terrible. I knew that Momma looked at things in terms of their potential, but she was really pushing it this time.

All I could think was "What am I doing here? What am I doing here?" But I knew the answer. It was my turn. I had to whip this place into shape and get a job; of course, I knew that that meant get **jobs**. There was no question that school was over, which in a way was a relief, but it also marked the passage of youth. It was my turn and people were depending on me.

At first I worked in my uncle's garage doing odd jobs of one kind or another. The only problem I ever had there was watching him weld when he clearly told me not to. I burned my eyes so badly that my uncle and aunt had to doctor them all one night, and I walked around for days with what felt like sand in my eyes.

It didn't take long to pick up a second job at an Esso station about three miles from the house. Mr. Turbeville from Whiteville had written a first-rate recommendation. I would work for my uncle in the day, work on the house and yard, and walk the three miles to the station to work there at night.

It didn't take long for me to learn that housekeeping was more difficult than it looked. Slowly but surely things did begin to take shape. I learned to contend with what the people in Florida called Palmetto Bugs. That all sounds pretty nice for bugs, but in reality they were nothing but the biggest cockroaches that I had ever seen. Small ones were as big as your thumb and they were everywhere. There were also occasional scorpions, but I finally became convinced that they were a lot less dangerous than they looked. Worse than the work and the bugs was the loneliness and homesickness. I may have been almost seventeen years old, but I still had never been away from my mother. As the house looked better and better, I could hardly wait for her to come and see what I had accomplished on my own with only a limited amount of help from my relatives.

My uncle and aunt tried their best to entertain me. He made what would amount to dune buggies today out of car frames, and we would take picnics to Dania beach across from Fort Lauderdale. There were a lot of transplanted Southerners in their acquaintance, so we were around people with a common background. Sometimes he would take an old car hood, tie it to the back of the dune buggy like a sled, and pull me around the beach. Sometimes we would fish the inlets. The water was so clear that you could see the fish swimming in great schools; you could catch fish until you ran out of bait, and then they would strike cigarette butts you had stuck onto hooks.

The beach was strictly segregated. Blacks stayed in their place and whites held the better places. But the segregation didn't end there. Sometimes you were made to feel that you weren't a "native," but some kind of outsider. Sometimes you couldn't help but feel that the real action of the world was across the inlet at Lauderdale. You felt extremely blue collar or less. And most of the time, everyone I knew was older—my aunt and uncle's age. The old feeling of being different never would quite go away; the old question of wondering exactly where you fit was always there. I was misplaced; the other kids my age were in school—I worked. The other kids were cruising the main drag on Ft. Lauderdale beach; I was going fishing with my uncle, afraid to venture out beyond his care, and proud to have someone I could lean on right then.

Momma stayed on until the end of the school year in Whiteville. Joe, my younger brother, wasn't old enough to quit school yet, and Kay was finishing business college in Wilmington. I needed to get a better paying job, but I wasn't old enough. Finally, my uncle worked a deal with a friend of his who worked at the huge refrigerated warehouses of Plantation Cold Storage and I got my first "real" job. You worked in an insulated snow suit and freezer boots, neither of which I knew anything about. My uncle had told me that I would need better shoes, so on the day before I started I went over to the Salvation Army store and bought a pair of old bowling shoes for 50 cents. Needless to say, the next day I came in from work with near frostbite. Who would have thought that you would come all the way from North Carolina to Florida to find better work and nearly freeze to death!

In late August, Momma, Joe, and Kay finally moved. One of the proudest moments of my life took place when Momma stood and looked at the house and all of the work we had done. Joe and Kay couldn't really appreciate it, but Momma had seen it before. She didn't say too much, but her look said it all. It was almost as if the cleaned and repaired home, the almost manicured yard, confirmed something in her own mind—confirmed that she had been right, that I was ready.

Kay quickly was able to get a job at a steel company as a secretary. That plus my two jobs allowed us to buy a car. It was a 1957 Chevy. Now, it would be a "classic" car; then it was just an old car. It was the ugliest color of yellow that I have ever seen, but for someone who was used to walking and thumbing, it was special. I would drive Kay to work and then go to work myself. In the evening that pattern was reversed, and then I would pick up extra work where I could find it.

A lot of the young people hung out on weekends at a Burger King that was near our house. I started going over there, cruising the parking lot like I had seen the other kids with cars do, and stopping occasionally to talk and listen to music. I met a guy named Cecil Hobbs and we became friends. He was also odd jobbing wherever he could and got me some work at a funeral home in town. "The Chapel of the Eternal Light" took its name from a fountain in its front yard that had a gas light in it that always burned. It was also always being blown out by the wind, and one of my main jobs besides general clean up and yard work was keeping the light burning.

Kids had begun to organize themselves into "gangs" in some of the schools in the Miami/West Hollywood area. Some of these gangs were like social clubs or fraternities, but other were more rough-cut and mean. One group was called the "West Hollywood Hoodlums" and they loitered around the Burger King a good deal of the time.

These guys were crazy. They were always prancing around like banty roosters, picking fights, and acting like minor league gangsters. I can remember on one occasion seeing one of their leaders take a penny and flip it into the air. Suddenly, twenty or more of the gang members were wildly fighting each other to see who would come up with the penny. There was blood, bruises, blank stares across semi-conscious faces, and occasionally a lost tooth or broken nose, but once the penny was secured they went away friends.

My North Carolina accent gave them a ready-made reason to pick at me. There were all kinds of cutting remarks about Southern "hicks," "rednecks," and "country boy." The term "boy" was particularly offensive because these hoodlums were the real boys; I was operating in a man's world except for those catch-as-catch-can moments of being a "normal" teenager when I hung out at the fast food restaurant. In addition, I had felt my black friends' blood boil when "boy" was consciously used as a racial slur. Then they started calling me "Bama," which was ironic in a way since I had never stepped foot in Alabama.

I really was letting all of this get to me, which was a little strange since I usually was able to brush off kidding, even when it got to the place of harassment. These were kids acting in totally kid-like fashion. There was not much that was unpredictable about their behavior. Most of the time, I could have handled that kind of situation. But maybe they were really striking a nerve. I didn't like the "country boy" image which I knew I had. I didn't like my accent. I was trying to change that and especially trying to get to know people who were a little more upscale. I wasn't trying to "get above my raising," nothing like that, but I was trying to grow or mature—although I'm sure those words would not have entered my mind at that time.

One night I had all that I could take. There were maybe 150 people either in the Burger King or sitting in cars in the parking lot outside. Some of them were people I guess I was wanting to have a higher opinion of me. Some of the hoodlums started in on the "country boy" and "Bama" talk and began to make threats about beating me up in front of everyone.

I started heating up and after one put-down too many pushed my way up close to one of the leaders: "I'll tell you what, boys. (I emphasized the last word.) You may kick my ass, but give me a few minutes to get my shit together and we'll see whose ass gets kicked." Had I not been so overcome with anger, I would have recognized that my standing up in the way I did had caused a visible backing off. No one stepped forward to take my challenge, and I simply walked away across the nearby field toward our house. No one even hinted at stopping me. In effect, although I didn't realize it at that point, I had won the day.

But as I charged back across the field, I was boiling-over mad. My uncle had given me an old double-barreled shotgun. There had been a rash of break-ins in the area, and he wanted something there for Momma's protection—just in case. With icy determination I walked through the house, got the gun, loaded it, and walked straight back out without hardly breaking stride.

Everything was business-as-usual by the time I got far enough back across the field for the parking lot lights to disclose my return. I'm not sure who saw me first but suddenly there was the look of awareness, then recognition, of what was happening on the gang members' faces. There was a half-way-sneaking, quick movement toward cars that was enough to send a message of alarm through the entire crowd. Most of the general crowd never saw me or knew exactly what was happening.

I raised the shotgun, aimed and cocked it, and then shot it off into the air. Once, twice, reloading, and then once and twice again. I was deadly serious, but the humor of what started happening brought me back to reality. I could remember what a large anthill was like when it was accidently kicked into by a kid playing in a field. Ants scurried wildly in ten directions at the same time.

That's what the Burger King looked like. People started ducking into cars, screaming, holding their hands over their ears and faces, and racing engines toward escape. In what seemed like only a moment the place was cleared. All that was left was a hanging cloud of exhaust fumes gathering toward the parking lot lights. Waste paper was still stirring all around the building and workers were peeping out from inside.

I just turned and walked back home. My anger and energy were spent. I put the gun away and sat down in front of the television. For the next hour it seemed that sirens and flashing blue and red lights converged from every direction. I could mostly see the flashing lights reflected in the glass of pictures on the walls. I never got up from where I was sitting. No one ever came to the house to ask the first question.

From that time on life at the Burger King went right on just as it had before, except for one thing, there were no longer any negative remarks aimed at me. All the stupid kidding stopped. I didn't brag about what I had done, and no one asked me any questions about it. There was, however, a sense of respect that had not been there. Finally, we all kidded about it. I got the name "Crazy Charlie," but no one messed with me after all that. Somehow I learned a new lesson, maybe one of the first that didn't come from my Momma; you had to be tough to survive—not mean and not ugly, but tough.

Maybe I now was coming to the place where I drove around with my head held a little higher. Maybe I was learning the ropes of this new place and feeling a little more confident. But don't get the idea that this "country boy" had suddenly become sophisticated and had everything under control. One day I was driving to work at Plantation. Suddenly, directly in front of me on the horizon as if it were falling from the sky was a huge metallic looking, cigar shaped object. My mind didn't think flying saucer or space ship, it thought "NUCLEAR BOMB!!" It had never crossed my mind to think much about what a bomb even looked like. I nearly wrecked into the oncoming traffic, jerked the car over to the side of the road, and jumped out. I starred into the sky expecting oblivion and holocaust at any second. There was no way that I was going to ask anyone anything, and everyone else seemed to be going on about their business as if nothing were happening. Hadn't anyone seen this but me? In a moment, as the large object floated closer, I could see the word "Goodyear" emblazoned on its side; it was one of the Goodyear blimps that I later found out was moored near Miami. It was a good thing none of the "West Hollywood Hoodlums" had seen this display.

By the time school started in the fall and Joe and all the other students returned to classes, it became even clearer that I was in a particular group that was singled out, those older teenagers who had to work. This became my circle of friends, but simply being out of school—which most of us had not had a very good experience with anyway—did not make us feel particularly deprived. Most of us worked days and nights and stole away for a little hunting, fishing, or just exploring the Everglades when we could. By this time I had been introduced to beer and drank enough either to get on the edge of being drunk or getting sick. Most of the time it was getting sick. We would go up to Fort Lauderdale to the War Memorial Auditorium for dances from time to time, but usually we just hung out on the edge of the crowd and watched.

What did make me feel deprived was the fact that I never had any money. Maybe I should say "extra money." There was money for food and gas and a little left over for cigarettes. If you were raised in North Carolina, cigarette money and food money were about the same. The rest was given to Momma to meet expenses. Russell had done it, Bobby had done it—even while he was in Korea, Kay was doing it, so I did it, too. It simply was the way our system had to work.

I had mixed emotions about all of this. I wanted things like I saw others having. I wanted to give the money to Momma and took pride in pulling my part of the load, but there were times when I resented giving it. In my mind, I wanted to be on the beach with the rich kids at Lauderdale on the weekends. At the same time I dreamed about making enough to move Momma and the rest of the family out of our small house into something better at a place like Miramar, a magical sounding subdivision community that was blossoming nearby.

Mostly, I felt deprived because I was always tired. Somehow it didn't make sense to be 17 years old and still be bone tired most of the time. I noticed that the other kids my age might dress better sometimes or drive better cars. I noticed the way that some of them spent money with great freedom. But above all, I noticed that they didn't look tired. When I looked at myself in the mirror in the mornings, I saw tired. It wasn't that I reflected deeply on the tragedy or unfairness of my existence—nothing as complicated as that. But somewhere deep inside it seemed like a small voice kept repeating, "Being 17 and being tired all the time just doesn't make sense."

In fact, it made total sense. There was no way, regardless of how much energy there is in youth, that you could avoid tiredness. You worked hard all day at the storage warehouse, you picked up work at gas stations or wherever, and the people at the funeral home were asking you to do more and more. Try crowding into that schedule even the most meager amount of teenager activities, and there simply is not much time left for sleep. Stretch this kind of schedule out over one month after another and a feeling of tiredness is there, deep in your bones, almost all the time.

You learn to survive. I worked my way up at Plantation Storage until I was responsible for pulling orders. This involved getting an order sheet and then moving with a fork lift throughout the large warehouse gathering stacks of boxes of frozen goods. Some people would have to race madly throughout the entire shift to get their orders filled, but I was able to do mine with maybe as much as two or three hours to spare. In that extra time I would pull the lift into a back aisleway, place a couple of pallets of boxes into the aisle, and then climb onto the high top of a back row of frozen goods. It was possible to set some of these boxes out and make a small igloo-like "cave." In all of your freezer outfit, you could slip back into one of these caves and sleep comfortably for sometimes an hour or more without getting caught or without really affecting your daily productivity. There were many days when these short naps were all that kept me going.

I was doing more and more at the funeral home. The owner, Dennis Stitely, had given my friend Cecil Hobbs increased responsibilities, and he quickly brought me along as his assistant. Cecil learned how to embalm and taught me. I was almost always scared in the embalming room, but I felt the need to challenge myself and this was one way to do it.

Stitely was a fine businessman who was interested in doing a lot more than just hiring cheap-labor teenagers to work around his business. He thought of us as apprentices and hoped that our experiences might lead to some kind of career in which we could better ourselves. He was always precise about what he wanted, but he was always fair as well.

The embalming room was eerie in one of the strangest ways that I have ever experienced. I guess it was all psychological or my imagination, but what I encountered there seemed totally real. The funeral home itself was air-conditioned, just as you would expect in South Florida. In order to save on expenses, many of the peripheral rooms—including the embalming room—had no special cooling. But the embalming room was always cold; cold like the late fall mornings in North Carolina when you have been used to it being warm and a sudden shift of air from the mountains dropped the thermometer thirty degrees overnight. Unexpected and different, and in this particular environment it was a coldness that you felt for maybe an hour or two even after you had gone out into the hot afternoon sun.

It might seem strange or even wrong to think of older teenage boys embalming in a well-thought-of funeral home. However, the work had to be done, others tired of it and found ways to avoid it, so if we would do it—why not. There was nothing bizarre or derogatory about it. Dennis Stitely had a great deal of respect for the remains of the dead and the deceased person's family. He taught us to respect the work that we did and to do it with the greatest care and compassion that we could have. I had the sensation of wanting to help the poor, emotional people that came in their time of loss; to do the best that I could with the embalming was my way to do that. We never joked about it and never brought friends around to give vent to their curiosity. I learned to have a special respect for the dead.

My most memorable, and difficult, experience took place one weekend when the body of a 350 pound man was brought in. He had been a piano player in one of the striptease joints between Dania and Fort Lauderdale and had died under mysterious circumstances. The local coroner had performed an autopsy. I knew what an autopsy was, but I had never worked with the remains of a person's body that had been through this process. It just so happened that on this weekend the regular embalming technician was gone. I had to do the job by myself.

In the autopsy process, a person is opened across the entire front of the chest all the way down to the stomach area. The head is also opened so that the brain can be tested. When the body bag was opened and the man's naked body was exposed, it was quickly apparent that the persons performing the autopsy had left all of the finishing work for the undertakers. The man's front had been unevenly sutured back together with heavy string and a good deal of the back of the skull was simply left hanging in place. All of this was difficult enough, but the layering of now grotesque fat made the embalming process—especially without any help—next to impossible.

I knew a little bit of what to expect. All of the internal organs and fluids—the viscera—would be in a plastic bag that was packed inside the rib cage. This would have to be removed and then replaced with any additional packing that was needed to give the body a proper contour. The heavy string sutures would have to be removed and then, following the packing process, new stitches installed. The skull cavity would have to be packed and the face pulled back in place with additional cosmetic packing that would make it look natural.

As I carefully opened the string ties, the weight of the fat at the sides of the body jerked the rib cage open and everything that was on the inside spilled out into the prep room floor. Viscera and fat were everywhere. What was I to do? It was the most awful scene I had ever seen. I could get sick and throw up. I could scream and panic. I could leave and never come back. In fact, all of these possibilities probably crossed my mind.

But, none of that would change the condition. It would still be there. Somebody would have to take care of it. Even this man— total stranger that he was—deserved better. His family deserved better. Where he had come from or where he was going were all beside the point. It simply had to be done.

I started picking up the mess. I repackaged it all. Nothing was thrown away, which would have been much easier and no one would have ever known. I worked with the fat to get the body back even again and after what must have been two solid hours of straining and pulling, I got the whole front evenly and cleanly stitched back in place.

This left the head. Repacking the skull wasn't difficult. The bone structure held its contour easily. But the face had to be rebuilt. This involved literally peeling the face down so that I could get in behind it to build it up. As long as I live, I will never forget the appearance of the man's head with the face peeled down.

There are simply no words to describe it. I must have wanted to stop and walk away a hundred times before that evening was over. But I didn't.

When the work was done and the room cleaned, I walked away with a satisfaction not unlike the house that I had gotten ready for Momma. No one would ever know all that had been put into that effort. But I knew. On numerous occasions, across the next year or so, as people inquired about who had done one particular embalming job or another, family members would come to me with great compliments about the way that I had worked with their dead loved one.

Sometimes I had nightmares. Sometimes the scenes from the embalming room would get mixed up with scenes from my childhood when I had slipped around to watch the hog killings. In my dreams the images would all run together and I would wake up with a coldness about my skin like the coldness of the Carolina fall morning when the men and women worked the meat of the hogs—like the coldness of the embalming room.

In late November of 1963, we were all getting ready for Thanksgiving. There was a festiveness in the air as we approached the holidays, even though it was still hot in South Florida. I could at least experience the cold that your body seemed to expect at this time of the year while I worked my shift at the warehouse.

All of a sudden things in the warehouse felt different. It was quiet and still. People were not running around like they normally did. Something was wrong. I sensed the same kind of alarm that I had seen on the distant faces of the people at the Burger King as I came across the field with the shotgun. Then the word reached me, President Kennedy had been shot in Texas. And then the word quickly thereafter, President Kennedy was dead.

Women were crying and men looked around like they were stunned and didn't know what to do next. The blacks seemed especially in dismay. It was like something had happened that they could relate to out of their past that wasn't in the white man's past. It was like the worst of that past was rushing back and the rug was being pulled out from under a lot of hope, or promise, or something. Everything just stopped.

I felt ten different things at the same time. I thought maybe something was going to happen to the world but I didn't know what. I thought maybe a war would start. I wanted to go outside and look around and make sure nothing was happening that I couldn't see.

More than anything else, life suddenly felt more real than it ever had. Sure, there had been plenty of struggle and hard work and not enough money and all that, but if you didn't have a great deal to compare it all to, it still seemed basically normal. Sure, I had taken my turn and felt the need to do my part, but still everything up until that point was youth and young and, in spite of a lot of things, naive and immature and fanciful.

From that point on, the sense of realism—that's the only word that comes close to fitting—that washed over me in that moment became the ground, the pre-condition, for everything that has taken place since.

President Kennedy was shot. President Kennedy was dead. Youth was gone. It was all adult now.

Chapter V

Sometimes I felt like I was at the center of a storm, but not the calm eye of the hurricanes that people along the Florida coast tracked on their maps and watched religiously as they formed near Africa and moved west toward America. My storm was more like the tornadoes that we had known back home in North Carolina. Retrospect is always 20/20, and now I know that most of the different kinds of conflict that I was experiencing are common to older teenagers trying to become adults. At the time it seemed like I was the only person in the world who felt like I was feeling.

First, there was religion. Momma had seen to it that all of her children were brought up in the church. She was convinced that the only way we had been able to make it since the death of my father was because of the help of God, and on more than one occasion the help of God's people. She prayed, read the Bible, and gave of what little money she had. The people in the churches we attended had a great deal of respect for her, and she taught us to respect the things of church.

Most of the time that had been no problem for me. Going to church was what most of the other people I knew were doing so I did it, too. The only time that there really had been a problem was when I had had a Sunday School teacher who made her students stand in front of the class and read sections from the lesson or from the Bible. I was so embarrassed not to be able to do this as well as the others kids that I began to skip Sunday School and then sneak back in for church so that Momma wouldn't know it.

It didn't seem that going to church was as important to people in South Florida, and by the time Momma got moved down there I had already gotten out of the habit. I didn't want to go into another environment where I ran the risk of being singled out as a "Badman," feeling like a total, awkward stranger, or having to see young people dressed better than I was and talking of school and social matters that were a hundred miles from what was happening in my life.

This created a great deal of conflict. I wanted to please Momma and somewhere deep inside there were a lot of the religious beliefs that were a part of me. Sometimes fear and guilt rose as leftover relics of the North Carolina revival sermons that were preached with great intensity from the community services held in the huge tobacco warehouses. Religion would catch back up with me or I would come racing back to it, but for an uncomfortable while it went its way and I went mine.

A second area of conflict occurred because of the diverse mixture of people living around Hollywood. In North Carolina there were basically whites, blacks, and descendants of Indians. I was so mixed up in the lives of all these people and developed such a sympathy for those that society had kicked down to the bottom rungs that there was little room for prejudice. I've got a feeling, however, that just about everyone develops some kind of prejudice, especially about people that you don't really know. I had developed negative feelings about Jews and Catholics and anyone who wasn't exactly a part of the America that surrounded Whiteville, North Carolina.

Those feelings all got turned upside down in Florida. All kinds of people had migrated to the Fort Lauderdale-Miami region a long time before it was discovered by true Southerners. By the time we got there a settled population of Jews, Catholics, Italians, and people of Spanish descent from Cuba and Central America had already developed. At first, contact with these people was intimidating and even frightening; you almost expected them to be wearing horns. It was almost shocking to find out that they had the same basic needs and feelings, the same kind of day-to-day experiences that you had. If there had been one thing that was certain, it was the roots and traditions and ideas which came from your home. It was unsettling, to say the least, to find so many of these ideas from home not panning out in the real world that surrounded you. You could not help but wonder how many other ideas from your past were not as they had once appeared. It was almost like you were having to learn life all over again. I'm glad for that experience now, as there is no doubt that it made me a more open and better informed person; at the time, it added fire to the fuel of self-doubt and the feeling of being out of place that was already growing in strength.

Conflict rose about those delicate but decisive matters of human sexuality. Sure, you knew about sex as a teenager growing up in North Carolina, but it all seemed to come along a whole lot slower. People still valued being a virgin—for both women and men—at the time of marriage. Girls wore virgin pins as a sign of courage and "good boys" respected them for it. There was extramarital sex without question, but it was either extremely discreet, totally unvirtuous, or something that "sinners" or "trash" became involved in. People still didn't teach or discuss in any objective manner the details of sexuality, and not having a father put me at a double disadvantage.

Suddenly, I was plunged into an adult working world where being discreet about sex had been thrown out the window. It was the main topic of conversation and consumed most of the discussions of the working day. Men talked, exaggerated, bragged about all kinds of conquests and activities that were beyond the horizon of anything I had actually even considered. Now, I know that much of it was done for the effect that it was having on me. I'm sure they laughed behind my back at the way my face must have revealed that I was believing every word. Beyond believing it, I was overwhelmed at the feeling of all that I was missing out on. What kind of a social cripple must I be, if all of this was going on out there in the world and I had experienced none of it? Sometimes the idea increased in my mind that I must be some kind of total jerk. Here I was waiting on marriage and the rest of the world was involved in a never-ending orgy. I smiled and acted nonchalant, as if I could relate to all that was being said, but all the while my head was spinning and my ears ringing with all that I was hearing.

My greatest sense of conflict rose from the odd division of friends I started making. On one side, there were the "country boys," those kids like myself who had migrated in from the rural areas of the South. We hung out together, consumed with our maleness, and did the things we had learned from the men of our homes; we hunted, fished, and explored the swamps. On the other side, there were the "town boys," those kids who were second or third generation Florida and knew the ropes of the South Florida coast. They went to dances in Lauderdale, got suntans on the beaches, were overwhelmed with the idea of "making it" with the girls, and found great adventure by cruising Burger King parking lots spoiling for a fight.

Somehow I was caught in a deep chasm between these two groups. I wanted to fit in with both of them, but never really had the feeling of fitting in with either. There was a careful division of those I would bring home and those that I never exactly told what neighborhood I lived in. They made their own divisions, too; sometimes I got the feeling that the thought was crossing some of their minds "Does Chuck belong with us or not?" Again, in retrospect, I realize that what I was experiencing is pretty common for teenagers, but at the time I identified with the television character, "The Fugitive," running from one place to another but never exactly belonging anywhere.

I got the feeling that you really had to be tough to survive. At least, you had to convey the image of being tough. It also didn't hurt, I concluded, for people to wonder if you were a little crazy. People did not quickly forget the image of me coming across the field with the shotgun. The only problem was that being tough or crazy wasn't me at all. I had always been a basically nice guy who liked to have friends and be fun-loving and peace-loving. A fight or some kind of bullying behavior was as far from the true me as night was from day. But if you get intimidated and scared by an environment, if you get unsure about yourself, that true person can be soundly barricaded behind a high and strong wall.

My best friends among the "country boys" were Dickie and Floyd Medlin, Fred Wright, Clyde Tiger, Buddy Walker, and Randy Johnson. My younger brother, Joe, was also getting to the age that he could be included in on some of our activities. Our favorite activity was to get off work and head for the swamps. It was not unusual for us to get together some odds and ends of food, a case of beer, and the basic items of camping and stay out from Friday night until Sunday afternoon. We would talk, kid, lie, dream out loud, drink beer, fish, hunt, explore, eat, sleep, talk, kid, lie, dream out loud, drink beer, fish, hunt, explore, eat, sleep—an endless cycle highlighted by impromptu wrestling matches and general horsing around that somehow blanked out the real world that waited on us out there beyond the swamps on Monday. We were still like a litter of new pups, growing and becoming stronger—soon to be men—but still as innocent and naive as those playful pups ever could be.

One of the strongest memories of my entire life took place while I was with this "country boy" group. We had headed to a favorite camping spot at a secluded spot on the edge of Lake Okeechobee with little more than two cases of beer, some oranges that we had picked at a grove that grew beside an old highway, and a small amount of bait. Beside the place where we camped was a huge pumping station that would suck the fresh water from the lake and send it out toward the water lines which reached all over South Florida. The motors and the suction were powerful enough to stir the surrounding water into an uproar. While the water was stirring, you could catch "specs"—speckled perch—as quickly as you could bait your hook.

Somewhere into the early part of the night, we ran out of beer and most of the bait. There was an old store nearby where we could at least get bait, so Fred, Floyd, Joe, and I walked off down there to see what we could find. When we got to the store, it was closed. We decided, probably under the influence of more than a little alcohol, to help ourselves and come back the next day and pay the old man who ran the store. As we fumbled around with the bait boxes, stumbling over one object and then another in the dark, the old man—who we didn't even know was on the spot— awakened and thought we were thieves. Out of the darkness he jumped, coming at us with a shotgun. We yelled, he yelled; we scattered down a strange road we had never taken, dodging holes, sinking in sandy dirt, and sure that our next sensation would be the burning of shotgun pellets in our backs. The old man never fired but we were well on down the road before we stopped running and now had to be concerned about finding a new route back to our camp.

We walked along in the dark for several minutes. I need to stop for a moment and give emphasis to the word dark. If you have never been in a swamp, far removed from the glare of city lights and without a street light for miles, you have no real idea of what "dark" means. Add to this the lushness of the trees, undergrowth, and hanging moss—plus the possibility of overcast skies or the absence of the moon—and you have real "dark." In my mind, whether it was South Florida or Vietnam, there is nothing like the dark of a swamp. With the help of a little alcohol, the sounds that you can hear without seeing their source can become downright spooky.

Almost out of nowhere we wandered upon the sounds and soft lights of an old bar. Suddenly, there was a much greater need to fortify ourselves with more alcohol than to find bait. We walked into the damp and dank room, and the faces of two or three customers acknowledged us only with a short glance of "where did this motley group come from?" For the most part, they seemed so many years into their own habits that our presence made little or no difference.

We asked for beer and showed that we had money to pay. Much to our surprise, the bartender wouldn't serve us. We were under age, but in most instances that never mattered. Why this man, far from the place that anyone would care what happened in his shanty of a bar, would refuse to take our money was beyond me. Maybe we had had a little more than I had thought, and he recognized it. Why go asking for trouble out of a bunch of kids? The sooner we "got lost," the sooner his place could get back to its own brand of "lostness."

I was ready to argue, which probably would have been proof enough that I had had more than I thought. Before I could get the words out, the door opened again and in stepped an old man in a top hat wearing a black tuxedo. This had now become the strangest night this bar ever had. A man in a top hat and tuxedo walking into a swamp bar now almost at midnight was like having a visitor from another planet.

The man explained that he had gotten lost, had gotten into a rut on a thick sandy stretch of road a couple of miles away, and was stuck in the ditch. It is next to impossible to get a car out of the deep sand of a back country Florida road. Once you get into a deep rut, there is no use fighting it; you simply grind off to the side where the rut takes you. Since there was no readily available help, the man offered the four of us $100.00 to go with him and help get him out of the ditch. He might as well have offered us the crown jewels of England; we jammed through the small front door, already revelling in what we would do with the money.

As we walked off into the dark, farther on down the strange road, the old man produced a full bottle of Jack Daniels whiskey. I knew exactly what this was but never had tasted it; it was too expensive. As we passed it back and forth, some of us could drink it better than others. It burned my throat going down, but I drank it anyway—again and again.

Then the strangest thing of all happened. The more I drank, the more the old man looked like the Devil. It never crossed my mind that the drinking was having this effect, but I became certain that it was all a trap and that somewhere on down that dark swamp road that we were all going to meet our doom. The swamp had never felt so eerie, the sky had never been so dark.

I began to pull the others aside and whisper my revelation. My total and complete seriousness was greeted with nothing but outrageous laughter. Even Joe wouldn't listen to me. My first impulse was to run away, but I felt that Satan had the power to strike me dead the moment I tried to escape. Anyway, I couldn't run off and leave Joe. Momma had made me responsible for him.

I kept my distance and watched for another several hundred yards—we were going deeper into the swamp, into the dark. You could tell by the feel of the road under your feet that very little traffic ever came this way. There was no car in a ditch; it was all a trap. Even the strange old bar had probably disappeared like something on "Twilight Zone" after we had left.

The other boys began to push around in a kidding manner with each other. The old man joined in with this. Everyone was in the highest spirits. Finally, one of the boys jerked off the top hat and a game of "keep away" commenced with the old man. He didn't like this at all, so I tried to whisper and signal for them not to do it. They paid no attention.

Suddenly, I could see something that everything within me wanted to deny. There along the front of the old man's receding hair line were two, ivory white nubs—horns! The more I looked at his face, the more I could see a reddish glow. When my eyes met his, it was clear that he knew that I knew. He smiled a frightful, all-knowing smile. The others were blind to the danger surrounding them; only I could see it.

I tried one more whisper to Joe, but all I got was a halfway shove and more laughter. Momma or not, Joe or not, I had to try to get away and get help. Why I thought anyone I knew could help me with the Devil, I will never know; at the moment, however, it made perfect sense.

We walked along together, all of the "play" continuing, but I stayed at the rear of it all. The old man—the Devil—kept turning around and grinning at me, as if to say "I've still got my eye on you—you're not getting away." Then I saw it, popping out at the back of his pants, a tail! The pitchforked end of the same tail I had seen in devil pictures since I was a kid.

I held back to the edge of the darkness. For every two steps they all took, I carefully measured out only one. In a moment or two they were at least twenty or thirty yards ahead, lost in the darkness. I slipped into the bushes beside the road and camouflaged myself as best I could. In a few moments they missed me and began to call out. Without an answer, they came back along the road—probably thinking that I had passed out from the Jack Daniels—and searched for me. After ten minutes of looking, the promise of $100.00 took them on down the road with the man—with the Devil.

For ten more minutes I didn't move. When I could no longer hear their drunken laughter, I jumped out of my hiding place and started racing through the dark back in the direction of what I hoped would be the camp. I ran as fast as I could. My lungs and heart felt like they would burst wide open, but I couldn't stop. I don't remember passing the old bar or the bait place. All I can remember is a sudden wall of barbed wire fence coming out of the darkness three feet in front of me. I jumped, probably with the idea of jumping over the fence. I went straight through it and came up off the ground, still running, stunned that I had not been cut to pieces.

After what seemed like an eternity, our campfire came into view. Two of the guys were still fishing away with not the slightest concern over our absence. I bolted into the camp area and tripped. It felt like I fell in ten different directions at the same time. I ended up in a hole at the end of the water only inches from the powerful suction of the pumping station that was roaring at full force. Whatever I had tripped over probably saved my life.

The fall at least had served to calm me down. The run had a sobering effect, but I was still convinced that the old man was the Devil. Maybe it was the intensity of the explanation, but my friends at camp listened seriously—finally somebody listened to me! We jumped into the car and headed back in the direction of my race through the swamp. As the lights darted right and left, uncovering one possible road to turn onto and then another, I was amazed that I had been able to find my way back.

Then, the car's headlights found them in the dark. There they were, an old man and three teenagers, pushing and straining at a car slid sideways off into a sandy ditch. I got out and helped, but still kept the car between me and the old man. Jack Daniels and I had an uncertain friendship from that time on, but there are still more questions in my mind about that night than answers.

Every young boy has to find some way to prove he is a man. My "country boy" friends and I did this in the out-of-doors with the kind of man-against-nature activities that our rural ancestors had known. We were hunters who could live off the land. We took the greatest pride in being self-sufficient. All we needed was the bare minimum of food and gear, something to fish with, and each other. We were learning something of that special "bond" among men that has been a part of human life since the beginning of time.

My town friends knew little about the world of the swamps; they had to find new ways to prove themselves. This often meant "making it with girls"—or at least bragging about making it with girls—fighting, or exploring the edge of one kind of trouble or another. This world was a lot more difficult for me to get used to than the world of the swamp.

We would go to dances and occasionally formalize our contacts with girls in terms of dates. This was awkward for me in some respects. I would see some of my friends extend their tough-guy acts toward their girls; they would talk rough to them and sometimes even push them around. I just couldn't do this; my Momma had taught me better. I could do nothing but treat whoever the girl might be in a respectful, or what I thought was decent, way. Strangely enough, I was usually the one getting dumped by one girlfriend and then another. Those that were getting the harsh treatment seemed to act like that was just part of their expected role and they had to take it. It didn't make any sense at all. There might be devils in the swamp, but that was easier to handle than the unpredictability of some of the town girls.

The whole business of fighting didn't make sense either. I wasn't afraid to fight and had had to defend myself plenty of times along the way of growing up. But just to fight to be fighting was insane. I've seen people get bones broken, teeth knocked out, and end up lying in a knocked-out heap on the floor. The thing that saved me time and again from having to participate in this ritual was my size. I was physically one of the biggest kids around, so I could depend on most of these people who tried to prove their manhood by fighting to try to prove it on somebody else.

I finally drew the line on some of these "town boy" activities. Destroying property just for the heck of it or stealing was just too much. I have been in cars that were driven at breakneck speed down highways and that were then steered straight into road signs. If you were skilled enough at this procedure, you could hit the signs just right, the rivets would pop out the back, and the signs would fly back over the top of the car. A wrong hit would simply make the sign bend over, slide under the car as it passed over, and lie springing in a rapid vibration on the curb behind you. That was a defeat. Guys would become angry when this happened and even more violent toward the next sign. It wasn't unusual on almost any morning to see work crews out in the hot Florida sun straightening and replacing signs.

It was also customary among many of the "town boys" to prove manhood by stealing newspaper stands. That didn't take much bravery or daring, not nearly as much as hunting in the Everglades with the fear of an alligator lurking nearby. We would find an empty or near-empty rack, shake or kick it to see if the coin holder had money in it, look around to make sure no one was watching, and throw it into the back of the car. Then, we would find some deserted section of the beach, break open the coin holder to get the change out, and throw the rack into the surf. On most occasions, there was hardly enough money to pay for the gas we had burned cruising to find the racks, racing to get away from the "scene of the crime," and driving the distance to the beach area.

I was not a saint and don't want to give that impression by any means, but all of this kind of action—or "antics" might be a better word—bothered me. I didn't care so much about signs or newspaper racks, but I couldn't get out of my mind that somebody was going to have to work to replace the signs and that the small amount of change in the coin holders was someone's livelihood. I had the strong sense that I was making life harder on someone who was probably already having a hard time. I just stopped participating in these kinds of things; I didn't go on some kind of religious crusade, I just stopped. Momma had always said that your real friends would respect you in times like this, and she was right about that. No big deal—I just stopped doing it.

If there was any good fortune in all of this, it came from my never getting caught by the police. I later found out that some of my friends had been caught and actually had police records to prove it. This fact, unknown to me, would play havoc with some of our most important plans on down the line.

By this time I had stopped working at Plantation Cold Storage. It wasn't a bad job, but I couldn't see myself doing it for the rest of my life. I was searching. For awhile I did construction work and helped build a huge incinerator and a cane mill back in the

Everglades. The worst job of this period was unloading crates of chickens at an egg farm. When Joe and I came home at night, Momma would literally wash us off with a hose before she would let us come in the house. Even at that, the whole house would smell of chickens—and I don't mean the aroma that rises from "Southern Fried" cooking in the pan.

Since I was accustomed to hard work, it was never difficult to get a job and hold it. The only time I ever got fired during this time was when I went to work at a tile making plant. My job was to pick up flats of wet tile on a fork lift and carry them to the drying room. It was a delicate balancing act, and if you did not do it just right, the wet tiles would get overweighted to one side or the other and spill all over the floor. Beyond the mess, the tiles became useless. After a few spills, the foreman—rather kindly I must say—told me that they "did not need my assistance anymore." I later came to find that bottom rung of chasing after one job and then another—bagging concrete in a Sakrete factory.

I can remember watching a lot of television through this period. My favorite shows were John Wayne war movies and a series about foot soldiers in World War II entitled "Combat." While some people my age were idolizing singing stars and ball players, the characters in these types of shows became my heroes. My particular favorite was the "Combat" sergeant played by an actor named Vic Morrow; he had a savvy and strength that was the stuff of a real man, the kind of real man that I was intent on becoming.

One reason that my idolizing would lean in this direction was undoubtedly influenced by my brother, Bobby. He had been very successful as far as the military was concerned. While we were in Florida, he was sent to be a Drill Instructor at Fort Gordon near Augusta, Georgia. He would visit us every time he got a chance. His uniform, drill instructor's hat, and bright medals were the most impressive symbols of manhood I had ever seen. In most respects, Bobby had achieved the most visible success of anyone in our family, and he was forever praising the opportunities of the Army. For Bobby, if there was ever any question, the Army would make a man out of a person. Spending half the night pulling chickens out of crates or the dusty monotony of filling bags with concrete made Bobby's uniform look all that much better.

Cecil Hobbs, Johnny Frazier, John Bludworth, Kenny Dormandy, Garret Bowling, and Angelo Marino were town boys. I hung out with them more and more. They knew their way around and were tough, not in a "tough around the mouth" way but real tough. Not mean, just tough. I was too, or at least wanted to be. We fit together well, and would not back up from any adventure or dare.

Sometimes we talked about the Army. Something like "Special Forces" or "The Green Berets" would be perfect for us. We could fight if we had to, have adventure, get paid for it, probably "get laid" for it, and have medals and uniforms to boot. We had heard of Vietnam but didn't know anyone who had really been there. Our ideas about Vietnam were so naive that I can remember one conversation in which we seriously talked about joining the Army, going over there and kicking ass, and then opening a Burger King. It seemed a sure bet to make a fortune.

On one occasion Bobby had talked seriously with us about enlisting. I didn't have to and didn't have to worry about being drafted; since I was the male head of our household, I would automatically be judged a "hardship case." Bobby said something about his getting five days leave for every person he could get to join, and to do something that would get us in good with Bobby was no small consideration. We had a romantic, television-and-movie, idealism about soldiers and war. We talked to a recruiter and filed his ideas away while we were coming and going in an environment that was quickly exhausting its possibilities.

I joined Cecil in working more or less full time at the funeral home. In our "apprentice" roles, we were doing everything that the regular workers did. I had a kind of love-hate relationship with the job. I felt good about working with the grieving families. I genuinely felt for their loss and tried to communicate that with the care I gave. On the other hand, though I pulled my part of the work just like everyone else, being around dead people kept me scared and on edge most of the time.

I hated to go pick up bodies. Sometimes a corpse could have "life" left in it. There might be a muscle twitch that could occur, air that was trapped that could escape from the mouth that made an audible sigh, and on occasion a corpse could pass gas. I know that has a humorous side to it, and it is humorous to me thinking back on it, but think about being in an ambulance or a room by yourself with a dead body and it suddenly passes gas, and you can imagine how funny that would NOT be.

The thought that frightened me the most was the possibility that the body that I was about to embalm was not really dead. I had heard and imagined all kinds of possibilities in this regard and so would cautiously keep a small mirror nearby. When no one was looking, I would hold the mirror under the dead person's nose and around the mouth. I had the idea that any breathing, no matter how slight, would fog the mirror. I'm not sure how I might have reacted if the foggy glaze of breathing had settled on the mirror.

One of the worst experiences I ever had took place one night while I was by myself. I had been watching Alfred Hitchcock—a favorite pastime —and then had gone in to do some work on a corpse that had been brought in. I had on a lab coat with large pockets and had the corpse laid out on a large table that was on rollers. I was up over the corpse doing some detail work when one of the arms fell loose and the hand dropped into my coat pocket. As I bolted back the hand stuck in the pocket; for all practical purposes—and all that would register in my mind—the corpse had grabbed me. I tried to run away but because the corpse was on the rolling table, it just kept following me around the room. For more than several moments the room was chaos with me screaming and trying to beat the hand away, while the dead corpse on its table followed every move I made. The only thing that saved the situation was that no one was there to see it—had they been, I would never have lived it down.

My friends, and Cecil in particular, knew of my fears. They weren't any different, so we were continually doing things to scare each other. I guess practical jokes in this kind of environment served to take some of its hard edge away. In addition, if you could scare someone, it became a way of reassuring yourself that they were as ill at ease with it all as you were. We knew few limits in carrying out our tactics of terror, although we steadfastly refused to act in any way that would have shown disrespect to the person who was deceased. We all drew the line at that point.

One occasion nearly ended in disaster; dead people might not be able to hurt you, but they could cause you to hurt yourself or someone else. Cecil knew that I was working one night late by myself. If there were no corpses to work on or families receiving friends, you had to catch a few loose ends of work, or wait around for the possibility of a call to pick up a body; for the most part there were long nights of watching TV in the casket room. On this particular night, I was back into Alfred Hitchcock again.

Cecil slipped in through one of the back doors, and I began to hear strange noises from the back of the building. At first, I figured that it was some kind of joke and whoever it was would go ahead and jump in behind me to see how badly I could be scared. Several long minutes passed and no one appeared. It would be deathly quiet and then there would be a noise again. There were all the time wierdos calling the funeral home asking questions about dead bodies—maybe it was someone like that. There had been a lot of robberies and break-ins from the growing population of unemployed migrants in South Florida—maybe it was a thief. Maybe, this time, it was the dead. Any interest I had in television quickly evaporated, and I sat there half afraid to acknowledge that I had heard anything, half afraid even to look back over my shoulder.

Finally, I couldn't sit still any longer. I called out laughingly a couple of times "Come on, I know you're out there. You're not fooling me this time." There was no response. As I stepped into the back hallway, I picked up the set of large, bronze praying hands that were sitting on a table near the doorway to the casket room. It had gotten dark while I had gotten into watching television and no lights had been turned on in the entire back part of the building. The light switch was at the other end of the hall.

I creeped slowly through the darkness with the praying hands raised high above my head. In the middle of the hallway between where I stood and the lightwitch was a circular stairway that led to the upstairs of the building. As I eased past it, Cecil jumped down on top of me with a yelling scream. Everything went icy cold and burning hot at the same time. I screamed and yelled, too, and all of the sounds echoed back in upon us from the surrounding walls in such a way that it felt like we were in a horror chamber of screaming death. With all of my might, might now fueled with the charging flow of adrenaline, I threw the object hanging on my back across the room against the wall. It crumpled to the floor and I was on it with the praying hands coming down toward its head with all my might. At the last millisecond, in the half light blinking of the television set in the casket room, I saw Cecil's face. My hand froze in space.

At that point we both sank together into a sweating, chilling heap. Maybe Cecil was capable of some laughter at having "gotten" me; maybe I was capable of some laughter of relief that it hadn't been a pervert, a thief, or the dead. For the most part we both sensed that we had leaped up on the edge of a tragedy and nearly fallen off. Can you imagine the obituary: "Cecil Hobbs, local man about town, was killed last night in a local funeral homes by a set of bronze, praying hands!" Although we made no formal pact, from that moment on Cecil and I pretty much held back on any funeral home practical joking we did with each other.

That didn't mean that we were immune to taking out our creative energies on someone else—especially Johnny Frazier. Johnny was openly uncertain about death and would have next to nothing to do with the funeral home. He seldom came around. On one rare occasion when Cecil and I knew that he was coming, we were ready.

Johnny had mustered up enough nerve to start asking to come up when none of the regular workers were there and see a corpse. We had told him that we couldn't do that, but he kept persisting in his requests. On one particular afternoon when he knew that everyone but Cecil and I were gone, he kept calling. Finally, we said "OK" and told him exactly when to come and which door to come to.

It was agreed that I would let him in and then direct him to the prep room. I would watch the outside doors so that I could warn him if anyone returned, and he would go into the prep room and see the corpse. What he didn't know was that Cecil would be under the sheet on the prep table and when Johnny got close enough, Cecil would jump up with the sheet covering his face and grab him.

It was hard to keep a straight face as I quietly met Johnny and took him as far as the prep room door. We had all the lights turned down about as low as they would go. I promised Johnny I would signal if anyone returned. He was so somber or scared that he never even asked where Cecil was. When I shut the door behind him, I immediately realized that one thing had happened that we hadn't planned for. A certain clicking sound in the door lock reminded me that the lock was not working exactly right and that it had locked from the inside. I couldn't get in now, but even worse—since he didn't know how to work the door, Johnny couldn't get out.

I stepped around to a small window that looked into the prep room just in time to see Johnny haltingly approaching the draped table. You could tell that he had extremely mixed emotions about pulling that sheet back and seeing what was under it. Cecil had not moved, not even the slight movement of breathing.

Just as Johnny touched the edge of the sheet, Cecil erupted on top of him, grabbing him with all of his strength and the sheet caught between them so that Johnny could not see who had him. Although Johnny was much smaller, he threw Cecil around like he was hardly even there. Cecil either wouldn't or couldn't let go as Johnny's howls got louder and louder. His panic was so great that even when the sheet dropped enough to disclose that it was Cecil, he didn't even recognize him.

Finally, he threw Cecil loose and I could tell even from a distance that the panic was out of hand; I had to do something. I have never seen such a look of horror; it was no joking matter now. I moved toward the door from my direction and Johnny was moving toward it from his. I tried yelling to him to calm down, that it was Cecil, that it was a joke, but nothing was heard. I could hear his first grab at the door but it didn't do anything. On his second grab, the door broke open and there stood Johnny with the doorknob in his hand. The door had come back with such force that when it hit him in the face, a huge blood blister rose like an egg filled with blood over his eye.

He never broke stride. I grabbed him around the shoulders and tried to stop him. It was like I wasn't even there. I'm not sure he even saw me, and suddenly I was lying in the floor, and he was headed out the back door into the garage with me struggling to follow him. He ran straight out the door and straight for the garage door toward the outside. The only problem was that the garage door was about two-thirds down. He must not have noticed that either as he ran at full speed directly into the door. It caught him about waist high and threw him back onto the concrete floor.

It should have killed him—could have killed him. Instead, he never stopped moving. Now, instead of being propelled by his feet, he was sliding on his back, feet first, pushing himself out with his elbows. As soon as he was clear of the doors, he was up and running again, out toward a large field and woods that were nearby. He never looked back.

Cecil and I were so stunned that we didn't exactly know what to do about what had happened. We fixed the door, straightened up the prep room, and waited. There is no question that we laughed until we hurt, but somewhere in the back of our minds we could not help but worry about Johnny.

In about an hour his girlfriend came to the door. She had come for his car but had hardly any details about what had happened. Johnny was at the Burger King and couldn't talk. She wanted us to come and see if we could do anything for him. When we got there Johnny was a mess. To add insult to injury, he had run through a huge briar patch in his terror of getting away. He was scratched all over, his clothes were torn, and he still couldn't talk. It was over an hour before we could get much sense out of him again. He basically understood what we had done, but never was totally able to put it all together. Needless to say, Cecil and I decided to let it drop. Johnny never came back inside the funeral home again.

All of this was great fun to be sure, but somehow we all realized that our lifestyles weren't really getting us anywhere. We were too young for the boredom that started rising from our routines. There seemed to be a whole lot more world out there yet to be seen; we were too young to start being adults in Hollywood, Florida. We could see where that had gotten those young people just a little older than us; we knew we didn't want that. We went back and talked to the recruiter.

The Army had what they called the "buddy system" at that time. It guaranteed that you could enlist with your friends and stay together throughout training and the assignments beyond. That appealed to us very strongly. Not only could we kick ass and take names in Vietnam, but we could build our Burger King and best of all—we could do it together.

The whole idea of something like airborne, special forces, or combat infantry stirred our imaginations just like they had been stirred by John Wayne and Vic Morrow. It's hard to convince a kid that television isn't real. If you watch enough of it, you easily conceive of yourself being a part of the action and glory. I needed some new action; maybe even glory didn't sound too bad.

I had more problems about the decision than my friends. What about Momma? What about Kay and Joe? Sure, I could send my

Army pay, but it wouldn't be as much as I was bringing home now, and Joe was not quite to the "man of the house" stage. My obligations were lessened a little by the natural distancing that was occurring between Momma and me. Sometimes I resisted her complaints about my late hours, or who my friends were, or any smoking or drinking that I was doing. That she still badgered me about going to church meant, to me, that she was still treating me like a little boy. When she would ask me where I had been, my stock answer had become "Nowhere. Just out shooting the bull." She came up with her own stock response: "Why don't you shoot him and kill him and get on home." By every indication, it was time for me to get out of the nest; I expect that although she resisted it, Momma understood this time a whole lot better than I did.

There was only one major obstacle that I focused on: the old Chevy needed tires badly. There was no way I could join the Army and leave Momma and Kay to have to drive a car with bad tires. The only problem about all this was that I didn't have money to buy a new set of tires. I simply couldn't go until there were tires for the car. Finally, John Bludworth loaned me the money, the tires were put on the car, and we went down to Coral Gables to enlist. When I think back about that period, it's amazing how we dealt with life on such a naive and simplistic level; imagine, new tires were the final, major factor in one of the most critical decisions that would be made in my entire life.

We all had to take physical examinations and passed without a hitch. Then, there was a series of tests that were supposed to show our intelligence or whether we could learn. I never had any trouble learning anything that I was really interested in, but I had also never been very good at taking tests. One of the enlistment officers came into where we were waiting and asked me to come with him into another room. The one thing that had never entered my mind suddenly hit me square in the face; I flunked the test!

There was a rush of uncontrollable emotions. I had let Bobby down and he would be disappointed and embarrassed. I had let my family down. I would be embarrassed in front of my friends. Finally, there was confirmation on paper that I was a failure. I began to cry and beg the man to let me in. I could not remember the last time I had cried.

One thing that you could say about this group of friends—Cecil Hobbs, Johnny Frazier, and John Bludworth—we might do almost anything to each other in the way of pranks and jokes, but when our backs were against the wall we took up for each other. They must have sensed that something was wrong and, uninvited, walked back into the room where I sat. I looked up through my tears and they were all standing there insisting on wanting to know from the sergeant what the problem was.

He explained the test score; they could go but I could not. I'm not sure which one of them spoke first, but quickly the "buddy system" that we had signed up under was invoked. If all of us didn't go, none of us went. At first the sergeant resisted and tried to con them into thinking that this was an exception and not a condition of the "deal." That did not temper their objection one bit; in fact, with a chorus of "we'll walk the straight hell out of here right now," the sergeant recognized that he was getting nowhere. Given the possibility of losing four warm bodies from his monthly quota of enlistments instead of one, he calmly and simply changed the test scores. We were in the Army now.

There were a few days back in Hollywood before we left for processing at Fort Jackson in South Carolina. At first, Momma didn't know exactly how to take the immediate reality of my leaving. In the end, as I probably could have expected, she told me that there were times when people simply had to do what they felt like they had to do. It was my time. I'm sure that when she thought about the Army that she saw it through the lens of Bobby's success. Maybe it would, in fact, help make a man out of me, too. I doubt that she had heard much of anything about Vietnam either.

The Army bused us to Miami and put us up overnight in a hotel before we were to catch the train for South Carolina the next day. We sat around the hotel room, drank a little, and reminisced about the past couple of years. There was a lot of macho talk about all we would do in boot camp and beyond with our toughness. We would be the meanest sons-of-bitches that "this man's Army" had ever seen.

Around midnight we went out walking on the street near the hotel. We hit upon one of the few businesses left open—a tattoo parlor. The other three guys immediately thought a tattoo was exactly what we needed: all of us with the same tattoo in the same place, a symbol of the bond that existed between us. At first I said no; I didn't want to get marked up with some kind of stupid tattoo. At their insistence, I relented. With the mixture of booze, remembrances of the past, and dreams about the future, how could I do anything but relent? An hour or so later we were walking back to our hotels and on out toward our futures, bearing small, Snoopy-like dog images on the lower outside of our left calves—a bond of friendship and expectation made concrete in yet another hero of our day.

Our mothers were at the train station the next day. As we gave our goodbye hugs and promises to take care of ourselves, stay out of trouble, and write, none of us had even the slightest indication of an idea that these four boys going off to the Army could not, and would not, return the same as we had left. The train pulled out of sight from Miami, our mothers—and a whole lot more than we would ever know. I found myself fighting back tears again.

Chapter VI

The train trip up through Central Florida and into South Carolina is nothing special. The countryside all begins to look about the same pretty quickly. There are a lot of orange groves, drainage ditches, and pasture fields that look scuffed rather than lush and green. Most of the parts of towns you see from trains are the poorest, oldest, most run down. There are faded signboards advertising last year's cars and small posters nailed to vacant buildings and power poles telling of events of little interest to the outside world that took place two or three months ago—wrestling matches, gospel singings, and one local personality or another running for constable or sheriff. Most of the people you see from the train windows have a look of desperation about them somehow. You wonder if they are reading your face the same way, feeling that your desperation is worse than their own. It is probably a toss-up.

This all sounds pretty melancholy, and that is about the best word I can think of to describe the trip toward processing at Fort Jackson. All of the romantic adventure we had built the Army up to be seemed to have pretty much drained away as our waving, tear-brushing mothers disappeared in the distance. The bravado of the night before had evaporated, though something of the tingling pain of the tattoo still remained as you shifted position to get more comfortable or as you moved to avoid the eye contact of your friends that held the reminder that they were thinking the same thoughts you were thinking.

There was a sense of breaking ties, a sense of suddenly not knowing these three people sitting nearest you as well as you had thought, a sense of private isolation that would not allow you for a moment to let down your guard, to tell another person what you were really feeling. We may have talked a little, but what talk there was was mostly forced. None of us showed any emotion to speak of, almost like we had now mounted a huge wheel that was starting to turn and with each turn gained a momentum that made it impossible to get off.

As night settled in, I thought of things I wished that I had said to Momma but did not. I was filled with guilt over the fact that her "Provider," and the one who was helping provide for Kay and Joe to a certain extent, was out chasing an adventure that suddenly was filled with more uncertainty than might make it worthwhile. We probably ate and had a beer or two—if you could even get beer on a train then—it's all pretty much lost in a vague fog now. The passing lights and rocking sound of the train finally lulled me off to sleep—like I was a big baby in the arms of a gentle metal giant; much more a child at that moment than a man.

The sun rose the next morning on a landscape that I had not seen in three years. There were mountains in the distance, or at least hills, and the vegetation of the trees and shrubs was distinctly different. My mind immediately raced to those times that Momma had let us go on a train to Wilmington to the Azalea Festival. That was one of the most pleasant experiences that I could recall from childhood. I had gone to sleep and awakened to the thoughts of Momma.

The train eventually pulled into the station at Columbia, South Carolina. Buses were already there to pick us up and take us to the new recruit processing center at Fort Jackson. I was a little bit amazed at the number of boys getting off the train and getting onto the buses. I guess that I had noticed these people, but they had somehow not impressed me as being bound for my own destination; they didn't look like soldiers—and maybe I didn't either.

The few days we spent at Fort Jackson were basically non-eventful. We stayed in large dorm-like buildings, ate three times a day—all we could eat, and listened to one piece of information and then another. We were welcomed by people in uniforms which brightly exhibited high rank. We were told of the place in our country's traditions that we were taking. We were assured that every effort would be made to give us a smooth transition from civilian life. The whole experience of the military service was explained as being one of great opportunity, and from the looks of these people—and from what I kept telling myself about Bobby—it must be. Maybe this would not be too bad after all. If "boot camp" wasn't anything more than this, then some of the rumors about its harshness that I had started thinking about on the train trip north must have been someone's idea of a bad joke.

There was a lot of testing in the first few days. This made me feel uncomfortable because I was afraid that I might have an experience like the one in Miami. I could see myself on a train back to Florida having to tell everyone that I had "flunked out" of the Army. We were assured, however, that these tests were used to determine what area of service we were best qualified for. At the end of the first week I was assigned a Military Occupational Speciality (MOS) of "11-Bravo-20" or, to bring the sophisticated terminology quickly down to earth, "Light Weapons Infantryman." I never learned anything about the test results, although the rumor had it that "11-Bravo-20" was the catch-all for those who demonstrated no skills in any other areas. It was what I had wanted all along.

The next set of directions I was given rang with what I felt was unbelievable good luck; such good luck, in fact, that I felt that maybe some of Momma's prayers—which I knew were cascading toward heaven over me—were working. We were ordered to load buses the next day for Fort Gordon in Georgia. Bobby was stationed at Fort Gordon and Russell lived in Augusta. This wouldn't be like going home, but it sure would be the next best thing. Even Cecil and the others were getting upbeat again and beginning to feel that there might be some "family" advantages for them as well. Little did we know.

When the buses got to our new training area, we were directed to "Company Area E42." This would be our address for the next eight weeks. As we got off the buses we were met by a couple of sergeants and low-ranking officers. They explained that we were part of a new training company that was being assembled, but that our group had gotten there early and the area was not as yet operational. We could put our bags in the barracks and begin to settle in, but for the time being we would have to use the facilities of the training company across the street. As soon as we had settled in, we should report to the mess hall over there and have lunch. As I looked around, it was about as I had expected: a system of streets with barracks on all sides separated by exercise and assembly areas where troops already in training were doing what I could only describe as whatever it is that trainees do in order to become soldiers. Everyone seemed to know exactly where they belonged, and though the general facility was old you immediately noticed how spotlessly clean it all appeared. Bobby was out there somewhere, and I could not wait to see him.

We left our belongings and settled in with the group that was drifting off in the direction of where the mess hall for the neighboring company must be. We had been issued uniforms at Fort Jackson, but nothing seemed to fit. We looked like anything but the pictures that we had seen in the recruiting office at home. A line of about 75 people had developed and, although we had had next to no instruction in assembling ourselves into any kind of formal formation, it was clear that the people in the line would march straight and upright when the line moved and stand at what we had heard called "parade rest" when the line stopped. We copied this as best we could, and the word was passed that some of the sergeants standing nearby would pull anyone out of line that was "slacking off" and have them do pushups on the spot. I had learned a long time ago to watch what everyone else was doing and do it myself. That strategy worked well, and we moved along without speaking toward the front of the line.

Chapter VII

Then I saw Bobby, standing off at a distance like the other Drill Instructors with a look on his face like he had been studying me for several minutes and was making up his mind exactly how he would respond in this situation. He was undoubtedly as surprised as I was. I moved up a few places in the line but our eyes never left each other. Everything within me wanted to yell out his name and rush up to him, but the formality and strangeness of the moment held me in place. He might need to be careful about how he responded around the other sergeants so I decided to let him make the first move.

In a few more moments his face began to move and I heard his unmistakable voice dominant above the general noise of the mess hall: "Matherson!" Our names were stencilled across the front of our uniforms, but why not "Charles" and why the same dead tone that the other sergeants were calling people out of line with over one indiscretion or another?

I stepped out of line and approached him. For some reason it seemed to make sense to stop short and copy the actions of the other young men I had seen approach one or another of the ranking enlisted men. Suppressing a smile over the unexpected coincidence that was bringing us together, I got my face together as seriously as I could and sharply remarked "Yes, Sir!"

His sharp, stunning response stopped me dead in my tracks and washed away all of the smile and most of the blood from my face, "Don't you call me 'Sir'; I'm not a 'Sir,' I'm a Sergeant. I'm not a 'Sir,' I work for my living. Don't ever forget it!" At first the thought crossed my mind that this was all just an act for the others' benefit, but as quickly as that thought came it was gone. Bobby meant business. I snapped back like a programmed robot, "Yes, Sergeant!"

He paused for a moment and studied me up and down. With near scorn on his face, he half-way spit his next words at me: "You look like a piece of shit!" I wasn't expecting this at all, and suddenly I could feel a hard knot rising in my throat. I expected my eyes to tear over, but everything within me fought for mind over matter—I could not cry. Not here. Not now.

Bobby went on, "You're not under Momma's petticoat any more. You're in a man's world now. We are going to make a man out of you or kill you trying. It's time for you to grow up!" Everything was running in a blur now. I wanted to say, "Thanks a whole hell of a lot, Bobby. I really appreciate all this." I knew better, but he must have read my thoughts. Somewhere in the midst of all he was saying and all I was thinking, I heard at least two more references to my appearance and a piece of shit.

His attention locked on my belt buckle. Something about it looked like shit, too. He called for an Acting Corporal, and immediately another guy, almost as young looking as I was, seemed to appear out of nowhere. He was sharp to attention and parroted the "Yes, Sergeant!" perfectly. Bobby ordered him to go quickly for a pair of scissors.

I couldn't imagine why. The only thing that crossed my mind was a scene from an old John Wayne movie when he was unjustly drummed out of the cavalry. Some officer took scissors and cut off all his buttons and medals in front of an entire fort full of soldiers. Surely to God Bobby wasn't going to do anything like this! It felt like every eye in the place was on me. Was I crazy? Was Bobby crazy? For a moment it seemed like the whole damned world had gone crazy.

The corporal returned with the scissors and Bobby proceeded to grab at my belt. As he talked he jerked my shirt and belt around while I still tried as hard as I could to hold firm in the attention position. He was explaining that there had to be a direct line that ran down the front of the buttons on your shirt, across the brass buckle of the belt, and on down the fly cover of your pants. If this line was not straight, you were not in uniform. He tightened the belt exposing even more webbing than had been hanging down. Nothing was to be hanging loose, no strings—which he termed "ropes"—and no leftover pieces of belt. He took the scissors and cut off the excess webbing. Even while he was jerking me around and cutting the belt, I began to feel something different—affection. It might have been a strange way to show it, but he was showing me that he cared and was trying to help.

Maybe something about my facial expression indicated that I was picking up on what he was really doing, so his behavior abruptly changed back to the way it had been. He returned the scissors, dismissed the corporal, and concentrated on me again,

"Do you see those barracks over there?" He pointed to the nearest building. "Yes, Sergeant!" came my correct reply. "There is a cup over there under that building. Get someone to go and get it out, and you bring it to me."

I might have wondered how Bobby knew that there was a cup under the building. In normal life, I would have said, "How do you know?" Maybe I would have figured out that he was involved in a tactic so common to Drill Instructors in this situation that a cup was always conveniently planted. I guess I realized this in retrospect, but at the moment I simple moved—halfway running and halfway marching—to the edge of the building where he had pointed and started sliding under.

He stopped me before much more than my head was out of sight, although I did clearly see a shiny styrofoam cup: "Are you completely stupid? I knew you were dumb, but this beats it all! Didn't you hear me say 'Get someone to get the cup'? Can't you even follow the simplest instructions. Now, you do exactly as I said to do!"

I slinked back out from under the barracks and raced over to Bludworth. I sorta whispered for him to come on. He knew what to do, but his face read "For God's sake, go away! Don't get me into any of this!" Bludworth got the cup, handed it to me, and both of us stood back to attention in front of Bobby. He dismissed Johnny back to the chow line.

He eased up closer to my face than any time yet. I thought, "Here it comes again." He was in control; whatever he did, I simply would have to take. Then, without changing the expression on his face, he spoke quietly, "This is not going to be easy. You hang in there. You're not a kid anymore." Here was the purest affection that this moment was capable of, but as he dismissed me back to the line with the others, I was never so glad to get the hell away from another person in all of my life. I didn't care if I ever saw Bobby again.

For the next few weeks, especially while we were confined to the company area during our initial training time, I didn't see much of Bobby. I couldn't go to him, and it was clear that he didn't want to come to me. I would occasionally catch a glimpse of him and one of the other instructors walking back to the general barracks area. I wasn't expecting favoritism, but I was at least looking for brotherly decency; instead, he had my own Drill

Instructor make sure that I was not named to the position of acting squad leader which I had worked so hard for in the first days of training.

It took me a long time to figure out what was going on with Bobby. What I finally understood was that he knew exactly where I was going and what I would face when I got there. There was a direct relationship between the roughness of training and a person's ability to survive in Vietnam. He knew that the harder everything was on me now, the greater my chances of living six months from now. In the end, he was absolutely right.

For the next couple of days, it seemed that we did little but stand in lines. There were shots, dental inspections, haircuts (or head shaves, as the case may be), and the issuing of one piece of material and then another. We were warned that we were responsible for everything, that any loss or unnecessary damage would mean extra time and still have to be paid for out of the next-to-nothing money that we were earning as recruits.

We were like cattle, a faceless herd of green moving with our files held securely under our arms from one colorless building to another. It was all confusing and disorienting; our uniforms didn't fit, we couldn't march in time, maybe we were as stupid as the Drill Instructors kept on insisting.

All in all, this wasn't so bad. Sure, we had to get up before sunrise, but we had all we wanted to eat three times a day. It was good food, and I especially liked the fact that we had all the milk that we wanted to drink. I guess we saw all the other training groups were doing, but it didn't exactly register in our minds that a different world was right around the corner.

That "different world" then suddenly came in like a series of unrelenting explosions going on all around you, keeping the earth shaking and rolling, without even the slightest hint of stopping or letting up.

The whole idea of basic training is to take people and totally and completely break them down. You are daily, hourly—literally from one minute to the next—called upon and forced to do more than you ever thought you could. We had all run the beaches to get in shape for special forces during the month or so before we had left home and were in pretty good shape—we thought. By the time our instructors ran us and marched us, ran us and marched us, ran us and marched us, I realized that I didn't know what shape was. I have come in in the afternoon with hands that were solid blisters from exercises on handwalking bars, only to get up the next morning to grab at those bars again as the blisters broke and the water and blood flowed down and mixed with the sweat and dirt on your arms. It was pure hell.

Besides the physical exercise, there was an unrelenting stream of verbal abuse. You were stupid, ignorant, dumb, a redneck asshole, a mamma's boy—it never stopped. You were constantly harassed with push-ups, and no matter how many you could get to the point of doing, you were always forced to do more than that. There were general inspections at almost any time, and everything had better be in the place for which it was intended. There was always cleaning to do on the barracks or in the company area. There was continual emphasis on personal hygiene, which for many in the group had never been a matter of major concern; cleanliness might not be next to godliness, but in combat it could mean some semblance of comfort and perhaps even an element in survival. There were always boots and brass to be shined.

We were issued two pairs of combat boots and told to place a small white dot on the back of one pair. This way, we could not get away with wearing the same pair of boots two days in a row. This also insured that you had boot cleaning work to do every night. It is no exaggeration to say that most of us spent two to three hours every night just shining boots. It was mindless, monotonous work that you finally hated. But it had to be perfect or the consequences were a lot worse than boot-shining. I never had to do KP, but plenty of my barracks mates did.

In the end it was all part of breaking us down. Finally, I guess I understood about the boots. If we were going to be "foot soldiers," then care of our feet and our footwear was one of the most important responsibilities we would ever have. If your feet ever let you down in combat, you were at a severe disadvantage. There is nothing like shining boots fifteen or eighteen hours a week to give you respect for footwear and the discipline to persevere at a task until it is done as close to perfection as is possible.

Everywhere you went, you were under the closest scrutiny possible. Even the least step out of line caused the harshest overreaction—at least we thought it was an overreaction. The humiliation of push-ups until you fell with your face in the dirt or mud, in front of all of your group, took place two or three dozen times a day. On one occasion, I saw a guy drop a cigarette butt on the ground and then have to dig a six-foot deep "grave" for it with a small entrenchment tool. After the "grave" was refilled, the instruction said to dig it back up and dispose of it properly.

There was nothing that you could do about it. You were told that anyone going AWOL would be caught before they got off the compound and that meant an Army stockade and duty that would make boot camp seem like "a holiday pass to Disneyland." It didn't take long to believe these people—you only went exactly where you were supposed to go. One guy in my barracks started urinating every night in his bunk. It dripped down on the guy below him and one fight after another followed. He claimed bladder problems, but the instructors had seen everything by now. Finally, it was easier to control his bladder and go on than it was to fight and still not get any attention. Only one guy in the whole training area "freaked" and shot himself in the leg; we never knew exactly what happened to him.

After they had broken us down to the place that Bobby's "piece of shit" had more dignity than we felt that we had, they could start building us back again—building us back their way. The amazing thing was the speed with which our young bodies responded. It was true that by the time "lights out" came you were so physically drained and mentally exhausted you simply fell into bed and were asleep within seconds. It was true that the whole process was so numbing that you really did not reflect on what was happening around you. In spite of all of this, you could almost see your muscles developing; after a while, you could even sense the stirring of pride and self-confidence that would finally flower before the training period was over. It was never really fun and often it absolutely hurt, but on the rare occasion of a good day you could pause for a half second and see that it was working.

And behind it all, as much as you had times in which you completely hated those men in their Smokey Bear hats and chevron-striped shirts, they still knew where you were going. All we knew was that we were being trained for Vietnam, but still we had no idea—no idea what "Vietnam" meant.

After a couple of weeks, we began to adjust to the routine. By now my friends and I had been separated into different platoons within the same company. As we passed each other in one training activity or another or had a random moment to talk over a meal, we expressed mixed emotions. We had gotten over the idea that Bobby had really "sold us a bill of goods" and we liked what we were experiencing of the "lean, mean fighting machines" that we were becoming, but we were still wondering if it was worth all the effort. It wasn't the same tired we experienced from working all the time in our ironically named homeland of "Hollywood," but it was tired all the same.

One of the most amazing, early experiences to me was the way we actually learned how to walk in formation. At first we had been like a clumsy sophomore at his first dance, but by a week or ten days we developed a smoothness that most of us thought never would have been possible. God knows we got enough practice; everywhere we went, we went in formation. At any time we were expecting formation marches to the toilets. The sergeants taught us some of the cadence songs and we picked up others from training companies ahead of us. A couple of the black guys picked it up first and took the lead. There wasn't much thought or anything said about them "having rhythm"; in fact, they could do something most of us whites couldn't and it helped us all. The very idea that an awkward, disoriented group of eighteen- and nineteen-year olds—especially from the South—could be marching out across a field singing and moving in a rhythm as intricate as any dance, and the fact that this all was being proudly led by a black guy, made you want to stop and shake your head in disbelief. The only problem was that you didn't have time to stop; if you did, some sergeant would be kicking your butt or, worse than that, the people behind would be walking right over you. Sometimes I still come up to the place where I might cross a street and halfway wait to hear the commands "Post road guard!" and "Retrieve road guard!"

Moving on into the second and third weeks of training, our efforts began to involve more than the punishing exercise of getting in shape. We kept on doing all that we had done in this area, but new information was added. We experienced learning how to use gas masks by going into buildings where we were doused by a sickening, thick smokey chemical fog. Besides being frightening and destroying most of your sense of control, it made your pores and sinuses run like tap water. You were told to take a deep breath, take your mask off, count to ten, put your mask back on, clear it, and begin to breathe again. There was no horsing around. You surprised yourself at how closely you could listen to instruction, trust the person who was giving the orders, and with great precision do exactly as you were told. Whether you knew it or not, the lessons learned in the gas chamber would have a chance to be put into practice again and again on the battlefield.

I was particularly interested in the first aid training that became a continual part of the middle and latter weeks of boot camp. All the interest that I had always had in medicine came back in the strongest way during this time. Some of the guys had no points of reference at all as to what the instructors were saying, but all of my work in the funeral home had given me a strong orientation to the workings of the human body and the use of various instruments to probe and repair it.

It was clear what the training was directed toward: the instructors were attempting to show every single trainee how he could be a front line medic in a battle situation—how he could perform life saving functions until more expert help might arrive. We were told time and again that on the battlefield we might be the only doctor one of our friends might have. It really came home to me, by the kind of wounds they were teaching us how to treat, exactly what we might be getting ready to be exposed to.

There was a great deal of discussion about bullet wounds to different parts of the body, wounds inflicted by various kinds of primitive boobytrap snares, and wounds caused by fragmentation devices like mines and grenades. We weren't talking about the scratches, blisters, and insect bites of my Boy Scout days that could be handled with vaseline and bandaids; we were talking about exit wounds as big as your fists, limbs being blown off, and gushing flows of blood that somehow had to be stopped in moments or someone would bleed to death right in front of you. I have never listened so intently to any kind of instruction in all my life.

For some strange reason there was one type of bullet wound we studied and had explained to us that I was most intrigued by. The training officers called it a "sucking chest wound." If a person is shot in the chest area, it is possible for the bullet to puncture the lung and then exit the body, leaving the entry hole, the passage and hole through the lung, and the exit hole. The lung continues to function, but it is no longer drawing air in through your throat but is "sucking air" through the exit hole. If the exit hole can be clogged, you will begin to breathe again unless the damage is too severe. If the hole can't be clogged, you smother to death. It was a gruesome thought.

In our first aid kits, we carried a large pad about the size of an envelope. When you broke this open—like you were pulling an envelope apart—you exposed a sterile, silvery coated interior. You were instructed in the treatment of many types of bullet wounds to make a compress out of the pad and hold it firmly against the wound to stop bleeding. For the "sucking chest wound," the idea was to press and cram the pad into the exit wound to stop the passage of air so that normal breathing would have a chance. For the first time, in the quietness that rose above the first aid training session, it began to strike some of us exactly what might be out there in the jungle.

By the third and fourth week of training, I was getting back enough of my strength and sanity to start thinking again. My basic thought was that "there had to be an easier way than this." I had always been good at finding that easier way; anybody who could create an igloo at Plantation Storage and get a couple hours of sleep during a workday could surely figure a way around some of the drudgery of boot camp.

Someone came through one day asking about volunteers to be company drivers. For some reason there was an immediate need for anyone who had ever driven anything besides a car. I thought to myself, "If you're driving a vehicle, you're better off than almost anything we're having to do." I gave them the information about my ambulance and school bus driving experiences; it worked. I easily got my military driver's license and began to be called on for one driving assignment and then another. I thought in the back of my mind that Bobby must be letting down his guard; this would have been "easy duty" in his mind, and he never would have let it happen.

What I hadn't expected was that missing a class did not mean that it would be avoided. It simply would have to be made up. I hadn't exchanged one duty for another; I had simply gotten to do two things now instead of one. My decision was made even worse when I realized that the training that I would first miss was weapons training—the one part of basic that I had looked forward to the most. I wanted Bobby to be proud of me, and in the back of my mind I had already determined that I was going to be the best weapons person that this company had ever had.

Instead I got behind on the M-14 training. The M-14 was basically a training weapon, a forerunner of the M-16 rifle that would become the primary infantry weapon in Vietnam. When the first proficiency testing took place, I scored so low that I had to be retested. Driving assignments would have to take second place; this was what I was going to do. On the second round, I made "expert," and although "best in the company" did not come up, I knew that these instructors did not hand out "expert" ratings very easily. Cecil, Frazier, and Bludworth were all doing well, too; without the interference that I was getting from Bobby, all three became squad leaders.

I also made "expert" on the M-60 machine gun. This was a larger, heavier weapon that had a great deal more fire power than the M-14/M-16. Usually, it seemed like the instructors picked out the larger, stronger men for the M-60 training. We guessed that when we got to Vietnam, that size and strength would make a lot of the determinations about what kind of work we would be doing or what kind of weapons we would be assigned to. The M-60 required four persons for its ideal operation. One man fired and carried the weapon while the other men carried the ammo boxes and helped feed the ammunition into the gun. The M-60 was usually fired from a tripod or bipod on which it was mounted; in an emergency it could be hand held and operated by one person. It was my favorite weapon, and I loved the feel of power that rose as it sprayed its fire across the target range.

We began to learn to operate as a unit or as a team. It was no longer each person trying to find enough strength within himself to get through the next set of exercises or the next day of training. Now it was impressed on us that we depended on each other; if one man went in, we all went in—when we came out, we came out together. Some of the scenes in the movies that have been made about Vietnam that depict someone in a company or platoon being left behind to fight the enemy alone offend me. It was carved into the marrow of our bones: you didn't leave one of your people behind alive. The Drill Instructors would run us more than ever, run us until someone had to fall out; when that occurred, the others picked him up and carried him. We all got there together.

The main event that I remember from boot camp took place about the end of the third week or beginning of the fourth week. We shared a training, exercise area with another company that was beyond its fifth week of training and was almost ready to graduate. They were a sharp, arrogant group, and had already been through the part of training that had to do with hand-to-hand combat. When we would do our morning exercises on the common field we shared, they were always directing some insult or generally smart-ass remark toward us.

We would do our exercise drills and then run in circles around the training area. Our company would run in one direction and their company would run in the opposite direction. On each trip around the field we would pass. As we passed their harassment would increase, and finally they came to the place that they were cursing us, spitting on us, and tripping or kicking. We would have people stumble, fall out of line, and break the order of our formation. Our sergeants, who probably knew exactly what was happening, would yell at us, make us run even more, or give us additional exercises. We wanted to fight the other company but knew better than to take on people who had had the hand-to-hand training that was still on down the road for us.

Finally, over one weekend when there were not as many of our sergeants around, our squad leaders got together with their squad leaders and made arrangements to "settle" our differences once and for all. No doubt, this was exactly what the other company had been baiting us for. It was decided that in the middle of the next week that the two companies would meet on the training field at about 1:30 or 2:00 in the morning and simply fight it out. If the sergeants ever got word of this, they never said anything about it; they probably would have seen it as being good for the spirit of both groups.

What wasn't common knowledge was that we had some people in our company from up North who had been in street gangs and who knew a lot more about "real" fighting than most of the rest of us who at most had probably gotten into a wrestling, drunken brawl or two at some nightspot on a Friday night.

A strategy was developed that had little to do with the meeting that had been arranged by the respective squad leaders. We got every large garbage can we could find and carried these to the nearby steam heating plant. There we filled the cans with large chunks of coal about the size of cantaloupes. About midnight or a little before we placed members of our company along with the cans of coal on top of barracks buildings that surrounded the exercise field. Everyone that was left then armed themselves with the entrenchment tools. We simply dressed in our underwear and combat boots so that we could distinguish ourselves from the other group. We waited.

Right after midnight we spotted movement around the other company's barracks in the distance. They grouped their forces and then came in an all-out, yelling charge across the exercise area. Without a doubt, the screaming charge was intended to inhibit and unnerve us to the place that we would be easy prey for the sweep of their charge.

We stood our ground. At the point that had been pre-arranged in our planning, the men on the barracks unleashed their bombardment of coal. You can imagine what it would have been like suddenly to have large balls of coal raining down on your head from every direction at once. Besides being hit, knocked down and out, and ripped apart in every way imaginable, the men were totally disoriented. They began to run in every direction—into each other—in the dark. They began to strike out at each other, stumble over each other, dodge coal. It was total chaos for them.

Then a signal was given and the "artillery" stopped as our "infantry" charged. All the hand-to-hand training in the world was of little use in view of their disorientation and injury and our entrenchment tools. Our fear and excitement simply caused us to strike out more wildly. Within only a few moments, they were running, pulling, and dragging each other back toward their barracks. We ended up having to pull some of our people off of their number that remained before someone was beaten to death.

The next day there was an uproar of investigation. In the riot, one man in their company had gotten an eye knocked out and there were several broken arms and legs. The number of people having to report to the base medical facility was so great that the other company was essentially unable to continue training for a day or two. Not a single person in our entire unit was even hurt badly enough to require treatment.

This was all such a big deal, however, that it could not be overlooked. The sergeant who had told us early on—as I am sure he had told every training company that he had every had—that he wanted us to be the "meanest Sons of Bitches on the entire base" had finally had his dream come true, but there wasn't much he could say about it. High ranking officers showed up to ask questions, we were restricted to base with all privileges revoked, and as much for our protection as anything until the other company finished training, our barracks were surrounded by concertina wire. It's razor sharp edges insured that the "battle" of the exercise area would not be repeated.

In the end, I had mixed emotions. I was all for having a little fun, even if it meant a fight. I was sorry though that anyone had really gotten hurt. You had to show that you were tough. If you didn't, someone would walk over you. Any sign of weakness was an open invitation to a beating. You could feel the pride building in our unit. Maybe in the end, the toughness and pride were what the rebuilding process was all about; maybe something of what happened on that exercise field would be a major component of basic survival in what for some in our group was an experience only a few weeks away.

Finally, our restrictions were lifted, the other company was graduated out, and a short pass was promised for the upcoming weekend. Bobby had gotten more friendly in the latter weeks of the training and had invited me to his house for the weekend. Russell would be there and Momma was coming up from Florida. I could not wait!

The day before the off-time was to start, I was in one of the small recreation centers we had been allowed to begin going to on rare occasions. Frazier and Cecil Hobbs were with me. We had a few drinks, although the low-alcohol beer was so weak that you would have had to drink two gallons even to begin to get drunk. There was a group of Puerto Rican trainees in the rec center sitting near us. I suddenly became aware that my helmet was missing, and I spotted it lying beside one of the Puerto Ricans.

Frazier and I walked over and I insisted that they give my helmet back. All I could think of was the possibility of having to report the helmet lost and losing my weekend privilege. There must have been ten or twelve of them, and they began to gesture and shove us around a little. They weren't giving up the helmet; I could go to hell.

I simply waded into the middle of them, pushed one aside, and got the helmet. There was no immediate resistance, and I walked on out into the front of the building and started across a major parade area that led back to our barracks. Suddenly, I was surrounded by all of the Puerto Ricans in a tight circle. The one man in their group that I had retrieved the helmet from jumped in the middle of the ring with me. There was no question that they had practice fighting like this. He was advancing on me while, all at the same time, they were kicking and jabbing at me. I was certain that I was about to get the worst beating of my entire life.

With that prospect in mind, I figured that I was at least going to take out one of them in the process. But, where was Frazier? It wasn't like him at all to leave us, even if it was two against twelve. Cecil was right there, though, ready to follow my cue.

I lunged at the one advancing opponent and begin to fight him with every force of energy within me. Immediately we were really fighting all twelve. The only saving mercy was that all of them could not get to us at once. I was getting it pretty good, but was still determined to take one with me. I locked onto his fingers with my teeth, and he began to yell and pull with all of his might. I never will forget the picture formed in my mind of his hand pulling back out of my mouth and the white, shining bone that was exposed as the meat of his fingers were pulled back with my teeth.

At that moment it seemed that the ring of kicking, shouting Puerto Ricans began to shrink back. I was anticipating a final, all-out attack. What was happening? The circle broke and light began to pour in. I could see beyond their kicking legs and here came Frazier—with the whole damn training company! Puerto Ricans scattered in twelve different directions with a half dozen of what six weeks before had been totally unattached strangers in hot pursuit of every one of them.

I figured that all passes were off and that I would probably end up in the stockade over this one. It was amazing that all of this had taken place right out in the middle of the main base parade field, and no one ever said a word. When I showed up at Bobby's house the next day, I was scratched and bruised in every way conceivable. Momma couldn't say too much. In the midst of her joy at seeing me for the first time in over a month, all she could get out was "Charles, are you all right?" Smiling through my wounds and own joy, I replied, "The training is a little rough, Momma. But I'm doing just fine."

Chapter VIII

I continued to be amazed by the attention to detail attached to the efforts of all of the Drill Instructors and training officers. Nothing was too small to be of significance. We memorized to the point that we could answer questions about everything from service numbers to the parts of our combat rifle without even thinking. The faster you could respond, the better, and any mistake was "rewarded" with more repetitions until you got it right. More times than not the mistakes were also accompanied by push-ups. If some of the people in the company could have been paid by the number of push-ups they were doing, they could have retired.

The only reward for correct responses and successful behavior was time. You might have a short moment or two to catch your breath or relax before the next assignment. But, one thing was for sure, until it was "right" you kept doing it again. If it took after-hours—if it took all night—you kept doing it again and again. Obviously, the best thing was clearly to listen with greatest care, watch every move the instructor made, and get it right the first time. You spent a great deal more time avoiding greater negatives than you did seeking praise or compliments. You found out the old joke about the "right way," the "wrong way," and the "Army way" was completely wrong—the Army way was the only way. It was amazing, however, how much and how quickly you did learn. Even people who had lackluster track records when it came to learning were surprised at how quickly they caught on and then mastered some technique or piece of information.

You were never asked about how you "felt" about something. Feelings and personal thoughts were left for someplace else; here you stuck completely to the subject at hand, offered no opinions, and spoke only when you were spoken to. There might be questions, but they had better be about the material that you were dealing with at that moment.

This whole training attitude extended beyond the classes to the space where you lived. No detail was too small to escape notice. The barrack's floors, bathroom surfaces, and toilets were scrubbed to the point that there was no way the kitchen plates could have been any cleaner. Every square inch was inspected and each task was performed perfectly or it was done again—the second time with an added dose of humiliation and punishment.

I started feeling like the instructors were more interested in the commodes than they were the people who sat on them. The commode performed a function; the people performed a function. And it was not always clear which function was most important. Maybe in their minds, a broken commode would create more problems than a broken person. I began to feel like a non-thinking, non-feeling machine.

And that was the entire point! We were being reduced to a function, and that function was being a well-trained, finely-honed weapon—a fighting machine. We had to function with the same efficiency and dependability, the same lack of emotion, as that spotless commode. There was no time for feelings and emotions. There was no time for unrelated questions. You had to be able to operate right the first time, to respond without thinking or questioning. Anything that interfered with this process of conditioning and response would get you killed before you knew it on a battlefield. We didn't understand that now, but we would soon enough. It sounds—and feels—all cruel and heartless; in the end, what this training did for us, given the kind of conditions that many of us would face, was the most humane act of goodness that one group of human beings could do for another group.

In the end, what they were trying to teach us more than anything else was concentration. You learned to give all of your attention to whatever detail was most important at hand. Everything else that could be a distraction was blocked out. By blocking out distractions and concentrating all of your attention on details, you lessened the chances of making mistakes or of missing something that could hurt or kill you. There is no question that you were on automatic, a sensitive mechanism with an immediate connection between stimulus and response, but for our trainers that "immediate connection" became the winning edge between survival and disaster. By the time ranking officers began to make their way into our training and bivouac areas late in the basic training cycle, and speak to us about how we were the most finely-tuned and indispensable weapon in the entire defensive arsenal of the United States, another element was added: we believed them; we recognized what they were saying as true; we now had self-esteem and self-confidence. We were ready, in fact, we wanted—to take our strength to the battlefield and confront any enemies of our great land.

Our abilities to avoid distractions and focus with a great deal of concentration on matters most immediately at hand were then made even more precise with our hand-to-hand combat training. What we had perceived as being mostly physical ended up being more mental. The first five weeks of training had taken care of the physical, and now we learned to control and channel that with our minds. All the physical strength in the world was of little importance if it could not be controlled and channeled.

The "O'Neill System of Physical Defense" was based on the most time-honored of the martial arts. We learned, through what appeared at first sight to be like the moves of a kung-fu movie, proper defensive positions, control movements, and the way to use the power and force of an enemy against him. Just as every other action and thought of our lives had been reduced to its most basic level, there was the attempt to reduce hand-to-hand combat to the most instinctive level. Our instructors talked about creating in us "the moves of an animal."

The possibilities of the O'Neill System were graphically demonstrated to us on the first day of this new class. Undoubtedly, this was a demonstration that introduced every class, but it was one that you did not forget. The instructor would be introduced by one of the company sergeants and, as was now standard procedure for our training, the new teacher would make a few introductory remarks.

Then, as was not the custom, this instructor began to taunt us a little. He told us that we probably thought that we were getting pretty tough now. We had survived all of this training, were getting stronger, were looking meaner. We were really impressed with ourselves, weren't we? In fact we were, but no one knew quite how to take this guy yet. He was only about 5'8" or so, and the thought crossed my mind that his stripes and ego had gone to his head. Still no one said a word.

He moved on to increase his bully-type attitude and gestures, directing attention to some of the men who were considerably bigger and stronger-looking than he was. Then, he issued the dare: anybody, the bigger the better, who didn't like him or what he was saying come on. He didn't care. Right here! Right now! What was the matter, were we babies, were we "chicken shit!!"

By that time, there was a volunteer. One of our ugliest, meanest, roughest products of the toughness of a hard upbringing and five weeks of intense physical training stepped forward and never broke his pace as he approached the considerably smaller martial arts instructor. It was almost as if here was the trainee's chance to take out on this instructor all his frustrations about the system we had been a part of for the past month. The instructor stepped back a pace or two and then a second pace or two, all the time taunting the now raging force in front of him to come on.

The larger man lunged, and for the next minute or so was tossed like a feather pillow from one edge of the training area to the other. It was like he was caught up in a tornado of moves and countermoves. In what seemed like a moment, he was lying in a dusty heap and the instructor had not broken a sweat or even slightly wrinkled his perfectly pressed uniform. With great meekness our "champion" was helped to his feet by the instructor, dusted off, patted on the back, and then allowed quietly and sheepishly to take his place back in our ranks. The sinking feeling that was written all over his face was being felt by everyone in our group. There were no more volunteers.

For the next several days we learned what control and attention to detail could mean in terms of self-defense. It was drilled into our heads that even though a situation looked impossible and there was no way out, to assume a defensive posture, stay in control, and calmly hold on and keep looking for options. What they put into us went deep and still remains; even though I would have no desire to test my belief, I still think that I could be confronted by ten men and have a chance to come away the winner in whatever fight might take place. It is not so much a feeling of foolish bravado but the deep-seated belief that they instilled in us that we could survive no matter what happened.

There was one crucial point that the instructor kept coming back to throughout the hand-to-hand training: do not panic! He stressed that panic was your greatest enemy. Panic was much more dangerous to you than a regiment of enemy soldiers. Once you panicked, you were beaten, at the mercy of whatever was happening around you. To stay calm, to stay in control, not to panic, he was convinced, would stand the chance of saving your life more than anything you had at your disposal. It was almost as if everything we had done from the moment we started basic training was aimed at this moment: stay in control, don't panic!

I am certain that not everyone heard that message and let it sink deep within their minds. I am also certain that even among those who did, who agreed with the idea and internalized it without question, that there were still situations in which the panic which rose within them was beyond their control. I can recall plenty of times when every ounce of my strength as a person was being called on—and then some—to control my own panic. But, in the end, it was the most important lesson of the entire experience: control your responses, never let yourself feel that a circumstance is impossible, don't panic! If you ever "lost it," you were probably done for. This was why they trained us with the single-minded determination that we met almost every moment of that first eight weeks.

Just as every great athletic coach has always taught, as flashy and dramatic as the offensive part of a contest may be, it is the defense that wins most of the games. If you don't have a good defense, all of the most sparkling offense does you little good. So, they taught us a defensive attitude first. Then, once we had learned to defend ourselves, we could think about taking the fight to the enemy. We graduated from hand-to-hand to four-foot-long poles with padded ends. The padded ends looked like huge, soft boxing gloves, and they even let us wear football helmets when we confronted each other. We probably thought there wasn't much to this until the blows began to land. Suddenly, you took very seriously the movements that you were being taught—the negative reinforcers this time were much greater than push-ups.

From the combat poles, we moved to bayonets. At first, the bayonet was looked upon as little more than a cumbersome extension of the rifle. Who would be interested in getting close enough to an enemy to fight with a bayonet when you could shoot from a distance? It might make a nice big knife to cut your way through undergrowth, but we did not first see it as a weapon. What we came to learn—and later to believe from experience— was that the rifle, even without ammunition, had a steel butt on one end and the bayonet on the other. This made it a powerful defensive and offensive weapon which, when used with the skills we were learning, could turn the tide of battle and ensure personal survival.

I'm sure I believed this, but this part of the training was the part that I remained most skeptical about. I would keep the bayonet and have it ready at all times. I would carry an additional survival knife that was not government issue; any country boy—especially one who has lived around the swamps—knows the distinct value of a good knife. But I would also carry plenty of firepower. When we would pack our gear to go on missions in Vietnam, others crammed in all the food and drink they could carry; I took ammunition. I was convinced that I could find something to eat out there, but there were no ammunition super markets in the jungle. It made a lot more sense to shoot from a distance than to have to use that bayonet up close. I typically went into the field with ammunition belts and packs fully loaded, and almost always added a reasonable assortment of hand grenades and Claymore mines.

Even higher ranking officers now were making their rounds. It was almost as if they didn't want to see us until we were worth looking at. Had they seen most of us early on in our training, they would probably have been ready to sign surrender documents presented by any enemy. Now, they could look at us and make their reinforcing speeches. We could now be told with some conviction that "the most potent weapon in the U. S. arsenal is the individual soldier." We now believed ourselves that "the machines of warfare are only as good as the men who operated them." We stretched ourselves to stand even taller when their speeches, sometimes fiery and dramatic, were concluded with the idea that "we had been trained to defend our WAY OF LIFE!"

The final two weeks of training fell into a basically settled routine. The training was still every bit as much as could be packed into a 24-hour day. There was still the demand for perfection and discipline on every side. Yet, it did not feel as hard. We were stronger and knew more about what to expect and what to watch for. We had learned how to respond, how to act to avoid some situations, how to act to escape others. Sometimes you wished you had never come; sometimes you were glad you were there.

The only training problems I was having now were with hand grenades and hand-walking bars. I never quite got over the fact that the hand grenade was everything but a huge firecracker. It had the capacity to blow you flat to hell and back. The uneasiness I felt around the devices was always there. I might carry eight or ten grenades and Claymores on the battlefield, but the thought was never far from me of what would happen if one of these went off or was struck by a bullet. The only thought that comforted me was that if this did happen, I wouldn't have to worry about it very long.

The hand-walking bars were a different matter. I had seen these things in children's playground since I was a kid. Usually there were eight or ten crossing bars that you could hand-walk from one end to the other. I was always strong enough to do this, and if you happened to lose your grip and fall off, it didn't make much difference. The army was different; no children's playground here. The bars were set up in rows of 20 to 25 bars, and when you got to the end of one row it wasn't over. You had to reach across to a parallel row of bars and begin the process all over again. Back and forth you went with always before you another row of bars.

You started out strong, especially in the last days of basic training, but by the time you got into the second row you were ready to drop. The only thing that kept you going was the knowledge that if you dropped, you went back to the first and started again. You fought through the pain simply not allowing yourself to let go. Like the combat training, the whole process became more mental than physical. I hated it, every minute of it. The pain was almost too much to bear. But, I did it. All the way to the end, with upper body strength and a power of determination growing at every turn. I simply would not let go, would not let it whip me.

During the final week of training we began to shut down our overall operation. There was a lot of paperwork to be done, new assignments made, and the inevitable cleaning up. It was announced that one person in each platoon would be recommended to leadership school. To be recommended a person had to have achieved "expert" level in most of the activities, get the commendation of his Drill Instructor, and be put forward by the rest of the platoon. The latter element was the most important. I received notification that I had been selected for this additional training. I was completely gratified by this, especially when—for the first time—there was a moment of praise in front of the other men as those designated for leadership school were singled out.

Bludworth got the same honor in his platoon, so we knew that we would continue to be together as this special training also took place at Fort Gordon.   Frazier and Hobbs had had problems. Information finally reached the Army that they both had previous police records.   It was nothing serious, but part of the Army regulations required that this be closely investigated. They were held back until the problem was resolved. We were all upset about this break in our plans, but by this time there simply was not time or opportunity to do anything about it. You had the idea that not only for these close friends, but for all the people that you had cried, sweated, bled, and fought with over the past two months, that your paths would take many, many different directions. Most you would never see again; those that you did, would never be exactly the same.

Bobby was there at my graduation. We marched proudly before the reviewing stands and received the congratulations and final speeches about commitment and valor from the commanding officers.   There were medals and ribbons to be presented that became concrete symbols of all that had happened to us in this place. I was most proud of the crossed infantry rifles that could now be placed on my dress uniform. For some this moment signalled a short time of leave they had been looking forward to probably for every one of those past eight weeks.   They were packing cars, greeting relatives, and heading for home. Bludworth and I didn't have money or cars for any of this. We didn't have time for South Florida now; our orders called for an immediate transition to leadership school and new classes that would start the following Monday morning.

Chapter IX

The way the Army had it set up, as soon as a recruit was finished with basic training, there would be a transition to AIT or "Advanced Individual Training." For most of the people that were going through with me and heading for Vietnam, that meant "Advanced Infantry Training." AIT would involve another eight weeks of more detailed training and a continuation of the program of physical conditioning.

To be selected for Leadership School meant that there would be a three-week interruption for some of us in this sequence. Instead of going immediately to AIT, our select group would be given a special training session designed to make us group leaders for AIT classes. We would have enough additional training with weapons and tactics, plus training in how to deal with people, that we could then be matched up with another AIT group and act as leaders or helpers in their training. It meant a little recognition and a little more control of the events that were happening around you, but it also meant that you would be separated from the group that you had spent the last eight weeks with and had gotten to know.

While this separation meant starting all over again in building new relationships, for me there was one plus—Bludworth had made Leadership School, too, so we were able to go in together and even bunked together in a smaller, less impersonal barrack. Hobbs and Frazier were still being held in a kind of limbo without much to do until the problem of their police records was finally cleared up. Bludworth and I had a little more freedom of movement now so we made sure to keep almost daily contact with Cecil and Johnny so their spirits would hold up. We would walk a couple of miles over to where they were staying and spend part of the free time we were now getting in the evening with them. There is a large hill at Fort Gordon that becomes famous to every recruit. You climb it, run it, and crawl it until you feel that you know every inch of it and have half of its sand and dirt mired into your skin. As we passed this hill in our movement back and forth to see our friends, we could see the new recruits in their awkward movements like ants all over that hill. A distinct feeling of joy and delight would rise in my mind each time we passed; I was glad that I didn't have to do that again.

In some respects Leadership School was just like basic training all over again. There was the same strictness and attention to detail, we were continually being drilled on one weapon and then another until we knew it by heart, and there was more and more physical conditioning. We would race against each other now, but not over fifty or a hundred yards; now the distance was increased to two miles and it was hard to believe how quickly you could cover this distance and still be ready to do it again. For the first time in my life I began to feel like I had really achieved something important. I was one of about 50 people who had been chosen from a group of ten to fifteen times that number.

For the first time in my life I had a real, definable goal—airborne! I wanted it so badly that I was more than willing to take anything that basic training or leadership school would dish out. It would simply make me stronger and more ready to compete with this special group. On down the line I could envision myself in the dress uniform that was accented by jump boots—the only dress uniform that could be worn with the pant bloused at the top of the boots. Not even Bobby had that. He would be a "leg," with dress shoes and pants hanging to the cuff; I would be airborne. Throughout Leadership School, I would add mileage and exercise on my own at the end of the day and over the weekends. I wanted to be right at the head of the roughest, toughest outfit possible. Later on in life, I found out that Bobby had been to jump school and had five jumps of his own, but since he had been assigned to a leg unit, he did not want to bring attention to himself. He had had the same kind of training I had, but I was too naive to know it. Maybe he felt that I needed to think that I had this kind of advantage that he didn't even have.

Bobby was giving me more and more attention now and that was the biggest reinforcement I needed. I went to him about Hobbs and Frazier, and he was able to make contact with the recruiting people in Coral Gables and get their problem finally straightened out. I spent part of the weekends at his house or at Russell's. I still wanted to make Bobby proud of me.

Every morning we did physical exercise from about 6:00 until about 8:00. There were still inspections at every turn, and the sergeants were still strict. Now, they looked for any sign of laziness or slacking off on our part. They told us that we weren't going to be hounded anymore, that now we were responsible for our own drive and pride. Even the slightest deviation from what they thought was our best effort, however, and they were on our backs like never before. Now, we were expected to be leaders, to be examples, to be better than anyone else. We were absolutely never to take advantage of less supervision—we were to use less supervision as an occasion to supervise ourselves, to drive ourselves, to create our own motivation. If you were a slacker now, you could be kicked back into a beginning AIT company so fast that it would make your head swim.

The remainder of our days were spent in class-like atmospheres. Sometimes they would be inside and at other times we would be in the field. We bivouacked for longer periods and began to do field problems. We spent more and more time with M-14s, M-16s, M-60 machine guns, and M-79 grenade launchers. I still favored the machine gun and was handling it with more and more proficiency.

When we got off in the late afternoon, it was more like getting off from work. There was time for relaxation, a few beers at our rec area, and an occasional trip into town. My only problem here was the same old one—money. There was never any extra. Most all of what I made, I sent immediately to Momma. A few beers and cigarettes, and the rest was gone.

On the last weekend before Leadership School was to be over, two or three of us planned a real blowout for the weekend. We would go into town, rent a motel room, raise a little hell, and leave a lasting impression on most of the female population of Augusta. Throughout the week we bragged about all that was going to be done. Hey, we were tough U. S. Regular Army soldiers now; there would be no resisting us. The weekend was fine—if your standard is a cramped room, bad food that you were having to pay for yourself, and—as was the case for me most of the time—getting sick before you got drunk. As for the female population of Augusta, they must have all been out to lunch. That part of our venture was totally unsuccessful.

Following graduation from my second school in a month now—not bad for somebody who had had so much trouble in regular school—we were hooked up with a new AIT company. Companies were divided into platoons and platoons into squads. Each of the Leadership School graduates was given a squad and assigned the rank of acting corporal or acting sergeant. Again, we were to be an example and help with the training or explanations when the others in the squad were having trouble. We got to march outside the rank of the squads when they moved from one place to another and call out the cadences. At times, we got to assign tasks as they related to one project or another. This gave little advantage really, and might amount to being able to choose to wash dishes on a KP detail rather than having to scrub pots.

Beyond such very small amenities, there was no special treatment. AIT was very much like boot camp again. We were restricted to the company area for the better part of the first month, all cars were confined to a special compound where they could not be used, and our civilian clothes were taken away. This was the business end of the army where we learned our speciality. Everything else had just been preparation for this.

Suddenly, you came to realize that Leadership School was a kind of honor, but it ended up putting you into a special kind of "double bind." On one side there were the training officers. They went in assuming that since you had been to Leadership Training you thought you were hot stuff and could get by with a little more than anyone else. They would prove you wrong on both counts. If anything, they demanded more of you and watched you more closely than anyone in the entire group. They knew what they were doing on this score just like their predecessors in boot camp. They knew that there was nothing they could demand of you that would not be demanded in Vietnam. If you were going to be a leader here, the jungle would single you out even more.

On the other side, the regular AIT company, the ones who had come directly from boot camp, knew each other and had built a special bond throughout all the training period. To these people, you were an outsider. They looked on you as someone that had privileged character status, as someone who had "brown-nosed" his way into a special treatment category. The real challenge of AIT for those of us who had been to the Leadership Training was gaining the respect of these strangers. This was the ultimate test of any leadership abilities that we might have. If you could break this "double bind" and win the respect of both the sergeants and the strangers in your own group, you must have something on the ball.

Some of the new squad leaders tried to demand their way into the respect of their group. This never worked. Some tried to "buy" their way in by looking the other way, letting people get by with a little less, or playing some kind of "you help me, I'll help you" games. This worked even less well. My approach was to keep my distance a little bit, do the job as best as I could, and just see what happened. At first it was pretty cool and having distance was no problem for them or for me. It didn't take long though for them to see that I could do the different tasks we were being called on to perform and I could do them especially well. This was especially true in the weapons work, and slowly but surely I began to win their respect. They realized that I knew how to do things in a way that could help them, and they started asking for help with one problem and then another. Within a couple of weeks, my squad was one of the tightest and most effective groups in the entire company. We may not have been glossy, but the sergeants knew one thing—give us something to do and it would be done. No questions asked—it would be done. That's what they were looking for out of me; that was what leadership was ultimately all about. Maybe not so much John Wayne or Audie Murphy, but getting the job done.

You began to get a better idea of what battle involved. There was more attention to weapons, to the point that you could take different rifles apart and put them back together in pitch dark or with your eyes blindfolded. There were classes in map reading, and especially in gaining the ability to find your way in strange terrain back to a place of safety if you got cut off from your own people. You learned the details of survival training, and it was packed into your mind on every turn that YOU COULD SURVIVE, even with nothing YOU COULD SURVIVE.

In our mock battle drills, we learned infiltration, camouflage, the correct way to establish and guard perimeters, the use of barbed and concertina wire, and how to work with both the creation and disarming of mines and booby traps. No one had to remind you to listen anymore, and there was no nodding off to sleep during lectures and explanations. The idea began to sink in now that what you were being told could very well make the difference between life and death.

It was all interesting to me. For the first time, teachers were striking a level of my interest. Learning was actually fun, and, I was absolutely learning it better than anyone. Even small things like stringing cans with rocks across open spaces to give a warning about approaching enemy sank into the deepest reservoirs of my mind. For someone who had learned to live in the swamps, you knew that there was no telling what might come up and you would need this information.

I was particularly intrigued by camouflage. Again, like so much, here was an animal instinct. If you could blend in, you could survive. How much they reduced everything to the level of animal instinct! If you could ever get to the point that those instincts could take over, you could stand the chance of living in even the most desperate conditions. But animal instincts didn't just happen, they had to be ingrained into the deepest parts of your system.

On one occasion they took us to the top of a rise overlooking a large field. The field was empty, or so it appeared. Then we were told to count the number of troops hidden in that field. Maybe— only maybe—some of us thought we saw a person here or there, three or four hidden soldiers at best. Yeah, we saw them. Two or three, maybe a fourth over next to that ravine. Then, a signal was given and soldiers in camouflage began to stand up all over the field. There must have been three dozen or more. That made a lasting impression: if you blend in, you survive.

A lot of time was spent on guard duty. This was all specifically planned, although we didn't realize it, to see the extent to which we could obey orders, no matter what the circumstance. What we guarded was never that important, maybe a motor pool or an ammunition dump, but we were given strict instructions about how to question anyone appearing at our outpost. We were to hold a rifle—unloaded at the time—on them until proper identification and clearance could be obtained. There was to be no deviation. Invariably, into the wee hours of the morning, some ranking officer—on the occasion that I was closest to, it was a "bird" colonel—would show up. He would be in a hurry, extremely demanding, and insist that he be allowed through. He would pull rank, rant and rave, threaten court martial and everything else. If you held to your instructions, you would be complimented. In this situation, an acting private could hold out before a general. If you bent to his intimidation, all hell would break loose and there would be every measure of humiliation and punishment imaginable.

After a month of AIT, we began to have some privileges restored. This included weekend time off, so some of us decided to go up to Darlington for the running of the Darlington 500 stock car race. This was a big deal—successful, training-hardened, self-confident soldiers off for a manly weekend. One guy even had a racy yellow Corvette, and who could help being impressed by four hot army studs in a yellow Corvette!

I can remember feeling part of a real important group as we roared off base, out of Georgia, and north toward Darlington. I had enough money for tickets to the race and some food; we would sleep as best we could at the track—who needed sleep anyway. It was a pretty good time and I came back feeling about as high as I had when we left. Then, there was a problem: as we got out of the car to head back toward our barracks, all the guys began to make up money to help pay for the gas. The Corvette owner asked for mine and acted like it should be there immediately. But I didn't have any more money. We were all tired. I felt everyone was looking at me. He wanted to be paid. I was pissed off because nothing was said about money. Suddenly the roller coaster was on flat bottom again. Here was hotdog soldier Matherson with no money? Could that be? Couldn't he carry his load? I felt like a down home, country jerk. It hurt our friendship, too. But there was nothing I could do about it; I didn't have any money. There would be no more invitations from this group, and the hardness of the next day had little to do with lack of sleep or too much to drink. Some of the old reality that had gotten filed away over the past couple of months came rushing back in.

During the last month of AIT, any sense of humor or levity was totally gone. This was business of the most serious sort. There were no fun and games anymore. We learned escape and evasion tactics, how to dig mines out of the ground with a bayonet without discharging them, and there was the continual emphasis being repeated on every side that panic would kill you faster than anything. As it became evident that some of us were better at some things than other, we specialized more and more. I spent increasing amounts of time with the powerful M-60. I could use it better than anyone in the training company.

We still didn't know much about Vietnam, but no one could miss the point that we weren't being prepared for flag carrying duties at a Fourth of July parade. The physical exercise was becoming unrelenting. It was getting on toward Christmas and getting colder, but they would run us and run us until everything about you wanted to drop. I can remember singing over and over again to myself every Christmas carol that I had every learned just to distract my brain from the painfulness of the running and the cold. At least in Vietnam it wouldn't be cold—or would it—how little I knew about this place looming more and more on the horizon of my life.

There was more and more emphasis placed on team work. You began to understand that you had to depend on all your own resources, but you also had to be able to depend on the resources of the others around you. It was like a very sensitive spider web, and if one part of the web collapsed, the strength and efficiency of the whole web was diminished. You had to be able to trust your squad members as much as you trusted yourself; they became almost an extension of your own body. The group bonding that took place was hard to imagine. You began to feel closer to the members of your unit than you had your own family.

Tasks would be assigned and your group would compete with other groups. There would follow a continual posting of scores and evaluations. I had never had the time to do athletics except for the short period in ninth grade. That had always bothered me. I felt like I would have been good at it, but never had a chance to prove it. This gave me the chance. I wanted to make something out of myself and my unit. Time and again when scores were posted we were at the top. It was like looking in the newspaper to see who had won a game in the World Series, and time and again we were coming out on top.

During the final week of AIT there were more physical examinations and the regular duties of closing down and cleaning up the training operation. I had volunteered for airborne—the only way to get in this special group—and would be heading for Fort Benning in Georgia. In some of his testing, Bludworth had scored out high in leadership skills and would be going on elsewhere for specialized officers training before going to Vietnam. The Army evidently needed officers, too. The old romanticism was returning: I would be a paratrooper and Bobby only a "leg"; I would get to Vietnam before him, set things up, and be ready for him when he got there. Our friendly rivalry had been over who would get there first, and it was clear now that I would be the winner. Little did I know the "set up" that was waiting on down the line. I had progressed a little beyond the Burger King in Saigon idea, but not much.

The word circulated that the most outstanding soldier in the AIT company would be singled out for special recognition at the graduation ceremonies. The brigade commander himself had established the tradition of spit shining a pair of jump boots and presenting these to the number one graduate. They were given to me. It was the proudest moment of my life, and those boots represented the single highest accomplishment I had ever made— not to mention the single most expensive personal belonging I had ever had. Then, the "icing was spread on the cake" as Bobby pinned a pair of his own highly polished and gleaming, blue-backed infantry shields on my uniform. This indicated my own particular degree of speciality—a combat infantryman. The look in his eyes as he pinned on those insignia was what it was all about— why I had left Florida, why I had stepped away from the security of home and Momma. This was what I was wanting to achieve. This is what I had achieved, and nothing would ever diminish this moment.

There was no stopping now. There was no money for trips home or vacation leaves like some of the others were taking. It seemed the buses for Fort Benning were ready to leave before we got off the graduation field. I felt a real sense of loss as we pulled away, almost as strong as leaving Florida. I had found myself here. My mettle had been tested and I had proven myself. If I could just stop now, hold that look that was in Bobby's eye, and go on back home, my goals would have been fulfilled and I could be on to something else. In fact, there was no stopping now. And this time, I was absolutely on my own. No Frazer and Hobbs, no Bludworth, no Bobby and Russell, and no Momma nearby. I felt a need for Momma on that bus ride unlike I had felt a need for her for a long time now.

When we pulled into Fort Benning, there was a huge sign out front that filled the bus windows: "AIRBORNE—WELCOME !!" My first thought was that they must have received word that we were coming; the roller coaster was at the top again. We dismounted from the buses in our dress uniforms—still not able to wear the jump boots and bloused pant legs—carrying our packed duffel bags.

Suddenly it was a different world. You could breathe it in the air of the place. There seemed to be a different gleam to the buildings, a different organization to the grounds, a different air of importance on the faces. And suddenly you realized that you were the "legs" and everyone in sight exhibited the unmistakable sign of importance for this place, the emblem of passage that really mattered—the jump boots and the proud blousing. Here came the roller coaster!

It was starting all over again. We were strangers in a strange land. No one said anything, but we looked over each other's faces. The bravado of the bus ride suddenly was gone. All of us were thinking the same thing, "We volunteered for this??" Two steps into the formation as we marched toward our new barracks assignment, the inevitable comment rose from the side, "Look at them! What a pitiful looking mess of sorry-ass legs." It was starting all over again.

Chapter X

Part of me welcomed the newness. After all, this was what I was looking for all along, and I was the only one in the group who had left Hollywood that had progressed in exact accord with the ideals we had set. Hobbs was still hung up in an AIT unit, Frazier was getting ready to follow his changed MOS to some kind of mechanical training, and Johnny Bludworth was off to Officers Candidate School. I had the jump boots and they would still be "legs." Part of me felt that, having survived the past nearly half-year now, the next three weeks couldn't be all that hard.

I held my head up high as we headed for our new barracks assignment. A couple of the people from the old AIT company were expressing dismay under their breaths, "What the hell have we gotten ourselves in for now?" Not Chuck Matherson—nobody was going to beat Chuck Matherson.

On the inside, another part of me wished that Bludworth was there. We had been through it all together now. It seemed like I had broken from the last remaining fragment of my old life, the last token of family. I would never see Johnny Bludworth again. He finished OCS, got his lieutenant's bars, and shipped out to Vietnam. He got his leg blown off in some of the first combat he faced and was back home almost by the time I got to Vietnam. Before I got back to the place where I could see him again, he was killed in a hunting accident. I never had a chance to repay the money he gave me to buy the tires for the old Chevy. That is unfinished business; I still haven't gotten it completely out of my system. Had I known all of this as I stepped out across the new ground of Fort Benning, Georgia, there would have been even more uncertainty to mask by the cocksure stride of my march.

Everything about jump school was refined to a precise art. It all aimed at five real jumps during the last week of training. That meant there was a tremendous amount of training and conditioning that had to occur in two weeks. First, there was a great deal of emphasis in raising the physical conditioning that we already had to a new plateau—especially the legs. You ran everywhere you went. Once your feet touched the ground outside the barracks, you had better be running—to formation, to the mess hall, back to your barracks, from one training situation to another—running, running, running.

All of this running—or "leg building" if you could convince yourself to think about it that way—was informal. The formal running involved the minimum of a five-mile run every morning. As we ran our daily course, we were followed by post ambulances. There were always two or three men who would simply fall out—I don't mean stop and walk for a while to catch their breath, but run until they absolutely passed out in mid-stride. The ambulances would pick the fallen men up and make careful record of their inability to complete the day's run—three drop outs and you were out of the program.

Sometimes I'm not really sure what kept me going. All that I can remember is saying to myself over and over again "if anyone else can, I can!" More than anything else, you didn't want to be the one who didn't make it. To stop, to quit, would have involved a feeling of shame that I simply could not have lived with. You could quit. In fact, they made it pretty easy to quit. All you had to do—and you were reminded of this every day—was tell your training officer that you couldn't take it any longer, that you wanted to quit. It was never "wanted to stop" but always "quit." Again, the certainty of the feeling of shame made this option no option at all.

In fact, in my entire training company, I am not aware that a single person quit. A few people were injured enough to be held up in their training, but no one quit. In spite of all the possibilities for serious injury and even death that would be involved in this level of training, I am not aware of a single person who had a chute fail to open or who died—or was even terribly injured—in the kind of accidents that usually jump into people's minds when parachute training is thought about. We were the toughest of the tough and the training was exceptionally perfected—it wasn't the kind of situation where people quit or where stupid mistakes were tolerated.

By the time our group got to jump school, all the smart-asses had been culled. There were no longer army versions of fraternity parties or Friday nights with good ole boys at the local beach bar. These were serious people and this was serious business. You listened more intently than you ever had in your entire life. Every square inch of equipment, every possibility within a process, every detail of movement was memorized by rote and could be performed or repeated on command without thinking or questioning. Your equipment became an extension of your body, and you knew it as well as your own body.

Besides information, the jump school training was designed to increase the level of confidence you were already experiencing. You had ingrained into your system that you were elite, that those jump wings you were aiming at were as exclusive as any set of pilots wings that had ever been awarded. It was important to see ranking sergeants and even officers training right beside us without any special privileges or recognition—jump school, jump wings, all of this was in a category that made badges of rank secondary. The two medals that really mattered were now within my grasp—the combat infantryman's badge and the paratrooper's jump wings. Nothing could keep me from this! I yelled the cadences with a conviction that sank to the depths of my soul:

I wanta' be an airborne ranger
Livin' on blood and guts and danger

All the way ! Airborne!!
All the way! Airborne!!

During the first week of training, beyond the running and additional conditioning, we worked in mock airplanes and learned how to get in and out of our equipment. We would climb into the planes and go through the same processes that would occur as we prepared to jump. Ironically enough, I had never been up in an airplane in my life. I had always liked to travel and watch the countryside. Flying meant for me seeing the countryside from a new and different perspective, so I looked forward to the real thing. For the time being, the inside of the mock planes looked about as I expected.

We learned about positioning ourselves in the plane, about following precisely the commands of the jump master who was stationed at the door, and about how to check our own equipment and that of those beside us. Then, above all, we learned the "airborne shuffle." When the command to stand up and hook our static lines was given and after we had made yet one more final check of equipment, we were commanded to move forward. This involved a deliberate, rhythmic shuffle that inched the entire line closer and closer to the door. It was all a mind game; you got caught up in the directions and the sound and movement of the shuffle and, in the process, were distracted from what you were about to do. More importantly, once that line started moving, you knew that there was no turning back. It became more like the operation of a giant machine than a line of men. There was only one way out—the jump. I never saw the first person chicken out or panic—the absolute, uncompromising, impersonality of the shuffle made it all but impossible to do so.

In that first week, when we got to the end of the line, we jumped four or five feet into a large sand box. We had to learn how to hit the ground. Most accidents that occur in parachute work occur on landing, and one thing that you knew for sure—you didn't want to be jumping into an enemy controlled area or behind enemy lines and the first thing that happened be a broken ankle or broken leg. The key term was "PLF," parachute landing fall.

We learned about "PLF rights" and "PLF lefts." These proper landing formations meant a roll on contact to the right or left depending on the direction in which the wind was blowing and thus the direction that your chute was likely to pull. You had to relax and get any stiffness out of your legs. It was a cushioned roll; stiffness would mean impact conveyed directly to the bones of your legs and under the weight of your falling body and the equipment that you would probably carry. This meant ankle bones and leg bones snapping like a dry twig or the chicken's "pully bone" which we broke for good luck when we were kids.

It became clear to me pretty quickly what jump school was really about. Sure there was more physical training and there were certainly new techniques to be learned, but more than any of this that it was a mind game. What you were really learning was a new level of concentration and a greater control by your mind of ever quiver of movement that your body was allowed. Here was the ultimate extension of listening closely, not panicking, the final degree of what had begun with the martial arts training. As long as you held your concentration, you could make everything work. It was all in the mind.

Toward the end of the first week, we moved from the PLF stage to a two or three story platform where our jumping harness was attached to cables. We were to jump out away from the platform into mid-air and experience the sensation of a chute opening. This drill also allowed us to continue practicing the timing involved in landing. It might seem totally unnatural to jump off a three-story platform into mid-air. What if something didn't work? But, if you totally trusted the instructors and the equipment, and if your entire system simply would not allow for the possibility of questioning, saying no, or quitting, it was almost second-nature. The equipment did exactly as it was supposed to, you timed your landing roll, and repeated the exercise over and over and over again.

During the second week of training, you learned how to control the chute once you were on the ground. They put us in front of huge fans, almost like the back end of the airboats that I had known from the Everglades in Florida. The flow from the fans blew into the parachutes we were rigged into and literally drug us across the ground. We learned how to struggle with this situation and control the chutes. It took a great deal of physical strength to wrestle with the air-filled chutes. You learned to pull on chute risers (the chords running to the chute canopy) in order to collapse the chute. You learned to hit the chest release on the harness so that you could get free and get back on your feet again. By the time this phase of the training was complete, most of us were scratched up all over and thoroughly exhausted from our struggles. With all the training we had had and with the way the muscles were bulging on most of us, I was surprised by the drain on your strength that an air-filled parachute could be.

Then, we learned something else about the risers. Not only could they be pulled to collapse a chute once you were on the ground, but they could also be used to help you guide your movement while you were in the air. This was very important. You wouldn't want to drift into the top of a tree or power lines; you certainly wouldn't want to drift into another chute and get all tangled up, and—above all—you wouldn't want to get stacked right above another chute and let it "steal" your air. I hadn't thought about those possibilities—and it was only the next week that the "real thing" would take place.

On into the latter part of the second week, they put us on the high towers that stood like huge space creatures in the middle of the massive training field. The mechanisms on these towers would lift you in your chute and harness up over 200 feet into the air and drop you back to the ground. It was the closest simulation of the actual drop that could be created. You were given the chance to get used to the height, the feel of the fall, and—again—the proper landing. The view and the sensation of the descent were beautiful, but all the time you still knew that you were attached to equipment; it was not the "real thing."

The third week came and we were loaded in trucks and taken to the base airfield. I can remember what seemed like tremendously long periods of waiting. We were told that other plane-loads of jumpers were in front of us, that landing zones had to be cleared, that the winds had to settle down, and on and on. I feel sure now that the waiting was intentional. Anyone who couldn't take the pressure of the waiting, didn't need to be out there in a real jump situation. In addition, you finally got to the point that jumping would get it all over with, and by the time you got to the jump you were past being ready for it to be done with. A mind game, all of it was a mind game.

Once the plane was loaded, you were so cramped and strained from the weight of the equipment that your back felt like it was going to break. The pain became almost more than you could stand. Match all of that up with the fear that you were feeling and—again—jumping and getting it all over with was something that you finally were looking forward to.

There was a lot of joking and kidding. It was all pretty much graveside humor. Was it true that parachute riggers drank a lot? What were your last thoughts going to be if your chute didn't open? Had you seen the newsreel shot of the paratrooper whose chute and safety chute had not opened? Didn't they lose six or eight people here every week in training jumps? It was going to be your time, not mine! It all reminded me of the humor of the embalming room—just another way of controlling fear.

As the plane took off and slowly climbed to jump altitude of 1200 to 1500 feet, all the kidding stopped. It became deadly quiet except for the rushing sound of the wind outside. You didn't hear anyone say anything, but there were a lot of people whose eyes were closed in prayer and whose lips were moving with final pleas and bargains being struck with God. I kept my eyes open and my lips didn't move—all the time, every fiber of my mind was praying for the nearness and help of God. I was scared but even more scared to say that I was scared. Regardless of what any of us had said or felt, stark fear was written on all of our faces.

Our sight finally became glued on the jump master and as he moved toward the side door of the C-130 transport, we knew that it was time. The red jump light went green, we were ordered to stand and attach our static lines—it was all business now, we were going to go.

Hold the static line in your left hand. Double check your own equipment. Double check the man in front of you. The man behind you. The door is open. Sky and air are rushing by. The shuffle has already started and you don't even remember it starting. You'll stand in the door, he'll strike you on the back, you jump out and away with all of your strength. Count to ten and then look up to see if the canopy is filling with air. Your only thought: it was a good idea to sit close to the door so you didn't have to wait long.

It all happens automatically. One after another of the shuffling line peals off of the side of the plane in front of you. You are at the front of the line. No time even to look. The strike on the back may be as much of a shove as a signal. The others in front have yelled "Airborne!" or "Geronimo!" or just yelled, so you do, too.

And before you know it, not even remembering if you have counted to ten, you are caught up in one of the most peaceful feelings you have ever experienced. You are floating on a soft cushion of air. You look up and the canopy is just like it is supposed to be. There is the strangest sensation of quietness that you have ever experienced. It is almost like a dream that caresses you and you would like to go on forever. You almost forget that it is time to think about risers and landing.

You time your landing just like they said. A broken bone might mean never getting recycled back into the program. You watch the horizon, not the ground. If you watch the ground, it will rush up too fast and you can't keep from bracing your legs with that undesirable stiffness. Watch the horizon, study the trees and the movement of the other chutes for wind direction so you can figure your PLF. Watch the horizon and time your fall. Just right now, touch, roll now, and you are on the ground with your chute collapsed, retrieved, and rolled up before you really have had time to think about what you are doing. You see smiles on all sides and realize that you are smiling as big as anyone. You did it! One of the finest feelings of satisfaction that you could ever experience rises around you like the perfume of a beautiful woman or opening the door on the aromas of a home cooked meal.

It was scary, no question about it. I believe that anyone who told the truth would tell you that. Every jump for me was a night jump—I always closed my eyes!

I had been watching two Marines since the first day of jump school. They had come in on some kind of special arrangement, and the rest of us were regular Army. They got a lot of ribbing, most of it in good fun, but occasionally you wondered if some real jealousies might not be coming through. I began to admire them for the way they held up under the added pressure. Then, on the third jump one of them broke both of his ankles in a poorly-timed landing. It meant instant out, and he knew that; no jump wings and probably no second chance.

With the help of his friend, he got off the landing field unnoticed and back into the truck. Somehow they got the jump boots laced up tight enough that he was able to walk. He jumped the next day and the next. Not until the fifth and final jump was complete did he report to the base hospital. He was in large casts within an hour, could not stand during the graduation ceremonies, but had earned his wings. That was the kind of determination that I felt that I had. They told us that one U.S. Army paratrooper could single-handedly take on ten enemy soldiers and defeat them every time. I believed it with all of my heart.

I will never forget the sensation of having those jump wings pinned onto my uniform. It was an even stronger sensation than the first jump itself. It meant so much to me because I had worked so hard for it. It was a living symbol of the fact that I could accomplish the most difficult tasks under the most difficult circumstances.

My next assignment would be Fort Campbell in southwest Kentucky, home of the 101st Airborne Division, the "Screaming Eagles." My earlier test scores had not allowed for the movement into Special Forces, but who could want for much more than the famed and fabled 101st Airborne. This was one of the most famous and most highly respected battle units in the entire history of the United States military.

There was another bus trip, another processing center, another welcome sign, but this time none of the harassment or belittlement directed at trainees every step along the way up until this point. The group that climbed off the buses at Fort Campbell, their jump wings gleaming and their boots and pant legs wearing the exclusive blousing of the paratrooper had paid its dues. We were soldiers now—101st.

The first thing I did was to report to the company commander and volunteer for service in Vietnam. I was intent on getting there as soon as possible, still intent on getting there before Bobby. I knew that part of the 101st had already gone over and that there would be an immediate need to replenish ranks with "new blood"—at that moment, "new blood" was still just a figure of speech.

The company commander welcomed my request in the most positive manner. He complimented me on the record that I had established and the spirit that I was manifesting at this moment. All arrangements could be put in place immediately. I would remain at Campbell for about the next month and then would be given a four week pass to return home before shipping out to Vietnam. He told me that I was to take care of getting new uniforms and basically relax. The company was "standing down" at the moment with a major part of its contingent gone. There would be no further training jumps before going to Vietnam. There seemed to be more paperwork to be processed than anything else.

In fact, I never jumped again after the fifth training jump at Benning. I am only aware of one major jump occurring in Vietnam. The terrain would not allow it, and in many of the areas where jumps could occur, the North Vietnamese had positioned "plungie sticks" made out of sharpened bamboo that could tear through your body like a razor. More than any of this, the helicopter had made parachute work almost obsolete. I was glad to be airborne, to have the insignia and jump wings—I had worked hard for all this—but, all things being equal, I was not sorry that my jumping career was over. I have never felt the need to prove myself in this particular manner again.

A great deal of care was taken with the new uniforms. Across from the base there were private tailors, and they could taper the uniforms until they fit almost like a second skin. There was no question that you looked good in your uniform. You should considering all of the training that had taken place. The ultimate confirmation was the knowing looks and "Hey, Soldier!" that came from girls everywhere you went. It was still not hard to get the idea, in the naivete and romanticism that still prevailed, that this was what the training was all about rather than some old jungle on the other side of the world. I still, at this late time in the entire training process, can't remember talking with someone who had actually been on the ground fighting in Vietnam.

The month at Campbell passed uneventfully and I was given a bus ticket to Hollywood and airline tickets from Miami to Los Angeles to be used a month later. On the bus trip home, I happened on a good-looking girl who was headed all the way to Fort Lauderdale. By this time, I had lost most of my inhibitions about girls to all of the confidence that rose during the training. I'm not sure where she had lost her inhibitions, but it ended up being one of the finest bus trips that the U.S. Army had ever arranged.

I had only been gone about six months, but in that six months a lot had changed. Joe had gotten married, Kay was still working at the steel company and had made many new friends, and several other of my old friends had headed for service. Momma was as glad to see me as a mother could be, especially since Christmas was just around the corner. But Momma knew two things: I was coming back a man, not the boy who had left; and, I was heading for real war in a month. She sensed the space that I now needed from her at this moment. She probably also sensed the space that she needed from me, a space that had established itself over the past half-year and, more importantly, a space that might protect her own feelings and emotions as a son went off to war. We mostly skirted the edges of the distance that was there now. I thought I wanted it and, to a lesser extent, she wanted it, too. It was all part of not being under that skirt-tail that Bobby had told me about back at Fort Gordon.

I hung out with Angelo Mario, and we made all the rounds of the old places. There were endless conversations over beer and cigarettes into the night about what we had done and what we were going to do. All the old acquaintances had to be looked up just so you could see the way that they looked at the "new you" and held you in a sense of respect and even a little awe. This was before the war fell apart; soldiers were still looked at through the lens of John Wayne and Audie Murphy.

And, of course, the old naive romantic that I was, I looked through the same lens. There was only one thing left to make the South Florida "Hollywood" experience complete—fall in love. And fall I did, all the way to engagement with one of Kay's friends. Most of our relationship was youthful fantasy, but a lot of it was real. We made our plans for "after Vietnam." We dreaded the parting that would come even before Christmas could be celebrated. We stole away all the time that we could—time away from Momma that I wondered later how she took. This was the love that would last. Vietnam changed all of that.

One of my friends had a brother who had been killed while I was away in training. We became pretty close during the month in Florida, and I got him to take me to the Miami airport. I wanted to say all of my goodbyes at home and have no one go with me but him. In no way whatsoever did I want to put myself at the airport, on the eve of Christmas, with my Momma and new fiancee, and break down. I was Airborne. Airborne held its emotions in tack and was tough all the way.

The trip to Los Angeles was lonely and about as sad as leaving home at Christmas time could be. Everything was on automatic again. There were arrangements for a bus trip to Oakland—lots of other soldiers were leaving home at Christmas. We did some final paperwork and medical work for about a week and then were on a flight to Vietnam. The whole fantasy of the experience was heightened by the Army's using commercial airlines to ferry us to Vietnam, commercial airlines with beautiful stewardesses that made battle seem a million miles away. In almost a moment it seemed that the pilot was informing us to extinguish our cigarettes and buckle our seatbelts for the descent into Tan Son Nhut. Vietnam!

Chapter XI

An airplane isn't really like a time machine. It doesn't so much pick you up and transport you from one time period to the other. It is more like a space machine. Here you are in one world with faces like you are used to seeing and voices like you are used to hearing. You may not know everything that there is to know about that world, but it is familiar to you. You figure that you could get lost, but you would be able to find your way around; you would be able to find your way back.

Then, suddenly you are in a new world with faces and sounds and smells like you have never experienced before. It is so different that it doesn't seem real. It's more like the plane trip has moved you through the initial stages of a dream. At any moment you expect either to wake up or have something happen that will make it stop just **seeming** real and actually **be** real.

The plane trip is like going under a doctor's anesthesia; everything becomes vague and although you try to push back the vagueness to clarity and sanity, "reality" somehow keeps staying just beyond your reach. At about the time you begin to sense the length of time the trip has taken, it is over, and although it has been long, it is not long enough to account for all the changes that have taken place.

It doesn't seem right sometimes to build an interstate highway across the top of a high mountain range. The truth of the mountaintop cannot really be experienced unless you have to climb the mountain. There is no time and not enough experience for the reality to set in.

The old timers from World War II talked about the great troop transports that carried them across the Atlantic to Europe. It took over a week to get there, and all the time they were tossed around by the great ocean. Sometimes they were so sick that they prayed for the tossing to stop. By the time they faced the Germans, they were ready to fight—if nothing else, to pay them back for the painfulness of the crossing.

The airplane takes all of that away. Suddenly you are in a new world. You looked out the plane window for what seemed hours, looking for a point of reference but being so high that you couldn't even tell where the ocean stopped and the horizon started. You wondered sometimes if you were actually flying horizontal to the ground; maybe they were really taking you up and away to another planet. The plane took away all of your orientation. Vietnam didn't give it back. The jungle, the people, the heat of the air that you breathed—it was like looking for a horizon that wasn't there. You couldn't tell where much of anything started or stopped. It was like you had gone back into a strange kind of womb, and until that plane came back and delivered you again into your own world with your own people, it simply would not be the same. Disoriented, uncertain, confused, waiting to wake up or for something real—Vietnam.

I remembered from the plane trip the difference between the younger guys and the older guys. The older ones were married and some of them had been here before. They must have known more about what was at stake, or it was just the way Christmas affected them, or something. They were quieter and more subdued, but they didn't seem to mind that the rest of us were not. It was almost as if they were saying "enjoy it while you can, it will be over soon enough."

All us younger guys were trying our best to make the last moments of America we were carrying with us on the plane as good as we could. We talked around about where we were from and what all kinds of training experiences we had had. Occasionally, somebody had been in the same place you had been or even had crossed paths with a mutual friend; this brought remarks about how small of a world it was. We bragged about all the girls we had had, although most of us knew we were lying. I don't remember anyone saying anything about what was before us. I can remember them saying that we were stopping in Washington to pick up some more troops and not even knowing for sure if they meant Washington state or Washington, D.C.—which way did you go to get to Vietnam anyway?

I can remember trading knives with one guy who I had never met before. I had a skin diving knife that I had used in Florida, and he had an Indian gurka. He seemed fascinated by what I had, although they were a dime a dozen in Hollywood; the Gurka knife, probably no great prize, was equally fascinating to me. Both of us went away satisfied that we had made an excellent trade.

I wrote Kay on a piece of Northwest Orient stationery that one of the stewardesses handed out:

Hi Old Maid. Well I'm up here with the birds. Flying at 39,000 feet. How are you and Al getting along? Did he call you again Christmas? Boy, if he did it must have taken his whole pay check.

Hey, what did Santa bring you? Ho, Ho! I bet it was orange peelings.

Hey, I just finished writing Linda. You'd never guess what I used for paper—a burp bag, because we didn't have anything else at the time. I really think a lot about her and will really be glad to see her again. Of course, I'll be glad to see you and Momma and the rest of the family, too. Tell Bobby I'll be waiting for him and to look me up if he gets a chance.

I remembered the lights of Tokyo as we landed there and refueled before heading on to Saigon. I wondered if the city was lighted up like it was all of the time, or if this was special lighting just for Christmas. Later, I learned that it was the biggest city in the world. I wanted to get out and look around, to explore new places, but there never seemed to be time for that. There must have been hundreds of different mountain tops or buildings or just places with people in them that I wanted to explore in Vietnam, but it was either off limits, too dangerous, not enough time, or none of my business. We had come there to fight, not to be tourists. Something about me still wants to go back and see what some of those places were about.

I remembered the details from my package of orders: arrive in khaki trousers and short sleeve shirt; have in my possession summer uniform, work uniform, and combat boots; 66 pounds of baggage allowable and 134 pounds of excess baggage—I wasn't sure if I had 134 pounds of possessions to my name; ID Card, ID Tags, Immunization Certificate; and, a minimum of $25.00 in cash to defray any initial expenses—the combination of the word "minimum" and $25.00 seemed strange to me, since $25.00 was to me at most times the same as a small fortune.

We sank down to the ground of Vietnam. You could tell by the settling of the plane onto the runway that it was loaded to its limit.

Nothing out the windows to make this look like anything but a military base. Not as big as I had expected. "Please keep your seatbelts buckled until the plane taxis to a complete stop at the terminal. Thank you for traveling Northwest Orient. Good luck to everyone. God bless you. Happy New Year." The stewardess's happy voice and cheerful smile still reassured us that everything would be just fine. Then we were up and inching our way— almost in the airborne shuffle—toward the front cabin door. "Please check around you to make sure that you have collected all of your personal belongings." It was too late for that now. The aisleway was full and with a silent determination everyone was pressing toward the light of the doorway ahead—to see the new world that was awaiting us beyond its opening.

Vietnam. The first thing that hit you was the heat. I was used to heat, but this wasn't like Florida. In Florida there was always a breeze blowing in from the ocean. Here, the only stir in the air was being caused by the exhausts of airplanes and the ant-like trucks that were crawling around everywhere. It was like the heat on the inside of a tent in the swamp when the trees were so thick that all the breezes were blocked off. It was like the heat that rises in wet waves off of hot pavement right after a rain shower. As you stepped away from the last hint of air-conditioning from the plane, it was like opening a shower curtain and stepping into a steam bath. Almost the exact second that the cool of the plane fell away from your back you could feel the sweat begin to pop out all over.

There was a pungent, fertile smell in the air. Immediately the scene came to my mind of a farmer in a Carolina field reaching down and cupping a handful of freshly plowed ground and smelling it. When I asked him what he was doing, he let me smell, too. It did smell wet and alive. "That ground will grow, boy, that ground will grow." This place was so alive that even on the taxiways which never ceased for traffic, grass was pushing up through the holes in the primitive steel stripping that still covered much of the as-yet-unpaved airport.

It all happened so suddenly that it was like taking a fast, express elevator from the top of a tall building all the way to the ground floor without stopping. I found out later that the plane had to make a quick, sudden descent in order to avoid the chance of being hit by rocket fire. In the back of my vague memory, I am walking away from the plane and look back to see the picture and name of a girl painted across the side of the nose of an airplane parked near the one we had landed on. Just like in the old movies—but I can't remember her name.

We were loaded on trucks and moved to a holding point at Bien Hoa just north of Saigon. As we drove through the city, I had never seen so many people crammed together in one place in all of my life. I didn't feel any fear, but was totally amazed at all the differences—how small they were, how dark black their hair was, all the children, even small infants, wandering around by themselves. We were all looking at them about like they were looking at us. At first someone would say "look at this," "look at that," "look over there." In a few minutes, it all stopped. It was just too overwhelming. What strange fate of politics and world affairs had made our paths cross.

The buildings were as crowded together as the people. There was seldom room to walk between them. It was clear that the bottom level was almost always a storefront of some kind or other. The people either lived in the back or upstairs. People and clothing were hanging out of windows everywhere. You could see piles and piles of what looked like bolts of cloth, maybe silk. I could find plenty for Momma and Kay here. On every street corner, people were selling. It was like one giant marketplace. I contemplated deals on cameras, knives, and all kinds of things. It would be amazing what a Burger King could do on one of these corners.

The smells of the town overwhelmed the farm, country smell of the airport and the road in. Motorcycles and trucks were everywhere. The exhaust fumes were so thick that when the truck we were riding on slowed or came to a stop, you could hardly breathe. Then, there was the fish. Fish cooking everywhere. Open flames in old oil drums ran five or six in number along every block. Smoked and dried food, along with all kinds of grains and vegetable, hung on hooks on the sides of buildings or were stacked in one huge woven basket after another. Flies were having a holiday. Part of me might have wondered why we would be fighting for something like this, but I am sure that I had been completely convinced by now that loss of freedom anywhere in the world threatened America's own freedom. It probably wasn't all that complicated though; the romantic John Wayne in me just wanted to fight, just wanted to get things ready for Bobby to come over.

Bien Hoa was a city in itself, a tent city. There must have been way over 10,000 American soldiers being processed through this holding area at any given time, maybe a lot more. We were all mixed up together—airborne, regular infantry,—all awaiting requests for personnel that would take us to one unit or another. The first thing I found out was unsettling and disturbing— airborne personnel were being assigned at random, with many or even most going to non-airborne units. This meant that in spite of all of the specialized training, that I might end up in a non-airborne unit—a leg unit. I was the last one in that original group of friends who had enlisted together whose plans had moved along in the direction we originally anticipated. It looked like my luck was about to run out. Of all things, and think about all the bragging I had done to everyone about not being a "leg."

The base was alive with activity. The air was full of all kinds of airplanes, and helicopters of every size were constantly landing, day and night. Trucks were moving around on every side, carrying people and supplies as if everyone knew exactly where they were supposed to go. I hoped that no one looked at my records and decided that they needed another driver. I had come to fight, not drive a truck. The ground was like red clay Georgia dirt except it was real dusty on top. Especially when the helicopters came and went, the dust would stir around everywhere. There was a fine film of dust on everything, distorting the army green with a dull red sheen. It only seemed to take a few moments in the morning for a sticky grit to form on your face and arms as dust mixed with sweat.

We were issued identification cards—mine read 6'1", 172 lbs.— the best shape that I had ever been in in my life, malaria tablets, and "script money." We would use these Military Payment Certificates instead of American dollars. Dollars quickly passed through the Vietnam black market to the Vietcong and North Vietnamese where it could quickly be used to buy weapons and supplies.

For several days we were given classes about life in Vietnam and how to deal with both the local population and any enemy that we might come in contact with. We were drilled in great detail on these matters. Our first lessons involved "Nine Rules for

Personnel of US Military in Vietnam." The front of the card that we were to carry at all times read:

> The Vietnamese have paid a heavy price in suffering for their long fight against the Communists. We military men are in Vietnam now because their government has asked us to help its soldiers and people in winning their struggle. The Viet Cong will attempt to turn the Vietnamese people against you. You can defeat them at every turn by the strength, understanding, and generosity you display with the people.

Then, there were nine "simple" rules:

1. Remember, we are guests here; we make no demands and seek no special treatment.
2. Join with the people! Understand their life, use phrases from their language and honor their customs and laws.
3. Treat women with politeness and respect. (From the looks of some of the women walking the streets, they were interested in a lot more than respect.)
4. Make personal friends among the soldiers and the common people.
5. Always give the Vietnamese the right of way. (I knew that the soldier who had driven our truck from the airport missed out on that point. He continuously motioned with his hand out the window for people to move, but he never slowed down. Later I would come to understand that when you drove, you always kept moving; it was more difficult to hit a moving target.)
6. Be alert to security and ready to react with your military skills.
7. Don't attract attention by loud, rude or unusual behavior.

8. Avoid separating yourself from the people by a display of wealth or privilege. (They didn't have to worry about me on that one.)
9. Above all else you are members of the U.S. Military Forces on a difficult mission, responsible for all your official and personal actions. Reflect honor upon yourself and the United States of America.

So far, there was nothing of "difficult mission" that I could see. Occasionally, you could hear a little artillery fire in the distance, but there was no small arms fire at all and none of us had yet to see any casualties or injuries. Especially with all these rules, it seemed more like Boy Scout camp. It was more like we were on a good will mission to help old ladies across the street than to fight a war.

After we had been drilled on how to make a good impression on the general population, we were told very specifically how we were to treat the enemy. In the end, I wish they had told us how to recognize the enemy. Vietnamese looked like Vietnamese, period. When I first came, they all looked like the curious and harmless faces of the old people and children on the streets; by the time I was done, they all looked like they could be hiding a weapon or a bomb or spying for someone to whom they would disclose where you were.

We were told that we were to comply with the "Geneva Prisoner of War Conventions of 1949." This allowed us to: disarm a prisoner, search him thoroughly, require him to be silent, segregate him from other prisoners, guard him, and, take him to a place designated by a commanding officer. We could not, under any circumstances: mistreat the prisoner, humiliate or degrade him, take any personal effects, or, refuse him medical treatment. I wondered if the enemy was having the same kind of classes. If they were, and people were able to get this far in their attitudes and treatment of each other, why in the hell were we fighting in the first place. And that personal effects thing, I was planning on coming back with all kinds of Vietnamese souvenirs.

We were given a second card that explained the Geneva accords in clear, specific language. We were to treat the enemy, if he came under our control, as a human being. We could expect the same kind of treatment. That all sounded fine and drew shaking heads of agreement in that holding area at Bien Hoa. It never came close to touching the reality of battle, especially when people—American or Vietnamese—go without sleep for long hours, are wet, dirty, and stink, or are absolutely scared out of their minds. We were taught several necessary Vietnamese phrases, and even had a short message from President Johnson about the "magnanimity" (what did that mean?) that Americans were capable of if the aggression by others would stop. There had even been a rumor that Johnson would build Vietnam another TVA along the massive river systems if the war could be stopped.

Finally, we learned about "Rogers Rangers." Evidently, in the French and Indian Wars of the middle-1700s, Rogers had been a colonial military commander. He had come up with a set of rules for fighting the Indians that we were being told would perfectly fit our battle situation. The small card with its silly drawings was a little hard to take seriously. By the time soldiers had been in the jungle for a day or two, you would see them shuffling around through their pockets looking for the card—it ended up applying perfectly to what we would do in Vietnam.

1. Don't forget anything. (And when we marched out on patrol with 80 pounds of equipment and supplies on our backs, we knew what he meant. You also learned to leave nothing behind—the enemy would either eat it or use it against you as some kind of weapon.)

2. Have your musket clean as a whistle, hatchet scoured, sixty rounds powder and ball, and be ready to march at a minute's warning. (You finally appreciated every moment you had spent learning to clean. You knew one thing for sure: when it came time to use the weapon, you wanted it to work.)

3. When you're on the march, act the way you would if you were sneaking up on a deer. See the enemy first. (When this wasn't followed, people died.)

4. Tell the truth about what you see and what you do.

5. Don't ever take a chance you don't have to.

6. When we're on the march we march single file, far enough apart so one shot can't go through two men.

7. If we strike swamps, or soft ground, we spread out so it's hard to track us. (I could tell Rogers a thing or two about swamps.)

8. When we march, we keep moving till dark, so as to give the enemy the least chance at us.

9. When we camp, half the party stays awake while the other half sleeps.

10. If we take prisoners, we keep them separate so they can't make up a story between them.

11. Don't ever march home the same way. Take a different route so you won't be ambushed.

12. Keep a scout 20 yards on all sides so the main body can't be surprised and be wiped out.

13. Every night you will be told where to meet if you are surrounded by a superior force. (There is no other feeling like being separated from your own people in a battle.)

14. Don't sit down to eat without posting sentries.

15. Don't sleep beyond dawn. Dawn's when the enemy likes to attack.

16. Don't cross a river by a regular ford. (There is no way to describe how this statement became the first commandment of our lives.)

17. If you are being trailed, make a circle and ambush your enemy from behind.

18. Don't stand up when the enemy's coming against you. Kneel down, lie down, hide behind a tree. (I know this makes sense, but when people panic it seems like the last thing they remember. Some were lucky when they stood up; others never knew what hit them.)

19. Let the enemy come till he's almost close enough to touch. Then let him have it and jump out and finish him up with your hatchet. (At that moment at Bien Hoa, it didn't really seem possible that we were even ever going to see an enemy.)

When I got a spare moment, I wrote home. I never was much to write, but it is amazing how that moment of letter writing does somehow make you seem closer. Some days you didn't think about home that much; some days you were so homesick that you didn't think you could stand it.

Assignments began to come down placing us in different units all over Vietnam. My main worry continued to be the possibility of getting placed in a "leg" unit. Each day more and more airborne went out to non-airborne units. Then my orders came through and I opened them with great hesitancy. There it was—101st Airborne, Phan Rang! Just what I wanted—"The Eagle's Nest," home base for 101st operations in Vietnam! Airborne all the way!

On December 28 we were up early and all prepared to leave. It seemed like we waited around half the day for the truck to come that would carry us back to Tan Son Nhut. Phan Rang was about 280 miles northeast of Saigon near the east coast of Vietnam, and we would have to fly there. Later on in the morning, I crouched in the shade beside a latrine—anything to get a little coolness from the shade—and began to write letters home. I didn't know what to expect at Phan Rang. All I knew was that it was located near strong enemy forces—the 101st was put there to intimidate some of the best soldiers they had. I closed my last letters from Bien Hoa with several PSs: "Take care of Momma and remember I love every one of you"; "Tell Momma not to worry about me—I am OK—I'll be back home pretty soon." It sounded like I was trying to convince myself more than my family back in West Hollywood.

Finally they loaded us back on trucks and we headed back across Saigon to the airport. I had noticed on the trip into Bien Hoa that the sides of the trucks had a steel stripping that I had not recalled on any of the trucks at the bases back home where we were training. I asked one of the sergeants who was accompanying us what the stripping was for. In the most casual tone he responded that it was to keep people from throwing things in at us. Not exactly understanding, I pressed on: what kind of things? Still in his casual tone, he responded—bombs, grenades, bottles of lighted gasoline. Somehow after that, those strange little people along the crowded street never looked the same again. No wonder the truck never stopped; no wonder those that knew better kept a careful eye on everything that happened around us. But, hadn't the cards said that these people invited us over here? Hadn't the cards said that the best way to get humane treatment was to give it? Maybe these people hadn't read the cards.

When we got to the airport, about 60 to 75 of us gathered in one area and got on an older plane for Phan Rang. The trip didn't take but about an hour, but along the way we learned that the 101st had not been in the area very long, that the VC controlled the high land about the area, and that the planes that had been in there earlier in the day had received some ground fire.

Still, I had heard nothing but distant artillery and was yet to see my first injured soldier. The idea of ground fire in the area was frightening but I tried to put it out of my mind. We were flying much closer to the ground now, and for as far as the eye could see there was nothing but lush green jungle and one stream, lake, or river after another.

The crew chief came back to where we were and informed us that we were receiving a little ground fire from the mountains and would have to make a special landing. The pilot would land the plane and taxi to the end of the runway. He would turn around, but not stop. The back door of the plane would open, and we were to grab any bag that we could and run off of the plane. We were not to stop until we made cover. I expected the back of the plane to open and VC machine gun nests blazing on every side. I don't doubt that there was ground fire, but in thinking back it was too loud on the plane to have noticed it anyway. His last expression, "Watch your ass!", was taken about as seriously as anything I had ever been taught in any of the schools; it would become the axiom upon which your very existence would depend from that point on.

When the plane touched down, we were already ready. The pilot did exactly as he said, and when the door opened we all began to tear out with every bit of speed that we could muster. I don't remember hearing a single shot, but all around I immediately noticed American soldiers. They were just walking around like nothing in the world was going on. Most were without shirts which was definitely not uniform, and there were some of the best tans I had ever seen. We had been had! Most of the soldiers on the ground stopped what they were doing to notice our arrival, and to horse laugh us for the gullibility that we were displaying. They had probably been in the same situation themselves. Not only were there no enemy machine gun nests, there was not even a weapon in sight.   Could this be the 101st on the fringe of enemy territory?

There was a huge open area that looked like it stretched for the better part of a mile on every side. It was covered with tents, all kinds of equipment, and a few makeshift buildings. Troops were everywhere.   It took on the appearance of just another huge training camp.   Beyond the large, flat area was the deep green jungle.   Overlooking it all was a rounded mountain with a small rise or point at its top center; it didn't take much imagination to realize why it would quickly have come to be called "Tittie Mountain." It was hotter than forty hells at Phan Rang, even more so than Saigon or Bien Hua.

We were gathered into formation.   There was some joking about what we had fallen for, but mostly relief.   Then, we were marched to the command headquarters where we received our various assignments.   I was assigned to a weapons platoon in Company B, 1st Battalion, of the 327th Infantry Brigade. Somehow the Army had circulated the information all the way to this point about my expertise with the M-60 machine gun.   Who said the Army wasn't organized?

The men in the platoon welcomed me and introduced me around to the people that I would be working with. They showed me where I could stay and helped me store my personal belongings under the flap outside the tent.   I was a little surprised at the friendliness I found.   I had expected that everybody would have their own friends and be a little suspicious about someone new. This wasn't the case at all.   They respected you for what you had done to get to this point. These were the cream of the crop, entirely all volunteers, regular Army.   These were all people who had wanted airborne just like I had.   These men were committed to the United States and to freedom itself.   They may have represented the best fighting group that our country has ever had.

The company itself was standing down right now.   They were getting resupplied and brought back to full strength with new personnel. I was replacing a guy whose time was finished, and he had gone back home without a scratch.   When you met someone for the first time, you would get a handshake or slap, and then the inevitable question would come "how short are you?" The first time it was asked, it seemed a strange thing to ask—after all I was 6'1". Then I understood.   It meant how much time did I have left.

All I could say was that I had just gotten to Vietnam. Most people could tell you the days and even hours and minutes they had left. Everyone talked about going home.

The most important, first questions had to do with where you had come from. If someone, especially the black guys—although we quickly were picking up on their language—found someone from near where they had lived, they would call them "homeboy." It seemed like everyone was searching for something—anything that would connect them back to home.

I was issued my weapons and combat gear. I was feeling more like a real soldier all the time and it felt pretty good. Over the next several days, we didn't do very much; mostly we did formation in the morning, ran in the compound area, and had a variety of clean-up type duties. I very quickly learned about the streams of black smoke rising out of halved 55 gallon drums. There were latrines like outdoor toilets, and they all had these drums under them and a small door at the back. Everyone had a chance to pull out the drums, fill them with diesel oil, and set them on fire. There were long sticks with which you stirred the mess to keep it burning. We called it "burning turds and stirring shit." I was much more interested in the volleyball courts and boxing rings that had been set up. I was also interested in the fact that most of the people in the company were older, or at least they looked that way to me, and had seen little heavy action. In the entire company up until that time only one person had been killed and only a few wounded. I was yet to see my first hurt person or the "enemy." We were told he was in the area, but the only evidence was the rare sniper fire that came in on occasion.

We rigged showers out of 55 gallon drums. There was so much heat that even late in the day the water was still warm. We learned to live out of our steel helmet liners, using them to wash and shave, but that was more adventurous at this time than troublesome. We got "three squares" every day, and the basic day to day necessities were even available at a makeshift PX which had been erected. The only thing that I didn't like was the way that Vietnamese locals were allowed on base every day to work or to try to sell us one thing or another. I kept thinking, how do they know this isn't the enemy? How do they know these people aren't spying on us?

The locals were mostly women, kids, and old men. The old women were called "Mamma sans" and the young women "Baby Sans." The Mamma Sans looked ancient; the young women were mostly about 12 to 15. It finally became clear that there were no men around, and where they were was not exactly clear. Some said they were in the South Vietnamese military; others were sure they were VC. For all I knew, it could have been both. There was a huge garbage pit back in behind our tents, and these people scoured through it like there were diamonds hidden there. I never really felt comfortable when they were around. The "Beatle nut" that they chewed causing red juice to run out through their rotted teeth all began to look pretty scary to me. They would just look at you, nodding and smiling, but sometimes I thought their minds were thinking something a whole lot different than whatever was being communicated by that smile.

After about a week, I was taken to an area that had the appearance of a shooting range and checked out on the M-60. There was no question that I knew exactly what I was doing. I was assigned to a four-man group. In the group there was a gunner—the star of the group who usually had been promoted and held a higher rank—and three ammo carriers. The gunner carried the M-60 and wore a .45 automatic on his web belt; the carriers were armed with an M-16 and loaded down with at least two cans of M-60 ammo with about 200 rounds in each can. Someday, if all went well, I would move to the gunner position and have my rank increased.

The gunner was a big guy from Elsa, Texas, named Rick Crossland. He had been in a little longer than I had but had seen next to no action. We became fast friends and across the next several days tried to get our tans to the place that they were equal to the short timers in the camp. I still had not seen the first person hurt. I was enjoying the hell out of myself.

It was now 1966 and I was writing Kay by candlelight:

> Sitting here trying to find a candle to write you with and finally found one. We aren't doing too much right now, but we are getting ready to go on some kind of big operation. They won't tell us what it is. It must be pretty big because we have received a lot of new men in the last few days.

I'm getting a good tan over here. Ha! Ha! Today I was
digging a hole in just my undershorts and I hit water.
People would think we were running a nudist camp
up here. Everyone has a great tan.

What have you been doing since I left to go on my
wonderful tour of Vietnam. Boy the U.S. sure is real
generous to let us come over here and visit with these
wonderful little demons. We learn more and more
each day about their filthy way of life. They even eat
up our garbage whenever they can slip in and steal it.
It sounds hard to believe but it is true.

The guys in Company C caught a monkey. He was real
cute and they played with him several days. They
don't have him anymore—they ate him.

Tell Momma not to worry about me. I'll be home by
Christmas!

Oh yeah, Happy New Year.

About the middle of January, we left the base camp for the first
time on what amounted to nothing more than an overnight hike
back close to the mountains. It must have been part of an exercise
to get the company back ready for combat again. We made no
contact with the enemy and saw no trace of their having been
around. Still there was a build-up and talk of a "big operation." The
first time out, you felt a little uncertain but not much. It wasn't
like the safety of the camp, but most of us didn't really have
anything to compare it to. A lot of the guys said more about their
fear of snakes than of the enemy. Snakes didn't bother me that
much as I had seen plenty of them in the Everglades.

We came back in, rested a day, and then prepared for a more
extended trip back into the jungle for three or four days. It is
amazing how much you have to carry for something like that:
ammunition for the M-60, your own M-16 and ammunition for
it—maybe 600 boxed rounds, 8 clips, and one or two bandoliers,
three boxes of C-rations for each day out, dry clothes, the steel

helmet cover, and, your P-38—your can opener. There must have been 80 - 90 pounds of supplies. And, always high on my list was extra ammunition, the first-aid packages which were provided, and two canteens of water.

We climbed around the mountains for three days, and it was treacherous going. Most of us were still trying to prove ourselves to the platoon leaders and what officers we saw, so there was little or no complaining. We kept up at all costs and still did everything exactly by the books of the training we had had. Again, there was no contact with enemy. Maybe it was still a training exercise, and the people in command knew that no enemy was actually there. It was amazing how tired and exhausted you became, but still—just like all the running you did in basic training—you were not going to allow yourself to be the one who fell out.

The deeper you got into the jungle, the more strange things you came in contact with. There were ant hills taller than a man's head. The trees were huge, large enough for people to live in. I kept thinking how easy it would be for a VC to be hiding in the trees watching our every move, or a VC sniper taking careful aim on the back of your neck. My biggest problem was the ants. I awakened in the middle of one of the nights out with stuff crawling all over me. It was ants—in my nose, at the edges of my mouth, in my ears, all over my hair and clothing. I jumped up and started knocking them off like I was attacking a fire. But, you could never get them all off. They became a fact of life, just like the air you breathed.

We came back in for a couple of days, rested all we could although it had started raining—pouring—all day and all night. Water was running everywhere and the ground had gone to pure mud. We took our turns guarding the perimeter of the camp. This suddenly became much more serious business, or at least I thought so. If I had been the enemy, this is when I would have attacked. We would have been mired ten feet deep in mud before we knew what was going on. But maybe this is not what the enemy wanted, fighting on our ground; maybe they wanted us to come looking for them, in the jungle on their ground. Still there was no contact whatsoever, only the sounds of artillery in the distance and the rare breaking of the night silence with small arms fire.

By the time we spent a third extended patrol on "Tittie Mountain," hardly any of the new people were taking it seriously. People had started getting loud, kidding around as if we were on some kind of picnic or family outing. Guys would throw their empty C-ration cans off the side of the mountains, and you could hear them echoing all around. I almost got in my first fight over that. It was stupid. If there was enemy within two miles, they would know exactly where we were, and we would never be able to hear them slipping up on us. I guess my nerves were getting a little frayed. Strange surroundings on every side, almost spooky surroundings sometimes, but still no contact. Maybe it wasn't a training exercise; maybe the VC were playing a mind game with us. I wrote Kay from a machine gun bunker on top of the mountain at 5:30 in the morning:

> It's going to be a beautiful day today. The sun is almost up and the birds are chirping. You wouldn't believe there's a war going on if it wasn't for the bombing and the rifles firing. The Air Force sure is dropping a lot of bombs in the distance. They must think that there is something big out there. Maybe that's where we will be going.

> I'm writing you inside a machine gun bunker. Jack is at my feet asleep and Rick is on the machine gun on guard.

> Gabe just came by my foxhole. He borrowed my cap. He's going out on a patrol. He said to tell you "Hi" and that he's going out and get a VC for you. I told him to be careful, but if he got shot not to get any blood on my hat. It might not sound funny to you, but we're always joking like that. I guess we have to. It helps us in some way.

> This should put cold chills on Momma. We shot a snake this morning. It was over five feet long. One shot blew him half in two, so Gabe and I opened him up. Guess what he had inside him—five rats. At least he wasn't hungry.

You said you were going to the Policeman's Ball. Is Linda going, too? Tell her to date other boys. I guess it is all right since there is no sense in her suffering sitting around while I am over here. It's a long time before I come home. If something were to happen to me, it wouldn't be right for her to keep waiting.

I went to church the last Sunday when we were in camp. I sure felt better after I went to church, except I was still tired. Send me some of your candied peanuts and some candles. If you can't get the kind I like, anything will do. Anything would taste good over here. If you need any money, take it out of my check that comes each month.

The picture of Bobby's baby sure is cute. When he comes over here, I hope it's 101st. The VC sure are scared of us. It's my turn to guard. Got to go.

Love you always, Your Brother, Charles

PS: It's raining cats and dogs.

The next morning we made contact! Prisoners! The word was passed down, and all of us were excited to get our first face-to-face view of the enemy. It turned out to be two women, and one of them was so pregnant that she looked like she was going to give birth at any second. Then, the platoon leader was calling out "Matherson!" What in the world could he want with me?

I was given instructions to take the women back to the main command post for interrogation. That they were "enemy" didn't scare me. That I was out on my own didn't scare me; I knew the way without any questions. It scared the living daylights out of me that this woman was about to have a baby, and what was I going to do if she had it on me right then? All the way back, she kept crying and pointing at her stomach and whining "Baby san, Baby san, Baby san!" I kept pushing on. Part of me wanted to stop, but I had been told clearly not to do so. If I stopped, I might never be heard from again. Never had that command center looked so good as it did when I came in sight of it with my two prisoners. I quickly left them with the proper officers and made my way back to my company, all the time feeling that God had watched over me in some special way and kept that woman from delivering her child.

When we got back to camp, we were allowed to go into downtown Phan Rang for the day. It wasn't going to be much compared to Saigon, but most of us were ready for anything that looked like the outside world even if it was Vietnamese. The moment we got outside the compound, it was like we had driven into the world's largest marketplace. All along the way were merchants hawking one piece of merchandise and then another. I believe you could have bought anything you wanted.

We passed an ornate and ancient Buddhist temple. It was beautiful and covered with all kinds of beautiful colors. I expressed an immediate interest in going up there and going through the place. These were the kinds of things I wanted to see in my off-time from soldiering. This was part of the world that the recruiting posters had promised to show us in the army. Quickly, one of the older guys told me in all seriousness that I had better not go there. Those old temples, he said, were full of deadly snakes and strange people. Part of me doubted what he said, but enough believed him that I never went.

Most of us just walked up and down the streets. We drank some Vietnamese beer and kidded around with the women. The beer was called "Tiger Piss Beer" and "Bombi Ba." It tasted like the former and had a kick like the latter. About all you could say was that it was better than the water. Many of the young girls were prostitutes and they were servicing one soldier after another just as quickly as they could duck behind a corner or into one of the small buildings. I didn't participate in this part, not because I was "holier than thou" so much as because I was broke. What little money I had went for beer and a few pieces of silk for Momma and Kay. After all, I hadn't been engaged much more than a month now. We had also been scared so badly about a form of Vietnamese venereal disease that would swell your testicles to the size of basketballs. No one wanted that!

You had to be careful where you walked. There were bicycles everywhere, people carrying all kinds of merchandise on their heads, and others who were hooked into shoulder yokes that allowed them to balance heavy loads on both sides of their bodies.

These people didn't slow down either, just as we hadn't in the trucks. You stayed out of their way. It was almost as if they wanted to act as if we weren't there. Maybe that was exactly what they wanted. There were no tourists in Phan Rang.

Right at the very end of January, we were loaded on trucks and driven east toward the ocean. Each time we went out we thought we were going for the big one, but each time we were told it was not quite time yet. As we drove toward the ocean, we passed one area that I was not expecting. There was a section of large Vietnamese homes that must have cost thousands of dollars. So, I thought, Vietnam has its "gold coast," too. Sure enough, there in the midst of all that was so primitive, stood structures that were in every way elegant and rich. No wonder we hadn't seen any VC; war seldom touches people in places like this.

We arrived on the coast and set up our bunker in a graveyard overlooking the South China Sea. Finally, there were breezes. We stayed at the coast for two or three days, never seeing anything that even slightly resembled an enemy. I went swimming in the ocean, collected shells to send to Dickie Medlin's mother, and got more homesick than ever thinking about the beaches at home. It wasn't clear whether this was actually a training exercise or a break that might better prepare us for the difficult time that was right around the corner.

While we were at the graveyard, a group of people came up carrying a red casket. From their crying, it was clear that there had been a death. They wanted to bury their dead, but the commander of our company had to make sure they were not carrying some kind of bomb. The casket had to be opened, and the people's grieving increased even more. It all took me back to the work I had done around the funeral home. I would like to have helped the people, even to have tried to comfort them; all I could do was look with curiosity from a distance. The homesickness mounted even more.

We came back to Phan Rang, rested for a day, and then they told us. We would be moving out the next day for Tuy Hoa aboard C-130 transport planes. Then, we would helicopter out to the mountains northwest of Tuy Hoa to carry out search and destroy missions against the enemy. They were suspected to be in the area to get provisions from the rice harvests that were just being completed. This was the "big one."

The movement to Tuy Hoa and the establishment of the camp was pretty uneventful. We could hear greater amounts of artillery fire in the distance, and now there had been contact by some of the other companies. One Captain and one Lieutenant had been killed and there were several missing men; still I had seen nothing. Then, the word came: we would fly several miles into the jungle the next morning. This was big—this was it!

Late that night I wrote to Kay in a letter boldly marked on the outside: "don't anyone else read this besides Kay."

Well, old girl, I've been lying out here getting a suntan on the beach. Ha! Ha! (Here was bravado and grave merry humor like nothing we had ever experienced at the funeral home or in jump school—on the inside there was very little that was brave or merry.)

(The tone immediately changes.) I haven't heard from Linda in over two weeks now. I guess she just hasn't got the time to write. Well, it may be better anyway as all I do is make her worry about me.

Kay, don't tell Momma this because it will worry her, but I've got to tell someone. In the morning we fly from this position into a VC stronghold. They're supposed to be two regiments of VC in there, and we are going in by helicopter and land right in the middle of them.

All I hope is that God will be with us. Kay, I guess we're all scared. You can't imagine how it is.

Kay, I guess I've changed some. At night, I have dreams just like everyone else. I don't know what's going to happen. All I know is we're all scared and we all pray that we'll come back safe.

Kay, if something does happen, take care of Momma and remember I love you and all the rest of the family very much. I'm lucky to have such a good family.

Well, I've got to get some sleep if I can. You'd never believe that I was your brother if you could see me. I'm dirty all over and need a shave. Well, Kay, write me and remember I'm OK, and I love all of you.

Love always, Your Brother Charles

Chapter XII

Had we known what we were getting in for, we might have been even more concerned. Our high command knew that the North Vietnamese and Viet Cong would be coming into our area following the rice harvest. To some extent, they would be coming to capture rice that had been grown and harvested for South Vietnam; it was never clear though—they could as easily have been coming to collect food that had been grown specifically for them. This was just one more instance of not knowing who were your friends and who were your enemies. The one thing that we did know—it was hot as hell! Humid hot, day and night, with no breezes blowing, no early morning or late evening cool that was noticeable. Sometimes the dampness that was all over your body would make you cold, but it was a chilling cold that didn't cool you off but rather added to your misery.

The North Vienamese were greatly dependent on getting local food supplies since they had no system of bringing in huge food supplies like we Americans did. If you could keep them away from the food or destroy it before they had a chance to get it, the idea was that you would hamper their ability to fight. In the end, about all that was accomplished was that you faced very hungry fighters rather than moderately hungry fighters—either way, these people always looked hungry.

It's pretty easy to get the idea of why we called them "search and destroy" missions. We were searching for the enemy and, of course, if we found him there would be a fight. But we were also out to destroy the enemy's resources. On this side of the coin, we were being asked to do things that, on balance, did not make a lot of sense unless you were there.

We would go into a village that was supposedly South Vietnamese in its loyalties, or—at most—of questionable loyalty. For the most part the village would be minding its own business. We would scare the people off or shuffle the very old and very young that remained into the center of the complex. Then we would meticulously search through all the hooches for anything the enemy could use. Seldom, if ever, did we find anything that resembled a weapon. I always thought these were gone before we got there.

We did find a lot of rice. Huge, woven baskets full. Some of the baskets must have held 500 pounds or more. It was beautiful rice, and its smell would make your mouth water. There is no telling how much work had gone into growing the rice and harvesting it. All that we could do was to burn it. A rich aroma filled the entire area as the flames of the burning hooches filled the sky. We would grab pieces of the popped rice and eat it like popcorn. By the time you had had nothing but C-rations for several days, it tasted pretty good.

The people just stood there and watched us. If they had any emotion, it had been washed away by the hardness of their daily lives. Their faces reminded me of the little kids on the beach who had so carefully and pridefully built sand castles, only to have them pushed over by some big bully. Sometimes I felt like a bully; sometimes I was so frustrated at all of the patrolling without any actual contact with anything but old women and children, that destroying the villages was at least something different to do. In the back of my mind, I figured that if these people had not been our enemies, they sure were now. It was like Sherman's march across Georgia all over again, and I knew from living in the South that those kinds of wounds don't heal easily.

More than anything else, it all seemed like a huge waste; all of that rice, all of the work to bring it to harvest, how much their lives depended on all of this, all of the effort to put the most mechanized army in all of the world into the field, just to burn Vietnamese hooches. But what were we to do? If we didn't destroy the stuff, the North Vietnamese would get it. The people, probably used to losing, were going to lose either way. So we stood there at odd angles to each other, they in their world and we in ours. All that we had in common was sweat, now flowing in thin rivers down our collars, along our backs, down into our pants, and into every fiber of our gear. The heat rising from the burning buildings was like standing in front of a great coal furnace.

One thing I learned to be happy about on these missions was the fact that my size had gotten me into the M-60 group. It might have been hard to carry all of the ammunition and help with the transporting of the gun, but the smaller men got to do something that was infinitely harder. Around every village, the Vietnamese either used caves that were available or dug them out in the ground around their hooches or the nearby hillsides. I guessed that they used them for storage or maybe bomb shelters. Because they had so many predators, they probably just used them for hiding places. These had to be checked out, and that's what the smaller guys got to do.

I've seen some little guy crawl back or drop down out of sight into the ground with a flashlight in one hand and a .45 in the other. It was dark and wet in the holes, and you didn't know what was there—a booby trap, someone with a gun, a snake or some other wild animal. It might also be old women and children. You had to make sure. People would crawl back out with a look of total relief on their faces. Most of the time the holes were empty. Later on, elaborate tunnel systems would be found that created the same as underground cities. Finally, we just got to the point that we would throw in explosives and destroy the holes so we wouldn't have to risk our men. There is no telling how many instant graves we created in this process. But, given the choice of going in and looking for yourself, it was probably the decision that most people would end up making.

One other thing that we didn't know—at least the foot soldiers didn't know it—was that the North Vietnamese had filled the area immediately in front of us with its 95th Regiment. This was one of the crack units of the entire enemy command, made up of experienced soldiers who were volunteers and who had had excellent training. They knew the jungle like the backs of their hands.

As I think back on it, the enemy knew they could not beat us when it came to physical and technological force—we were simply too overwhelming. They also knew they could not beat us in any normal fighting environment. So, they would try to beat you mentally, and they were positive that if they drew us deeper and deeper into the jungle that we would get more and more out of our element. We would be wet, tired, hungry, exhausted from sleeping on the ground. In turn, we would become frustrated and disgusted, and then we could get careless and subject to surprise.

It was all in the mind, and they knew this better than we did. It was hard not to think that with all our great manpower and equipment and training we could just walk straight over these little, delicate people. But they had been toughened by the jungle for their entire lives. They knew nothing of air-conditioning, hot baths, cases of cokes and cold beer, and lying around on the couch watching baseball games on television. Their skin was like the hide of a wild animal. They could run barefooted and in little more than their black pajamas through an area that was so filled with saw briars and briar bushes (we called them "wait-a-minute bushes") that it might take our platoons hours to get through. I thought of Brer Rabbit in the briar patch, his home sweet home; in this instance, we were in the briar patch and they were the rabbit.

The stupidest strategy that our higher-ups pursued during this mission was the way in which they let the enemy know we were coming. I had never heard, or could not have conceived, of any army doing anything like this. They would fly helicopters or transport-type airplanes out ahead of the areas we were in. The air would fill with what looked like, from a distance, snow. Actually it was small leaflets printed in Vietnamese. This told the people that we were coming into the area. They could move to a safer place, surrender, or retreat.

In some respects, this gave the locals a chance to get out, although we kept finding the same women and children in the villages. All I could see it doing was giving them a chance to dig in, hide weapons, or make decisions about their own troop movements. The rice was too heavy and cumbersome to move, so it seemed like we were more interested in destroying food supplies in hopes that the enemy would be pushed back north than we were in fighting. Only on the rarest occasion would someone hold up one of the leaflets as a sign of surrender.

In some instances this tactic might have saved American lives, but not this time. The North Vietnamese had evidently sent their crack 95th Regiment in to challenge the famous 101st Airborne. If they could compete with this group—among the best the Americans had—they could gain a great psychological boost to their war effort. Of course, we didn't know this—yet. We were still just finding rice-filled hooches that we could burn down. We were still just cursing the warning leaflets. If they would just give us our head and let us fight, we could be in Hanoi in six months. Maybe some of the guys were right. Somewhere in a big office back in the States, someone was wanting to drag this thing out—it was good for the economy and a lot of fat-cats were getting well-heeled.

All we wanted was to fight, what we had been trained to do. All we wanted was to pay someone back for the rain and heat, the blood-sucking leeches that filled the creeks, the ants and flies that felt like they crawled in your body at one opening and out at another. You had to pull the leeches off. Sometimes they were six inches long. In a mudhole after a rain, you could stir the water with your bayonet and it would roll with leeches like carp shoaling next to a lake bank. You couldn't use up all of your repellant on them because you would need it at night for the bugs. Everywhere you pulled a leech off your skin, it would leave a sore. It was hot, it was sickening, it was god-forsaken, god-damned awful. Still, as we were coming to the end of the first week of February—I had taken time to draw Kay a valentine and send it to her—I had yet to see my first enemy soldier or see any American injured in the slightest way from battle. We ached all over from the wet, the heat—so much so that our clothing and boots were actually starting to rot— the leech marks where we had burned them off with cigarettes, all that we were carrying and climbing with, the incessant brush of the jungle undergrowth, and the tiredness that came from days and days of inadequate sleep. No wonder they had trained us so hard.

Finally, we started running short on water. In the heat, you started to dehydrate, so your water demands were more than they would normally be. Although the taste was not very good, we started using their creeks. You would fill your canteen, drop in the purification pills, and have something that was at least wet and supposedly not dangerous. On one day, we had drunk from a small creek and then moved on up it finishing our planned advance for the day. We turned a bend right beyond where we had stopped to drink and the creek was filled with the decaying body of a dead water buffalo and the bloated remains of a human being— maybe the first actual enemy soldier we had seen. People were overwhelmed on every side and stood bracing themselves against trees, cursing, and vomiting their insides out.

Late the next afternoon we stopped in a grove of coconut trees. I had been around coconut trees before and liked the liquid on the inside of the nuts. We called it "monkey juice" or "monkey pee," and it was almost as much of a delicacy as the chicken's "pulley bone." Although I could tell that the nuts were not quite ripe, the liquid on the inside would have to be better than the water. We cut down one of the trees, opened the nuts with our bayonets, and I drank my fill.

We set up camp for the night along beside the diked waters of a rice patty. I was guarding with the M-60 in our foxhole of a bunker when the coconut liquid started having its effect on my stomach. I started to have some of the worst stomach cramps I had ever experienced in my whole life. I had to use the bathroom—an odd term when there is no bathroom for a hundred miles—right then. Right then! I quickly woke a couple of the others and explained very, very carefully that I was going to walk over to the side of the dike and get rid of all this pain. It was dark as pitch, so I explained again exactly where I was going so that they wouldn't mistake me for an enemy and start firing. At least, for me, a man hated to make love or use the bathroom in front of someone else.

I slipped carefully to the edge of the dike and started out across it. Then I heard the soft "tuth" sound—like a cork easing out of a bottle or the sound of the tongue as it flips out from the roof of your mouth and releases air—the sound of the trigger on an anti-personel mine! These mines can blow a man's legs off in a split second! Light erupted all around me, but faster than it takes time to think I had instictively jumped in a reflex movement straight up and back—off the dike and flat into the soggy, muddy water of the half-drained rice patty. It was a trip flair. In the process, with the force of adrenalin and fear, my bowels exploded in movement.

That was Vietnam, one mess exchanged for another and not even a place to get cleaned up. My friends laughed until they cried—at least I had given them some kind of distraction if only for a moment. I finally laughed too, more glad to be alive than anything else—you might as well laugh, crying didn't get you anywhere.

You got to where you hated to see night come. Everything about you wanted to sleep, but you couldn't really sleep. You knew the enemy was getting closer all the time, and you began to sense that you weren't chasing them as much as they were luring you into a trap. You would fight, but on their terms. In the now-near distance, we could watch "Puff the Magic Dragon" planes as they fired into the jungle in front of us.

The planes were converted transports that had been filled with rapid fire machine guns that were built on the principle of the old Gatlin guns of the American west. It was possible for them to fire thousands of rounds per minute, to create a literal wall of raining lead. Every fifth round was a tracer shell so it looked like the planes were pouring out fire. Basically, the "Puffs" were out there laying down instant death to anyone who might try to sneak in on us during the night.

Occasionally, flairs would go off out on the perimeter to check for any movement. You loved the light, the way it opened up the dark, and you especially loved it when no movement was revealed. You hated it when frogs and crickets suddenly stopped making their sounds. Something was out there. You hated it when whoever it was blew a bugle somewhere back out there in the mountains just to awaken you, just to let you know they were there.

One night we suddenly began to hear movement in below our position along an old roadway. The movement increased and then there were voices—Oriental voices. We could see them moving along fifty yards beneath our position. More and more kept coming into view. This was it! We didn't make a sound. Everyone was suddenly at the peak of alertness, waiting for the command to fire.

Nothing happened. We looked from one position to the next toward the command position. All we got back in return were gestures for silence and motions to be still. Surely to God, I thought, they aren't going to let these people go. Surely, they aren't afraid to fight. This is what we've waited for and we have the element of surprise! Everything within me wanted to jump up and start firing away.

In a moment or so the voices and then the sounds passed beyond us and were gone. We sat there for the rest of the night not knowing what the hell had happened. The next morning, word was passed: a group of South Koreans had passed through our area. Somehow, our command group had known. The South Koreans were wild and crazy fighters; no one else would have been out like that walking around at night. Had we gotten caught up in a fire fight with them, it could have been a disaster of monumental significance.

Our helicopters would come in in the mornings. We loved to see them come. They were our contact with reality. As long as they came, you felt that help and something of home could not be too far away. They brought warm food, fresh water, and mail. We reassured ourselves that if we did get hurt, the helicopters could have us out in moments.

I noticed the door gunners with great envy. They were always clean. They wore fancy polished and painted helmets and expensive-looking leather gloves. Somehow they seemed like guardian angels coming in from heaven. John Wayne would have made an excellent door gunner. They would smile and wave and always seemed willing to try to help with whatever was going on. How much different from all of this wading through heat and mud. The very idea of lifting off, leaving it behind, and riding through actual breezes back to a clean base.

Everything got the same. Day after day—the same. Night after night—the same. I can remember only one time, sitting down beside a clean little river and eating all of the sweet sugar cane I could hold, that anything even seemed halfway normal. Still no enemy, but he was out there. Mentally and physically we were all getting exhausted. We wanted to find them! We wanted to fight and get it over with!

It was time for another short letter home. Somehow with all that the helicopters were bringing, they were bringing us writing paper. A strange place to write a letter home:

Well Hello Old Maid:

Guess who? Yep, it's me, the best-looking soldier in the U. S. Army. Guess what? I got us some souvenirs. A VC knife and some bamboo arrows. I'll send them home. But don't touch the end of them. I don't know if there's any poison or germs on them. OK?

Boy, the VC are really afraid of the 101st. I don't know why, but all I know is that we put a lot of lead in their behinds.

Well, it has happened to me. I have fallen in love, and I'll give you two guesses who. Well, you are right—Linda. I can't seem to get her off my mind. Every time I close my eyes I can see her, and all I do is remember the good times we had together. Kay, get her to tell you our dreams of the future about the house and all.

Tell Al when he gets out of service, that we'll have to get together and take you and Linda out on the town in Miami in Linda's Stingray. Oh yeah, tell Linda that I told Momma in my letter that I loved her and if she wants to she can tell her the same.

Take care of Momma and everything until I get back.

Airborne all the way!

Love, Charles

Chapter XIII

Two or three more days passed, and still no contact. We would break camp in the morning and maybe advance our front line four or five miles. It was always slow going. You would measure every step and not leave any bush or low place unturned in your search for any trace of the enemy. Almost always you sensed that you had just missed him. At most there might be a little, sporadic rifle fire in the distance but nothing more—it could easily have been a sniper, someone who was suddenly scared and fired at an animal that suddenly moved in the deep foliage, or just a bored GI trying to relieve some of his pent up tension. It was almost like going hunting but never finding any game—after a few hours you were ready to shoot your weapon even at an imagined target just so you could say that you had shot at something.

Word was passed on occasion about some distant contact and maybe even someone getting wounded, but nothing that directly affected any of us. You finally got to the place that you almost quit expecting much to happen, although you never ever got to the place that you felt comfortable moving in that jungle. You couldn't see thirty feet in front of yourself most of the time, so you never really felt secure that someone might not be hiding just ahead, already drawing a bead on your head. There was always the funny feeling that ate away at your insides that your next step might set off some kind of booby trap.

There wasn't much talk during the day time and then at night you were afraid that any noise, no matter how slight, would give away your position. Sometimes you felt like if only you could get away somewhere and sit down and shoot the shit with your buddies for a couple of hours, a lot of the tension could be relieved and you would feel a lot better about everything.

In the day time you were isolated from everyone else most of the time by ten or fifteen feet of jungle. You watched all the movement around you and communicated with hand signals with the people on both sides, but we had been warned not to bunch up and give the enemy a chance to shoot several of us at once. A single soldier was never as much the target of choice for an enemy whose firing would give his own position away as a group was. You were almost continually in a defensive, guarded crouch, as if you would uncover something the next instant. You yearned for the chance simply to stand upright, throw your rifle back over your shoulder, and walk off down the road like a normal human being—but there were no roads, only jungle.

This searching and looking and sneaking and half-crawling would go on for hours. Your senses were peaked, letting every intuition and instinct merge with the total environment that surrounded you. Watching, listening, smelling—he was out there somewhere, but where? But where?

At night an ambush perimeter would be established around some kind of central area where the company commander established a command post. Usually the perimeter encompassed a trail that you had hit upon that looked like it had been used by the enemy. Since they moved a great deal at night, the idea was to sit out there in the dark, wet jungle with weapons carefully set up to avoid any crossfire on your own people and wait for the enemy to walk into your trap. Silence and stillness—but careful alertness—was of highest priority.

You had to be careful about watching things out there in front of you too long. If you got to staring at a tree or bush, it would seem to start to move on you like it was somebody. You had to stay constantly aware of moving your eyes from one point to another or they would play tricks on you.

You can't imagine the pain, the bone-deep hurt, of being worn out from the nerve-racking searching, crouching, and crawling your way through the jungle of the day, yet still having to sit there—essentially by yourself—and watch for the enemy suddenly to appear in front of you.

We set trip flares and Claymore mines, took turns trying to sleep—although it works on your mind to think that the guy next to you who is supposed to be awake is as tired as you are. What if he drifts off? You can't yell over and ask if he's awake; they would know where you were. What if the enemy happens to step over your trip wires? What if the next sensation you have is a knife in the still of the night slitting your throat? Sometimes you wake in a jerk feeling at your throat to make sure that the knife isn't already there.

You can't imagine how hot it was in the day time. There was no release, no breezes, humidity so high that you could almost reach out and move it around with your hands. God, how the breezes that were always on the beach seemed like a dream ten million miles away. You were drenched with sweat ten minutes after you started out in the morning.

Then the night was just the reverse. So cold that you wrapped yourself in all you had. You had cursed it for having to carry it in the day, and then you cursed it because it was never quite enough to really get rid of the chill in the night. If you could have just gotten everything dried out, then you could have gotten warm. That never happened. On this particular mission it never stopped raining long enough to get anything dry. Your underwear stayed damp and you were always galded or nearly so. Your boots and clothes were starting to literally rot, and there was no way you could run off the field and take a break on the sidelines and get a clean jersey. There was no way that you could duck into the office toilet in the middle of the afternoon, wash your face, and knock off your five o'clock shadow with an electric razor. You stuck your head down into your poncho, pulled your boonie cap tight over your head like an umbrella and slipped a smoke. No one had to tell you to be careful to keep the light concealed. You blew the warm smoke down into the personal envelope that the poncho was trying to make and imagined that somehow the warm smoke was chasing the chill away.

You learned things they never put in their books. Rice dikes are made for 100 pound Vietnamese, not 200 pound Americans loaded with battle gear. Everyone knew, without even turning to look after a while, the disgusting curse that rose when the dike gave way and someone slid off into the cold, stagnant water. This seemed almost always to happen just as it was getting dark and you were getting ready to stop for the night and just getting a little dried out from the sweat and rain of the day.

When those night flairs are set off in the sky, you jerk to cover one eye. Look with the flair's help for any movement of the enemy out in front of you. Keep the other eye blinded so that your night vision won't be lost. The enemy closed their eyes, then moved as the flair died out. If you could not hold your own night vision, they could be on you before you even saw them.

You covered your remains when you urinated or your bowels moved just like an animal would. The enemy could smell you almost as easily as he could see you. God, how you wanted that cigarette—God, how you feared that its odor might make you even a better target.

You missed the strangest things. I'm not sure I had ever had a craving. I had heard about them, especially pregnant women craving ice cream or pickles, or some strange combination of foods. I had never thought much about it. Then I started craving popcorn. It was unbelievable. I would have given any amount of money for a bowl full of popcorn. Given the choice of wild sex or hot, buttered popcorn, the sex would just have to wait. The smell, the salty taste, the warm texture as you chewed it—all they had to do was drop popcorn on any objective that they wanted achieved out there in that damn jungle, and my getting there would not seem nearly so bad. Maybe my system was craving the salt, maybe the popcorn somehow subconsciously represented the simplicity and security of home—I couldn't get it out of my mind!

In the intensity of the moment, it didn't take long to become close friends with those around you. Rick Crossland and I became closest of all—the closest that I had come to anyone since Cecil and Johnny Frazier and John Bludworth and Bobby and Joe. What were they doing now? I hoped they were anywhere except some damned jungle. Rick and I talked when we could. Sometimes about girlfriends—sometimes serious stuff and sometimes bullshit born of our fantasies. We would count our days and think together about what we would do when it was over. Sometimes it got quiet and we tried to laugh off the new-learned fact, passed from someone in another company, that the first target on the enemy's list was the machine gunner and his carriers. If the machine gun could be put out of commission, the whole unit's cover was all but destroyed. High on the enemy's wish list was our M-60; it was the battle trophy they most wanted to capture. Get the machine gunners first, then the radio man, then the medics, then the lieutenants, then the sergeants; everything else would fall apart in confusion. We didn't talk about that much, but you never exactly got it out of your mind either. Why did the son-of-a-bitch have to tell us that? But maybe it was better to know it than not.

You learned to be careful about "short timers." At first you liked to be near them. Maybe some of their good luck would rub off on you. If they could make it, you could too. They were kind of a link to the outside world. As they left, a little of you seemed to leave with them. Then, you found out that short timers were dangerous. They got too careful sometimes and stopped being able to respond to what was happening around them quickly enough. At other times, they got the idea that they were invincible. Sometimes just the thought of two more weeks or two more days was a distraction from what was happening around them. It was amazing how many guys ended up getting shot or killed in their last month. It was so much so that the Army started rotating a person out about a month before they were actually due to finish their time in Vietnam. This didn't work; the soldier just got an informal out time set in his mind, and all the other problems became evident again, just one month earlier.

You even had to be careful about your garbage. You learned to take your knife, cut up your C-Ration can, bury it, and then cover the spot with foliage. If you didn't, the VC would come in where you had camped and get your waste and figure out how to use it against you. A C-Ration can could easily become a bomb. We started booby-trapping our garbage, and maybe fifteen or twenty minutes after you had marched out of a camp, you could hear an explosion in the distance as the booby-trap got its victim.

You learned—two or three trips into the jungle—two or three weeks in there without relief. You learned. If you didn't, you died.

The morning of February 7th came clear and cool. The cool wouldn't last. Maybe an hour at best. We heaved down some half-hot coffee, tried to shake some of the sleep and stiffness out of our bodies, and headed back out. Just like yesterday, the day before, and the day before. The sun was just slipping up behind us, but it would be there with all of its force plenty soon enough. I wondered what would give out first, my boots or my back. Surely, if we didn't find anything today or tomorrow they would send us back to Phan Rang. What I wouldn't give for a night in a tent, a bath, some dry clothes, a hot meal, a new pair of boots! My moment of contemplation was quickly erased by the groaning sounds of hundreds of pounds of equipment being hoisted onto soldiers' backs as we moved off into the next five miles of jungle that this day would carry us through.

We moved down into a wide valley that had large groves of trees on each side and mountains in the distance. The valley narrowed in the direction in which we were moving. If you had been a tourist fresh from an air-conditioned hotel in clean, fashionable safari clothes, it would have been beautiful. For most of us, it looked like exactly what we had been seeing for the past week. It was about 9:30 or 10:00 o'clock in the morning.

We were deployed along with another company or two in a large "V" shaped formation. The front of the "V" was moving toward the neck of the valley. The entire formation must have been several hundred yards across. The point moved very slowly, almost so slowly that you wanted to yell out "Hell, Go on! There's nothing! Let's get it done!" I was close to Rick, maybe ten yards away, and the other two carriers were in behind us somewhere. We were about half-way back on the right side of the "V" as it moved across the valley.

About noon word was passed that there was some enemy movement ahead of us. Hell, we all started looking. There was no sense of fear. If I had come this far, I wanted at least to say that I had seen an enemy. It was almost like riding along in a car or on a train and someone says they have seen a deer or a bear. At a minimum, I wanted to be able to go back to South Florida and talk about that day in early February when I saw some "enemy."

We didn't see anything, anywhere. It must be wrong; somebody thought they saw something, a rumor, something to chase away a little of the monotony.

About 2:30 or 3:00 o'clock we began to hear a little small arms fire. Word was passed that the front left of the formation was receiving some fire from the distance. Several enemy would appear in the trees and underbrush, fire off their weapons, and then visibly retreat on into the narrowing neck of the valley.

If you had stopped to think about it, there would have been little question that we were being lured into a trap. Yet, we were not worried about traps. It was our job to move in the direction of fire, to engage that fire, and then neutralize it. In all that we had learned, it was a simple as that. Maybe we got a little quieter and watched around us a little more closely, but we had no inclination to do anything else but to move straight ahead. The greater part of the formation was still forming a buffer in front of us. Put the bastards out there in front of us. We were airborne. We were ready to fight. By God, let us at them. They put us through hell to get here, now let's pay them back. Still, we had received no fire that was anywhere close at hand. Still, we were yet to see a wounded American soldier.

We slipped forward over a small hill then down beyond a large bomb crater that was reasonably new. The jungle had not had time to grow back over it, but it had been there long enough to get partially filled with water. It must have been a huge bomb. The crater was at least eight or ten feet deep. There were a couple of large ditches running parallel to the direction of our movement, so we moved away from these, not wanting to have to lug our equipment through them. It seemed like there was the sudden need to imprint exactly on your mind the ground that you were passing over at that moment. If you had to get back, you would know what was back there.

Suddenly, in the split second it takes for a sensation to strike your eyes and begin to register on your brain, there was something different happening all around us. It was like some great sickle or scythe was loose in the underbrush around us. Grass and leaves were clipping off, springing into the air, and falling back to the ground. There was a rush of air, mud, dirt, pieces of limbs, twigs, leaves, and weeds—almost like a huge collection bag carried on a giant mowing machine had exploded. Since you had never seen anything like it before, it was almost like in that split second that your mind was trying to sort through all of its past experiences and determine what this particular one might be.

Then there was a loud popping sound all around your head and face, like you had stepped into the midst of a thousand million firecrackers on the Fourth of July. Bullets were popping the air apart on every side, and finally it all registered as the flash of the muzzles of guns firing took on the appearance of hundreds of cameras flashing off all around you. The flashes were so thick that it was impossible to pick out where any one single flash was coming from.

The trap was sprung! We were under attack!!

The sights, the sounds, the flashing lights all acted together with every instinct that would throw itself in gear to push you like a huge, slapping hand down to the ground. At that moment everything that had been trained into me for over half of a year worked. Sure it scared me shitless, sure my heart leaped into my throat, sure every fiber of my central nervous system was yelling "This is it!!" But still, I was down there with Rick and we were moving together without any talking like we were puppets on the strings of a master puppeteer. We eased back, still under control, toward the small hill and rolled over into the relative safety of the bomb crater that had been to our rear.

Still there was no panic. There was nothing to be said. There was no look of desperation. No question about what we would do next. No inclination to dig into the bottom of the crater and disappear from this part of the earth. We squared the gun around and began to return fire. That was what we were programmed to do—return fire—and the program was playing to perfection.

Over and between the sounds of the gunfire, you could hear people screaming. Cursing, commands, cries to God, someone yelling out "Momma!" over and over again. Careful, controlled cries that asked for the medics and corpsmen by name—it came back in this moment that a simple cry for a corpsman or medic was a deceptive enemy trick. But no time to think about the source of these cries, all that they unquestionably implied. Return fire!!

After a moment or two, it was possible to slip a look out of the edge of the crater. The evidence of the trap was there. All along the ridged up dirt at the edge of the distant tree line and along the dirt island at the sides of the paddied field were the open slots of machine gun bunkers. Long slots made from heavily disguised bamboo—some six to eight feet long and two feet high had fallen back on hinges to open us to their field of fire. Now, they were empty and the enemy was falling back to another set of bunkers from which their fire was still raging. This was precisely where they had lured us for days. We had come to their home field, and now the abuse of their advantage was destroying everything in its path.

I have been asked a hundred times and have thought myself more times than that what I felt in that moment. I can't really say that I felt anything. That had been the whole point of the training, not to feel anything. Had everything not been pure reaction, I have no doubt that I would have been cut down like the grass and weeds that were falling all around me. Enemy fire is not choosey about what it does with anything in its way.

I can remember seeing people fall, but for all I knew they were diving for cover just as I had. I may have somewhere along the way thanked God that it wasn't night. At least I could see what was happening around me. I remember distinctly never having even the slightest inkling of the thought that I was about to die; I am absolutely certain that it never even entered my mind that I might be the next one shot. It is absolutely amazing how, even under this kind of terrifying circumstance with every second fraught with instant death, that your mind is still telling you that things like death happen to other people—not to you. You return fire. That's all. You return fire!

You have to think to be scared. It is a conscious act to be scared. When everything is on pure instinct, pure reaction, you don't have time to think. Somehow the strange idea crossed my mind that I ought to be scared, but I wasn't. The program worked; without any command or direction, you did exactly what you were trained to do—you moved in the direction of the fire. There was no inclination to retreat, to run away, to hide—you moved in the direction of the fire. It wasn't macho, it wasn't pride, bravado, or an old John Wayne movie—it was the program. You returned fire!

Rick and I eased along through the undergrowth, staying low and getting all of our equipment back in order. One of the other carriers was back behind us several yards hugging the ground behind a low rise of muddy dirt. The third carrier was nowhere to be seen. It was beyond question now that the enemy had carefully chosen their target and gone directly for the machine gun. They must either have moved back or concluded that they had gotten us; the fire, though still heavy all around, was not the wall of burning, slashing lead that it had been a few moments ago. We were careful not to give ourselves away as still being in action until we could get to a little better cover.

We crawled in behind a low hill, just enough to cover our faces and bodies if you were on a flat plane away from us. A half-circle of palm trees that were randomly growing along the side of the field provided a little more cover. We were able to get the gun in place up over the low rise and began to spew out a field of fire across the whole area in front of us. You couldn't see to tell if you were hitting anything, but you knew that this was what you were to do. It felt right. There was something infinitely strong about that moment. This is what it had all come to and you were doing it, doing it precisely like it was supposed to be done.

After a while our supply of ammunition was running low. There was too much return fire to try to advance and any advance would demand more ammunition. I finally got the attention of the other carrier and motioned for him to come on up. He refused.

He would not move and it made no sense at all for me to simply lie there and yell at him. There was no time for arguments, threats, or value judgments about him being a coward or afraid or panic stricken.

I went back for more ammunition, crawling and holding low to the ground, all the time being careful not to expose any more of my head or body than was necessary. I don't know if the enemy saw me and tried to shoot me. There were bullets smacking in the air all around, but it had been that way for maybe an hour. It didn't really occur to me that what I was doing was brave or stupid. I certainly didn't think about John Wayne and Audie Murphy any longer. It was simply something that had to be done. I didn't feel defiant or desperate, returning fire and moving in the direction of fire meant more ammunition. There was no one else around to do it; it was my turn.

All along the way from the position that Rick and I had established and back again, in what took maybe fifteen or twenty minutes of careful movement in a field of fire. I picked up one metal container of ammunition after another. It was almost like it had been dropped by some kind of great sprinkling machine. Maybe it had all been on the third carrier, and he had dropped it to run. Who knows? Anyway, it was all that I could carry and drag, and by the time I got back I had hundreds of rounds of ammunition. Gunfire was still raging in what seemed like every direction except our immediate rear. We fired back. Surely the enemy would have to budge loose and we could reorganize and mount a more efficient attack. If we could get them on the run, we would be on their backs straight to hell if that's what it took. You kept expecting to see retreat, not on our part but theirs. They hit and run, but for now they just kept hitting away and we just kept hitting back.

Another hour passed. All the smells changed. No longer the ripe green lush smell of a growing jungle almost thick enough to see; now there was smoke everywhere and the heavy, wet smell of gunpowder. It hung like a film and mixed with the sweat on your face and in your clothes to make a sour smelling stickiness. The air seemed full of pieces of grass and trees and dirt, almost suspended in the thick smoke, falling in near slow motion with every new stir of bullets in the air. Rick and I were lying as close together as we could get, not talking, not exchanging any looks;

every sense organ alive with intensity watching for anything that would threaten or anything that would signal us to press the battle on. We were operating like two people who could read every thought in the other person's mind. Me, Rick, the gun, all operating in perfect solidarity.

Everything eased off for a minute. You expected it to start back up. Across the entire afternoon, it had eased off and started again, eased off and started again. This time it stayed quiet, almost too quiet. We didn't move. Nothing moved. Maybe this was it? Maybe they were turning to run? There was no movement on either side and since they were in a well-defined defensive position just waiting to cut us down or on darkness so they could slip away, it was not likely that they would charge straight on. It wasn't their way of fighting most of the time. Maybe they were finally running out of firepower and slithering back into the jungle?

We had been fitting a million pieces of the puzzle of that moment all at one time. Feeding the machine gun, watching the tree line in front and the perimeters beside, listening to all the voices on every side, planning out in our minds all the options if we had to move. Rick and I probably were talking, but more than likely we were working on instinct, like two perfectly meshing gears in a well-constructed machine. I had been seeing it all, trying to see even more, with every sense on its fullest alert. Two men, a million miles away from home, in the middle of hell—depending on each other more than most brothers would ever have the chance. And in the moment of sudden quiet you could feel yourself almost relax, at least sag down into the ground and catch your breath, feel yourself alive again.

Every particle within you wanted to sink down into the mud. If you could sink into the mud, everything would be all right. At the same time, other senses were crying out "Keep going! Advance on the fire! Return fire!"

I guess you had to look. Somebody had to look. We are curious and impatient people. We don't know about waiting like the Vietnamese do—and they knew that.

Rick slowly raised his head. Maybe two inches, maybe three. Just enough to get his eyes above the ledge of dirt in front of us. I looked square into his face. I would tell from his expression exactly what was out there and what we would have to do next. Almost like a periscope coming up out of a secluded, deep ocean spot, I watched his face. It would tell all.

I saw the damage being done even before the sound of the gunfire rang in my ears. "Oh my God!" Like a slow motion picture imprinting and then pushing an image deep into my mind never to be removed. Like frames of a camera film, jerking one instant after another into never-changing reality. Dead center. Smashing, wrinkling into the metal of the precise front middle of Rick's helmet. In one moment that I am sure he was never even conscious of, the helmet and the top of Rick's head peeled and tore straight back. The helmet scattered on off through the underbrush behind us, rocking and spinning and twisting out there somewhere while my attention was still riveted on his face. The helmet didn't even have time to be bled on. The top of Rick's head fell back toward his neck and shirt collar like a huge slab of flesh cut loose by a butcher except for the one, dangling connecting link that ran down into his shirt collar.

In one, uninterrupted slump he fell over onto his right side. It was almost as if someone had carefully and very easily set down a large, infinitely valuable object. There was a loud, sharp exhausting of air and then a low moaning sound. He never said a word. He never heard a word. With every pump of his heart, blood gushed out of the top of his head like water squeezing out of a sponge that someone had stepped on. I was covered all over, on my clothes, in my face, in my mouth, my nose, my ears, all over with his blood and brains. I'm not talking gore here, I'm talking death. When it's someone you know and in that moment you realize that you have become inseparably bonded to them for the rest of your life, it's not gore, and it's not some kind of sensationalized pornography of violence—it's death. The rushing blood gurgled to a still pool that only seeped to an overflow and ran down his face.

All the time, instantly, without even the slightest moment to scream, cry, pray, curse, run, or anything, I was reaching for Rick's bandage pack and then my own. Everything that I had ever experienced in the funeral home was running on automatic. I would put this head back together just like I had put a dozen heads back together before. I pulled the scalp gently and easily back up from behind, being careful not to let hair or dirt or metal catch inside the crevice of the skull. I got it all back even and perfectly in place all the way around. There was nothing to do about the dent and tear in the front—maybe in my mind I just avoided that—but the side and back came together and fit. I took his bandage and wrapped it tightly in the back, and then took mine and wrapped it from the front. It all was back in place. Rick held a strange gray appearance that I had never seen any color exactly like in my whole life.

I guess that part of me knew there was no use. It was too late the microsecond after he was hit. I guess I knew that all the putting together of that skull was useless. Rick was splattered all over me and his blood had already run out and was sinking into the dirt all around us. But what do you do? You do everything in any of the power that you have to save life in any way that you can. I did everything for Rick in that moment that one human being could do for another. I know that as a fact, and I guess it sometimes can be a kind of relief. But it's hard to avoid the guilt, too; the nagging wonder, it's really a wish against death, that you could have done more. I held the pressure points we had learned about in the first aid training until my hands cramped stiff. When I finally took them off his stiffening body, with all the cramping and caking blood, it seemed like they would never start working again. If every power of my concentration and wanting and hoping could have brought Rick back to life, it would have in that moment. Every fiber of my soul was focused on him, and the blood which had long since stopped pumping stopped seeping, too. The heat of the jungle seemed to make it start to thicken right in front of my face.

Maybe the next thing that happened was panic, but I didn't feel panic. Maybe somewhere inside something was saying nothing mattered anymore, but really nothing mattered any less. In fact, because Rick had given his life, everything mattered more. I don't think it was exactly panic, desperation, hate, or any surface emotion that you can talk about. Maybe it was a combination of all of those, an overflow of emotion, and those emotions being controlled by other emotions. Maybe I didn't have a chance either, but then I wouldn't allow myself to think that. It all hit at one point at the same time.

I stood straight up with the M-60 and began to fire it with all of its power in the direction the bullet had come which killed Rick. Thinking back, it's hard to believe. Bullets were firing on me from every side but I wasn't even nicked. Where was the diabolical bastard who knew some American would have to look in that moment of quietness, who was waiting for that first hint of raised helmet, who could hit it with such masterful dead-centeredness? Why could I stand in full view and him not pick me apart. Was Rick killed by a now-deserted marksman or a random bullet fired with no aimed intent?

I emptied the gun and fell back to the ground. It is a wonder that I had not charged the enemy position with my bare hands. The absolute exhaustion of that second sank me so low that the ground and I almost became one. I almost felt like that ground could have absorbed me, I could have disappeared, and nothing would have changed. I wondered if that might be why a soldier is never found, especially in the jungle.

As suddenly as it had begun, it all stopped. I heard nothing. For all practical purposes, I might just as well have been out there in that entire valley by myself. I was by myself. Always before, Momma or Bobby or Cecil or Rick, always before someone had been around. Here I had Rick's body, the M-60, the ammunition, my own rifle. I couldn't stay here and I couldn't leave anything either.

I began to crawl and pull everything back. The bomb crater was back there somewhere and then the hill. If there was anyone left, they would go back to the hill, regroup, and make some kind of stand or attack or something. I drug and pulled and scraped. Now, I was afraid, but I was still under control. Everything about me kept saying Rick was dead, he needed to be left, I had done everything, but I couldn't leave his body yet.

Finally, I got to the crater and rolled Rick's body into it. Still the gunfire had all but ceased. It could be a trick or they could be gone. At least this crater was a certain enough spot that I could now go for help; we could get someone back to Rick's body now. I could leave it there because I knew I had done the best I could do, as much as I believe Rick would have done for me.

I got back into the large ditch. I could stand up here and walk for the first time. I had given up the high ground and anyone could be on top of me in a moment or meet me coming in the opposite direction, but just to walk for a moment was worth the risk. The gun was on ready; just the slightest movement or gesture and I would set it off. Ever since before Rick had gotten shot, I still had not seen another GI.

There were washouts in the side of the ditch plenty big enough for someone to hide in. It would be easy to ambush someone here. I moved along so carefully and deliberately that the foot deep water in the ditch barely rippled or dripped. I heard voices above me.

American voices. I called out something to identify myself and they responded. It is a wonder that we didn't open fire on each other. I knew both of the guys. They were friends and especially friends of Rick. They were coming to help us. I told them: "Rick's dead." It was almost like they didn't hear me. I told them all about it. I told them this was Rick splattered all over me while I pointed to my shirt and face. Still, it was like they didn't hear. They wanted to go get him. I said no. We had to get back to the hill and regroup. It was like they didn't hear me. It was like they were out looking for Easter eggs or something and why didn't I just come on along. They didn't get it. I finally said, "Hell no! I ain't going!!" There was no inkling of an indication in their faces that I was afraid to go back—which I was but I wasn't. There was simply no need to go back. There was no indication that my not going back was a demonstration of a lack of emotion on my part or loyalty on my part to Rick. They just didn't get it. They went back in the direction I had come toward the crater. I warned them one more time not to go. I turned and started on up the ditch. I began to hear sharp gunfire behind me again. It sounded as if it was all starting again. Maybe they were chasing us now, trying to capture any retreating stragglers that they had not killed in the ambush.

There was a sharp bend in the ditch line right ahead of me. I thought I heard some noise or something move around that bend. God, who knew what it might be? I eased to the corner, knew that I wasn't going to stick my head around to look, and jumped in a crouched position around the bend with the M-60 square out in front.

There stood three Vietnamese—an old woman, an old man, and maybe a five-year old kid. I'm not sure what was worse, the look on Rick's face the instant the bullet struck home or the look on these people's faces. For the life of me, I can't imagine in a million years what kept me from pulling that trigger. Maybe it was the grace of God or that training that I keep coming back to. I began to motion for them to go in front of me. We would have to get out of this together.

Then there was a rushing, frightened noise behind and above us. I pushed them back into a shallow washout with all of my strength. They didn't make a sound, not even the kid. It had to hurt. My ruck sack and steel frame were crushing them back against the dirt wall. I got the gun barely pointed around the edge. If something moved in that ditch, it was dead.

Voices started yelling "Matherson!" It was the same two guys. Now, one of them had his arm nearly blown completely off. It was just dangling there. Now they got it; now they understood. No more Easter egg hunts.

There were five people to get back now. We followed the ditch line until it stopped. As we slipped up its side, the hill that I was heading for was immediately back up to our right. We crawled again and eased back up through the slime and smoke along the side of the hill. Probably we were obscured from enemy fire by that time, but we were taking no chances.

An American sergeant whom I had never seen stood in a half crouch to meet us. He directed the civilians one way, the injured soldier and his mate in another, and asked me if I was all right. When I responded yes, he told me to take the M-60 and set up on the right flank of our position. He made it specifically clear that that was my spot and I was to hold that spot under all circumstances.

By now it was beginning to get dark and everything had quieted down. I don't remember any crying or moaning or screaming through this period although you guessed that there were others still out there. On across the hill, you could hear or sense the movement of other GIs but no one was talking. You really felt alone. Back off to my right there was another company still operating in the distance, engaging the enemy and carrying the fire into the night. Maybe the focus of the battle had shifted there, but there was no question that the enemy was still out there somewhere in front of us. There was a gray haze of thick fog hugging the ground all out in front of us. The fog seemed almost like it was pushing, crushing everything that was left out there down into the ground where it would be lost forever.

In a little while word was passed for us to get down and lie low. I'm not sure if I knew what that meant, but I didn't ask any questions. In fact, if I could have gotten any lower at that point I would have been a blade of grass.

Suddenly, without any warning and almost absolutely out of nowhere an A1E "Skyraider" skimmed in across the hill and into the heart of the neck of the valley where we were moving earlier that morning. You could literally look up and see the inside of the cockpit, the pilot had brought the plane in so low. You wanted to jump up and yell "Thank God"; you weren't out here by yourself, somebody knew you were here and was doing something. You could see the bomb dropping almost in slow motion, and the pilot was banking the plane up and away.

It was gone before the huge tanks of napalm broke apart in an exploding inferno right in front of us. Had you not been down, the concussion from two hundred yards away would have knocked you down. If you looked in the direction of the roaring, leaping, sticking fire for more than a moment, you felt like your face would burn off.

The fire was like pictures you see of the sun. The flame was rolling inside itself, twisting and turning. Above it hung a huge black cloud, and the fire kept sucking the black back into itself. There were balls of flame pushing out and pulling back like some huge demonic hunch. You wondered what kept the red-orange wall from pushing out and encompassing you. In a moment, as the ball of fire consumed all that was there, everything was a grayish ash. No vegetation remained anywhere, and glittering gray globs of a gooey plastic-like material was flowing everywhere. It reminded me of the glow reflecting from the insides of animals that had been run over which your headlights would catch as you drove down a back country road on a dark Florida night.

The screaming returned, even above the sound of burning. There were enemy screams. Undoubtedly, there were American screams as well. There was a literal wall of fire. The enemy might do a lot of strange things out here in his jungle, but for a moment, at least, you relaxed in the knowledge that he wasn't coming through that jellied fire that was raging.

The night was long, as long as any I have ever spent. There was no relief and no opportunity for the slightest possibility of sleep. You could hear people crying, praying out loud, calling for their mothers. The medics were moving about here and there, but there were more injured than they could ever get to. You would get familiar with a certain moan. Every moan was unique. At first it might be loud, then it weakened, then it was gone and another moan took its place in your attention.

I did exactly what I was told to do that night. I held my position. Sometimes I have felt like I could have done more. I have said to myself more times than I can count that I should have told that sergeant that I was going back to help someone, that I was going back for Rick's body. I'm sure he would have told me no, that the position was more important. I guess maybe I should have put him in a position of having to say that. I don't know. Maybe this is the survivor's guilt that everyone talks about. I was scared, scared to go back. If I had been ordered to go back, I would have. There's no question about that. I'm not saying anyone else went back, but then I'm not anyone else. Maybe I ought to just realize that it is all right for me to have been scared about going back. How could I have helped but be scared? But, it's still hard. You want to have been able to do more, but you simply could not. You feel guilt even though you know it doesn't make sense to feel guilt. Nothing made sense that night.

The next morning a fresh company was dropped in by helicopter and we advanced right back into the same area. The first gun shot wasn't fired. It was as if an enemy soldier was nowhere in a thousand miles. There were puddles of gray muck everywhere. It stuck to your boots and clothing. There were rags and splashes of blood, but no dead bodies.

I was totally surprised. We didn't have any kinds of materials or any bodies of our people. Maybe someone else had gotten them out, but I don't know when. Someone had heard that the Vietnamese came in during the night and dragged off the dead bodies to confuse and demoralize us. Without question they had scavenged for anything they could use to help them fight. The smell of burning napalm and burned flesh was everywhere. The dull gray ash stuck to everything around. I can't remember who gave us orders or who was making the decisions about our movement. I can only remember that suddenly I was looking around on every side all day long and I didn't recognize anyone I knew. By now I had found out that this village that we had been moving in the direction of was called My Canh 2.

On up in the day it started getting hot. You would see a large knot of flies here and there, and you began to realize that they were feeding on puddles of blood. I wanted to get some of this battlefield death stuff off of my clothes, but it was no use. The flies were on me all day long, on what remained of Rick all day long.

Still, it was the strangest thing: it still didn't seem like they were all really dead. You couldn't find their bodies to prove it. Even when we came upon the enemy bunkers and command centers and located fresh graves, they were of people who had died days ago and been dragged there. We felt complete obligation to dig into the graves to see if any of our comrades in arms were there. It was gruesome. The stench would surround you as you broke the ground. We knew there might be hidden bombs, so we had to attach ropes to dead legs and pull from a distance. Once you got one decaying body out, you usually found a second one under it and had to start the process all over again. In one grave there were four people buried. None of them were Americans.

The rotting smell was so penetrating that it would get into your taste buds, and every time you ate over the next two or three days you would taste the reminders of death that lingered. You wanted to throw up, but even more you wanted to wash it all away. Sometimes I still find myself wanting to wash it off. It still, somehow, is there.

I could remember working at the funeral home, and sometimes we would get bodies that stunk with the beginnings of decay. We wiped Vicks Vapor Rub into our nostrils and mouths, and it would take the smell away. I would have given anything for some of that salve that day. All we could do was dig up another grave and move on. All the good that it did was to give some officers that were standing at a clean distance with pads and paper a chance to confirm enemy dead and add to the body count that we were continually being made aware of every day.

Where were our people? Maybe they hadn't really died? Maybe they had sent helicopters in the still of the night and they had rotated out? You almost had to tell yourself that this was possible in order to go on. It was all so confusing and vague, and you couldn't talk to anyone about it or ask them questions—they didn't know what you were talking about.

They moved me to gunner. The M-60 was mine. I would have the carriers. It is amazing how, in spite of everything that had happened, that you were still struck by a sense of pride that you had come to this position. You somehow escaped thinking about the fact that you were now the target.

Chapter XIV

Finally we pulled back about a mile from where all of the heaviest action had been and established a small perimeter camp. I know that we had been operating in and out of the area of the large battle for only a few days but it absolutely felt like months. All of the fatigue, all of the reminders of death, the suddenly absent-without-a-trace enemy, the heat and wet damp—all of it worked together to make you feel that days would never end, only to be followed by nights that would never end.

It was clear what was happening. The enemy was still out there, just one more step on down the road. We would rest, resupply, fill the gaps in our ranks with replacements, and go after them again. Somehow you blocked that reality out; all that was important now was rest. It was impossible, however, to get normal rest. You wondered if there would ever be any real rest again. Every time you closed your eyes and drifted toward sleep, you were met by the ghosts from the attack. You finally slept, but it was not real sleep.

People have a way of being able to have things that really mean something to them. Even in that back mountain perimeter, some guys seemed always able to come up with a can of beer. I had Winstons when nobody else did; I traded one item or another out of the C-rations for the small cardboard four-packs. Most of the time, I kept the side pockets of my field pants stuffed full. Being out of C-rations was one thing; being out of Winstons was quite another. Some guy had been able to hold on to a small tape player and one tape, something by the Supremes. You heard the tape over and over so many times that as soon as one song finished you were humming the notes of the next song before it started. Even though it was the same, it was a welcome attachment to the outside world. We didn't have "Radio Saigon" where we were at that time; after a few minutes of silence, someone would call out for more Supremes. Even today, when those old songs come on the radio, my mind leaps back to that back mountain jungle.

Every morning we would form into platoon-sized groups and feel our way out into the jungle in front of us. At night we would come back and take turns guarding the perimeter. On some days our platoon would stay behind to guard the camp. It was never clear if it was safer to be with the group that went out or the group that stayed behind. In all of this, still there was no enemy contact. There wouldn't be any either; they patiently waited for you to come to them. Some of the time you slept or sat around and talked—girlfriends, family, what you would do when it was all over. Nobody ever discussed the political implications of the war. No mention of those who had been lost came up; you left that alone, as if by doing so you could convince your mind that they were simply rotated out. Even though they had died, somehow you still didn't really feel very vulnerable yourself. If death came, it would come for someone else.

Some high-ranking officers began to come in and inspect our company area and talk to us about what we were doing. In the end, we found out that we had been a major part of an ongoing operation called "Van Buren." We had faced one of the most elite groups of the Army of North Vietnam, the 95th Regiment. These were battle-hardened veterans who claimed as much pride in their units as the 101st Airborne did in its own. In the speeches, it was clear that we had won the victory—if victory meant taking the ground and holding it. In the back of our minds, we could not help but feel that we had really simply walked into the first stage of an enemy trap. We had been hit, and they had run. That was their plan, and it had been perfectly executed. We would follow, and they would hit and run again. Maybe their officers were talking to them about victory, too. Maybe our officers were simply telling us what they did so that our morale would be increased and we would be willing to fight again tomorrow.

On one of the visits, a full colonel stepped into the midst of the troops and began to talk to us personally. He asked me straight out if I needed anything that he could get for me. I showed him my boots and the way that they were by now almost rotted off my feet. He promised: "I'll have new boots for you here tomorrow," and he wrote down my name and size. My friends expected that it was all a show, and that I would never see this guy again. Not me. I was still gung-ho. I trusted everything that was said and had no question that the man would keep his word. Sure enough, the first helicopter that came in the next morning had the boots. I felt a great deal of pride in those boots and in being a part of an Army in which promises like this one could be kept.

There was warm food and clean water, and a chaplain came and conducted church services in the open field. I went straight there with no question about going. Most of us were suddenly rediscovering a sense of religion that might not have been the most important part of our lives in many years. Some of us were rediscovering what praying was all about and were finding many opportunities to practice this rediscovered art.

One old boy had this thing for flying saucers. He knew all of the constellations, when satellites would be passing over, and more about the night sky than I had imagined. He was convinced that there was intelligent life out there and that we were being monitored. His descriptions were so vivid and real that you almost halfway expected something from another world to land at any time. When we were all in a group together, I laughed and kidded like everyone else; when I got out in the dark by myself and studied that sky, I wondered. Sometimes it got spooky like that night the devil chased me in the swamp, like that night on guard duty when some huge object came out of nowhere and tore by me in the jungle. It shook the ground, nearly stepping on me, but I never saw it. I figured that it must have been a water buffalo or a huge elephant, but I had never been sure. Anyway, I finally philosophized if it did land and take us away, at least it would be getting us out of here.

There was time to write. I put it off as long as I could, wondering whether or how to talk about what had happened, but I had to get something of it all out of my system. At least I had to try. It would be easier to talk to Kay than Momma, so I started with her:

> What are you doing besides living it up? HA! HA! Well, you know me, as good looking and kind and such a nice personality as I have, that I'm OK. [Maybe if I could convince Kay of this, I could convince myself in the process. Maybe by coming off funny, the blow of what I was about to say could be softened.] I've had a lot of close calls. I guess you and Momma—and myself—are praying me through this war. But we all know who is looking after me. God is.

Kay, I'm OK. But I'm still shook up from the last battle we had. I lost a lot of buddies. You remember Rick, well he's dead. But Gabe is OK. He's back at Phan Rang, that lucky dog. He didn't come out on this operation because he was on rest and recuperation leave.

Did I ever tell you about Rick. Well, he was one of my best buddies. But he's dead now. He died in my arms. Kay, when you have those pictures developed you'll see him as a real big guy, and he is probably beside me holding the machine gun. He was a real nice guy.

If I don't write for a long time, don't worry. It will be because I can't. OK? I've got to go eat. You guessed right—C-rations. Boy, I'm sick of them. I can't wait till I get home and eat some of Momma's cooking.

I signed the letter "Good Looking." If Kay could have seen me at that moment, it would have been the last thought to cross her mind. Then, I turned to Momma:

I guess you thought I'd never write. Momma, we've been out on a big operation. We lost a lot of men, but I'm OK. I know God was with me, and I know you all were praying hard for me because I made it back without getting hurt.

Momma, I've never been so scared and I've never prayed so hard. But I still did my job. I'm gunner now.

Momma, do you remember me talking about Rick Crossland? Well, he was one of my best buddies. He was gunner and I was his assistant. Momma, he died in my arms. I prayed for him and I prayed for all of us. Then, I took over the gun and I've had it ever since. We wiped out the VC.

Momma, you asked me to tell you about our operations. I'd rather forget them if I can. All you can do is pray for us and don't worry too much because God is looking out for us all. Well, that's enough about this place.

Has Bobby got home yet? What company is he coming to? Momma, I wish he wasn't coming over here.

I think I might make Spec 4 pretty soon because I'm machine gunner now.

The letter writing was a mixed blessing. It made you homesick as hell, but it also made you feel a little closer to the people you loved. I could almost imagine Kay or Momma standing there talking with me and responding to the things I was saying. The Army was amazing, too; they kept a steady stream of mail and even packages coming to us while we were on our mission. The camp was quiet enough to hear a pin drop in the several moments following mail call. Nobody had to say anything; everyone's thoughts were in the same place.

As I became familiar with the encampment over the next few days and began to look around and notice the people, it seemed like I could only recognize maybe 15 out of over 175 that had been with me back at Phan Rang. When I have looked through the old records at Fort Campbell, there is nothing to indicate that that many people were killed and injured in our battle, but I still can't account for whatever had taken place. Maybe going through what we had all gone through in the past week or ten days was so powerful that it had changed our appearances somehow. I certainly wasn't the same person in many ways that I had been. Maybe they weren't either. I didn't recognize them; maybe they didn't recognize me either.

I thought about what all the enemy had in place waiting for us. As we searched through and inspected their fortifications, you could not help but appreciate and admire their craft and workmanship. There was a primitive beauty to the polished finish and artistic efficiency of their gunports, cross firing patterns, and intricate system of tunnels. They had been preparing this battle ground for years, and then they had simply waited. We had walked right in, taking our bullish American initiative, just like they knew we would. Now, they were waiting again, probably in a setting just as intricate and deadly as those we had already faced.

As the new replacements began to come in, I was assigned three carriers. This was a little unusual. The typical number was two. Maybe there was a shortage of M-60s. Maybe carriers and gunners were becoming more of a target than I had even come to understand when the bullets had gone through that field like a huge mowing machine. Maybe by some gruesome mathematics it had been determined how a gun could be better kept in operation; with one more man who could die and the machine still function.

These guys were all black guys. It didn't take long for them to understand that my being a white guy from the South created no problems. Blacks have a special defense mechanism, a radar, that lets them spot bigots and prejudice a hundred miles away. My Momma had taught me better. Our lives depended on each other now. I wouldn't have cared if they had been green. We were all men with a job to do. We were Americans with a common bond, a bond that got deeper with each new step we took out into that jungle.

They were at a much worse disadvantage than I. They had been trained as supply clerks and cooks. I couldn't understand this; all the combat training they had even come close to was the almost game-like stuff in boot camp. Beyond those first eight weeks, they had pursued their own specialties, and now here they were in the middle of a Vietnamese battle zone. It didn't sound quite like the Army of the colonel who had sent the boots.

I was given two or three days to make them ready to go into battle. There was no way to tell them what it would be like; the words weren't there, and I didn't want to scare them to death before they even stepped out into the field. I could explain the gun, explain it till they knew it like the shape of their own faces. Finally, they could take it apart and put it back together blindfolded.

We spent a lot of time talking about the sounds of the jungle. They had to know to watch and listen for everything that was around them. I emphasized listening for animal sounds to stop; if they stopped, the animals saw something. Then, they would have to be able to see whatever the animals saw for themselves. I reinforced what little they had learned about first aid; they knew everything about their bandage pack before I was finished and how it could be used in an emergency. I talked about getting down and staying down if the gunfire came. I emphasized lying there, not panicking, and using every fiber of their minds to think about other options—but never for running away, always for moving on the enemy. I ingrained into them everything that I had been taught about returning fire and moving in the direction of fire; I thought about Rick rising up to look.

Some of it registered, but not much. They could work the gun, but I knew that this was only a small part of the bigger picture. So much of all the rest just went in one ear and out the other. But, how could it have been any different? There was no way they could really realize what I was talking about.

We also got a new lieutenant and new sergeant. That was unusual, too. Most of the time, they tried to keep at least one of the people who was immediately in charge of a platoon or company as someone with combat experience. In many respects, the sergeant was more significant than the lieutenant. But both of our men had been wounded or killed. You couldn't help but feel a little insecure about all of this. What would all these new people do if the raining hell of bullets came again? We all looked to a Sergeant Louallen, a "buck" sergeant with three stripes who had experience and had been with us all along.

On the 13th of February, which was looked upon as not a very good day to do anything, we moved out with the contingent of new troops. The idea was just like before: search and destroy in villages during the daytime, set up ambushes along suspected trails at night. Day and night, day and night, but no enemy.

A part of me hated going into the villages. You really weren't scared, because the enemy was always long since gone. At most, there were women, children, and old men—ancient old men. We burned their rice and their hooches. They stood off and looked at us; they couldn't do a thing about it all. Loud cries of "why?" were written all over their faces, but they didn't dare change one wrinkle of their stone cold stares. Maybe I was scared, but there wasn't really anything to do about it. You just kept doing what you were told to do; you just kept pushing on. I hated the smells most of all, the smells of their own dying. It reminded me of the field where Rick died. Everything was so lush and beautiful, but it could all change in the moment it took to pull a trigger or finger the pin loose from a grenade.

They didn't have anything, but what was there we were destroying. We had to be watchful for any kinds of booby traps. If we saw something that we wanted, a knife or something that looked valuable, we would carefully tie a string around it and stand off at a distance to pull it toward us. The first few times, their stuff was fascinating; finally it all looked alike and wasn't worth the trouble. Let the new guys get the war prizes out of their system; you could sit down under a tree and watch it all with your own kind of blank stare that looked but refused to really see. Maybe "why?" was written all over your face, too.

The more we walked through the area, the more evident its intricate plan became. There were spider traps everywhere. These were small holes that had been dug to a size to conceal one man. The enemy would hide in these, wait for you to walk right in on them, and then jump up and start cutting you down. Before you could really recover your senses, they had run from one place of hiding to another. You got the idea that they could find these little holes in pitch darkness. All that we seemed able to find was the same river. On one night alone, the new lieutenant led us across it three times when we were supposed to be going in a straight line. The leeches were as big as small snakes and we couldn't even burn them off with cigarettes for fear of giving our position away. Everywhere you pulled them loose, you left a stinging, bleeding cut.

Plungy pits had to be avoided, too. These pits didn't hold people but sharpened bamboo sticks. These sticks had then been covered with human excrement. If you stepped into one of these pits, the shafts would go right through your boot. The excrement insured infection setting up almost immediately. The Army finally redesigned the field boot with a steel plate in the sole, but the Vietnamese came along and quickly redesigned the pits with longer barbs coming out of the sides of the dug out space. The unrelenting spears then dug into calves, knees, and thighs. It would not kill a person, but the whole movement of a platoon would be greatly handicapped for a good part of the entire day getting the injured person help and then being overly careful about avoiding other traps that might be in the same area.

We came into one village late one afternoon, and although the people had moved off out of the way, we stirred up a small Vietnamese pig. The same thought must have crossed everyone's mind at the same time—barbeque. People started firing on the pig from every direction, but it squealed and zigzaged almost like a cowboy dodging bullets in a western movie. Somebody yelled, "Take him, Matherson!" I brought the M-60 up and must have fired a hundred rounds. The pig just kept moving. If I had had any doubts about what the ammunition carriers might do in battle, I'm sure that they must have had doubts about me now. You just kind of grinned and went on; it was the first time I could remember grinning in weeks.

For ten days we continued to push our way deeper into the jungle. Still there was no contact. It was like the enemy had never been there before. Word began to come around that we were going to change strategies. If the enemy was staying out of the villages in the daytime and coming back in at night, we should start setting our ambushes outside the village entrances. If anything moved, they would have to move through us. The officers wanted contact; contact was all that would justify our being out here to begin with. We wanted contact, too—but each day that we didn't find them, there was also the unsettling sensation that you were using up the odds that were in your favor. Sooner or later, even if you had to march all the way to Hanoi, you were bound to find them—or they would find you.

I sensed a new intensity. This plan would work, no doubt about it. If I had been making the plans, it is what I would have done. Somewhere deep inside, I wished they hadn't thought about all this—we would meet them again. There was time for a final letter or two:

> Momma, I went to church yesterday. The sermon the chaplain preached was about lifting up your head unto the hills from whence cometh our help. Our help was in the Lord who made heaven and earth. He told us as we walked up these mountains to remember that God was with us. It's a good thing to remember.

It's a shame we're fighting over here. I'll just be glad when it's all over with and we can come home. Boy, I'll be glad to see you.

Boy, I felt like an old man letting my younger brother beat me to getting married and going to be a daddy soon. But you know me, I'm not ready for that right now. I'll wait until I can give my wife a nice home and I want to have a good job. And when I do get married, there's going to be two women in the house to keep me straight—that's you and my wife.

No, really Momma, I do want you to stay with me. I sure would be happy because you're the best Momma in the whole world. I thank God every time I pray for letting me have such a good Momma.

Momma, if I don't write for a while, don't worry. I'll be out on another mission. We're leaving tomorrow night. But don't worry. God is looking over me and I pray to him all of the time. I ask him to take care of you all, and I know he will.

Oh yeah, tell the preacher at the church that I'll be glad when I get back so I can go to church. And tell him that we are giving offerings in church over here. The money is going to be used to build a mission over here, and I think they might even get a missionary.

Well, I've got to go. Write soon and God bless you all.

I had started sending small items in the letters. On this last evening before our new set of missions, I included packets of instant coffee that were in our rations and even some toilet paper. I sent Kay a can opener, the "P-38," and told her that it was to be her wedding present. This probably didn't make sense, but it was my way of sending something of what little I had maybe to pay them back for what they were sending me. Can openers, instant coffee, and toilet paper make a strange "widow's mite," but it wasn't like there was a K-Mart on every corner.

Then finally, before sleep, to Kay:

> What's going on in the Sunshine State? I've been
> sitting here on the river bank today getting a nice
> suntan. Boy, I bet you wish you had a suntan like
> mine. But don't worry, I'll give you a little of mine
> when I get home.
>
> Tomorrow night we leave and go back into the hills
> again. I wish I could get sick so I wouldn't have to go
> back up there again. That's where we lost about half of
> our company. But I'll be back OK because God is
> looking over me and you all are praying for me. And,
> of course, I'm praying for you all and myself, too. But
> don't worry; I'll be OK.
>
> Well, old Sis, I'd better close. Write me soon, even if I
> don't get to write you back right away. Kay, we leave
> tomorrow night, so I don't know when I'll get a
> chance to write you. But don't worry; I'll be OK.
> Remember I love you all, and I pray for God to take
> care of you. Write soon.

On the night of the 24th of February, 1966, we headed out for a
night ambush that was fully routine except that this time our
objective was the entrance of a small Vietnamese village. It was
dark and pouring rain. The intensity of the new strategy—the
likelihood that it would work—had everyone tense, especially the
new lieutenant. We were slipping and sliding off dikes, sogging
along in the soft, soaked ground. There was groaning and
complaining out of some of the new men, new men who had yet
to come close to seeing an enemy.

The lieutenant kept communicating back along the line: "Shut
up!" "Keep quiet!" "Hold it down!" He was getting irritated with
us, and within an hour we were getting irritated with everything
that was taking place around us. I didn't say anything; I wanted to
say: "YOU shut up! Go fuck yourself! They already know we're
here!" I had no doubt about that last thought. They knew where
we were better than we knew ourselves.

We kept passing water buffalo. Sometimes there would be 20 or 30 of them huddled together in the rain. Occasionally, one would be wounded somehow and standing off from the others with a startled look on his face. Sometimes, the old bull would look at you like you were invading his turf. Their big eyes followed your every move. They snorted fog into the air. They could charge, but you weren't supposed to shoot them under any circumstances; what were you to do? Take all the water buffalo you want; give me the devil in the swamp any day.

In spite of the rain and everyone being basically pissed off at the new lieutenant, it seemed like our plan was working. We worked our way across an intricate pattern of rice paddies that typically lead to a larger village. Then there was a long trail coming out of the edge of the paddies through a clear area and then to the entrance of the village. The moon was full and you could see everything around you. I had little question that we were coming in undetected; we would have made too irresistible of a target otherwise.

There was a huge wooden archway across the trail at the entry of the village proper. The name of the place was written on it in Vietnamese that I couldn't make out. It was old and had probably been erected there maybe decades before to ward off evil spirits. Such obstacles made little difference to the US Army and we slipped on in.

There were several hundred yards of jungle now covering the trail that led on into the town itself. All that stood on the outskirts was a scattering of rickety hooches that looked like they had long since been abandoned for the safety of the numbers in the town. The lieutenant and sergeant arranged us in a kind of open horseshoe which closed on down the trail into the village. My group was placed on the front left prong facing out toward the trail and rice paddies. If anyone came along, we would see them first.

Joe Kearny had an M-79 grenade launcher across from me on the other prong. He also had new men. I hoped that when the placement was done that everyone knew what they were doing. Being hit by the enemy would be bad enough; we didn't need our own crossfire to boot. Joe and I were close. He was another black guy whom I had come to appreciate. He was a hell of a fine soldier, but he had the same fears about new men and new leadership that I did. The only other person I knew real well who was out there with us was Kenny Desart. He had come up to a machine gunner position just like I had. His placement was on down the side of the horseshoe toward the village.

You get used to the idea that nothing is probably going to happen. In spite of all that had happened, the fact remained that in two months, I had seen part of one day in actual combat. Part of me felt like this was going to be just one more night. I walked back to one of the abandoned hooches and pulled off part of the thatched roof. I placed this on the soggy ground, and it gave us a relatively dry covering to lie down on. I took the first watch about nine o'clock. The carriers slipped off to sleep.

The rain slacked and stopped and the moon came out with all the force of its bright fullness. We were back in the dark, and everything was lighted up before us. You could see 200 yards. I loved the light. If you had to be out here, make sure you were concealed and everything else was lighted up so you could see. For what we were having to do, for once, this was the perfect set up.

After about an hour or an hour and a half, I nudged one of the carriers and told him to take the gun. We swapped places, he leaned in behind the rear of the gun on his stomach. His M-16 was beside him, and I stretched on my back with my feet up toward his face. I pulled out my .45 automatic and cradled it across my stomach. In the coolness and slight easy breeze that followed the rain, it was easy to go to sleep. It was so dark back in the jungle that it was almost like being in a deep cave.

Maybe an hour passed and suddenly I was lying there with my eyes bulging wide open hearing Vietnamese voices. Maybe they were twenty yards away, maybe less. They were coming toward me down the trail. What in hell was going on?

This was a free-fire zone; anything that moved was to be fired on at will. You threw grenades first so as not to give your position away. Why weren't my men waking me, throwing grenades? Why weren't Kearny's men doing something? Had we all gone to sleep out here? Had the rest of the platoon folded up and forgotten to awaken me? Was I dreaming? No, these were enemy voices and they were getting closer all of the time.

As easily as I could I raised up and began to roll toward the gun. There would be no way they would see me. Suddenly, the carrier who had relieved me was pointing his M-16 square in my face. The end of the barrel was an inch from my right eye. He was whispering in dead earnestness that if I moved he would blow my head off. I never understood that exactly. Maybe he panicked and just lost it all. Maybe he knew I would open fire and he didn't want to fight. There wasn't much I could do. He was serious for whatever reason.

I could see the Vietcong, three of them, walking along just as completely unconcerned as anyone could be. They were talking loudly and carrying on like three old buddies who were just coming in from a late night party. They had weapons, but they were slung back over their shoulders. They had no idea we were there, and they were making enough noise that we could have been talking or moving and they probably would not have even noticed. They passed right on by our position, and all I could do was just sit there, hanging in a halfway crouch with a rifle barrel in my face.

Now, there was a double problem. Not only had our perimeter been penetrated, but any firing that took place now would create a crossfire in which we were firing on ourselves. I slipped my hand around the M-16's barrel and moved it away from my face. The carrier was visibly coming to himself now. I calmed him and the others and slid behind the gun. I still had a clear shot, but it was right straight toward where Joe Kearny and his men were positioned. There was no way I could shoot now.

I told the carriers to lie still and to be quiet. I was going to move down along the prong of the horseshoe and let the other people know what was happening. They couldn't shoot either, but if I could get word on down to Kenny Desart, his firing would be from the back of the horseshoe out toward the open end. He could take them without any chance of hitting our own men.

In retrospect, all of this sounds damned scary and maybe even a little desperate. In fact, it was amazing how much under control you can be. The old training coming back; the old working principle of Momma—take whatever you get and do the best with it you can. I don't remember being the slightest bit afraid. It had to be done, and I was the one to do it.

I eased off toward the next position. The Vietcong were still joking loudly along their way. I kept abreast of them, kept them in the corner of my eye, and didn't make a sound.

Maybe I had gone ten feet when one of my carriers cried out at the top of his voice "HALT!!" All hell broke loose! Fire rose from every direction. I'm sure most of the people that were out there were firing because they were startled by the scream. Stuff was hitting all around me. The Vietnamese bolted forward and disappeared on down the trail toward the village. It was clear that nothing was coming close to hitting them.

There is no telling how many hundred rounds got squeezed off in the next two minutes. The whole canopy of jungle lit up like a million flash bulbs going off. People were yelling and hollering like raving maniacs, not in pain but in total confusion. I was crawling back toward my original position, but the ground all around me was popping up from gun fire like coffee percolating into the glass dome on an old style coffee pot.

If I could get hold of that carrier, I would kill him on the spot. Now's when he needed to get that M-16 in my face. I was cursing him and calling him everything I could think of. As I rolled back unto the thatching I had layed on the ground, I yelled square into his face: "I'd blow your fucking brains out if you had any!!" He was petrified and couldn't respond or blink his eyes or anything. I shot my fist at his jaw as I pulled the front of his fatigue shirt and face toward my fist. I had never struck anyone like that before. He fell back unconscious.

Suddenly, rising out of the gunfire you could begin to hear the repeated yelling of "CEASE FIRE!! CEASE FIRE!!" It took several moments, but the fire finally stopped. It was quiet and still again except for the falling pieces of bark and palm branches that had been cut apart in the crossfire. Miraculously, none of our own men had been hit. Even more miraculously, no one had gone beserk enough to start throwing grenades. One thing was for sure, there were no Vietcong hidden out in there with us or waiting on us to give away our positions. Had they been anywhere in ten miles, we would have been sitting ducks.

I was so pissed off I could hardly stand it. This wasn't my fault, but then it was my fault. They were my men. Who was ever going to believe that my whole group hadn't been sound asleep. Hell, ninety percent of the whole patrol must have been asleep. The other two carriers were just staring straight out toward where the Vietcong had been. They were too stunned to even move. The third carrier began to come to and eased back away from my reach. I pounded the ground, threw my helmet down. I cursed. I sat there in a totally god-forsaken stew. Damn it! Damn it all! The stupid, son-of-a-bitch bastard! I told him to be quiet!!

Sergeant Louallen made his way around to us. The only thing he asked me was "What happened?" I will never forget the tone of that question. There was not the slightest, even the slightest, sentiment that I had screwed up. It was like he knew that I would not have made a mistake in that situation. There was not one iota of blame in his voice toward me.

That was enough to calm me, to get me back to rational, in a second. I was not a screw up, and could not tolerate the thought of being pictured in that way. I quickly told him what had taken place. He didn't have time to start throwing out criticism at anyone else right then either. It was over and done; it couldn't be brought back. It would have been simple enough to ambush the Vietcong, and since nothing had happened since our little firestorm, that would have been the end of it on this night. We could have gone back with our body count, and everyone would have been happy about how the plan had worked, how contact had been made, and how none of our men had even been wounded. Suddenly, it all got more complicated.

My idea would have been to wait until morning and go into the village or to stay in our positions in the dark and see what might come to us. The lieutenant had other ideas; we had to go in and get the three Vietcong. He ordered Louallen to have me get someone from my position and Kearny someone from his, and send them in to flush out the three enemy soldiers.

Maybe the lieutenant saw it as a punishment or as our responsibility. Maybe he figured both Kearny and I had had someone asleep on the job, and we could send that person. I doubt that he would have ever sent in a machine gunner if he had thought about it. Louallen specifically told me to send someone with him.

Given my frame of mind, there was no one to go but me. It was my position. That I had carefully stayed awake on my watch was beside the point. My position screwed it up; I was going in.

Louallen and I went across to where Kearny was set up. The sergeant explained what was taking place, and Joe said to me—like we were going out to the country club to play a round of golf, "You goin' in?" I said—with no show of emotion or no real feeling of fatalism, "Yeah." He finished the conversation with "I'm with you," and Kearny, Louallen, and I headed down along toward the village parallel to the trail. We passed through the mess of trees and underbrush that our gunfire had cut up, crouched a notch lower like we were passing through some kind of low threshold, and entered the pitch black darkness that lay out ahead of us. Somewhere out there were three Vietcong—and who knew what else.

There is no way to describe how dark it was with the moon back behind thickening clouds and the dense canopy of jungle growth. You could literally not see your hand in front of your face. I took the point with Kearny maybe five yards behind me and Louallen back yet another five yards. I was feeling my way along in a kind of sliding stagger step. It was like every energy of concentration in my mind was out there on the end of that left foot that I was using as a probe. The M-60 was cradled in my left hand and my right forefinger was close against the trigger. Even the slightest movement ahead and I would lay down an erupting fire of lead. Silent inch by inch we made our way in.

It was stupid to do what we did, but everyone was wanting contact and at least we knew the enemy was in there somewhere. We had fished around in empty holes for the better part of three weeks now. The bird wasn't in the hand, but at least he was in the bush. The only problem was that we didn't know which bush.

I was acutely aware of plungy pits or spider pits or trip mines. The very idea of excrement-covered bamboo shards ripping into my feet and legs sent chills up my spine. One more inch, then two, then another—I knew Kearny and Louallen were back there. I hoped they could tell it was me. Even with all the night vision that had been restored since the left-over glare of the firestorm had died away, I still couldn't see anything but the surrounding outline of huge palm trees backed by an horizon of general jungle undergrowth.

Then I felt it.

There was something different about the ground. My foot was easing up on softer dirt that had been raised up. There was some kind of hole in front of me. Maybe the edge of a bomb crater, but there was no evidence in the underbrush and trees of this area having been bombed. Maybe a plungy pit. Maybe the edge of a spider pit, but if there had been anyone in it he would have fired by now. I eased my foot a breathless inch ahead. Still no fear: total, concentrated carefulness. One more inch and I would know.

What can I say? No word is going to work. Should I use all capital letters and a row of two dozen exclamation marks? It just happened, as matter of factly as your next breath, as real as a red light turning green at an intersection. No deliberation, no judgment, no sense of the movement of a conscious will. It just happened.

It exploded.

It exploded.

It exploded.

It exploded.

Not a bomb, a grenade, a trip mine. In the light of the fire I caught instantaneous glimpses, split microsecond glimpses of three men in a foxhole down under me, one firing up straight into my body and the other two firing out toward Kearny and Louallen. Whether it was the three men walking along the trail, I have no idea. It was like sitting astride an erupting volcano, only the spewing lava was streaking lead.

I had the sensation of being hurled upward into the air. I don't know how much of it was the impact of bullets and how much of it was every force of my existence leaping backward. It felt like I was fifteen or twenty feet up into the lower limbs of the palm trees, flipping over in slow motion. I don't know if it would be possible to hurl a person that far up in the air or not, but I would swear that I was nearly as high as a short telephone pole.

Parts of the M-60 went one way and then another. I could almost see them scattering away like clipped frames of an old movie as the whole space leaped from light to dark and back to light again as the enemy weapons fired. I felt my body arch over like a basketball at the top of its flight, and then I felt a ballooning fall like the ball heading back down toward the hoop. There was absolutely no awareness of pain whatsoever and I had yet to make any sound.

My knee crushed down into the metal of the M-60. Then there was pain. It felt like my knee had broken in two. I waited for it to fall loose or for blood to begin to gush. Neither happened, just the pain of being hit in the knee or shin by a powerful hammer. The pain began to fade almost as quickly as it had come. In fact, it was not so much the pain fading as my consciousness going out. I blacked out. No doubt, my attackers must have thought I was dead and so stopped firing on me. I was out for only a moment and then began to experience the sensation of hearing again.

Kearny was hit and he was yelling, partly about being hit and from the pain, partly for me. The yelling simply made him a target and all the fire was training in on him. I didn't make a sound. Let the Vietcong think I was dead. They weren't five feet away.

Fire was coming from our other troops now. We were in a damn crossfire again. There was panic again. Kearny was yelling, Louallen was yelling. The Vietcong were firing and trying to get out to a better place on back toward the village. I was trying to get the end of the .45 up over the edge of the foxhole. There was so much mud and stunned disorientation that it just wouldn't go like I wanted it to. I got it up over the edge and started to fire. Maybe they were gone or maybe I shot them. I don't know. In a moment the enemy fire was coming from ten or twenty yards on toward the village. They were no longer in their foxhole, or the ones in the foxhole were dead and we were taking fire from a group in behind them.

I suddenly became aware of the sensation of not being able to breathe right. Then, I could hear it, air sucking in at my back! Oh, my God!! Sucking chest wound!! I felt for my back and there was a hole that felt like I could stick my fist in it. How could this be? There was still no real pain. I would finally learn that I had been shot at point blank range. There would be no telling how many times. Had I been maybe two, maybe three feet further away, the bullets would have gained a rotation and speed that would have torn holes in me large enough to drive a truck through. There would have been nothing of the entire middle part of my body left. As it was, holes had been ripped and one had torn through my lung and out my back. My lung was still trying to draw air, but it was drawing it in through my back.

It is amazing when I think about it that a human being could keep from panicking. Maybe the only thing that saved me was knowing that if I did panic, I was dead on the spot. Even though Kearny and Louallen were still yelling and all hell of gunfire was breaking loose all around us, I was still able to realize that my life's breath was slipping out of me. I dropped the pistol and reached my right hand around as far as it would go toward my back. I could feel the edges of the exit wound and pushed and crammed hand, shirt, flesh—anything—back into the wound. I could feel suction like putting your hand down over a carburetor on a small engine and the warm wetness of my own blood and body fluids. But the breath came back. I held on with all of my strength and began to try to maneuver with my left hand.

My first sensation was to see if the enemy fire was distracted from me and being directed back toward our main force; it was. The Vietcong were returning fire but trying to get back away from our main firepower at the same time. I could crawl toward where Kearny was screaming and then get back to where Louallen had taken cover.

I didn't make a sound. As soon as I got enough cover from the darkness that my position would not be given away, I called out to Kearny: "I'm hit but I'm OK. Stay where you are. Don't come in to me. I'll get to you." I yelled to Louallen that we were coming.

When I got over to Kearny, there was no question that his wounds were serious. He had been hit in the shoulder and the entire area around his shoulder blade had been blown back and exposed. We latched on to each other, both of us knowing exactly what kind of a jam we were in.

Just someone else being there to help seemed to calm him some and we started out. I was crawling in front without either the M-60 or the .45. Kearny was holding on to my leg with his good hand and arm, and I was pulling him. It was hard going. There was all of the weight, the mud, and the sensation of crawling through a corn field where the stalks had been cut off three or four inches above the ground. The only problem was that is wasn't corn but bamboo. In the end, I'm not sure whether I was crawling through some kind of trap or simply an area where the bamboo had been blown away or partially cleared for some reason or another. I pulled and Kearny pushed and somehow we drug each other out.

Finally, we made it back to Louallen where he was covered behind a large coconut tree. He hadn't been wounded. The gunfire was finally dying down now; the Vietcong had moved to another position, and Louallen was able to help us both back through the lines to a small hooch where the lieutenant, his radio man, and the medic had stationed themselves as a command center.

As the medic began to ask questions, I responded that I was OK and that he should help Kearny. I wasn't trying to be John Wayne; there was next to no sensation of pain still and the breathing, though a little forced perhaps, was actually about back to normal. The medic examined Kearny with a small flashlight, dressed his wound, and gave him a shot of morphine to ease the pain. Kearny quickly quieted into an easy stupor.

Then he came to me. Almost immediately I could tell that there was more to what had happened than I had ever imagined. As the medic, a fine guy from Hawaii who later was killed, cut and ripped back the clothing from the upper part of my body, truth was written all over his face. The sucking chest wound was just the beginning. Gunfire had caught me all across the front of my stomach and chest. There were wounds everywhere. Not only was my lung all but exposed from the back from that exit wound, but my stomach area was so shot up that parts of my intestines were hanging outside my body cavity. My spleen was blown to bits and what extra blood I might have had quickly ran out making a sticking, clogging puddle all around where they had laid me on the ground. The crawling with Kearny had raked the sharp bamboo stalks across the whole front of my body and pulled and cut the intestines even more. Everything was full of mud and grime.

Louallen could tell, too. He began to open up with a steady stream of talk that was meant to reassure and convince, but because his honest tone could not be concealed it had the opposite effect: "Man, you got the big one this time, the million dollar big one. You'll be on your way home now and back on the beach before you know it."

Somewhere in the distant memory of that last battle, I had heard people talking to dying men just like this. He lit a Winston and stuck it in my mouth. I couldn't draw the smoke. Then I knew there was a bad problem. In cutting off my clothes, the small four-packs of my Winston collection began to spill out; they were Louallen's favorites, too. "Shit, man, how'd you get all of these. You've been holding out on me. Listen, since you're going home anyway, why don't you leave all of these with me?" I agreed. Louallen halfway began to put on the act of collecting his new-found bounty, all the time talking and trying to joke: "You old son-of-a-bitch. Look at all these cigarettes!"

In the background, I could hear the lieutenant on the radio: we had received enemy fire, two men had been badly injured, they had to get one of them out of there right then. I knew he wasn't talking about Kearny who was resting peacefully on the compacted dirt floor of the hooch next to me.

The medic stayed huddled over me. Louallen stepped outside as if he could take it no more. Then he was back again to help if he could. The pain was beginning to come, but he couldn't give morphine. You can't give morphine if there are stomach wounds. There was no blood or any kind of IVs that were carried by a medic on this kind of mission. All he could do was keep applying the field dressing, try to clean at the wounds a little, and use the pressure points to try to control the bleeding. I can remember the silver lining of the field dressing gleaming in some kind of light; the moon had come back out.

It must have been 12:30 going on 1:00 in the morning. I lay there and finally began to understand how bad everything was. I could feel the blood and body fluids filling my lungs. It made me think of the water rising in the flush box of a toilet. You could feel its warmth coming closer and closer to the top. I knew that if it ever came up to that "top" I would drown in my own blood. I prayed, with everything in me I prayed. I promised God everything I could think of: I'd never smoke again, never curse again, never run around with women. I went the whole nine yards. I would be a missionary, a preacher, anything. Anything! If he would just let me live! In between the praying and the hurting, I listened as intently as I could for the first whisper of helicopter rotors. I knew we were miles out, but that was nothing for a helicopter. There was no enemy fire outside at all; maybe those three had been the only ones around.

Oh, my God, how I listened for the whipping sound of the helicopter rotors. Only the foot soldier knows how wonderful this sound is; like the sound of angel wings coming to save you.

It wasn't too long until the helicopters came. The radioman gave our exact position. The people on the choppers could see pretty clearly because of the moon. The medic said that everything was going to be OK, and I think he believed it at that moment. They would take Kearny and me out of the tree line and down into the clearing near the rice patties. The chopper could land there while the second one provided any cover that might be needed. We were wrapped in ponchos and carried into the clearing. Kenny Desart was there with his M-60. The choppers were coming closer and closer. Maybe they were coming to get us all out.

They were holding us up above the paddie water waiting on one of the choppers to set down in the middle of a large open area surrounded by dikes. I was looking straight up and could see perfectly the silhouette of the two choppers as they hovered above. They threw on their spotlights to look for a safe place to land. If a chopper got a skid in the side of a rice dike, the rotor would cut into the ground and the chopper was immediately inoperative. The lights glared down on us.

Suddenly, the tree line all along the side of the open area exploded in gun fire, our troops jerked into response—we were caught right in the middle. Vietcong had come from somewhere, and just like always before, they seemed to know exactly what we would do. Everyone dropped and Kearny and I were back down in all of the mud and slim. I was still looking straight up, although I could feel the dirty water puddling up all around me. You could see the sparks of gunfire chipping off on both helicopters. They pulled off immediately, and then there was all kinds of yelling over the radio: they were hit, they now had wounded, there was a fire on board one of the choppers, they were leaving. The spotlights were extinguished, and the roar of gunfire directed straight in at us. In a moment it all stopped as suddenly as it had started.

There was nothing else to do but crawl and be drug back into the jungle. There is no way to describe the misery, the pain, the hurt. We got back into the same hooch. We would have to wait. No more helicopters would try to come in that night. The rest of the company was alerted and was moving out in our direction, but they were at least five miles away. There was nothing else to do. I came to the realization that I couldn't make it. I knew enough about first aid and dying. There was no way. Rick had bled to death in ten minutes. How could I possibly make it much longer than the two hours that had already elapsed? No one could help us for at least four hours. There was no way.

I started thinking about Momma; what was going to happen to her? How was she going to make it? The $10,000 life insurance policy that the Army had on us wouldn't last anytime at all. This time when I prayed, I prayed for Momma. Please God, help her. I reminded God about what a good Christian woman she had always been, about how she had already lost a husband and suffered all kinds of hardships. I prayed that for Momma's sake, not my own, that He could somehow see fit not to put her through my death.

There was a weak and dizzy feeling, and I passed out. I was in and out like someone suffering through a deeply troubled sleep. I would wake up and accept the fact that I was dying. I would remember what I had heard the old preachers say about making your peace with God, about how with God it was never too late. With the greatest sincerity I could muster, I asked God to forgive me of my sins, to save me, and to let me go to His heaven.

I was overcome by a sense of euphoria, a feeling of total peace. I wish that I could somehow get that feeling in words on a piece of paper, but it is impossible. From that point on, I lost the fear of death. I didn't want to die, but I was no longer afraid to die. The only word I can think of is "comfort." Without a shadow of doubt in my mind, I don't think that this feeling could have come from any other source but God.

I could hear voices around me, but it was like I was off in a world by myself. I had never felt like this before in all my life. I'm not wanting to get pious here or sensational; I didn't see any angels or have any visions or experience any strange lights glowing at the end of some tunnel. I simply felt total peace, the feeling that everything—death included—was going to be all right. All the fear went away. It seemed like this feeling went on forever. I can't explain it for anyone else and don't feel the need to. What I felt needs no defense or any further confirmation in my own mind; it was without question that "peace that passes all understanding." I feel the need to say it for my children and anyone else who might believe me without looking at me and thinking that I'm some kind of a religious nut or damned hypocrite. Without a doubt in my mind, I believe that God in heaven was with me and let me have those feelings of comfort and reassurance. From that moment on, for me to say "I believe in God" meant something for real. Before, it was just a thought about an object that I had never seen, an object that I had talked to but who had never talked back.

From that moment on, "it" became "He," the object became a person—a kind of background shadow that might or might not be, became real. What more can I say. My language is exhausted before the reality.

Morning light came. The rest of company came. I was in. I was out. I could hear voices, but I couldn't respond. I tried to respond, but I couldn't respond. There were no Vietcong to be found anywhere around. Helicopters could come again. In and out. In and out.

The company commander's medic began to do his work, although this was little more than just repeating and checking what had been done. I heard someone, maybe the lieutenant or maybe Louallen ask if I couldn't be given morphine anyway—so I could at least go out in peace.

Everything within me was hearing them, but trying to say to them, "No! No! I'm still alive! I'm still alive." I was afraid that the morphine would stop whatever determination or body functions that were still keeping me alive. I don't know what happened: maybe they caught drift of a murmur or a shaking of the head; maybe they felt no need to waste the morphine; maybe the helicopters came again. No morphine was given. I am convinced they thought I was dead.

The next sensation I had, and I don't know about time frames anymore, was being lifted and tossed like a huge duffel bag unto the floor of a helicopter. My mind was still working enough to be confused over this kind of harsh treatment. Then, other people were being thrown and laid in on top of me. What the hell was going on? We were lifting up and I was out again.

Nothing. Time passing. Who knows how much. Nothing to me.

I felt myself coming to. I could look up to the top of a huge tent. There were no sounds or movement anywhere around.

I could ease my eyes slightly to both sides, and all around were high tables with people lying on them. There were no doctors or attendants, no sound. The people lying on the tables were perfectly still.

I knew enough to know! It was a morgue!!

Who knows what controls responses in that moment. You would think that someone would bolt up and start screaming for help. I couldn't move or speak. A morgue!!

My right arm moved up and across toward my shirt pocket. I can remember distinctly reaching for my Bible, my watch, and the little pack of rosary beads a young girl had given me back there somewhere—if someone had given me a yamaka, I would have put it in my pocket, too. The only explanation that I can give for my hand moving toward that Bible, signalling my life, was the power of God.

There was the sensation of rushing people all around, and I was out again. Rushing people all around. Rushing people all. Rushing people. Rushing.

Rushing.

Chapter XV

Then there were people rushing me off of a helicopter with a lot of hollering. The prop wash must have stirred me somehow, but the next thing I knew was that I was lying in a hospital bed with all kinds of tubes running into my body and bottles of one kind or another hanging on every side. There was nothing but solid bandages from my neck to my waist. It was like a strange swimming dreamland with nothing that would exactly come into focus.

I could move my head to the left a little, and the first thing to come into focus was the man in the bed next to me—a gook, a Vietnamese—my first thought was that I had been captured. I later came to find out that the man was a Korean officer who had been blown all to pieces. The whole ward was filled with the worst injuries imaginable.

There was a feeling of a warm flowing of liquid on my right side like something was suddenly gushing out. A bandage or some kind of stitching must have come loose, and I was bleeding again. I halfway moaned or called for help. The medic showed me the colostomy bag that they were trying to get in place; I could see the protruding, red end of the intestine sticking out of my side.

It took a moment to realize the bag's meaning. I had never heard of a colostomy; the bag and I would be continual companions for months to come. I was out again. The medication, the shock to my system, the fever from all of the spreading infection—in and out, in and out.

A half world away, a car with the markings of the U.S. Army was pulling up to Momma's home in West Hollywood. A young man got out, all very routinely, with a yellow telegram paper and headed for the door. Of all the most exceptional coincidences, Bobby just happened to be there, home on leave awaiting his own movement to Vietnam. Had he not been there, Momma would have been all alone.

Momma had gotten up early that morning and was preparing to go to the doctor; she had been unexplainably ill, and Bobby had all but told her that while he was on leave he was taking her whether she liked it or not. It was about 6:30 or 7:00 o'clock in the morning. Bobby was in the living room, and Momma was just walking into the room from another part of the house.

Bobby knew what it was the moment the car stopped. Not death, a team of notifying officers made that visit. Captured, missing in action, injured—in that moment, an injury was the least offensive of all of the other options. With Momma on the edge of stunned panic, he read the telegram—clear-cut, precise, military correct:

MRS. CARLENE D. MATHERSON
HOLLYWOOD, FLORIDA
REPORT DELIVERY
DON'T DELIVER BETWEEN 10PM AND 6AM

The secretary of the Army has asked me to express his deep regret that your son, Private First Class Charles D. Matherson [then there is x-ed out "became seriously ill—was seriously injured"] was seriously wounded in [large black space filled with] Vietnam on [large blank space] 24 February 1966 as a result of gunshot wounds of the chest and abdomen sustained while in defensive position and he was hit by hostile small arms fire.

Prognosis [large blank space filled with] fair. Please be assured that the best medical facilities and doctors have been made available and every measure is being taken to aid him. A report of his condition will be furnished you in a few days. If there is a significant change in his condition you will be advised immediately.

J. C. LAMBERT, MAJOR GENERAL, USA
THE ADJUTANT GENERAL

Bobby sat Momma down on the couch and tried as best he could to comfort and reassure her; it could have been worse, the telegram did say "fair," some of the best doctors in the Army were stationed in Vietnam, just thank God he wasn't captured or missing; missing, he went on, would have been the worst news except for death itself.

There was no way to tell the extent of my injuries from what was written. There was no way to contact the 8th Field Hospital on the other side of the world. There suddenly was unleashed into everyone's mind a tremendous number of uncertainties. There was crying, praying, the wrenching feelings of wanting—desperately needing—to do something, but there was nothing they could do. That was probably the special horror of it all; they knew but they really didn't know anything much at all; they would have done anything but there was nothing they could do. There were rushed phone calls to all of the immediate family and their phone calls then reached on out like ripples from a stone thrown in a pool all over the Southeast; Charles had been wounded; no, we don't know how badly; pray for Charles. Tell the people at the church to pray for Charles; we're waiting to hear anything, pray for Charles.

Bobby started trying to pull what strings he could. A call to the Department of the Army itself in Washington did not even get as much information as they already had. No one knew anything. Every response was kind enough, but it was also business to them—everyday business—and Bobby was told that in this instance no news was good news and they were sure that if there was any change, he would hear immediately. Somehow Bobby knew better. In this man's army, it was the squeaky wheel that got greased; he kept pushing for more information, but none was to be had.

The girl that I was engaged to at the time worked for Bell Telephone. When word of my injuries and all of the problems about getting information got around where she worked, one of the supervisors gave permission for her to take time from her regular duties and use the Bell System lines without charge to call anywhere in the world to find out anything that was possible. Phone call after phone call either found no response at all or was referred to someone else who knew little more.

It was almost time for Bobby's leave to end and for him to head for Vietnam himself. He could not leave his family in that kind of lurch, and he certainly would not leave the country not knowing what was happening to me. He even began to talk of going AWOL if that was what it took to hold the family together.

Finally, someone was able to turn up a piece of information that I was being transferred to Travis Air Force Base in California. Bobby would leave early and head on out there and look for me.

They placed my bed up at the head of the ward. Everything that took place had to pass by where I lay; I was in continuous view of the main nurse's station and with any passage to deal with other patients the doctors and nurses were continually stopping to check on my every move. There was no question from the looks on their faces that this was serious business, but I never really had or was given any idea of how bad I actually was. When they checked the dressings, I could see the railroad track of heavy metal and rubber sutures that covered the whole front of my body, but all I could think was "give me a machine gun and let me go back; just don't let anyone see me like this."

You were acutely aware of people dying. They didn't seem, on the surface of things, to have as many dressings or tubes or bottles as I did. I wondered if they were giving up or what. I knew, if I knew anything at all, that I wasn't giving up. There was, however, a complete loss of the sense of time. I would wake up and have no idea if moments, hours, or even days or weeks had passed.

What I didn't know was that there were two problems: the wounds themselves which included the lung, the intestines, and a spleen that had been blown away; but more significantly, or at least grossly complicating everything else, the unbelievable amount of infection from the dragging through the mud, being dropped and dragged through the rice patty, and the lying out without any cleaning up through the night in the jungle and part of the next day in the morgue. The fever kept coming back higher and higher. The body's defenses were shutting everything else down, including my consciousness of what was going on, to fight against this raging fire inside.

One afternoon when I was conscious enough to be aware of the activity in the passageway near my bed, a guy walked by who had been in my original company. We had been in the first battle where Rick was killed and outside the village the night that I was shot. I got his attention.

It is impossible to describe his reaction. He turned white as a sheet and halfway collapsed in the floor. He reached for the wall to support himself, like he was seeing a ghost. All that he could say for a moment was, "You're dead! You're dead!" In a moment or two, when he came to himself a little more, he went on to explain that he had helped throw my body on the helicopter the next morning when they were carrying us out. Everyone, he said, had been deeply moved that Matherson had "got it"; the whole group just didn't seem the same anymore. I was startled to hear him talk about my carriers: evidently they had hidden to avoid the fighting that took place on into that night. The next day they were found huddled in a group—decapitated. I wondered if some of the bodies that had been thrown in on top of mine might have been theirs.

He didn't have any information about Kearny, and I have never been able to find out anything about what happened to him. That's one of the realities that makes this whole thing linger on. Combat leaves missing pieces to a puzzle that forever remain important to get put together. Those pieces get lost out there and can't be retrieved. It's like you remember where you left something, but you can't get back there to look for it. And then even if you did get back, you have the feeling that the pieces that you lost wouldn't be there and you would be driven to look for them somewhere else. It all just hangs there like a heavy cloud.

Later, the fact of their certainty about my death would explain a lot of things. All paperwork about my promotion to Spec 4 that would have normally accompanied the elevation to the position of gunner had stopped; it would be the better part of a year until this was resolved. There was no good reason, given the crush of the moment, to attend to any business of decorations for going into that dark trap on that night or, even more importantly, pulling Kearny out while we were still under fire. At that moment, however, promotions or decorations were of little concern. It gives you a strange feeling, nonetheless, to have someone explain that you are supposed to be dead.

An officer came by, said a few words like a priest pronouncing some kind of ritual, and pinned a purple heart to my pillow. I guess that meant something to me, but more than anything else, it made me aware that it was the only thing I had that was mine. I had been separated from everything else. My personal belonging had been stripped away somewhere in an attempt to get at my wounds and save my life. All of my other belongings were supposed to be back at Phan Rang—my dress uniform, tapered with upgraded silver buttons and crossed infantry rifles, my jump boots for having finished highest in my class, my personal clothes.

I wondered what they did with a dead man's possessions. Send them home? Divide them among those who were left? Throw them on the dump to be claimed by ravaging Vietnamese? I never saw any of it again. The whole sense of being separated from family and home was raised to a new level with the realization that I had been separated from everything that was mine. It was like my identity was scattered out there somewhere—with the lock of a girlfriend's hair that I had carried for good luck, with the parts of my body blown away in a dark, wet jungle. Before it was all over, the purple heart was even lost in the rushed shuffle of saving life.

The doctors had the basic idea that my situation was so desperate that I needed to be at the best facilities the United States had to offer. In spite of all of their advanced technology, there was simply not enough in the Vietnam hospitals that had been established really to give me a chance. I didn't know this; I found it out later. In the end, they were caught in a delicate double bind; they had to move me or I would die—if they moved me, they were nearly certain that this would kill me.

Finally, somewhere around the end of the first week of March, they had to try it anyway. The idea was to get me as quickly as possible to Walter Reed Army Hospital in Washington. Some of the best people in the world were there. Except for refueling, it was to be a direct flight.

I only made it as far as the Philippines. In all likelihood, my lungs collapsed. That seemed to be the most perplexing problem which they couldn't get right. They kept forcing me through the pain of blowing water from one bottle to the other to strengthen the lungs, but they still kept collapsing. The plane was forced to land and they immediately had me hospitalized. I really can't remember this. I recall the doctors in Vietnam; the Philippines is a total blank. I must have been about dead at that moment, but I didn't know. Everybody thought I was going to die, but I don't recall ever having that thought.

They finally were ready to try again, but this time they made it only as far as Hawaii. I do remember something of this. When they were taking me off the plane, I'm sure along with some other men, there was a military band on the tarmac of the airport. They were playing prideful military music that made you want to get up and march, to salute a flag, to do close order drills with your rifle.

Everything about me wanted to stand up and march with pride; in the deepest frustration, I couldn't even move. The fever was back and I was out again.

After several days in Hawaii, they got me as far as California. While I was there, undergoing new treatments, trying new techniques, there was a steady stream of dignitaries and movie stars that made the rounds of the wards. Except for one instance, I can't remember much more than the movement of smiling faces and reassuring pats on the shoulder. They told me that Audrey Meadows was coming in to see me. She came in, but I was in such pain that I couldn't even concentrate enough on her being there to respond. Somehow I asked her to give me a few minutes and come back; she said she would. The nurses gave me a shot for the pain and several minutes later Audrey Meadows was back just as she said. Someone made a picture, and it eventually made its way to my family. In it, there is a beautiful movie star going out of her way to help try to cheer up a wounded GI; there's the GI, too, secured to every kind of medical device imaginable, suddenly dwindled in his ordeal from 176 pounds to 115.

When Bobby got to California it was as if my trail had gone cold again. There was one mix-up after another. Still, my family had next to no information about my condition, only that I had been wounded and was receiving the best of care. Bobby was determined and pushed every button available to find out what he could and to get where I was. In the calls back to Florida he began to talk about AWOL again, and it took everything Momma and his wife, Ann, could do to convince him to go ahead and follow his orders and not jeopardize his excellent military record.

In what amounted to his last ditch effort he was able to get in touch with a man at the Pentagon in Washington who did take some personal interest in helping our family in this situation as it had developed. He not only found exactly where I was but took all of our family information and promised to keep in touch with them about whatever was happening. Bobby headed for the hospital where he was told I would be; he got there late in the afternoon only a few hours after I had been flown out for Walter Reed in Washington.

There was yet a fourth forced stop in Texas; I was dying again and they had to get to a hospital. There is simply no memory at all of any of the events or people surrounding that stop. It annoys the hell out of me to know that a significant slice of my life somehow just never got registered in my memory; in some ways, though, maybe it is better that it did not.

At long last, I can remember landing in Maryland at the air force base outside of Washington and being loaded along with several others onto a huge stretcher bus. When we pulled into the hospital, we were immediately surrounded by a huge group of doctors who were quickly looking through and sorting out the incoming patients in one direction and then another.

In a moment it seemed like the attention of the whole group was centering on me. I didn't know why. I really wasn't feeling anything. The lungs had collapsed again. There was yelling and rushing and a sensation of something about to happen.

One of the doctors suddenly was over me with a scalpel and was cutting, almost digging straight into my chest. Some of the others were holding me down. There was a severe look of determination mixed with desperation on his face.

For me, there was horrific pain. I was screaming at them—why were they doing this to me? I was yelling for God—what had I done that was so bad that I was having to be hurt this way? They were cutting me open without the first hint of a shot or anything that would deaden the pain. Nothing in my entire existence had ever hurt like this.

I could feel my chest opening back like a huge crack in the earth pulling apart in an earthquake. The feel of warm blood running out of the chest cavity and down the sides of my stomach took away any sense that I could have any control in this moment. They began to push large tubes into the open wound. I felt the air that I had only suddenly missed flowing back in. In a moment, a nurse was there with morphine and I eased off into that calm netherworld where nothing matters, but more importantly where nothing hurts.

A second word was now reaching South Florida, this time much more ominous than the first. The man at the Pentagon had kept his word; he had followed my progress across country and had a Dr. Lapenta on the phone to Momma moments after they had completed their initial work on me. The doctors offered little hope; if my family wanted to see me alive they had better come as quickly as possible. There was a phone on rollers which could be brought to the ward. Someone brought the phone and I talked to

Momma. I didn't say much at all. She had to tell me about the conversation later as I had no recollection of it at all. For maybe a short instant, Momma wondered if all the praying had fallen on deaf ears, but this mother would never give up on God, her son who had fallen in battle, and a second one just finding out about that damnedable jungle for himself. Preparations immediately rushed into place for a quick trip into North Carolina where family would be waiting to bring her straight to Washington.

When Momma arrived at the train station in Miami, there was a problem: seats were reserved and everything booked solid all the way into Washington. It was the height of the college spring break period, and there was simply nothing available. Momma explained her situation, even going so far as to suggest that she would stand if she had to. It didn't take but a moment until people started making arrangements right and left. There was seat changing and one move after another all the way to North Carolina, but this woman's son was dying and they were going to get her there no matter what.

I remember the next couple of days, the days before Momma came. I remember them better than anything I had remembered in a long time. The hospital must have been full. They put me in a ward that had been created out of the side of a long corridor. The ceilings were high and sometimes it was drafty cold; it must have been cold outside because I could lie there and watch the streams of water run down the steamed up windows above the doors at the end of the corridor.

I had all the tubes, the colostomies, big soft rubber drainage tubes running out of my lungs, two poles on either side of my bed crowded with one kind of IV and another. Something was running in and out of me all the time in a curious interchange of life.

Then, there was the stench, the smell of rot, the odor of death. I remembered it from the funeral home and the hard death cases that we occasionally got there. I remembered it from the days after Rick's death when we uncovered the shallow graves. There was burn rot, infection rot, bowel rot. This was a death ward.

Maybe the second day, I could pull myself up a few inches on the bar that hung over my bed. To my immediate right was a sergeant named Jerry. He had had his face literally blown off in an artillery explosion. They had saved his life, and now they were trying to give him a new face. He had a huge hunk of meat hanging off his forehead across his left eye and cheek and sewn into where his chin had been. He had been there about as long as anyone. I was amazed at his tracheotomy, the first thing I guess I had really noticed outside myself since the jungle. He kept a cigarette in the hole in his throat and successfully smoked it. He even took pride in being able to blow smoke rings through the hole. There was even greater pride in being able to feed himself with a small tube without any help from the nurses.

I just wanted to be left alone. I didn't want to talk to anyone. Let me suffer in my own private hell. Let me work out a way of accepting that they're never going to be able to put this Humpty Dumpty back together again; the "great fall" had just been too much. There were too many unknowns and I couldn't handle it.

Jerry brought me out. He got me to talking, and before long showed me that all of us were a part of a special fraternity who had to try to kid away reality. If anyone else said the kind of things to us that we said to each other, I guess our feelings would have been crushed. With the odd sounds and even odder aromas of my colostomies and intestinal infections, I was christened "Stinky." Jerry was already "Frankenstein" and there was more than one "Peg Leg." My easy response to any onslaught of kidding from other patients and the equally grave-merry humor of the nurses and doctors was the threat to hit someone with one of my "shit bags."

It was gruesome, but when the pain wasn't overwhelming it helped. One guy six beds down was held suspended in the air between boards that clamped him together. He had literally been blown apart, and the boards were holding everything together until his body could begin to mend itself. One poor kid across the way had been "stirring shit" on latrine duty, and the excrement and diesel fuel mix had exploded like a morbid kind of napalm; his face and arms had burned away nearly to the bone. At a bad moment, when the best kidding didn't help one bit, you felt like you were in an absurd, cruel kind of freak show—people made too misfit ever to come back into a normal world.

I would tell the nurses and doctors, even beg them at my lowest moments, not to tell anyone I was here, not to tell anyone anything about me, and—for God's sake—not to let anyone see me like this! I can remember crying out in the middle of the torture of the pain: "Give me my gun! Leave me the hell alone! Let me go back to Vietnam and die in my own misery!!" The combination of morphine, self-pity, fever, and the dwindling of hope was as bad as the injuries themselves. I had lost my watch back over there somewhere, and I had to go back and find it. It's strange the kind of tricks that your mind can play on you; it was only a Timex, but I hadn't had a real watch of my own like this one—if I could get it back, maybe I thought on some level that I could get a lot of everything else back with it.

At times I felt myself turning into something that I wasn't and something I couldn't control. I felt myself feeling spiteful and saying things that hurt people, and then feeling a great rush of guilt for what I had said. I had never intentionally hurt anyone in my whole life by something that I had said. Now, it would just jump out and I couldn't do a damn thing to stop it. God, how I hated it all!

I had gone off to sleep on the second or third night, the day before Momma came. Somehow I remember being conscious of actually going off into a peaceful sleep. Then, I was in Vietnam again. It was real. All the people, the familiar places, the same conversations, the heat and wet. It was real. Then suddenly there was a grenade, right in on top of me! I screamed, leaped, cried, and was out of the bed ripping everything that was tied to me out and down, trying with all that was within me to get away from the grenade.

Then Jerry had me. Holding me in his arms. Hugging me. Talking me down. Bringing me back. Telling me that it was all going to be all right. Keeping me from hurting myself even more until help could come. And I was out again.

There had been a couple of more phone calls as Momma worked from one relative to another on her way to Washington. I knew when she was coming, and there was no way under God's heaven that I was going to let her see me like this. A little before the time that she was supposed to get there, I drug myself up out of the bed. I can't remember exactly how I did it, and propped myself between the two IV poles that stood beside my bed. I got on out toward the hall so that I could watch the door that opened onto the ward. I carefully draped something—a robe or gown or something—over the patchwork of steel, rubber, and cloth that was spread across my stomach and chest. I waited, maybe against the wall, or sitting on the edge of something—I don't know, the memory simply isn't there.

When she walked through the door, I moved toward her. If she could see me like this, she wouldn't think that I was in such bad shape; she wouldn't worry as much.

She saw me. She had had to steel herself against so much already, and she knew that going all to pieces when she saw me would do nothing but make me think even worse of my condition and my chances. We embraced—as best she could through all of the tubes and tape—and there were tears in both of our eyes. But from the very beginning there was that old spirit; you couldn't always do anything about what came your way, acting like it wasn't real didn't make it go away, we would face this head on, she would help—between her and the power of God this would be overcome just like so much had been overcome in the past. It must have nearly killed her to see me—still her baby—about as close to the point of death that a person could be, but she seized the moment and set herself on a course to help in any way that was possible, a course that would admit only one possibility in the end, getting her son back to a place of total physical health and mental sanity. It was no easy task at that moment, but she was not there for a short visit—she had come to stay.

Then, the doctors and nurses recognized me, and everyone came running, asking me how I had gotten out of bed, bouncing "Oh My God!" looks off of each others' eyes, and carrying me as I collapsed back into the ward.

The first thing Momma did, beginning almost the moment that she came into the room, was to start cleaning me up. Although it had been almost a month since I had been wounded, there had been so much bleeding, peripheral wounding, and the left over remains of that last stretch in the jungle that I still had blood in my hair, rough scabbing on my back, and thick callouses almost like shoe soles on places on my feet. She cleaned and bathed me, worked with the minor sores that the doctors and nurses had not always gotten to, and found razor blades to begin to cut the callouses away. I felt the strength that only a mother's care can give. All the other human contacts I had had up until this time were efficient and directed by logic; this contact was life-giving, affection compelled by love.

Some of my aunts and uncles had brought Momma on into Washington, and in a few minutes joined her in the room. There was talk about me needing anything. The only thing I could think of was popcorn and barbeque. A doctor was called and asked about this possibility, and with total frankness he said to give me anything I wanted—it was too late to do anything but try to pacify me.

Had Momma come the next day, she would have walked into a completely different situation. My fever skyrocketed again, there was tremendous pain, and I was nearly delirious. The doctor called the guest house where she was staying and told her to come quickly; I was getting readied to be taken back into emergency surgery. There was, he said, little hope of recovery.

I made it through the surgery as I would one time after another, as I would so many times that I lost track. And every time I came back Momma was waiting for me. While she waited, she prayed. While she waited, she became a kind of guardian angel or mother figure—maybe they are one and the same—to many of the other men on the ward. She encouraged them as they encouraged her; she shared from the bounty of food and candy and cards that were soon coming in from friends and family all over the Southeast.

A great stroke of luck—Momma called it the will of God— occurred while she was transferring from one relative to another in North Carolina on her way to Washington. She found out that an old school friend named Rose Smith was a nurse at Walter Reed. Not only could she help Momma work through any red tape that she might encounter, but Momma could stay with her for as long as she wanted. This great gesture of kindness made it possible for Momma to avoid many of the frustrations and discomforts that come with being away from home. She stayed with me in the day and at Rose's at night. She helped with the house cleaning and cooking in exchange for the place to stay. She would hold herself together for me, always strong and certain of my recovery; she would stop at the chapel every day when she returned to Rose's to pray. Sometimes she had to sit down on a park bench or lean in the new, spring shade against a large tree and simply cry her heart out.

I can remember the Mommas and Pappas singing group and their famous song from that time "Monday, Monday." It seemed like every Monday they were taking me in for another round of surgery. The infections kept coming back, the fever rose, and they had to go in and take out some more of the poison that was trying to kill me. There were good and bad days. Sometimes Momma and I would talk for hours about home and the good old days when I was a kid; sometimes the nurses would stop her at the door and tell her that it would just be a lot better if she didn't even see me that day.

At one point in the process, the doctors became so amazed that I was still living—about how I had lived in the first place—that they asked permission to take films of my insides. Some surgeon in Vietnam had done some kind of repair work they had never seen used anywhere before. It was probably what saved my life to begin with. The films would be distributed to other military surgeons with the hope that this could save American lives. The vision of a desperate physician working away at a dying man came into my mind. He had tried everything but it hadn't worked. With nothing to lose, or in a moment of high genius, the new procedure was born. I hoped that this information might help save the lives of others.

Such thoughts didn't last long. Even Momma's encouragement was losing ground to the endless round of draining surgery. I sensed that this was going to be the story of the rest of my life, and that would not be long. I would simply go off to surgery one more time, and would not come back. Someone else would fill my bed, and life—or death—would go on. I began to wallow in long bouts of self-pity. This wasn't me, but I couldn't seem to get enough stamina together to do anything about it. If there was hate directed at the overall situation, it began to slip over into more and more negative feelings about my own self.

A second "guardian angel" came on the scene in the person of an Army nurse by the name of Captain Eber. Now I know she was a caring saint who knew more about dying soldiers than they knew about themselves. At that time I was convinced that she was the hardest, least caring, son-of-a-bitch of a bitch I had ever seen in all my life. God, how she made drill sergeants look tame; God, how I would have loved for her to have gotten hold of a couple of the sergeants that I had had along the way—maybe even Bobby that first day at Fort Gordon when he had called me out of the mess line to get the cup from beneath the barracks.

She started taunting and ridiculing me, even in front of the other men in the ward. She was loud and there was a keen look in her eyes and a sharp tone in her voice that felt like it was digging into my very bones. At first, I took a completely "fuck off, fuck you bitch" attitude toward her, as if I was not even hearing what she was saying. I figured I could convince her that I didn't care and she could go straight to hell. For most people that would be enough to make them say "fuck you" straight back and take their harassment somewhere else. I'm sure that on bad days every thing I thought about her, I said to her face.

But she wouldn't quit. Thank God, I know now, she wouldn't quit. I can hear her now, "I thought you were tough. I thought you were one of those hard-ass paratroopers who could take anything and do anything. Airborne. Airborne bullshit. You're a quitter just like a hundred other quitters I have seen get carted out of here. You couldn't get up and get out of here if you wanted to. All you're going to do is lie on your pitiful ass and let someone wait on you!"

It went on like that almost every day. I hated to see her come on the ward. I knew exactly where she was headed—straight for me, "See you're still here, Matherson. It figures. Wasting my time and the government's money. Pretty good free-loading trip you got going here. Wouldn't you say, Matherson? Talk to me, Matherson, or maybe you're not feeling good enough to talk today."

If I could have gotten out of that bed, I would have tried to kill her on the spot. She was getting to me, and I hated her twice as much for that. Nobody got to me! I would show her. By God, I would show her. I would get out of there if for no other reason on God's green earth than to spite that damn, hard bitch—which was exactly what she wanted all along.

It finally got to the place that the only thing on my mind was getting back to Vietnam. There was part of me that couldn't believe all that I had seen there; not just the war, the fighting and dying, but the people and the buildings and the land itself. Something in my mind could not totally accept that I had even been there. It was like a dream that you suddenly had awakened in the middle of, and then struggled with everything within you to reconstruct and bring back to the front of your conscious mind. It was all there, you were sure of that, but it wasn't complete, it wouldn't come back so you could somehow square it all away. To go back would confirm that part of me that I had left there—that in some respects is still there. I yearned for the kind of completion and closure and personal affirmation that I became obsessively convinced could only be had back in Vietnam.

Even though I could look at myself and see with my own eyes that it had been real. Even though I could finger my sutures and feel the pain piercing from my wounds, there was still something left to do. It wasn't totally revenge, though that emotion was there with a lot of others. But simple, hateful paying someone back is not enough of an explanation for someone to want to go back to hell.

At the same time, it wasn't some kind of death wish either; to draw that conclusion is simpleton bullshit. It wasn't death that I wanted to find there, but something of life that had been lost. I couldn't get the people out of my mind. Why were they having it so hard? Why had life dealt them one sorry hand after another? Why? The old people who came crawling though our garbage dump to try to reclaim something that would advance their lives, sometimes simply something to eat—the old man and woman and child whom I met in the ditch after Rick was killed—the look of fear, horror, and fatalistic resignation to whatever cruel fate they might meet in me—all these people and the looks on their faces walked back and forth through my mind every time I closed my eyes and drifted toward sleep.

The girl who had promised to marry me was wanting to come. Momma had told her at first that it might be too soon, and she had waited. Now, she was becoming more and more insistent all the time. We talked on the phone a little, but it wasn't the same anymore. For her it was, but what I had was gone. It hurts me now that I did her the way that I did. It wasn't really me and it wasn't really her; it was Vietnam. I doubt seriously that we would have ever really gotten married; it was all a kind of boyhood infatuation, not the stuff marriages are made of. But still, what I was doing had to be cruel in its effect. I wouldn't let her come. There was no way. She would never see me like this. It didn't matter that she was Kay's best friend. It was over. It was all off. On some level of truth—whatever that is—it's not possible to have an ultimate, absolute commitment to two things at the same time. I couldn't get to anything else until Vietnam was over. My concentration, my absolute concern, was Vietnam.

Captain Eber finally did it, or Captain Eber and my obsession with Vietnam. I started getting up. I could walk with the support of the two IV poles, and finally could creep around like a weak and broken old man all over the wing of the hospital. I could make it to the vending machines, could walk Momma out to the door when she would leave each day, and could get around to one person or another on the ward. I learned how to clean my wounds and clear the external infection spots with peroxide. I could clear the colostomies by myself now.

The tubes were all still there, but I learned how to control the irritation. There was an exact way to move the tubes in your nose so that pain in one place of irritation would stop, so that they would not come all the way out and you would have to experience the severe pain of having them put back in place again. I was afraid to try and straighten up for fear of pulling loose all the stitches and sutures, but some doctor would come along, stick his knee in my back, and pull my shoulders back, "Straighten up, Matherson! Straighten up!" I thought Eber would change, compliment me or something, but it didn't happen. She kept agitating, and I kept swearing to myself that I would show her.

As I began to improve, there were more people who started coming around. Football players from the Washington Redskins came through the wards on a regular basis. I seemed puny next to them and wished they could have seen me at my battle-ready prime. I wished they could have seen the man who won the commander's jump boots. There were programs with a variety of singers, dignitaries, and movie stars. I hadn't paid much attention to this sort of thing when it showed up in the war movies or on Bob Hope telecasts, but it really did help and none of these people had to do any of this. There were baskets full of cards from friends and people in Momma's church. Cecil Hobbs's mother came to see me. That helped me, but surely it scared her beyond words to wonder what this war might, right then, be doing to her own son. My Uncle Herman came and, though I begged otherwise, got me to laughing so much that I literally pulled stitches loose; it was worth it.

The girls who worked in the government offices in Washington had, through three wars, made it a practice to come to

Walter Reed and try to provide some company for the soldiers who were there with their injuries. Someone should write a book about all that they did to help, without a dime's pay or anyone making them do it. They would come in and talk about their homes and your home. They knew about Kansas farms and Colorado mountains, Maine in the winter time when the maple syrup was collected and California beaches. They smiled, they generated an infectious and positive attitude, they smelled good.

But I was afraid, afraid of what the colostomy bag might do with its unpredictable sounds and smells. I didn't want to be embarrassed in front of these girls. I began to hold my hands under my sheets the minute they came in. By tightly gripping the top of the opening from the intestine into the colostomy bag, there was no way that I would be embarrassed. But then I would begin to hurt, like the pain of desperately needing to have a bowel movement but not being able to. I would hold it till they left, but finally I had to tell the nurses not to let them see me. It hurt too badly. I wondered sometimes, between the taunting of Eber and the dreams of Vietnam, if I would carry this embarrassment the rest of my life.

Buster Carter and Eddie Jones came up from North Carolina to see me. My oldest childhood friends, I had not seen them since before Florida. When they came into the ward, Buster turned white as a sheet. I don't know if it was the smell or the sight of human agony that suddenly was spread out in front of his face. Even before he could say hello, he blurted "I've got to get outside," and he rushed into an outer corridor. I got up and went to him, a kind of ironic thing to happen under the circumstances. I was genuinely happy to see them and talk with them. Here was something that really did help. I'll never forget them for coming the way that they did. You would hang on to something that happened on a good day and carry it with you into the next day or the next several days. My friends' visit got me on a good high that lasted over the better part of the next week.

It had finally turned spring, late May, and all of Washington was alive with the beautiful budding of new blossoms and leaves on the trees. The past three months had been more of a painful blur than anything else. I was getting my sense of humor back, and starting to cut up with the other men, starting to help and reassure the new men coming in like I had been helped. I stole an officer's maroon robe and wore it instead of the enlisted man's blue robe. I would sneak food from the vending machines I was not supposed to have. There was an ongoing—and now I see, a very purposeful—competition between me and the doctors and nurses. I would hide the contraband and they would make the pretense of looking for it. It was wonderful when you could actually take a shower.

Those of us who were able began to look for distractions. We gambled on anything that was available, not any big money but enough to help the day pass. Our main activity in this regard was wheelchair racing. There was one long circle through two of the wards that made a perfect track. We would race two at a time in a kind of elimination event. It was racer against racer, but also the patients against the staff finding out what we were doing, the inside world learning how to make life work without the help of the outside world.

My favorites were the guys whose legs had been blow off, the guys that we "Stinkys"—the ones with stomach injuries—called "Peg" or "Shorty" or kidded about not having to buy shoes or whether anything above the legs had been blown off, too. They loved it and fired back, "We might never dance, but we won't smell like shit." I can remember lots of times when someone would wreck—maybe a guy with new stubbs would go crashing into the wall—and there would be great pain and doctors coming from every direction. The entire ward knew what to do. Help would come, but we had it made up to act like we didn't know what was happening and to go on like we had not even heard the "accident" occur. The doctors and nurses would raise hell, threaten to bust a person in rank or dock pay; in the end, I would bet they knew exactly what we were doing and saw it in terms of recovery.

They told me that I could go home. Almost all of the tubes were gone now, and I knew how to care for the colostomies. There was no way! I wasn't going home with a plastic bag stuck on my side and carried around like some kind of absurd holster. I wasn't letting anyone see me like this. When I went back—if I ever went back—it was going to be like the Charlie Matherson who had left.

At least Momma could go back. She looked tired, and there was no way that all of this time since the first part of March could do anything but be taking its toll. She expressed some doubts about leaving me, but not as many as I really expected. She would head back to Florida—not much of an argument at all but would be back in a moment's notice if I needed her.

What I didn't know, and what would have explained why Momma was not so hard to convince about leaving, was that she was sick, too. She had been all the time, but I didn't know it—had no idea of it at all. She needed surgery for a pinched nerve and some sort of tumor in her back. She never made it to Florida, but had to stop in North Carolina where things got so bad that the surgery had to be performed immediately.

The tumor was OK, but she had to be placed in traction on account of the nerve problem. While she was in traction in the North Carolina hospital, one of the men in the ward that knew me was able—without my knowledge—to find her and keep the promise of letting her know about my condition. I was critical again, getting ready for emergency surgery—the fever and infection was back. She got out of the traction, checked herself out of the hospital, and was back in Washington by the time I was coming out of surgery.

This time my recovery came quickly. They were able to resection my intestines and get rid of the colostomies. There is no way adequately to describe what that meant; only someone who has gone through it could understand. The very fact of being able to sit down on a toilet and have a real bowel movement, given all that had happened across the past three months, was one of the proudest moments of my life. It could only compare to the pride of a woman having a baby. For the first time, I sat there and knew that this would not be the end of my life as I had known it—I would be back!

They had to watch me for about another month, but there was all kinds of new freedom. I got a new uniform and new jump boots. I would spend hours spit shining them to perfection. The other guys on the ward kidded me incessantly about this, but I proudly came back that they were "just damn 'legs'," and what did they know. I walked around a lot with Momma and we spent time outdoors—the foliage of Washington in spring a million miles away from the jungle.

I would walk over to the eye section of the hospital where Momma's friend, Rose Smith, worked. While I was there one day, I ran into a guy from the old platoon who was shot on the same day that Rick was killed. He had had one eye completely blown out, and had been in and out of the hospital almost as long as I had. He knew his way around much better than I did.

Several Congressmen were having a party on a huge paddlewheel boat, and he had been invited. Did I want to go? Even as I quickly was saying "Hell, yes!", something deep inside was pulling me back. When I saw all the girls and liquor available on the paddleboat, I knew what it was. What about all those promises that I had made to God back there in the jungle? He had kept his end, would I keep mine? I had maybe one or two very uncomfortable beers and just briefly talked with a couple of the girls.

My old friend was getting ready to leave for home on a month's convalescent leave. He could hardly wait. To show their thrill over his return, his parents had bought him a brand new Chevrolet Super Sport. In the few days right before he left, we made all kinds of plans. He would return with his car and we would turn Washington upside down. There was great excitement when he left and even more in a couple of weeks when he was due back. On his way back in, in the new sports car, there was a terrible automobile accident—he was killed. Depression came rushing back in. All of the questions—why this, why that? I had to get out of there. I had to get beyond all of this.

I was discharged for a month of convalescent leave right after the first of June. Some of my kinfolk came up from North Carolina with a station wagon. Momma had made a bed for me in the back and her plan was to stop several times along the way at one family member's home and then another. I was anxious to get back to Florida, to put all of this as far behind me as possible, and it dug at me when Momma kept trying—when everyone kept trying—to treat me like I was a baby or some kind of invalid. I was amazed how strongly all of the old promises kept flooding back as we drove away from the hospital. I was going to be OK—what was I going to do about it?

We stopped at my Uncle Jack's and Aunt Helen's in Whiteville. He had been a World War II veteran and they had a son in Vietnam. He talked about his war experiences and about his son. I envied the son. That was where I needed to be, not waiting around here until Momma thought I was strong enough to make another leg of the trip back. My frustration was heightened when my Aunt Nell's son, Max, stepped on one of my jump boots and disfigured the shine on the front. I had to get out of there. Finally, I told Momma that either we left for Florida or I was walking to the highway and thumbing my way back. I didn't tell Momma much in that kind of tone; maybe she was a little uncertain about how all that had happened was affecting me, but quickly arrangements were made to go on. In retrospect, it is interesting that little Max went on to be a paratrooper himself—and then to understand my response to his scuffing of my boots.

Florida greeted me with more mixed feelings than I thought were possible. I guess I thought on some level that the innocence and ease of childhood that I had known there would be back the moment I crossed the state line. It wasn't. I would never go anywhere again like the kid who had left there hardly a year before.

First things first. I had to face the girl I was engaged to. There wasn't any reason to play that one out, to mislead her in that moment, or to use her in the flow of emotion of my return. There was also no reason to be cold or cruel. I was neither. She came over to the house almost immediately. We sat and talked about Vietnam, about my own confusion, about life in general, any kind of relationship or future in particular, and about my going back to Vietnam. That was the only real thing that was on the horizon, the only point of focus. I just simply couldn't do any better by her or myself than to sort all of that out first. She cried. The deep hurt was obvious. My sister was hurt, too. How much hurt all of this had turned out to be, and I was at the center of the hurt feeling more guilt than I had ever experienced in my life. It was over, but it was all that could be done.

Then I had to face God. All the promises were standing on one side, but the reality of wanting to get back into the flow of all that was happening with the old people and the old places was there, too. The conflict was tearing me apart. The doctors had told me repeatedly that they simply did not know how I had lived—I did, God had made it possible. But here I was being drawn, no longer to the Burger King, but to the West End Bar where my old friends had graduated to a whole new level of experiences.

Sometimes I found safe haven at home, but then everyone kept treating me like I was so fragile that I was about to break. I had to get out. I had already started smoking again, so one promise broken made the next one even easier.

But did I ever show up at the bar in a way that no one, myself included, would ever expect! I decided to go in and preach to the people. Maybe it was a good thing that it was a bar; had it been any kind of place that expected "normal" behavior, I would probably have been arrested. But drunks and near drunks hanging out in bars on afternoons when everyone else is at work will listen to anything. It doesn't register with them, but they will listen. By the time I had finished my "sermonizing," I felt like a damn fool; I was also ready for a drink, but left without it.

I was back the next day. I wanted to drink beer so badly that I felt like my tongue was hanging out on the floor. Maybe just being around it would get me by. Let somebody think they can't do something, and they'll want it twice as badly. Even if I didn't like the taste, I still didn't want to think I couldn't do something I wanted to do. Then there was a disturbance of some kind down the bar from where I was sitting. Some guy and his girl friend were having an argument that was erupting into some pushing and shoving on his part; she was holding her hands up to protect her face and trying to pull away from him.

He was a huge, strong-looking guy and she was much smaller. I would normally have marked it all off as bar business and nothing that was any business of mine. But I couldn't distract my attention elsewhere. The near violence that was taking place was senseless, absurd. Then, he reached back and smacked her across the face with all his strength. You could see her head flip to the side and then spring back with a look of sudden shock.

So I stepped in; what the hell was he doing, leave her alone, you didn't go around doing that to another human being, was he crazy, stop it, stop it now! It was not hard to imagine his response, especially considering that I was barely above my hospital weight and probably looked like someone who had just been in a hospital, nearly dead, for the past three or four months.

There was almost too much difference in our size and apparent strength at that moment for him to react immediately. He started telling me to mind my own business, to go to hell, that he would wipe the floor up with my face. There is not much question that he could have done that, too.

I said for him to wait a minute, that I would be right back. That has never made much sense to me, even though it was the second time something like it had happened. Why would anyone wait for someone to go out in the midst of a confrontation and see what would happen when they came back? Would someone think that the person leaving was going out for pizza for everyone, or going to get a camera to take a picture of this situation? But people who are drinking don't always think.

As quickly as I could I went home and came back. I brought a .45 caliber semi-automatic pistol with me. When I eased back into the bar, I'm not even sure he noticed me that much. They were both still at the bar, and he was still berating her and gripping her arms and face with his hands until you could see the hurt it was causing on her face. Any tears that she might have shed had long since stopped; there was nothing but sheer terror written on her face now.

I came in beside him and in one motion of my hand and arm brought the .45 out of my shirt and stuck the barrel of the gun right into his mouth. I jammed it back into his throat and got my face right in his own: "I ought to blow your fucking head off!"

Nothing moved in the whole bar. A pin dropping would have sounded like an avalanche. Looking back, I'm not sure why I just didn't go ahead and pull the trigger. She got loose and ran out. We stood there pressed against each other like statues for what seemed like fifteen minutes, and I ripped the gun back out of his mouth. He halfway collapsed, halfway leaped off to the side and cowered down without saying a word. That was it; I turned and left.

I went off down to the beach by myself. I sat there, who knows how long, looking off across the water into the distance. It was all screwed up. I sat on this beach and thought about over there; I sat on that beach and thought about over here. Had what I had just done meant that I was crazy or that I was the only sane person in that bar? It was all a mess. I was overwhelmed by the confusion and lack of clarity. I got up and turned to leave and could hear myself—almost like I was some kind of outside observer—repeating over and again, "Fuck it all! Fuck it all. Fuck it all......"

I started drinking again—not enough to really even count under most circumstances because I didn't even like the taste of beer all that much, but enough to break the promises. I got with Angelo Marino and Bob Alleva, and we crammed in all of the partying and cruising Fort Lauderdale that time would allow. I was amazed that the thirty days of leave passed by so quickly. I went to church maybe two times.

When I was getting ready to catch a military plane out of Homestead Air Force Base back to Washington, I ran into a couple of other enlisted men and we began to talk. There wasn't much room on the plane we were waiting for, and we were on stand-by. All that meant was that we had a ride if no officers came along and bumped us. If they did, we sat and waited for the next flight.

Three or four young lieutenants, no older than I, came in and it was clear that they would get seats. I was feeling kind of sad about leaving, and all of this got compounded by the fact that it looked like this flight would go off and leave us sitting there.

As it turned out, there was room and after the officers loaded on the plane, we got on. There was a first-class for the officers, and then we went on toward the back. We could see into the first-class cabin, and there was a young, blond Airman First Class making on over the officers and they were coming on to her just as quickly. When another enlisted man would come through, they all looked like they were being bothered and interrupted. I sat there thinking, "just one more instance of us grunts getting kicked in the ass."

The plane was ready to leave, and she moved back a step or two toward the door to help close it. Evidently, there was some kind of prop wash or suction, because a strong gush of air ripped off her hair—her beautiful blond wig that is! She was ugly as homemade sin. Chopped off, black, butch hair that now made her face look like a gaudy, over-made-up clown face. Suddenly, the entire back cabin erupted in howling laughter. There was nothing the young officers could do but bury their faces in the nearest magazines. Maybe sometimes a grunt gets a break, too. All she could do was chase after her best feature as it kept scurrying away from her in the wind like a leap frog or a piece of paper caught in a draft.

This time there was only minor surgery at Walter Reed. The pockets of infection were still a problem, but nothing like before. There were plenty of scars and plenty of bad memories that were reawakened when I walked back in the place, but I was gaining my weight back, getting stronger, and feeling better about myself. They placed me in the convalescent barracks, and about all I had to do was spend time by myself and let them check me out every day or so.

I thought more and more about Vietnam. By now the newspapers and television reporters, some of the college kids my age in the street, were beginning to get more and more openly critical of Vietnam. That hurt. It was my country, too. I loved it, too. I wasn't a war monger, a killer. I didn't feel any hate toward what they were saying. They just didn't understand. The only thing they were right about as I could see it was the way too much politics had gotten involved. If the politicians had given the military its way, we could have been in Hanoi in six months. Everyone over there knew this. The people starting to cry out in the media and on the college campuses wouldn't take time to see the trees for the forest, the soldiers for the war. We weren't all that different at all.

I kept talking to the doctors about how much better I felt, and how I was ready—ready to go back. There must have even been some place right there in Washington—maybe Bobby's friend at the Pentagon—where I could volunteer. They understood and weren't cold about it, but the answer was no. It didn't matter how much I put on the good ole boy convincing act, the answer was still no. Almost any kind of wound, they explained, with all the damage that had been done already and my having no spleen to hold a supply of blood, and I would be dead. They couldn't agree to put my life in danger, and it wouldn't be fair to put me in a position in which I might endanger someone else. There was no convincing them.

Instead of Vietnam, I was assigned to Fort Carson in Colorado. The high altitude would be good for my lungs; make them work harder and get stronger faster. But, I protested, it was a mechanized unit, a tank and armored personnel carrier unit, a leg unit! My protests didn't make an inch of headway.

Since another leave was built into a change of station, I was back on my way to Florida after having only been there a month before. I was on stand-by at Andrews Air Force Base, but nothing was opening up for Homestead. I got to talking to a girl whose father was an officer in Vietnam; she had been waiting for a flight most of the day, too.

Nothing came for either of us, and I was planning to stay the night. She invited me to go back home with her and come back the next day. I agreed. It was the nicest house I had ever been in. Her family was as kind to me as people could be; I might as well have been a brother or a son. It seemed like doing something for me, because I had been in Vietnam, was like doing something for the father who was gone. There was nothing sexual about it, nothing like the movies—just nice, almost like home.

As soon as I got back, the party scene started again. The reminders of the promises weren't as strong this time, but they were still there. The faster I ran, the less I seemed to think about God. I would wring the hours out of the day until I was exhausted and would not have to lie there in the dark at night, not being able to sleep, and have to think about it all.

One afternoon I had a date with a girl I had dated before Vietnam. We had planned to go over to Davie to a new tourist attraction that had a kind of Western movie setting. There were people dressed up like cowboys and indians, all kinds of Western gift shops, and a train ride on what was built to look like an old-time steam locomotive with two or three passenger cars and a red caboose.

The girl and I got on the caboose and climbed up into the observation room. We were sitting there talking, and I wasn't paying much attention to anything that was going on. I hadn't thought about how a regular part of something like this would be a mock holdup with actors playing parts. Before I knew what was going on, one of the actors had run into the caboose and was beneath me firing a shot. I leaped on him like a cat, disarmed him, and had him pinned to the floor of the caboose before my senses came to me. What a damn fool I felt like, besides scaring the girl and the poor guy half out of their minds. I apologized over and again to the people standing in the caboose who had been previously enjoying the whole show. They edged back and gathered their children closer to them to give this "crazy man" more space. Needless to say, the girl was interested in exactly no more dates with me.

My reflexes were so keen for survival that the slightest lapse in attention to exactly what was going on around me and I was set off. To most of the people who didn't understand, those same instincts that had saved life in Vietnam were comical here. They would point or whisper or even laugh out loud, but something that strong just didn't turn off on demand.

All it took was a car backfiring or a firecracker going off, and for a split second I was right back in the jungle. It's funny now but wasn't a bit funny then. I was up on a ladder painting the side of the house and had gotten into one of those kind of near trances that painting can bring on. Momma suddenly came around the corner of the house, flashing into my peripheral vision unexpectedly. I was off the ladder on her and had her on the ground in a moment. She didn't say anything, and all I could do was not look at her and climb back up and start painting again. That was a miserable feeling.

I got to Fort Carson in late July of 1966. At first it was fine, leg unit and all. The mountains were beautiful, and you could stand and look at Pike's Peak and get almost the same kind of overwhelming feeling that you got looking at the ocean. The company was just forming, so there wasn't much to do. They gave me a private room in an empty barracks. There was no work to do, no formations to stand, no one needing me to report to them.

It was like being lost. There was no increase in rank, no medals, not even the Combat Infantryman Badge I could now wear with a silver wreath because I had been in combat. About the only thing that gave me any contact with what had gone on before was the continual pain in my side. I had medication for it, but most of the time it didn't work all that well. I got tired of explaining how I felt and trying one more, different pill to see if it would work. It was easier just to tell them that you were doing OK, even though you were not.

I began to get the idea, especially when I discovered more and more people like myself who were there, that it was all a kind of military, bureaucratic charade. If they sent you up here and left you till your time was up, they didn't have to give you a medical discharge that would cost them money for the rest of your life. It was almost as if they had created this place to be a kind of shelf where you would be set back out of the way until it was all over.

It didn't do a bit of good, but I would regularly go down to the company commander's office and volunteer for Vietnam. I wanted to go back. I wanted to go back as a door gunner on a helicopter. They needed volunteers for that. It was dangerous enough duty that airborne-trained volunteers always got put to the head of the line. There was no cooperation, almost as if they had been given their orders about what to do with me. Still I went back and still they said no.

The new men began to drift in, and I was kind of a novelty to them. When I got out of the barrack's shower, they would see my scars and look with a kind of wonder in their eyes. There was one lieutenant in particular. He wanted to get to Vietnam almost as badly as I did. Way into most nights he was on the foot of my bed or sitting in the floor leaning against the wall, wanting to know it all and asking a million questions. Part of me wanted to tell him to stay away, to do anything to stay away. He'd be sorry if he went. Part of me understood exactly what he was feeling, only more.

My promotion to Spec 4 finally came through; that is, they finally figured out that I wasn't dead. The delay in getting the new classification took so long that it had cost me a lot of money, but they didn't trouble with that.

Finally, I got so stir crazy that I went asking for something, anything to do. They assigned me to a supply sergeant, an older man who had also been to Vietnam. He took me under his wing, and there was at least someone that I had something in common with. We would get up in the morning, drive into the field with whatever materials were needed for the various units for the day's training, and then have the rest of the day pretty much to ourselves.

He would take me into town at night, and I admitted to him how I was still hurting. He smoked pot and convinced me that it could help with the pain. I hadn't really seen anything like this before. When I was in Vietnam, if it was there I didn't see it. There was no good reason not to try it. I hadn't made any promises about pot, so I started smoking a little. It really didn't do anything. I wished it had, if the pain would stop. I got a better "buzz" off of the beer that I really didn't like all that much.

They moved a roommate in about halfway through the training cycle. He had been in Vietnam, too. After a while, I got to telling him about the pain since he had been a medic. At Fort Carson, he was serving as a Specialist Fifth Class medic and working in the base hospital. He told me I had better tell the doctors all about it, but if I did he knew that they would never, ever let me go back. He had access to some stronger medicine, and finally there was some relief. I was wanting to get off this hill. It was getting on toward the late fall and getting colder than any boy from the South ever wants to be. I couldn't imagine spending the winter trapped up in those mountains.

Amazing coincidences can happen sometimes when you least expect them. I say coincidences because it was for sure that God didn't owe me any breaks. I was getting checked out for the hundredth time at the Fort Carson hospital, when the doctor who was doing the checkup—a new man that I had not seen before kind of nonchalantly looked up at me and told me that he had worked on me in Vietnam. He had been at the field hospital and remembered how I should have been dead, how I was thought to be dead. He knew how many times they had given up on me during that first several hours, but tried one more time, one more technique, and it had worked. Now, I had someone that I could talk to, someone who could help me perhaps; at least I could tell him everything except about the pain that just wouldn't go away.

It took about a month, a month of almost everyday contact. I would try to explain why I had to go back, and he would halfway understand and then not understand. I would have him almost ready to clear me, and then he would back out. You simply didn't send a man without a spleen back into combat. He said it again and again, but I persisted. Finally, he gave in, the clearance papers were prepared, and it only took about four weeks for the new orders to come down. It was back to Florida for the standard leave, and then I was to report to the same departure point as before in Oakland, California, on February 28, 1967.

The last leave pretty much drug out, not like the ones before that were over before you knew it. I would go to the Everglades and ride airboats with my friends; we would do some partying around, but my mind was somewhere else. Momma didn't know what I was about to do until only a few days before I left. She told me later that when I said I was going back she thought my mind had been affected. What she told me at the time, characteristic of her own strength and determination again, was that she didn't understand, but I had to live my own life. She hated it, but I had to do what I felt I had to do.

"I just have to, Momma. I just have to." It was all I could say. It was all that I knew myself. . . .

There was a two-day layover in Oakland waiting to go out. I watched a lot of TV. There was more and more about Vietnam. I was magnetized by it all. The TV pictures created new images in my own mind. I sat there in the room, attention riveted on the set, my images mixing with those in the tube, creating a fantasy fog of memory and expectation as the smoke from my cigarettes mixed with the stirring, blinking light images of people half a world away; a world that I would be in before week's end.

As the plane lifted off and the lights along the shoreline disappeared below us, as we chased the sun already lighting that jungle over there, I breathed a sign of relief. All along the last several days I had expected someone to come up and tell me that it was all off, that I had been found out. I was chasing something else too—a new clarity that had been lost in all of the confusion, a clarity about Vietnam and about myself. Maybe in a way, I was chasing God, too. I hadn't kept the promises, but I could do this. Maybe it would help.

I also was running—from that self that had been bred in the point blank fire of that Vietnamese foxhole and had come to fruition in more hospital wards than I could remember.

I also was running—from God, from all that I had said I would do and hadn't.

Running from God.

Chapter XVI

As the plane landed at Tan Son Nhut, it was like a different world from what I had seen less than two years before. For all practical purposes we might just as well have landed at Miami International or Wright-Patterson in Washington. Everything was as modern as all of the new technology in the world would allow. No more steel stripping on the taxi ways or runways; everything was the finest concrete now. No more hastily built control towers or hangers; only the most solid and new structures that money could buy. Even as I looked out the window at the new and modern runways, construction equipment in the distance was building more.

I remembered the old smells of the pungent, alive jungle that moved in through the warm humidity when I had gotten off of the plane before. This time there was nothing but the smell of jet fumes and burning diesel fuel, so thick that you could hardly get your breath. There was mad rushing on every side as people quickly removed luggage and equipment in a race to get this plane out of the way so that the others creeping through the landing pattern that was stacked overhead could get on the ground. I was wrong; Miami International at its peak hours was nothing like this.

Stretching out from the airfield a new city had grown up since I had left. As far as the eye could see in every direction, American military architecture had taken over the land with every kind of barracks and warehouse that could be imagined. I was absolutely overwhelmed. I could not imagine that it was even the same place.

Still, in the midst of all of this, I was excited; the first real excitement that wasn't forced or totally put on that I could remember for months. Now, finally I was on my way back. People talk sometimes about a "sense of place" —maybe about their old homeplace or somewhere that has special memories—that's what I was feeling at that moment. I was back where I should be. It sure wasn't home, but I had left something of myself here that I had to try to find again.

We were almost raced off the plane to waiting trucks and carried across Saigon to a processing center just like before. The old sights were there again—the roadside shops, the mass of bicycles, the high-pitched voices of barter, the fish smell. But there was more this time, more Americans. Intermingling with and appearing to outnumber the Vietnamese were every color and type, every rank and insignia of the American military that was imaginable. It looked like the entire population of Fort Gordon or Fort Campbell had been turned loose on liberty all at once. I knew that Johnson was sending more troops all the time, but I had never kept up with the numbers. It was amazing.

The traffic on the sidewalks that overflowed into the sides of the streets was matched by the traffic in the streets that threatened to overflow onto the sidewalks. Jeeps, deuce-and-a-halfs, large flatbeds, American cars, expensive foreign cars—and running around like ants in the midst of elephants, more and more bicycles. I had never been to New York City at rush hour; in fact, I'm not sure that I had ever been in much of a rush hour anywhere, but it had to be something like this. It must have taken us half a day in the heat and noise to go ten miles. Unbelievable!

I had assumed that all my plans and orders were as they were supposed to be. When people asked me where I was going, I told them to some assault helicopter company as a door gunner. That was the plan; that was what I had volunteered for. People started filtering out to one unit and then another, and I was simply waiting around the processing center, watching all of the air traffic in and out of Tan Sun Nhut, confidently expecting my helicopter assignment at any time.

The assignment finally came through, but it was everything except what I had expected. No helicopters for me, but a job as a Security Police unit operating in Saigon itself. No helicopter, no field duty in a battle zone, not even Military Police—damn, do-nothing Security Police watching Vietnamese unload cargo and trying to make sure they didn't steal anything. Somebody had screwed me over. Somebody had passed the word. I should have known better—they weren't going to send anybody with my injuries into a battle zone. The doctor at Fort Carson had told me that; the commanding officers, too. I guess it was easier for them to get rid of my constantly being a pain in the ass, knowing all the time that when I got over here it would be for some shit-duty assignment like Security Police.

I was carried back to Tan Son Nhut where the company headquarters had been established. We were housed in an old soccer stadium that had been made over into a barracks and assembly ground. Compared to any of my previous Vietnam accommodations, this was like staying at some kind of grand hotel. There was absolutely everything that you could have found in any medium-sized American town: hot water, hot meals, private rooms, fans, movies, bars, even churches.

The only thing I noticed that seemed strange was that all we had built was carefully enclosed behind high walls. The walls had barbed wire and concertina wire strung on top of them, and when the concrete had been poured what looked like broken pieces of thick coke bottle glass had been placed in it. If anyone tried to get across that wall, they would cut themselves to shreds. What were they expecting or afraid of. Surely to God, "Charlie" wasn't anywhere close to us. There was just no way that all of this America which was spread out around me could be penetrated by any enemy. It seemed strange.

My duty assignment was just like having an ordinary civilian-type job. We got up at the same time every morning, showered and had breakfast, and then were taken by truck into the city. We relieved a night shift, and then sat in warehouses along the Saigon River and watched "coolies" unload ships. They stationed us at desks about a hundred yards apart. You could yell to someone else if you really needed to, but for the most part there was no contact with any other Americans for most of the day. You carried an M-16 and wore an "SP" armband and symbol on your helmet. I finally got to the place that the Vietnamese could have carried the whole damn warehouse off and I would not have cared; my biggest enemies were boredom and fighting off sleep.

I hated it, and what I hated most was the way the natives were always watching your every move, always staring at you. It was like they knew something that you didn't know, were planning something that you could not know about, talking in their strange sounding whispers about private information that you would find out about in their own good time. Their yellow-toothed grins and fake smiles were getting on my nerves—and they knew it as well as I did. You didn't have to worry about leeches here or ants crawling in your every body opening, but they were like ants finally—crawling all over you, hovering, scooting in and out of shadows without making sounds. I hated it.

Everything fell into a kind of boring routine. To work, to barracks, to work, to barracks. Watching Vietnamese, being watched by Vietnamese, watching Vietnamese. In the end, more than anything else, I began to feel degraded by the assignment. Finally, you didn't care much about anything, and I despised that feeling.

We would go into town occasionally. You had to be careful to stick to the main streets and watch what was happening around you all the time. There had started being some of the terrorist type of activities, and you would hear of a bombing or a killing here and there. The main streets, which you began to feel were filled with the enemy, were relatively safe in the daytime; they didn't want to kill their own people, so you were safe, too.

The best safety idea that was passed around was to find a young Vietnamese boy to walk around with you. Although they might be no more than ten or twelve years old, they were working for the North Vietnamese and Viet Cong. This might not have been true in every case, but you never knew. If you paid them, they would show you around to the best places to eat or the places where the best bargains were on anything you wanted to buy. If there was going to be trouble, they somehow knew when or where. There was a great desperation to get American dollars, so it was just a pragmatic trade-off all the way around; you paid for safety, and they got U. S. money. In the end, they could buy weapons on the world market with those dollars, so what you paid for now would reap double dividends—safety for a few hours in Saigon and the hostile fire that would be directed at you later on. I knew about this money business and simply refused to do it. A lot of people did. I didn't mind giving the Vietnamese piasters and they probably kept hanging around thinking that American money would follow—but it never did, not from me.

In spite of the possibilities, I always felt close to the kids and tried to be kind to them. I thought that most of us didn't have any idea of the hardships they had been brought up under. I would go into town and buy candy to give them, and before you knew it they would have you surrounded. Finally, you would have to throw the candy up into the air away from you to keep from being trampled.

The black market in Saigon was unbelievable. Anything that you could buy in any store in the United States was right there on the street. The prices were unbelievably low, but since it was probably all stolen there was 100% profit. Everyone was making money off the war. There were payoffs on every side. The Americans, Vietnamese, and North Vietnamese might be trying to kill each other on battlefields, but here they had found a higher God. Men were reinlisting just to keep their blackmarket scams going. Families were sending all they had to soldiers in the city, where American money could be tripled in its value in a moment. It was all illegal, but drop five bucks here or there and all of the appropriate authorities would look the other way. The black market sometimes looked like it had brought more American civilians than Vietnamese.

I wasn't interested. Somehow I got the idea that somebody who was here for the right reasons was the first one to get taken in when the schemes started coming down. I bought a few trinkets to send back home and contraband cigarettes, but that was about it. I would eat some of the food, and most of it was very good. However, this place needed a Burger King; that instinct from long ago had, at least, been on target. Sometimes I would buy drinks for a "Baby San"—usually in her late teens or early twenties. I knew full well that what I was paying for was watered down "Saigon Tea," and even though the English was broken and the smiles usually forced, it was at least someone to talk to and pass the time. I didn't have money for anything else. Very carefully, the majority of the small amount I was being paid went straight to Momma. There was still the compelling need to pull my part of the load.

I finally had all of the boring routine I could stand. One more day watching Vietnamese watching me, and I would go out of my mind. The boredom, the tension of doing something that was not me in any way, kept on mounting, and as it did, the pain in my side got more and more severe. If I didn't have to think about it, I didn't notice it too much—unfortunately, all I had to do was think about it.

I went in to the captain of the company. I explained with great passion all that had happened and why I had volunteered to come back. I felt that a commitment had been made to me. I had done my part, and then some, but the Army hadn't done its part. I wanted to be back with the kind of people I had trained with, that I had fought with. I wanted to be with a unit that had some sense of pride. Then I guess I went to far; this unit had no pride.

He simply listened, and then just as simply denied my request. I didn't know why. Maybe he had orders on me restricting my combat exposure. Maybe I pissed him off with my comment about the unit having no pride. Maybe he just didn't care. It would have to be my problem. The pain mounted.

About a week passed, and I went back in. I had made up my mind that I was either going to a helicopter unit or I was going home. When I went in to make my plea the second time, the pain was so intense that it was all that I could do to stand straight to make the proper salute.

He listened again, unhurried and maybe even sympathetic. Was I making progress? Then, just as unhurried—denied again. I fell flat in a heap in the floor. I don't know for how long, but I began to come to while a group of medics were putting me on a stretcher to carry me out.

The medics took me to the main hospital there on the base, and efforts started being made to check out my records, give me something for the pain, and start treatment with some antibiotics for the infection that was evidently coming back. I am convinced now that attitude and infection somehow work together; the worse I felt about what I was doing, the more pain that came. If I could do what I came to do, I felt sure the pain would go.

What I wanted seemed to make no difference at all. It was clear within hours that they knew exactly what they would do with me; I was going back home.

The next day the captain of the Security Police unit walked in and stood beside my bed. We looked at each other for a moment, and then he pulled a chair up and sat down close to the side of the bed. It was almost like he was deciding to say something but hadn't totally decided to say it. Then, swallowing and deciding to go on with it, he leaned closer. Could he talk off the record for a moment? "Why not," I responded, what difference did it make now.

He explained that he had seen all of my record and had looked it over with great care. He could understand where I was coming from, but he felt like he knew better, that he was doing me a favor keeping me out of the field. All that talk about pride, I was exactly right. The Security Police was a shit detail, no doubt about it. He had been an infantry officer in the field himself. For reasons he didn't go into, that had all stopped. He was as frustrated as I was. Watching people unload a boat was no place for a soldier.

He was prepared to pull whatever strings I needed, but he wanted to let me know one more time that he was against it. What about the pain? Was it too much? How could I fight with pain?

My answer was easy. Give me a chance to get back in it the way I want to, and the pain will not be a problem. It might even stop all together. I didn't need to go home. I needed my chance and that was all that I was asking.

"OK, soldier, OK," and he shook my hand and left. Most of the pain seemed to walk out the door with him.

Whoever was in charge of the ward came back around not long after that. He had heard that I was feeling a lot better and was ready to return to my unit. Had the Captain already told them that? Were they just going to let me go that easily? I played the role right on out: "Yeah, I'm fine. Must of just been some kind of virus or something I ate." Hell, it didn't really make all that much difference to them; just one less patient to have to keep up with. I was ready and gone before they could change their minds.

I waited around the soccer field barracks for a couple of days, and my new orders can in. I had been assigned to the 121st Assault Helicopter Company which was a part of the 13th Aviation Brigade located down along the Mekong Delta at Soc Trang about one hundred miles south of Saigon. There was a short helicopter flight to Can Tho, a command area for the group, and then on out to Soc Trang.

All the way down, I started feeling more and more at home. The countryside leveled out like the flatlands of Florida and the Everglades. It was especially pretty. When the French had been in here, they had dug canal systems for irrigation and had helped the people put in farmlands. It all looked just like the canals running out of the Everglades and Lake Okeechobee. If you weren't riding in the midst of all the Army green, you could swear you were somewhere south of Jupiter heading toward Miami.

The French had built the base at Soc Trang, and the first thing that caught your eye as the base came in sight was part of their creation—a swimming pool, a damn swimming pool! This was more like it—a hell of a lot better than sitting on your ass in a warehouse staring at "coolies."

There were helicopters everywhere. The overall company had gunships, troop carriers called "slicks," and large two-bladed Chinooks for transport. All of them carried M-60 machine guns in one pattern or another. The slicks were UH1Ds that carried a pilot and co-pilot, a crew chief who served as mechanic and gunner, and a gunner. Its primary objective was to take in and bring out groups of ten or twelve troops. Because of its slow speed at landing and takeoff, it had to have defensive weapons. The two M-60s, one mounted on each side, constituted that defense.

The gunships were Huey UH1Cs and were designed to be offensive weapons of the highest order. They were smaller and faster and were not designed to carry troops. Besides the free handed M-60s, a new experience for me which allowed the guns to be fired without the limitations of the mounts and which I liked— you felt more like the weapons was a part of you, this helicopter could be outfitted to carry two rocket pods with seven to fourteen rockets in each pod, and two M-60 "flex kits" that were controlled by the pilot. With the configuration of weapons, the chopper had a fire power of 2400 rounds per minute. The Chinooks were CH47Bs, and they carried troops, supplies, and acted as sky-wreckers to pull out damaged slicks and gunships. When they were used in this last capacity, they were referred to as "shit-hooks." The Chinooks sometimes had side gunners with M-60s, depending on how they were being used. Later on, Cobra gunships came in, and they were even sleeker than the Huey's. Rapid fire "Gatling Guns" or automatic grenade launchers could be mounted under the noses of these choppers and their deadliness was increased all the more.

It didn't take two minutes after landing to know that you were around a class operation. Everything was organized and clean. The people you talked to knew what they were talking about. I was immediately taken to the head gunner, and something about his whole dress and the way he carried himself let you know that he was the clearing house. If he liked what he saw, you went on; if not, some other different strategy must have already been in place.

He looked me over, and all of my credentials were right there for him to see: the shoulder chevron of the 101st Airborne, the jump wings, the Combat Infantryman's Badge with its surrounding wreath indicating combat under fire, a bar of battle ribbons from the first time in Vietnam, and the "expert" badges for the M-16 and the M-60. We talked. I was welcome. He found out all he needed to know.

The next stop was the company commander's office. What the head gunner approved, he approved. His welcome was genuine, as was the feeling he had for his company, its importance in the larger scheme of things in this war, and the place that was mine and the way they were depending on me. He stood and we shook hands. This was where I needed to be.

The rest of the afternoon was spent with the head gunner. He took me around the base and showed me where everything was. All along the way there was one introduction and then another. The people seemed real. The officers and enlisted men seemed to blend in together better; there wasn't as much saluting or detailed military protocol. A dozen or so people were lying out by the pool, like college kids on spring break in Lauderdale. There was a large mess hall and PX, generators for lights, and—of all things—a shower. I might be up in that helicopter with people shooting at me, but there would be no leeches or ants or mud; I could, by God, come home at night and take a shower and sleep on a bed. That the idea of "home" slipped into my thinking seemed strange indeed. I never felt that way at the soccer field.

We checked out a slick. That would be my first assignment. Prove myself there and the gunships might be a possibility. The M-60s were no problem. I could literally run them blindfolded. The mountings and ammunition feeding system were a little different, but I could handle the gun. I might not have confidence in some areas, but I could handle the gun. He saw that. There was no problem. He showed me how to hook the "monkey belt" around my waist and secure it to the floor of the chopper. There would be many times when it was your lifeline, especially when the angles of fire got severe and you were standing outside the troop compartment on the skids firing away.

There was strong caution about the back blade and keeping a respectful distance from it. It wasn't going to hit you in the hand or leg, he explained; it would hit you in the head. Before I left Soc Trang it happened, and some poor guy was killed instantly.

Then came the first real perks. We went to the supply building and checked out some of the equipment I would need: a flight jacket, a bullet proof vest, long, soft leather gloves, an M-14, and—literally the crowning piece—the flight helmet. In fact, I got two, one to wear while my personal helmet was taken into town to be personalized in the colors of my own unit. John Wayne would have loved this. There were other perks, too; Vietnamese women who did your laundry and shined your shoes for $5.00 a month; an infantry company continually patrolling and securing the base's perimeter with the help of large German Shepherd dogs.

You could absolutely lie down and sleep without worrying whether your partner would stay awake, worrying whether you would wake up with a North Vietnamese knife slitting your throat. This "Eden" lasted for quite a while, until enemy ground to ground rockets were introduced in the Delta and we became an immediate target.

We would leave early in the morning. Getting ready and getting into all of the uniform, the fiberglass protective plates that fitted around you, and hooking into the belt and gun made you feel like an astronaut getting ready to go to the moon or a professional football player gearing up for the Superbowl. The gun and the helicopter were an extension of you as a person; you never felt that you were an extension of some kind of impersonal machine. You felt confidence and power. And the mobility and being able to see so much—not like the pitch black jungle at night—gave you a feeling, not exactly of safety all of the time, but of options and options meant freedom.

And as much as anything, when you took off, built speed, and began to move off to your particular assignment for the day, there was always a good, strong—cool—breeze. You didn't spend days soaking in your own sweat. You didn't stink!

We would move first to a troop staging area; sometimes the troops would be brought to our base. Our unit was mainly working with South Vietnamese infantrymen—maybe eight or ten in a group with one or two American Special Forces advisors. We would sweep into a landing zone with maybe twenty other choppers, lay down cover fire when it was necessary, and let them out. Off we would go to get more troops, or to return to base. Late in the afternoon, like the most punctual taxis, we returned to pick them up and take them out. In some respects, it was the same thing every day, but on a more significant level, every day with its new mission was different.   It was everything that I had envisioned it to be.

The highest feeling of all: sweeping in out of the clouds along a tree line, the ground full of fire below you, and the people down below depending on your coming for their very lives. Feeling like a savior coming to rescue dying men—a savior. How many times I had wanted to help in my life. How many times I had wanted to help and could not. Now, I was helping every day, sometimes ten times a day. That which had been empty and incomplete was now being filled. It was the nearest thing to a religious experience I had ever had. It was only surpassed by that moment when I was lying in the field bleeding to death and I experienced the presence of God in the total peace that had come convincing me that I would be all right. Now, I felt the peace that rises in those circumstances when people do exactly what they feel that they are somehow supposed to do. All the psychologists in the world, with all their talk about self-actualization and self-fulfillment, ought to have this experience. It is precisely what all the books are talking about.

Chapter XVII

There was no way to keep up with the number of missions we flew. It was like an over-the-road truck driver trying to keep his travel log up to date. All we knew was that we flew everyday, sometimes three or four times a day. On a rare occasion, the helicopter might be off the line for repairs, but more times than not the head gunner of the company would assign me to fly out with another chopper. From time to time there were even volunteer missions, and I repeatedly found myself being asked to go on these. Usually, they didn't even have to ask. It wasn't so much that I was gung-ho; it just seemed like it was the thing to do.

We were given air medals for the number of missions we flew. After so many missions a new medal was awarded. The first two or three were special, and I was very particular to keep up with them and wear them at the appropriate times. After a while, I lost track of how many there were.

Most of the time we were flying with South Vietnamese regular army and special forces troops. A unit of South Vietnamese were then accompanied by an American Special Forces advisor. I could identify with these men much more than the rest of the crews that I worked on. I had been exactly where they were—and where they were going. I knew the quiet looks on their faces as we prepared to set down into a landing zone reflected what they were thinking inside. I knew how their hearts were beating and what the lumps felt like that were rising in their throats. Part of me wanted to go out that door with them; there was another part that thanked God when the chopper was empty and we were back on our way.

I especially felt for the American advisor. He was essentially by himself. Sure, there were a lot of experiences that you didn't need to know the language to talk to someone else about. Sure, on some basic level they were all human beings caught up in those desperate kinds of cruel life experiences that bring everyone to the same level. But it sure did help to have somebody to talk to that knew where you came from, that could appreciate the things you liked to eat, that knew what a baseball game or a best girl were all about, that you could talk to about your brothers and sisters or your mother. If you got hit out there, you somehow wanted your own people to be around you, especially if it might be your last moments.

We worked all over the Mekong Delta, and as my time progressed in the unit, we started going closer and closer to the Cambodian border. The North Vietnamese could come down through Cambodia almost the entire length of Vietnam without ever experiencing any resistance at all. Then, all they had to do was raid straight across to the east. When we struck back, they could jump back into Cambodia, and we had to stop at the border. I wondered why they could use that border to their advantage any time they wanted to, and we had to respect it like it was the Great Wall of China. Real wars don't have borders. It was like playing a game with one hand tied behind you. Like playing checkers with two sets of rules—one for you, one for your opponents. About the best we could do was to drop the South Vietnamese in with their American advisors, and let them try to keep the backdoor to the whole country protected while other groups, like those that I had been in, carried the fight to the North Vietnamese along the Demilitarized Zone and in the mountains.

One morning we dropped into a staging area to routinely pick up our first group of the day. A whole line of choppers approached, and the various groups were spread out along a long roadway in groups of ten. We landed, an ARVN unit piled onto the chopper, and the American advisor—a lieutenant—climbed on behind them. There was always a little scramble for the best seats, which meant a place where you could hang your feet out the door onto the skids and get a good cool breeze.

I recognized the American officer. He was the same lieutenant who had stuck so close to me with all his questions about Vietnam at Fort Carson back in Colorado. He had finally gotten his wish. We both looked at each other for a minute, and then it dawned on us both at about the same time where we had met. We were happy to see each other. Really, "happy" isn't exactly the right word. Anytime you had contact with someone you knew from back home, it was like the very existence of "back home" was reaffirmed. We talked and laughed around like two school kids while we made our way on toward the landing zone. After fifteen or twenty minutes, it was like we kind of ran out of anything to say. We both knew that we were almost there. I went back to the gun and got ready.

The landing zone was "hot." They knew we were coming; they almost always knew we were coming. You could see the gunships working their circles in the distance, low along the tree lines, coming in, sweeping by as they spread their fire, pulling around, and running another sweep. The smoke and fire of tracer bullets were picking at the tree line. You could see a little flash or smoke of return fire; not much though. They were dug in now. Their return fire would come at us when we landed.

If a zone was as hot as this one, two more things would probably happen—if we were lucky, and more especially if these ground troops were lucky. A group of four or five jets would come in, almost out of nowhere, and lay down a line of napalm along through the trees. It would not kill all the enemy soldiers, but it would stop things for a moment or two. Then, a smoke chopper would come in—if the landing zone was wide enough—and lay down a smoke barricade between the tree line and where we would land. It all helped, but it was so obvious where we would have to come down that they could shoot at us with great accuracy without even seeing us.

We entered the patterns of the jets and gunships. This is when you had to be really careful. You had about as much chance of hitting your own people as you did the enemy. The idea was for the helicopter gunners to eat away at the tree line with their M-60s. This should cause the enemy to at least keep their heads down while you landed and unloaded. Most of the time, if the initial saturation was strong enough, the process worked pretty well. You were receiving fire, but there were not many choppers or their crews that were lost at this point.

We were on the ground. Dust, smoke, noise, bedlam was roaring all around. This wasn't going to take but a short few seconds. We were ripping away with our guns and people were piling off the chopper all around. They wanted down on the ground at that moment. Hovering like we were made everyone a sitting duck. In fifteen seconds, they might be looking up at us as we pulled away, but at the moment of landing you didn't have to ask people to get out of the chopper and take cover. They were good troops, and this was their home. They leaped into the landing zone and toward the enemy in the tree line with a vengeance.

The lieutenant was the first one out. In the midst of it all, him on the ground organizing his unit and me at the door blazing away with the gun, our eyes met. Part of him wanted to go with me; part of me wanted to go with him. He looked a lot older than I could remember. And we were gone.

The chances of us running into each other again were very slim. When you let people out in the mornings, you always wondered what happened to them. You might come back to the exact landing zone that afternoon or in the next couple of days, but it seemed like the people were never the same. Maybe they changed while they were on the ground, especially the new ones that had never been out before. I never saw the lieutenant again.

The hardest group missions were those when you were having to get people out at the end of a battle, and the enemy was still pressing the fight in around your exit spot with all the fury of having someone on the run and being ready to annihilate them. At one and the same time, you had to be providing cover fire, and also be getting panicked and wounded troops on the chopper. You also had to be careful about how many got on. More than about a dozen and there was too much weight for you to climb. That made you, under a difficult rescue setting, too good of a target. You had to do something about this kind of a situation, or you were almost certain to lose everyone on board and the chopper, too.

Late one afternoon they scrambled us out a little more quickly than normal, and we headed up the delta to the northwest. You could tell from the speed of the choppers—about a dozen or so of us—that we were needed somewhere in a hurry. We talked back and forth over the intercom, and found out that a small South Vietnamese outpost was under attack and about to be overrun. We had to get them out.

The South Vietnamese would go in to what looked like the middle of nowhere and build outposts along the river. There would be a kind of triangular, fort-like structure pointing out toward the river, mostly made out of high mud banks and sandbags. These outposts would allow the South Vietnamese to keep an eye on the river and hopefully prevent the enemy from using the waterway to infiltrate or move supplies. Because the river was so important for these purposes, there was a continual attempt on the part of the North Vietnamese to knock out the outposts.

The real problem in this kind of situation was that the South Vietnamese soldier's family would follow him to places like this. Beyond the fort-like structure there would be a small field full of makeshift hooches. Women and children would be all around, almost like settlers creating a small village. When the outpost came under attack, and you came in to rescue, it wasn't simply soldiers you were trying to deal with—which was hard enough; there were women and children, old people and sometimes people who were crippled or hurt—this made matters infinitely worse.

It was pretty easy to tell what you were about to be in for when a situation came fully into view. In this particular one, the South Vietnamese soldiers and their families were backed up nearly into the river. Sometimes at distances of what looked like no more than a hundred yards, the enemy was crawling like invading ants toward them. There was fire all around. As we came in, a good deal of it started being directed at us. You could hear the sound of the bullets, and feel an occasional plinking sound as one round and then another penetrated into the underside of the chopper. We always counted bullets holes when we got back to base; there would be some serious counting this time.

In this kind of operation, the rescuing choppers were pretty much on their own. The enemy and the people that you were trying to rescue were too close together to drop napalm, and the gunships were only marginally helpful. You just simply had to go down in there and get them out. It was like going down into hell, but by God we went right on in. No hesitation. Go in and get them out.

You could land and shoot at the same time, providing some degree of covering fire. Maybe it helped, but it didn't seem like it. The main thing you had to do was to get the people on the chopper. At that point, you were completely in charge, and your decision ruled the day. No sooner had you set down than people were swarming in the dust and gunfire all around the chopper: children, old people, people carrying everything that they owned, people who were wounded, panicking soldiers.

Like those doctors who met the ambulances in the corridor at Walter Reed, in split seconds you were having to decide who could get on and who would have to wait—probably who would live and who would die.

I went for the children first. You could get more of them than soldiers. Then the women. Then the old people. Then the wounded. That all sounds pretty orderly, like you are putting up cue lines and everyone is standing exactly where they are supposed to. Of course, that wasn't the case. Everybody wanted to live, and that helicopter represented the only chance they had. They knew, beyond wounds or anything else, that if the North Vietnamese got hold of them that nothing on earth could fully describe what would happen.

I can remember coming in on one rescue when we were too late. The outpost had already been overrun by the time we got there. All we could do was pick up the pieces; the enemy had gone. Right out in the middle of the area where we would have to land, almost like a warning sign that had been posted, was a South Vietnamese soldier. He had been stripped of his clothing, lifted up and jammed down onto a sharpened bamboo pole. Blood was pouring out of his rectum and his feet were jerking just inches off of the ground. If that were not enough, the North Vietnamese had cut off his privates and stuffed them in his mouth. He was dying, but he wasn't dead yet. And there by his side was a wife and a small child, screaming, wailing, hugging at his jerking, twitching body, not being able to get him off the stake, not being able to do anything but scream as he choked to death on his own genitals.

That's what these people were running from when we landed to rescue them. That's what harmless old farmers and ancient "Momma Sans" were running from; the horror and terror of death that did not known how to be simple or easy, or dignified. People were stumbling, crawling, fighting, pushing—anything to get on the choppers. And you had to decide who left and who waited.

We would get all that we could, especially as many of the children as possible. Always there were more, and while you were trying to lift off, you were having to push away begging faces; having to cram your hands into the middle of the most desperate pleas that it is possible for a person to make. You didn't have any choice.

Always you had more than was safe for you, and the chopper strained and pulled as if the huge blades were going to bend and break, as if the motor was going to explode from exhaustion. Always two or three men—usually the soldiers—would grasp at

the skids and try to hold on. Anyway to get out. You didn't have
any choice. You were going to crash back down and everyone
would be lost. You didn't have any choice. You had to start
stomping with all of your might on their hands to make them let
go. Some fell off immediately. Some were able to take more pain
than you could imagine was possible. They were yelling and
pleading, their hands were bursting apart under your blows. I can
remember one time in particular when one man was up well
above the tree line when he finally fell loose. The scream fell away
and disappeared into the din of the last desperate moment of
resistance below. He never looked away from the chopper until he
hit the ground. You didn't have any choice.

On this particular rescue—although that word sounds greatly
qualified now—there was one little girl, maybe she was nine years
old. She was right in the edge of the weeds where we set down. I
grabbed her into the chopper first. I noticed she was carrying a
small cooking stove strapped on her back, and normally I would
have thrown it out. In the melee there was not time; there were
other kids in the weeds.

When we finally got airborne and pulled away, I began to notice
her. Somehow someone in her family had scavenged some high
octane jet fuel, and had been using it to cook in the stove. It was a
wonder they had not killed themselves with what was little more
than a bomb. At any rate, in all of the firefight and rush for safety,
the fuel had begun to leak out onto her back. It was literally eating
her skin off. The pain must have been terrible, but she sat there
and did not make the first move. She didn't cry. She didn't move.
She took the pain. She probably knew more about pain than I had
learned in all of my life—all of my battle wounds notwithstanding.
I tried to help her, but couldn't get to her. I couldn't tell her or any
of her people to help her. She just sat there and rolled her big dark
eyes around. When they fell on me, there was even a hint of a
smile—as if somehow this big American who reached down and
pulled her up out of the weeds had saved her life.

Which in fact he had. That same big American who would
have done anything in the world to relieve her pain in that
moment. That same big American who had, five minutes before,
stomped on dying men's hands and sent them in a slow-motion
slide back into hell.

And what did we do with these people? Sometimes take them back to a base or to some kind of hospital area. More times than not, it was just a few miles away from the fire zone to another outpost—where they could probably count on the same thing happening again. Maybe tomorrow. Maybe in two weeks. But it would, inevitably, happen again.

Then, there was the blood. Everywhere. Rolling off you. Saturating your clothes. Standing in puddles in the floor of the chopper. Dripping over the edges of the doorway where the passing breeze sucked it out and dried it in creeping stains on the outside of the chopper. The first thing you had to do when you got back was to wash out the blood. If you waited in the heat, it coagulated into a thick sticky mess that was almost impossible to clean off. How foreign to everything you believed: to think of the life substance of another person as a mess that had to be cleaned up. But even through all the blood, even through the realization that you couldn't take them all of the way out, came the eyes—eyes saying "Thank you," "God bless you," or whatever eyes say when someone knows that you have just gone into the very depths of hell itself and brought them out. Maybe not forever, but in that last instant of life in that outpost fire zone, "forever" was the last thought on anyone's mind.

Occasionally, there would be a scramble call or a call for volunteers for a one or two helicopter mission. You almost always knew that these were going to be somehow unusual and without question dangerous. On one of these occasions, our chopper was scrambled, and we headed for a small hamlet up on the northwestern fringe of the delta. We knew there was a Special Forces unit stationed there, and they had been using patrol boats to watch the area up close to the Cambodian border.

When we arrived, a Special Forces major, the commander of this station, was waiting to climb on board at the landing zone. He carried an M-16 and wore a deadly serious look on his face. As we became airborne, he spoke through the intercom to the pilot. Directions were given to follow a small river that snaked into the delta out of Cambodia. He had sent an LRP (long range patrol) of four men on a small boat up the river the night before, and they should have long since returned. He knew that they were in trouble, and we had to find them. This particular pilot was new to the unit, had been a little hesitant about this mission, but took us on up the river maintaining an altitude of about 1500 feet—our typical "safe" running altitude that decreased the possibility of our being hit by random ground fire.

The LRPs were designed to be small, very secretive missions. They wanted to find out about enemy movement, but they were not designed to make contact. I had seen small reconnaissance boats shot all to hell, and felt that the chances of our finding anything good on this trip were pretty small. You could tell that the commander felt the same way.

Then, we spotted the small boat. It was obvious what had happened. The men in the boat had rounded a sharp turn in the river. In front of them, placed so they had no time for any real warning, the North Vietnamese had cut trees across the river. The men had turned to run back the way they had come, but other trees had been cut in behind them. They were trapped, and there was nothing that they could do. The boat was empty.

We began to circle and slow down enough to look for any evidence of life. The pilot carefully maintained altitude, in spite of the commander's request to go lower. Although the pilot was outranked, in this situation he was the "Aircraft Commander" and this status made rank on board beside the point. We kept looking.

Then, there they were. On a small triangle of beach that reached into the river, you could see four men, stripped nearly naked, staked out in a spread-eagle fashion. It looked like four large "X" marks on a tic-tac-toe board. The men weren't moving, at least from our altitude you couldn't see movement. You couldn't see blood either, so it was not clear if they had been shot.

God, I thought that my heart was going to pound out of my chest. I could almost feel what they must be feeling if they were still alive. They must be lying out there burning up in the hot sun. They must be thirsty, half out of their minds. Everything in creation must be crawling all over them. Now, they had heard the sounds of our chopper coming. Now, they could look up and see us hovering over them. They knew that we could see them, too.

But there was no question in anyone's mind that it was all a trap. There was just enough room for us to land, but the tree line and surrounding underbrush was bound to be full of the enemy, just waiting for us to pull an all-American rescue. The minute our chopper set down, there would be nine dead Americans, one downed chopper, and new weapons and ammunition to be used on other Americans. There was no question that it was a trap, but these were our people—and especially people just like I had been less than a year before. We had to go in after them.

The Special Forces commander started off talking to the pilot telling him how to make his approach and what we would do as we came down on the ground. The crew chief and I would blaze away with our two M-60s to provide cover, while the commander jumped onto the beach and freed the men. He talked as if it were all set and there would be no question.

The pilot spoke back, as calmly and as collected as a person could possibly be, that he was not taking the chopper and the men under his responsibility into that situation. Everyone would be killed. It was not a statement of cowardice in any way, simply a statement of fact. As the pilot read the circumstances, there was no other choice.

The commander tried to pull rank, but it did no good. The pilot simply reminded him that he was the Aircraft Commander. There was the threat of court martial and all kinds of other threats, but the pilot was not swayed. I wanted to go in, the crew chief wanted to go in—the very thought of those men staked out down there looking up to us for help absolutely took away any thought of personal safety. It didn't make any difference what we thought at this point; we weren't even players in this game.

The major yelled and cursed and hit at the back of the pilot's seat, but the pilot never even looked back. Finally, the commander pleaded with the pilot at least to go down closer so that he could see what was going on. We were ready at the guns to return any ground fire. The chopper began to drop altitude, maybe to a 1000 feet or 750 feet. The Special Forces major was hanging over the side looking down, pointing with his M-16.

Then, he opened fire. We opened fire. We hung there in space for maybe a minute throwing out every ounce of firepower we had. And we left.

No one said a word. No one looked at anyone else, at least not in the face.

Twenty years have now passed since that day. I can't really say with absolute certainty what happened out there. I wonder sometimes if part of me is still avoiding, still blocking out what happened. Maybe it is more than I can actually face. Maybe that's the special living hell of war: putting young men in situations where things happen that they can never face again.

I know what that Special Forces commander did. He shot his own men. Maybe they were already dead. They probably were. But, in the end, he did what he thought was all that he could do for them—even the best that he could do for them: to make sure that they didn't stay staked out there for another minute, to make sure that they would not be subject to the greater tortures of the enemy, which would now be increased because we had not taken their bait.

I'm not able to say for sure what I did, or what the crew chief did. I think the memory that stands out in the front of my mind is the tree line and the underbrush all around the clearing being cut and chewed and burned all to pieces by the fire of our M-60s. I'm afraid to look beyond that front of my mind to the possibility of something lying behind it that I don't want to see. Did I shoot our own men, too? I don't think so. I hope not. I would not have wanted to—but, on the other hand, had I been staked out on that beach, I would have seen what that commander did as an act of highest mercy. I would—without any question whatsoever—have wanted that for myself. I could conceive the act of mercy; I cannot conceive the alternative of being left in the hands of the enemy. I just don't know. Something about me wants to know. Something about me doesn't want to know. Mostly, I just want to forget it all. But it just keeps coming back.

We rode on away from the small beachhead toward evening. The beating of the chopper blades created a box of isolation; all you had were your thoughts and the image of the men staked out on the ground. We stopped long enough to let the commander out at his station. He didn't say a word or make any kind of eye contact; he simply walked away.

At the end of most missions, you spent time talking about all that had happened. Sometimes there was basic information, sometimes a lot of the relief of bragging, but there was always talking. It was a kind of way of getting everything out of your system. When we landed, we went about the necessary activities of securing the chopper, cleaning the guns, and storing our equipment. Nothing was said. We did our work in silence and walked off in four different directions. The mission never came up in conversation again.

For twenty years it has hung there like a ghost. I felt great guilt. Not the guilt of firing on the men; I don't think I really did that. But there was the undeniable and unrelenting guilt of not going in for them. Part of my mind now knows that the pilot made the right decision. I ought even to be thankful that I am alive today because of that decision. Another part of me could rest easier with having died trying. Seldom a week passes without the recollection of that mission leaping back into the front of my mind. Part of me died out there on that beach that day, and the mourning of that loss is as real as the air that I breathe.

There are other ghosts, too. Most of the time you shot cover fire into tree lines or covered underbrush long enough for troops to jump off of the chopper and take up their own firing positions. There were occasions, however, when you could flush the enemy out into the open or catch them on the run. They were sitting ducks and had no way of outrunning the chopper or your string of bullets.

Part of you felt that it was your time to pay them back for all the hurt and pain that you had seen inflicted on your own people. They deserved to pay—they were the enemy. You really never thought about this being another person, with hurts and fears, with families and friends, just like you. Maybe war wouldn't work if you allowed yourself those kinds of feelings. It was especially difficult to have feelings from the air. From the air, you only see people fall over in a heap. You can't always really be certain that you have hit them. You don't see the actual destruction that an M-60 round can do to a human body; you don't have to go in and pick up the pieces.

I can recall on one occasion catching a fleeing North Vietnamese in a wide field between two lines of trees and deep underbrush. The field was full of what looked like piles of straw that had been heaped up to dry out. The man ran, zigging and zagging, as the helicopter settled in behind him. The pilot drifted off to the side, and the running, stumbling figure came up right in under my side of the chopper. It would be an easy kill.

Somehow the running man must have felt that if he could get to one of the stacks of straw that he would be safe. I held back on my fire as the pilot held the chopper on a steady parallel line with the running man. It was clear which of the stacks he was now running for. I settled my sights in front of it and waited. He more or less ran straight into my line of fire as he reached the stack. Maybe he had time to think he was safe now. Maybe he had had time to let the thought cross his mind that something must be wrong with the guns on the chopper because no one was firing.

If those were his thoughts, they were his last thoughts. The fire from the M-60 caught him with the first rounds, went up his back, and threw him up against the stack of straw. He was pinned against it like a large flat dart piercing into a dart board. The tracer round smoked into the dry straw, and it ignited. We were by it all in a second and worked in the area for the next several minutes.

As we came out, we flew right back over the burning—now almost completely consumed—stand of straw. You could look right straight down on it. The co-pilot had seen it first and was telling us to look down. There in the middle of the stack was the dead, burning body lying on its back. The arms and legs were protruding out to the sides in an agonizing stretching grab. It looked like a huge cockroach caught in a terrifying trap.

I can remember getting back to the base and, as was almost always the case, the word getting around about this unusual kill. I must have repeated the story and the description of the dead man a dozen times. It was like the description of a bone-crushing tackle in a football game, or the knockout punch in a boxing match. There were congratulations all around.

On another occasion, we flushed out an enemy soldier in an open field where there was no place to hide. He had evidently been walking along without any thought of trouble, and we were suddenly on top of him. He did all of the running, twisting, and turning to avoid being shot. It didn't make much sense. He would have been better off to stop and turn and start firing on us. That would not have been much of a chance, but it was the only chance that he would have had. Instead he kept running and we kept closing in.

I started playing with him. We would pass and I would circle him with fire. The bullets would tear the ground up all around him, and the tracer fire was following him like a cloud. Part of me wanted to put him out of his misery. He must have finally known exactly what I was doing. Part of me wanted to punish him, wanted to transfer the pain that I had seen on so many others that had been wounded and tortured by the enemy. On about the third pass, something was said about our being out of there—it would be the last pass. Cleanly, if something like this can be clean, I finished him off. He was doing his job. I was doing mine. Some mutual respect because we were both soldiers. He took his chance, and I took mine. Were the tables turned, I doubt that he would have been any easier on me. No hate really toward him; no feeling really at all.

It gives me a great deal of pain to recall episodes like these. In many respects there is a hardness about them that comes close to the recollection of those difficult feelings that rose from Rick Crossland's death. There was always a lot of bragging about body counts back then, but that time is long past. I take no pride in having killed or added to the torment of another person's life. Those men in those fields are dead and gone; it is true that I go on, but it is also true that I carry something of them with me every day that I live. The cruelty of war stopped for them out there in the middle of those fields; the cruelty continues for me, and I expect that it always will. In all likelihood, had we had a chance to meet under other circumstances, we would have tried to communicate, we could have smiled in each other's faces, and probably had more in common than not. War took away those possibilities, and told us to kill each other. And we did our job—as they did—with painful efficiency.

One afternoon about dark, one of our pilots came into the enlisted men's club we had there at the base looking for me. He had been assigned to a special mission and wanted me on it as gunner. I didn't have to go; he was looking for volunteers. I didn't ask many questions, but I was interested in what was coming down. He didn't have any information. We would be told in flight. When that happened, you knew it was a big deal.

When I got to the flight line, two helicopters were being prepared. We were told to remove the doors, something that was a completely new practice to me. When the officers got away at some distance where we could talk, the crew chief explained. This didn't happen very often, but when it did it meant that the chances of our going down were so great that at least getting the doors out of the way increased the chances of our getting out of a downed chopper.

We would also be flying without lights, something the pilots didn't care a lot about doing. The lights could give you away, that was correct, but they could also serve as a marking to your own people that might give you some safety. We finished preparing the choppers and were ready to leave.

A civilian car pulled up alongside of where we stood. At that point I thought I knew what was going on. There was a CIA station outside the base on the edge of Soc Trang. We were getting ready to ferry some civilian dignitaries to Saigon. This might not be too bad after all.

What got out of that car defied description unless you have spent a lot of time in Rambo and Chuck Norris movies. Four American mercenaries stepped out of the car and walked straight to our chopper. Nothing was said by anyone. The car just drove away. Its lights were still off. I had never seen anything like it before in my life. They all four were covered with long, shoulder-length hair and heavy beards. Where the hair didn't touch, there was dark blackish-green camouflage paint. They were wearing black pajamas, just like the enemy. They were barefooted. Each man carried a sawed-off shot gun and there were bandoleers of shotgun shells crisscrossing their chests. They looked like Mexican bandits. No one said a word.

It was like something out of the lowest budget Hell's Angels movie that was ever made. Charles Manson didn't have anything on these men. The sky was heavy with clouds, and there wasn't a star to be seen. I always worried when there were no stars, because I felt that in spite of the sophisticated equipment, if there were stars, I could help find our way back in the air or on the ground. We flew off into the pitch blackness without any indication of what was taking place. All I knew was that the two men up front and the crew chief to my back had the reputation of being the best in the entire unit.

We were airborne for maybe five minutes, and the co-pilot switched his radio to an unusual frequency. I could hear the talk of coordinates on the map, but they seemed to be a lot further to the west of anything I was familiar with. I couldn't really see much down below because it was so dark. Occasionally, there would be the lights flickering from a fire in a house or something burning out in the open. It seemed like we were going faster than usual.

Then, as quickly as we had taken off, we were setting down in a small open place maybe a mile from what looked like a pretty sizable village. Whoever was there must have thought they were pretty safe as there were lights of every sort burning without caution. The four men were on the edge of the chopper and out on the skids ready to get off. Even before we touched down, they were gone in the dark, melting away like a sinking ship into a sea of black.

As we came in, the pilot had simply said "Get ready!" He didn't have to say what for; I had already figured that anything could happen. Nothing did. We were up and away, picking up the other ship that was covering for us, and were gone in a moment. For all the people in the village knew, we had only flown by. At least, that must have been what we wanted them to think. The crew chief knew about these kind of things, and he explained that it was an "elimination" mission. There was a Vietcong commander and politician in that village. They would try to kidnap him, and if that wasn't possible they would kill him. We wouldn't be going back after them. They always had a way of getting out on their own. I had dreams and images slipping in and out of my mind all night; those men moved in and out of my dreams like they were out there moving in and out of the night. Where had they come from? Who were they? How many of those kinds of actions were taking place out there in the night? When it was all over, I hadn't gotten the slightest indication of where we had even been. The pilots didn't talk about that.

Not everyday was this bad. Many were not. I don't know if we could really have stood it if they had been. When we weren't flying in with troops or bringing them out, we would normally pull back near a small village or some staging area near a camp and wait. As soon as we landed, the children of the camps would come out to talk to us and play around the choppers. We always welcomed them, and sometimes would spend hours entertaining them. We made "toys" out of whatever was available. There were always plenty of genuine hugs and pats on the heads to go around. It was almost as if we were on recess and these were our playmates.

The contrasts that could occur in not much more than a matter of minutes were unbelievable. We could be out using all of our skills to kill in one hour, and then be back on the ground playing leap frog with a bunch of kids the next. I never saw an American soldier be anything but totally kind and generous with those Vietnamese kids. I have seen fear on their faces when we rescued them out of a fire zone, and I have heard their desperate, mourning whines when they were hurt or separated from their families. I have also seen their joyful glee and high spirited laughter as they leaped and jumped and played like war was a million miles away.

I never really knew what irony was until I thought about the fact that these kids that I was playing with all afternoon had fathers, and I had helped carry their fathers off to battle that very morning. Some of them were out there dying right at the moment I was playing with their children. I would go out in a while—we would carefully get the kids away from the chopper blades before we started up—I would have said goodbye to our little friends and playmates, and I would go to pick up their fathers, uncles, and brothers. Some I would bring back alive, others would be shot all to hell—some would never come back again. Would these kids, now so happy, cry themselves to sleep on this very night? Those fathers that rode out on my chopper should have been there that afternoon playing with those kids. What was taking place over there on that scratch of land dangling off the body of Asia had a way of quickly cancelling out an awful lot of "shoulds" or "ought-to-bes."

Not only would there be secret or dangerous kinds of missions that the unit commander would ask our chopper to go on, but he would also pass around to us "perks" from time to time. It got to the place that we became almost the private "taxi" for one South Vietnamese infantry commander. We would carry him to various points in the field to check on troops or to make determinations about the progress of battle. Then, in the evenings or on the weekends we would take him home to spend time with his family. "Home" for him meant an absolutely exquisite palace overlooking the South China Sea.

It was amazing how you could move in and out of battle; at one minute you were pulling him out of the middle of a firefight, and within less than an hour or so you were setting down on his own private helicopter pad with servants scurrying around to meet you and take care of all of your needs.

He would invite us in to eat the evening meal with his family before we left. It was like sitting down on a Hollywood movie set. Most of the time we were eating food that I had never seen before, but it was good—it sure beat army food. We would stay around into the evening and enjoy the cool breezes blowing in off of the waters. It was quiet and peaceful; you hated to leave. I've often wondered what happened to this place and to this man after the Communists took over the country. My suspicion was that he was so well-connected and had greased all the right palms, that this eventuality was already long-since taken care of.

One day our commander came in and called us out for a special mission to Rach Gia, over on the Gulf of Thailand. That was a long way out of our normal flying areas, so it must be important. We were expecting dignitaries or maybe even more CIA mercenaries. It sounded big.

We got the chopper ready. I checked the guns especially well to be sure they were all prepared. Then our specific orders came. The officers were planning a big party and shrimp was going to be the main course. Some of the best shrimp in the world came off the docks at Rach Gia. We were to fly up there, make some prearranged contacts, and bring back what seemed like half a chopper floor full of the biggest shrimp I had ever seen. I have seen lobsters that wouldn't rival what we brought back. It was a "secret" mission all right, but my spotless, at-ready guns would not be necessary.

As a kind of reward—and probably in exchange for our keeping our mouths shut—we were given the day in Rach Gia. It was a beautiful resort and fishing town, almost totally untouched by the war. The cleanness of its streets and softness of its people compared to what we were used to in Soc Trang and Saigon was remarkable. It was almost like walking the streets of home, and our "commission" or "carrying charge" on the officers' shrimp wasn't bad either.

Finally, after about three months of pretty hard going, our flying group was given a four-day pass to Con Son Island in the South China Sea. Con Son was an isolated, radar and navigational site that might as well have been a million miles from the war. There were a few people stationed there, but you absolutely felt safe. We could get out of our military clothes, fish or lie in the sun, watch movies, and have all the plain old, fried American steak and potatoes we wanted.

The most interesting activity was the fishing. We would take six or eight hand grenades and walk out unto a small jetty. All you had to do was throw the hand grenade out several feet, let it explode, and go out and pick up all the fish that you and half the other people on the island could eat. The peacefulness and security of Con Son made you not want to go back across the short stretch of water to the war. Part of me was beginning to feel that all I had come back for had been accomplished. At least I knew that the slicks had run their course. I didn't know if picking up one more bloodied half-corpse or another parentless child would be possible. You could only be a savior—although it was very temporary and short-lived salvation you were offering—so many times.

Maybe the gunships would be better. At least they were cleaner; in a deadly, antiseptic way they were cleaner. I was doing awfully well in the slicks, had the respect of the whole unit—but the gunship didn't land. Somehow they offered a sense of greater detachment that those days on Con Son underscored in my mind and I was needing desperately.

Our main E-6 made up my mind for me not long after I got back from our short R&R. He put me in charge of all of the gunners. I would assign missions, orient the new arrivals, and be able to pick and choose my own missions and flying crews. Beyond that, I would immediately go to Corporal and then be able to use the NCO club that was on the base. It wasn't much status, but there wasn't much status to go around in Vietnam for enlisted men like myself.

It all worked well for a couple of weeks. My promotion had not gone through, but it would soon. Then, this E-6 had one of his old buddies show up on a second tour out of Saigon. Some of the people knew him. They didn't care for him very much; he was a general slacker. But the minute he showed up, I got rolled off all the lead gunner responsibilities.

That did it. I would do whatever was needed to get to the gunships—to the Vikings, "The Blue Diamond Demons of the Delta." Beyond that, I decided that I was due a little bit of a break, maybe in Saigon. Since there was almost always enough pain to need to get checked, it was a pretty simple procedure to check in with the base doctor, let him give ten seconds of looking at my medical record, and I was back on my way out to Saigon. To hell with the E-6. In the end, there was no way that he or I could have—in our wildest imaginations—dreamed of what was waiting in Saigon.

Chapter XVIII

When I got to the hospital in Saigon, I was told to report to the emergency room. There was a beautiful, blonde—round eye nurse who was doing the in-processing. She was polite and we took up an easy conversation. She was an officer, but didn't act like that made any real difference. She talked about her California beaches, and I talked about Florida. I always was a sucker for a nurse in a white uniform, and blonde on top of that.

Around a hospital, it's always feast or famine; either too much activity to ever talk or enough dead time that you could tell your whole life story without interruption. This was a dead day, so while I waited to be checked over, we sat there and talked the afternoon away.

After the initial checkup, I was assigned to a ward. We spoke again in the hall and since she knew there was not a great deal wrong with me, she invited me to come back around and see her sometime. That was all it took, every time I had a spare second, I was headed for her desk. Before the day was over, she had me helping her with some of her paperwork—the majority of which I'm sure she had to do over again. What the hell—maybe she was as lonesome on this day or as bored with the routines of war as I was. I probably would never see her again anyway.

When you go to sleep in a hospital, you don't expect to rest. You expect to be awakened eight or ten times during the night by someone "just checking" to see if you are all right, taking your fever, or monitoring your blood pressure. There are all kinds of noises as people work their midnight shift, need help for one reason or another, or are up moving around because their days and nights are mixed up. The fact that I was off this time in an area that afforded a little more privacy held out the promise of a good night's sleep. There had been one check-up earlier in the afternoon, and a couple more were scheduled over the next few days. It would be a good change of pace, and then I could get back and think about moving to the Vikings.

The night went by without interruption and, as I competed with morning coming on for a few more minutes of sleep, there was the sudden sensation that something was going on with one of my feet. At first, it felt different or pretty good and, since I was still half asleep, I just held still until I could focus in a little more clearly on exactly what was happening. Somebody was sucking on my big toe!! Hell, was I dreaming! What was this all about? Sucking on my toe!!

Without moving my foot, I eased the cover back and looked toward the foot of the bed. I had to shake my head to clear my senses. I must still be dreaming. A blond vision was almost tenderly holding my foot, stroking it with her free hand—with my damn toe in her mouth! Two, wide-set round eyes—I hadn't seen many round eyes in Vietnam—met mine and, what can I say, what could anyone say in a situation like this? I was totally dumbfounded, but I sure as hell wasn't going to ask questions, move my foot, or tell her to stop. She might be a pervert and getting ready to bite my toe off, but for the time being I would take that chance. All that time helping with the paperwork sure had paid off. My in-processing nurse was involved in a kind of "in-processing" that was totally new to me in this man's army.

I'm from North Carolina by way of the Everglades. I may have done my share of bragging in my time just like everyone else, but I wasn't ready for this. I guess I had a goofy, down-home look all over my face. Before you laugh, what kind of a look would you have had on your face? It didn't seem to matter to her. She just kept on, and I would not have cared if she had gone on forever. Maybe I had died in the night, Momma had been praying, and I had gone to heaven!

Almost any "round eye" was beautiful in Vietnam, but this woman was indeed a classic. She was 35, which would have seemed old to me at that time, but she would have passed for 25. No questions were asked about the difference in our rank, or no attention was paid to the fact that women officers and male enlisted men did not associate. I had ten thousand questions that I could have asked, but I wasn't crazy. If she had me mixed up with someone else, if she thought that this was her calling from God, if she was crazy—who was I to look the proverbial "gift horse" in the mouth, especially when that "gift horse" had my foot in her mouth? Damn! If only Hobbs and Bludworth and Frazier could see me now! And, they would have to see me, because this was one "war story" they would never believe.

She found some new warrant officer's clothes that I could wear, and we would walk out of the hospital together like we owned it. She had a small apartment in Saigon, and we stayed there. Officially, I was AWOL and could be court martialed for the deception of my uniform, but at this point it was worth the risk. I don't think I had ever broken an Army rule before in my entire service time, but I guess there had to be a first time. She was so clearly in charge and knew everyone, that there seemed little reason to worry.

We hit every high spot Saigon had to offer and then some. I had been here before, but not on this level. She paid for everything, never even hinting about whether I had the money to do so myself—which I did not. I would be back in the hospital in time for rounds or appointments in the morning, and then as soon as her day was finished, we were off to "wonderland" again. We even found an out-of-the-way bunker on top of the hospital that was quickly transformed into our secret meeting place; some days, she couldn't wait for the shift to end.

It doesn't take much for a kid out of the unsophisticated South—at least the part that I had come through was not all that sophisticated in what the preachers called "the ways of the world" —to fall in love. It might have taken me all of fifteen minutes into that first meeting in the hospital. I was taken, I was bitten, I was down for the count.

Life has some funny turns. In only a matter of a couple of days she was talking about love, too. We started planning an R&R to Sidney, Australia—she could pull all the necessary strings. And then there was talk of marriage. Out of the clear blue sky, she produced the ring that her mother had given her father years before, and we were "engaged."

"Heaven" could not last forever, and I had to move back to Soc Trang. Parting may be sweet sorrow, but that was a pretty rough parting. I was ready to go AWOL again. All she had to do was say the word, but the Vikings probably made more sense for now—at any rate, Sidney would not be too far away. The last thing she did was to attach a set of special coded instructions onto my dog tags so that if anything happened to me, she would be notified and I would immediately be taken to where she was in Vietnam.

When I got back to Soc Trang, there was a series of missions on the slicks before my transfer to the gunships was finalized. There wasn't much need of telling my friends what had happened, they wouldn't believe it. I had the ring for proof, but you could get a ring anywhere. They all thought I was putting them on. After about a week, a beautiful picture arrived with "War is Hell" and "Love" written across the front of it. That made some of my doubters wonder, but still most of their comments were that I was pulling their legs. With great and growing curiosity, the comment that kept coming was "Come on Matherson, quit kidding us, this is all a trick, tell us the truth." My insisting that every detail was the absolute truth left them shaking their heads and occasionally drooling over the possibility that it just might be true.

About a week later as we were coming in from an early evening mission, a corporal from the base main office was waiting for our chopper. This usually meant some kind of message for the pilot—something was up. But, no, it was for me. I had a radio call from Saigon. This never happened, and it must have taken all of ten minutes for word to get all over the area. By now, even the officers—who heard everything—were getting interested.

I went to the radio operations center and the connection was made. It was her. She had managed that highly irregular, personal call on restricted military communications lines like she managed everything else. There was no big deal. This was simple, business-as-usual for her. While I talked in the large, open room, no less than a half-dozen men were "working" nearby, hanging on to every word that was said. When we finished talking, there wasn't much I could do or say. I just turned around and walked out—followed by eyes all the way back to the unit compound.

What I didn't tell them was that she had worked out a ride from Saigon and would be there the next day. Maybe she was a spy or something—how had she known that we would be rotated off the next day for repairs. I told them when I got back, but no one believed it.

Just like she had said, when the early helicopters came in from Saigon she was on one. It was probably the event of the year at Soc Trang. She was as striking as I had said, and as we moved in and out of the base clubs and to town and back, there was no other topic of conversation. The officers didn't like it; they were jealous. The other men were probably jealous, too, but when they saw the officers' reactions, they loved it all even more. Had I gotten a dollar for every question I answered in the next week, I could have retired from the Army. It was amazing the amount of respect that suddenly was coming my way, even from the officers. I could have told those people anything now, and they would have believed it.

A part of me liked all of this attention, but—as crazy as I'm sure it must seem—part of it was feeling a little too confining. I wasn't sure what kind of game she was playing, or if she was playing any kind of game at all. Once I got back to Soc Trang, and all that was going on around us with the war rushed in to fill my mind, I guess I just wasn't as interested in playing along with much of anything. The war had again become the compelling reality.

I kept wearing her ring, and kept answering all the questions, but my mind was going elsewhere. Maybe whatever we had, if we had anything real at all, was just another victim of the war—but it was real! There were other calls and letters about Sidney and my coming back up to Saigon—it just never got exactly worked out on my end.

It wasn't too long after these thoughts began to change that we were on a huge mission that involved our units at Soc Trang and units from other bases in the area. We had flown wave after wave of South Vietnamese troops into an assault area, and had pulled back into a huge field to await new orders or to be ready to assist in their getting out. The field looked like it had a thousand helicopters in it. We were mostly checking our equipment and talking around to people that we didn't know.

Several people had eased over toward where an officer was talking about something; I drifted on over myself. He was talking about being in Saigon in the hospital and meeting up with the most beautiful woman he had ever seen. She was a Captain and a nurse. They were going to Sydney and getting married. He showed his ring—it had been her father's ring.

I eased up near the front and said "Like this," and held up the ring on my hand. We had the same ring, the same picture—it even had the exact same writing on it. I thought it was all pretty funny, and I had my out that I had been looking for anyway. He got so mad he couldn't see straight; of course, he was the one who had fifteen people gathered around listening to all his bragging. The same thing could have happened to me.

I want to be as straight up about this situation as I can. I'm not trying to create a negative stereotype of women in the military or military nurses. My life has depended on too many of them too many times. Almost without exception they were perfect ladies and highly moral women. My Captain was a classy person, a good person, and I never felt that what she did with me was any less than moral or lady-like; she was more than that. It is certain that every American female in Vietnam did not act as she had acted; the stereotype of "fast," sexually-charged nurses has very little accuracy and demeans the role these women played. Not everyone was like her; yet for that moment in my life, thank God, she was the way she was. That officer went away mad; I went away feeling that she was a pretty damn sharp woman—an angel of mercy in nurse's white.

What had happened to me on an individual basis, the Army decided they would try, in principle, to make available to our units as a group. This meant bringing in USO shows that were filled with girls in skimpy costumes who would dance provocatively in front of us to American rock music. We never got the big, Bob Hope type shows. In fact, we never even got Americans. There was a steady train of shows featuring Philippine girls.

These "morale boosters" had a mixed effect. Sure, you enjoyed the music and who was going to turn their backs on women; not many eighteen and nineteen-year-olds that I knew anything about. But we wondered why we didn't get American girls, and when they left—as suddenly as they had come—all that was left behind was a bunch of horny soldiers with little or no outlet for the feelings that had been stirred. Soc Trang had plenty of girls, but there were more lectures about avoiding sex with the natives than there were USO shows. The Army circulated all kinds of rumors, too, about hidden razor blades, people with venereal diseases that were untreatable, and all kinds of scare tactics to keep you at a distance. It worked with me for the most part, but a lot of people I knew had the idea that if they were going to get killed anyway, VD didn't make a hell of a lot of difference. What the Army shows stirred, the Vietnamese girls of Soc Trang often became the outlet for. I can understand their feelings: if you thought you were going to die, you felt the pressing need to cram as much of life as you could into whatever time that you had left.

In many respects the time on the gunships was the best time in Vietnam. It seemed like the fighting was settling down to some extent; some people were even speculating that the war was about to be over. More than anything else, the gunships let the killing and the bloodshed stand off at a distance. You never landed in a fire zone with a gunship, you never took on wounded and dying, you never had to wash the blood out before it congealed on the floor of your chopper.

When I first came in, there was a great sense of pride. You didn't get into the Vikings without being voted in by the crew chiefs and other gunners. When I had been taken out for a test check on the weapons, I had performed flawlessly. The vote was unanimous, and getting to wear the black tee shirt was better than any promotions or, in fact, engagement rings. I loved to wear the black beret and Viking emblem that we proudly displayed on our hats. This was a class act. The fact that we freehanded the M-60s and the knowledge that a North Vietnamese and Vietcong bounty was on all of our heads simply heightened the positive feelings that came from being a part of the unit.

These were good days. Little did we know that the end of the war was nowhere close. Little did we know that what we were experiencing was just a lull before a major firestorm. But that was on down the road; on down the road toward a Vietnamese New Year's celebration called Tet.

The Vikings would take liberties that really were against a lot of the rules, but it was part of the spirit of the unit. We would be out flying between missions and would swap out responsibilities. I got my first chance to fly a helicopter and fell in love with flying. On one occasion, a company clerk kept bothering us about going out for a flight. We finally took him, but by the time we had set down on the Mekong River at over 100 miles per hour to skip across like a water skiier leaving a trail of spraying rooster tail as long as a football field, he decided that a desk was a much safer place than a gunship.

People started feeling at home enough to begin to accumulate pets. Some guys had snakes, and occasionally there would be a good old American favorite mutt of a dog that would show up. Unfortunately, the dogs didn't last very long. The Vietnamese would steal them and eat them. On one occasion we were doing some work with a group of Navy SEALS, the Navy's special operations group. When they left our area, they gave me a pet Otter that I named "Oscar."

When I first got the otter, he was just a baby, but he grew quickly until he was about three to four feet long and probably weighted twenty or twenty-five pounds. He was one big otter. He would sleep with me at night, have the run of the camp while we were out on missions, and loved to take showers with anyone who would let him around. Sometimes we would take him on the helicopter, and, even though we might get into hellacious fire and be making all kinds of offensive and defensive maneuvers, Oscar would just lie there like he was having the time of his life. When we would get back in from a mission, Oscar would stick close to me. He knew my habits. Some of the guys would immediately go to eat, but I always cleaned my guns first and then fed Oscar. He seemed to appreciate the fact that I got his crabs and lizards before I fed myself.

Oscar's favorite hangout was the club that we had on base. He would go in like he owned the place, and everyone knew him. He loved beer. I had to worry about Oscar like a mother worries about her child. He would keep late hours, come dragging in drunk, and have every manifestation of a hangover the morning after. There is nothing quite like a drunk otter.

The only trouble that Oscar and I ever had was his tendency to get too friendly sometimes. He meant it for love and play I'm sure, but on one occasion he got too involved with my ear and nearly bit it off. I punched him right in the nose and knocked him half way across a room. I felt badly about that later, but Oscar seemed to understand. We had no problems after that.

One guy in a barracks area across from where I stayed had gotten a large baboon somehow or other. He kept it in a huge bamboo cage in his sleeping area. It was wild and could pitch every kind of crazy fit imaginable. He was pretty tame around the guy who kept him, but nobody else had better come close. The very idea—a guard baboon. Most people were, in fact, afraid of the crazy animal.

When we got in from one mission, the baboon had gotten loose. It was like a wild vandal had gotten into everything within the better part of a city block. It had destroyed everything in sight and, worst of all, had eaten up everyone's carefully cared-for goodies from home. People were madder than I had ever seen them after an enemy rocket attack or an unsuccessful mission. This probably goes to show what was really important to us and how personally we would take any invasion of that part of us that related to home. The baboon was dead meat.

Finally, some of the gunners captured him. Someone knew about how to turpentine a mad dog, and JP4 jet fuel that we used to clean the guns was used on the baboon. As he ran screaming for the jungle in the distance, the gunners opened up on him with their M-60s. He avoided the fire but not the concertina wire wound into the top of the fence. The next day he was gone; either having tricked us into thinking that the concertina wire had gotten him or as the fine centerpiece of a Vietnamese feast. I hadn't personally helped to get rid of the baboon, but I was delighted about his departure.

At first I was a floating gunner, which meant that I flew with a variety of pilots and crews. You learned a lot about people in this situation, and the coolness under fire of these people was amazing. It wasn't unusual to go in on a fire run and be so close and moving so fast that what you were firing on was exploding all around you. No one was phased by it. You were into and out of exploding fire and debris like the troop carriers had eased in and out of clouds. But, you never had to land and you never had to fly like a slow target. More than anything, you never had to kick people off whose only chance of life was getting on your chopper.

Sometimes what we did was pretty heroic. Late one afternoon we were scrambled to an outpost up the river from Soc Trang. The enemy was on the fringe of the river encampment and about to overrun it. By the time we got there, you could see the invaders already breaking through the town gate and crossing the bridge to the village area itself. The defenders were backed up into a church yard, and the special forces commander—an American—had already called in fire on top of himself. It would be a few minutes before that order could be executed, and by then it was clear that they would all be dead.

We came in at point blank range firing everything in our arsenal. The pilots were blazing away with the automatic weapons and rockets and the crew chief and I were working all sides. The gunships were completely loaded with ammunition, and the automatic feeds allowed us to hang out the side and fire hundreds of rounds without stopping. It was our gunships against the entire invading force of enemy, most of whom were smelling victory and were vicious in their last assault into the center of the town.

You didn't have time to think, to plan, or to execute some kind of strategy. You fired, moved, fired, moved, all in a graceful kind of dance with death. We spewed all kinds of fire and received all kinds of fire. There was the continual pinging, ripping of bullets tearing into the chopper. What those pilots did in maybe thirty minutes was amazing. There is no way to describe the positions they brought us in and out of, or the amount of fire that came out of our choppers.

But it was enough. In a few minutes they were retreating, the artillery could be called off, and the jets with their napalm were chasing them back into the jungle. When the Tigers got in to pull the remaining defenders out, they brought word that most of them were preparing to commit suicide rather than be captured just as we had arrived with the gunships. As we had pulled back and circled for a final run before returning to base, you could see the river full of floating bodies. We had killed on this day, but we had saved life—even one American life—as well.

I wish it had all been like that. The whole ideal that I had fostered in my mind, since those first dreadful days in the mountains where Rick had died, of helicopter crews being like saviors dropping in from the sky would have come true if that had been the case. Unfortunately, there was a terrible down side as well and, all the lives saved notwithstanding, it is the terror of that down side that keeps repeating itself in my mind.

We had scrambled again, and roared out of Soc Trang with a half-dozen other gunships toward that inevitable outpost up the delta. It took us longer to get there than usual, and the slaughter that was going on was nearly complete. The compound had been overrun, and as we broke the horizon the enemy began to scatter and run back for the surrounding jungles and whatever cover that might be available. They had almost gotten away with it all, but now they would pay.

We moved into an attack formation and began to make one pass after another. Soon the clearings between the village and the tree lines were ablaze with the fire from the tracer rounds. The pilots moved the choppers in and out among the trees, the buildings in the village, the fire and smoke, and each other like some delicate ballet. You wished you had the chance to stand off at a distance and watch them work; there was an amazing intricacy to their timing that words cannot easily describe. What was equally amazing was their coolness; most of them didn't even sweat. Sometimes in their concentration they didn't say very much; there was, in fact, a deathly silence that often pervaded the entire chopper in the highest pitch of battle. This was the only edge that seemed to exist.

Finally, the enemy was gone. A stir of life was becoming evident in the village again. We began to widen our patterns to pick up on whatever fleeing enemy we could find. As we came out of the tree line and back toward the village, I spotted a fleeing sampan on the river. My first thought was that some of the enemy had jumped the small boat and were getting away. The movement of the sampan was directly back toward where the enemy were fleeing on foot.

I spoke to the pilot over the intercom, and he broke off in the direction of the fleeing boat. As we settled in behind and above it, I opened up with the M-60. The boat came still in the water with my first rounds and, as the pilot slowed for an easy pass to the left of the boat, the target sat right off to my right, best angle of fire. The rockets and flex kits fire from the pilots had already made their mark. Then, my M-60 ripped it apart, and the tracer rounds ignited the bamboo thatching of the boat's roof. No one jumped or fell wounded into the water. The sampan erupted as the fire reached the fuel tanks of its small motor, and the smoke was rising in the distance as we pulled back toward base and passed the Tigers and their transported reinforcements on their way in. We hovered at a distance and moved back in as was needed to give support to the ground troops.

We got back to base, cleaned the weapons, and ate supper. It was typical to wait for the men who were carried back with the Tigers to come in and give some kind of ground report. When they came back in later that evening, nothing was being said. You knew the pattern: if everything had gone well, there was a lot of horsing around, bragging, and kidding; if there had been a problem, people didn't look at each other in the eyes, no one said anything, and no one asked questions in a group. You got someone off by himself and found out what had gone wrong. Someone must have been lost, but all the choppers had returned. This was a strange one.

Then the word drifted around. A sampan had been shot up. It was carrying nuns and children. They were trying to escape from the enemy that had already broken the last lines of defense. Nuns and children! My blood went cold. It was like every energy of my existence ran out in the floor. Nuns and children!

No one said anything. The subject never came up again. There was absolutely no blame. There was no way to know. It was battle. They knew what kind of person I was. They had seen me taking almost more time than anyone with the kids. There was no blame. There was also no escaping in my own mind what had happened, and every rationalization in the book—no matter how accurate they might be—did not help. The only saving grace was that I had not seen their faces. But, they had been so close to getting away and the Americans had come with their flying guns. And one American was a master at his craft and responded exactly as he had been trained.

I may live to be a hundred years old and may build a life of memories so numerous that Vietnam becomes only a fragment. I will never get beyond thinking about that day, what in great commitment to what I thought was right that I did, and what those people must have felt. Heroism is blind from a racing helicopter in the midst of raging war two hundred yards away from your target. The war raged that day. Twenty years later, that part of the war is still raging. The legacy: the hurt and pain haunting the mind of the man who was trying with all that was within him to be a savior. A savior!

About a week later I was out on a single helicopter mission along the delta late in the afternoon. We had gone into a heavy enemy territory and knew it going in. The pilot was an older man with a great deal of experience and good reputation. I can remember feeling relieved when I saw him in the cockpit as we were preparing to leave.

The mission itself was uneventful, and we were heading back just as the sun was going out of sight in the distance to the west. We had received a little ground fire on and off all afternoon, but it had not amounted to very much. This happened quite a bit; it was simply "Charlie's" way of letting us know that he was down there in the jungle somewhere.

Suddenly the pilot was coming over the speaker system telling us that we were going down. There was as much calmness in his voice as you could ever imagine; like this was just business as usual, something that happened every day. "Tighten up, engine failure, going in." No excitement—just the settled fact of a matter that he had the situation under complete control.

He set the chopper down in the middle of a rice paddy, and we prepared to receive fire immediately. Had there been any enemy forces who saw our descent, we would have been an easy target for them. After a few moments, nothing but the early evening jungle sounds could be heard. No one was nearby or the birds and frogs would have told us.

We got the guns loose from the helicopter and started back toward a special forces camp that the pilot knew from his maps was nearby. The place was probably crawling with enemy, but this was our best chance; it wouldn't take long for a downed craft to be located by someone. The feeling of being back on the ground and making our way through the jungle brought back a lot of haunting feelings. This was the way it used to be, the mud and the heat again—the deep dark that veiled everything except the next ten feet. The other three men kept saying how glad they were that I was with them. It wasn't a feeling I shared.

We heard sounds coming our way and took cover. It was clear in a moment that it would be more people than we could stand off. With anxious expectation, we watched for insignia to appear. In a moment, an entire squad of South Vietnamese special forces appeared in the clearing before us. Holding our cover, we identified ourselves; they had been sent out to find us.

We went back to the encampment, got a hot supper, clean clothes, and even enjoyed the small bar that had been built. These kinds of accommodations back this far in the jungle were exceptional. A Tiger unit came in later in the night and took us out. I fell asleep on the floor of the chopper on the way back in. The next day a Chinook pulled our downed craft in. Some of the hydraulic lines had been severed by ground fire. It could have happened anywhere along our mission. We had been lucky that the breakdown occurred where it did.

The pilots were in a terribly exposed position in the front glass canopy of the chopper. We were trained to pull them back into the back of the gun area and administer first aid if they ever got struck by fire. I had become best friends with a pilot named Sonny Mayer, and we had flown a number of missions together. He kept telling me that he was depending on me to get him out if there was ever trouble. Sonny was a great pilot, but he was always aware—as were all of the pilots—of the dangerous position they were sitting in.

We were out on a morning mission and everything was going along fine when suddenly we came under strong ground fire. You could hear the bullets chipping away outside, and you started hoping you would fly out of it in the next second or two. Suddenly, Sonny was yelling. He was hit.

My first impulse was to get the gun secured and reach into the cockpit for Sonny. The co-pilot couldn't help at this point since he was having to fly the craft now. Sonny had been hit in the foot or leg, and we had both seen people lose feet and legs at moments like this. He was thinking the worst and I was, too. In a half-panic I jerked him back into the back of the craft. He was yelling and scared. This was serious business.

Finally, when I got to where I could see what was happening and examined his foot and leg, I began to laugh—as much in relief as anything. He had been hit and, without question, the force of the bullet had jolted him good. But the bullet had simply torn through the canopy and into his boot. The skin itself was not even broken. It took a moment or two for us to convince Sonny that he was all right; it took weeks for him to live down our exaggerated reenactment of his brush with death.

One of the more exciting assignments was on what they called "firefly missions." We would take a larger chopper and arm it with a .50 caliber machine gun and what we called "coffee grinders." These were automatic grenade launchers. Then, we would strap on large spot lights and go out at night. These missions were strictly volunteer.

The idea was to create what some called a "suicide ship." We would fly into a suspected enemy area and turn our spot lights on like we were searching for troops. It was a kind of search, but more than anything else we were creating a target that would have been difficult not to fire on. When we drew fire, we would open up with the .50 caliber and the grenades, but more importantly we would be accompanied by a couple of gunships flying behind us in the pitch dark without lights. As soon as we began to draw sufficient fire they would come in and do their tricks. We were the bait; they were the trap. Every time I came back from one of these missions, I felt that the old cat had used up another of his nine lives. We were told of the effectiveness of this tactic, but I was happy when the enemy finally discovered what was happening and stopped firing on the lighted choppers.

Christmas of 1967 and New Years of 1968 came and went. I had only a couple of months left. Things started changing around Soc Trang. For the first time since I had been there, we started getting a larger amount of mortar and rocket fire on the base. The system that had been worked out was that sirens would begin to sound the moment fire started coming in. The enemy had such pinpoint accuracy that you knew they had people inside the base plotting out the exact coordinates of the places where people would congregate. Most of the base moved for shelters and bunkers when the incoming rounds began to explode. The Vikings were to scramble and find the source of the fire. We always got airborne in the midst of the fire, but by the time we got up to a vantage point so we could tell where the fire was coming from it would stop. All we could do was return to base, empty handed and not a little frustrated. Charlie was playing with our minds.

When those sirens went off in the middle of the night, it was like you started running before you totally awakened. You would be halfway to some kind of hole for protection before your mind totally realized what was going on. For a long time after Vietnam, my first response to any kind of siren was not that ambulances, police cars, or fire engines were on the move somewhere, but that I was in the midst of a rocket attack. It has taken the better part of twenty years for that finally to begin to go away.

Word came down that I was to go up to Bein Hua for special training on the armament systems of the new Huey Cobras that were coming on line. I wasn't too happy about going. This meant school, and I wasn't too interested in school. What did they have in mind. Yes, it was the best gunship ever made, and maybe it was true that they wanted some of the more experienced gunners to be the first to check it out before it went into action. With only a couple of months left, I would just as soon have stayed with the Vikings. But someone, I guess, had to pass on the information that could be gained about these new systems. After a couple of weeks near Saigon, I was sent along with some of the new ships down to the major base at Can Tho. There was a lot less flying, and I didn't like this. My old friends would fly in and out to refuel or pick up troops, and I was stuck in the heat. They said they envied me, but boy did I ever envy them. It probably didn't make all that much difference; in only a few weeks, I would be out of here anyway.

Chapter XIX

The compound at Can Tho was the largest American installation I had been on in Vietnam with the exception of the processing center we had gone through at Ben Hoa. Can Tho was the main headquarters of the 13th Aviation Brigade and most of the American and South Vietnam Special Forces activities in the delta region. It had everything that the most modern bases in the United States had. There were barracks, training facilities, huge mess halls, theaters, and one of the largest hospitals outside of Saigon.

My first experience at Can Tho had been when I had first gone on the slicks as a gunner. We occasionally came in and out to refuel or pick up troops. You could be certain that you would come here if there had been an unsuccessful operation with a lot of casualties. This was the main hospital spot for the worst cases. I have literally seen the runway streaming in blood when large contingents of helicopters came in loaded with wounded.

The base at Can Tho got the latest equipment and finest materials the Army had. For most it was an easy duty station, so many strings got pulled to get people into this compound. Consequently, there were not very many people on base who had had real combat experience, especially ground experience. It seemed so safe that lack of combat training made little or no difference. In fact, we were not even allowed to have weapons in our barracks. Any weapons that were used had to be carefully checked in and out of the base armory. Not having a weapon nearby, just in case, seemed a great underestimation of what the enemy was capable of doing in my mind; it made me feel naked.

The compound was situated to the rear of the main city, which itself was about halfway between the Laotian border and the South China Sea just east of the convergence of the Mekong and Tonle Sap Rivers. The base itself was surrounded by fences topped with concertina wire, hundreds of yards of head deep sawgrass and marsh, and machine gun stands along the outer perimeter before the distant jungles took over the landscape.

A large contingent of South Vietnamese regular army units patrolled the perimeter and kept the machine gun guard posts around the clock. There was a continual movement of troops, often with vicious looking guard dogs, working the perimeter. Can Tho was equally important for the South Vietnamese, as it served as one of their major provincial capitals in the southern part of the country.

Everything about the base seemed secure. Besides the guarding troops there was the terrain itself. The marshy lowland would have been almost impossible to cross. At least it would have been for equipment laden, two hundred pound Americans; I had seen Vietnamese move through these kind of obstacles almost as if they weren't even there. I told people about this a couple of times, but they passed my warnings off as being totally inconsequential.

I could not help but feel uncomfortable. Not only did I feel safer in the air than I did on the ground and not only did the loss of weapons give a sense of vulnerability, but there was a huge prisoner of war stockade on the compound. In fact, it was located right across the street from my own barracks. The prisoners would seldom say a word or even become engaged in some kind of activity. They crouched in their tail-slung-low, flat-footed posture for hours at a time and just stared at us. It wasn't a curious stare or an evil glare. There was no emotion to it at all. You knew that they were trying to psyche you out, and the best thing to do was simply not to pay them any attention. Unfortunately, that stare was like a sharp place on a tooth; you couldn't stay away from it. I hated that stare. I hated the thought that was behind it. Everything about Can Tho seemed like one great big target to me.

It all felt like being in South Florida in hurricane season, but no one paid the slightest respect to what a hurricane could do. I had seen it in Florida. Announcements would come and go from the weather bureau, and nothing would ever happen. It would finally become a big joke, and even though the announcements would come, people would take no precautions. Those that did were laughed at. It even became fashionable in some places to throw hurricane parties and wait for the "big one" to come. I never appreciated that bravado. I would much rather take down the hurricane protection a dozen times than not to have it up the one time that it was really needed.

I was "short" as far as my time in Vietnam was concerned; I took precaution. I got with another guy who, like me, had seen the kind of action most people at Can Tho had only heard about, and we went out beside the barracks and built an elaborate bunker.

Sand bags were raised above the trenched out dirt, and steel runway stripping was used as a cover; additional sand bags were then layered on top of the steel.

We dug out shelves that we could put our bedding on and carefully constructed a grenade pit. If a grenade was thrown into the bunker—the typical way of killing anyone hidden within—it could be kicked down into a long tunnel where its explosion would do little or no harm. It was the best bunker I had ever seen—fit for a general. I slept there at night. Though plenty of people laughed, I could see no reason for taking chances. There was a big hurricane out there somewhere; I could smell it like the salty humidity in the Florida air.

Can Tho was too much like a regular job. We were up every morning about six, showered in motel-like facilities, and ate breakfasts better than anyplace except home itself. Then, it was off to the heat of the flight line where the new Cobras were stored in their protective vats. There was still a great deal to be determined about the new weapons systems. Two weeks of school in Saigon had only scratched the surface; it was still mostly learn as you go in a less-than-perfect, trial-and-error system.

On almost the first day, several rounds were lodged in one of the mini-machine guns that hung under the pilot's cockpit. I knew better than to stand in front of the gun while it was being worked on, but I didn't know all that it might be capable of doing. It wouldn't move by hand, so I was prying with a long screwdriver. Suddenly, whatever was stuck gave way, there was movement sufficient to engage the trip lever on the firing mechanism, and the gun fired.

Not twenty-five yards away, some guy was nonchalantly walking by. The bullet could not have missed him by three feet. He fell flat on the ground, looked around, and got up. He dusted himself off with no more consideration for what had happened than if he had been splashed by a car passing on a rain-filled street. In fact, it was much less than what you would have even expected in that situation. He didn't say a word; just walked away like nothing had happened.

I couldn't understand this. It was my mystery for the day. Had that been me, I would have been ready to fight. Such carelessness or lack of thinking should have at least been rewarded by a severe cursing out. I could hear any one of two dozen of my friends, "You dumb ass. If you don't know what you're doing with that thing, you better get away from it." Why had the strolling man not responded? Then, it struck me. He had probably never been shot at before. He had probably never seen anyone shot at. In no way did he understand the full implication of being shot at. Can Tho was that safe.

I was afraid someone might think I was bringing them bad luck. Almost as soon as I had finished the bunker, things started happening. At first there were sporadic rocket attacks; not anything terrible, but regular enough that large backhoes were brought in to dig trenches near the barracks that people could dive into when the attacks came. Suddenly, people were a little more interested in the premium space available in my bunker.

On the flight line itself, we began to pick up on a little sniper fire from the distant jungle. The ARVN troops would respond and we would occasionally get a chopper or two into the air, but by that time the snipers and those firing rockets were long gone. It was becoming a nuisance and interruption, but seemed much more like a random harassment than a prelude to something bigger that was on the way.

There were several large conex containers along the runway where we were usually working. These were about eight feet high and maybe five feet by five feet on top. My idea was to build a sandbag bunker on top of one of these and get an M-60 down there with us just in case. It took a couple of days, but we finally got a powerful piece of "high ground" together that gave me a little more security than I had had ever since coming to the new assignment.

What I didn't know, or at least didn't think about, was that I had created a rather noticeable and predictable target. It would not have taken a genius in the enemy army to know that a shot fired generally in our direction as we worked would bring someone up and into the bunker. With careful aim, a sniper could set up his line of fire and pretty well be sure that someone would climb right into it.

In the middle of one long, hot afternoon, about the time that you could begin to feel that you had this day made, sniper fire came in. I was off and running toward the conex container. I would get the M-60 into action and show some people what battle was all about. I climbed straight into the line of fire. Whether something had agitated my movement in behind the M-60 or the sighting had not been true, the bullet that was fired missed maybe by fractions of an inch.

I threw myself backward off and away from the top of the bunker. All the time, I expected the searing burning of a bullet wound, or—like before—maybe I was already shot and didn't even know it yet. There was a wide area behind the flight line that we called a "slush pit." It was filled with stagnant water, oil, airplane fuel, and all matter of putrid crap. It gave every appearance of being a cesspool or the ground level outcropping of a broken sewer system.

I fell in a huge splash, and felt greasy mud flowing in all around me. Somewhere out there in the jungle, a North Vietnamese or Vietcong sniper was probably laughing his ass off at the digging, slinging, cursing, and yelling that I did getting out of that mess. It was probably better for him than had he hit me to start with. All around me, the looks on a couple of the guys faces that were watching seemed to say—to me at least—"wonder if all of those airborne, black-shirted Vikings are like this?" It must have taken two hours to get cleaned up from that mess, and to add insult to injury, when we left the flight line we had to go by the armory area and turn the M-60 and its ammunition in like good little boys.

The rocket attacks became more regular. It was clear from the way they came in that the enemy had amazingly precise coordinates for the large gathering places. The mess hall was the main target, then the theaters, and then the barracks. We ate in smaller numbers, stopped having movies, and those in the barracks were ready at a moment's notice to bail out into the trenches. Still, for most people, it was all a matter of inconvenience more than war.

The potential horror of it all came in strongly early one morning as we were awakened by the incoming rounds of another attack. There was one guy in a barracks area up the road from where my bunker had been dug who was a particularly religious guy in the best sense of that word. He was especially kind to everyone and had this special kind of large, decorated Bible that he read from and kept by his bunk all the time. He was a real Christian.

I'm not sure why he didn't move, or if he simply did not have time. A rocket ripped into his barracks and hit him square in the chest. There was nothing left. It was like he just suddenly evaporated. What struck me as being really sad was the fact that not only was there nothing of him to send home, but the Bible that had been a gift from his family was so blown to pieces and saturated with his blood and fragments of his body, that no one had the heart to scoop its pieces together and send them back. It was the first death that many of the men on the base had seen.

From that point until close to the end of January, the enemy action increased. It seemed like no one was taking it seriously. The only extra precaution seemed to be the trenches that were dug and that people raced toward at the first sign of a rocket attack. No extra men were put on the gates, there was no sign of extra reinforcements on the perimeter, and still they issued no weapons. About the only time that I felt any safety at all was when I was securely in the bunker at night or near the M-60 while we worked on the flight line. I saw the army treating the symptom but making no attempt at getting at the causes of what was escalating around us.

As we had just left the flight line early one evening, the screaming of an ambulance could be heard in the distance coming from the town. It was not an unusual sound. Ambulances came and went with great regularity to pick up wounded soldiers and carry them to the large hospital. Maybe it registered a little in my mind that it was only one ambulance and it was not strange for there to be a dozen or more coming at one time, but it still wasn't totally out of the ordinary.

You could follow the progress of the ambulance by its sound, even though you never saw it: on toward the base from Can Tho, through the gate unhampered by any checks, and on to the flight line. The next step in the process that my mind was somehow almost subconsciously waiting on was the sound of helicopter rotors breaking the air in the distance bringing the wounded. That sound never came and maybe I noticed the difference, but it was hot and we were busy. Again, it didn't exactly register.

Suddenly, the flight line was erupting with explosion as one heavy charge and then another was dropped from the speeding ambulance—filled with enemy soldiers in South Vietnamese uniforms—along the landing zone and as close to choppers as they could be thrown. One chopper and then another exploded in flames. In the moment it took for the knee-jerk of response to take place as people realized what was happening, the ambulance was back at the front gate and gone in the distance. Most people stood around stunned. There was nothing that could be done about it but clean up the mess.

Then, everything you heard had to do with Tet. This particular holiday, which combined the celebrations at the end of the harvest season and the lunar new year, was the biggest holiday in the Vietnamese culture. All the preparations and enthusiasm that the people seemed to be getting caught up in reminded me of Christmas. Of course, there was nothing like the elaborate gifts we were used to seeing in the States, but families spent a lot of time together, there was feasting, and lots of decorations and fireworks. Almost everything stopped at Tet. The enemy went back into their jungle hideaways, and the South Vietnamese sent most of their troops home. A truce was called and everything stopped.

I went back in the barracks. At least, it was cooler and since everything had about stopped anyway, it made more sense to be around a good time and a little more companionship. Even their celebrations put you a little in the holiday spirit, and that meant you were a little more lonesome for home than normal. The barracks would be fine for Tet.

All the newspapers and news magazines that were lying around were full of LBJ and General Westmoreland. Westmoreland felt that the truce, initiated by the enemy to a large extent, carried with it the promise of a winding down of the war. We were winning and finally the enemy was having to recognize that. The President continued to talk about a "light at the end of the tunnel." Most of the attention of the war was being directed at a Marine base near the Laotian border called Khe Sanh. It was a large outpost near safe haven for the enemy and along one of their most important supply trails. If anyone stood the chance of catching hell from an enemy invasion, it was those guys. Khe Sanh would be infinitely more interesting to me than Can Tho if I were the enemy; as we relaxed and counted down another day of "short" time, Khe Sanh seemed a million miles away. I drifted off to sleep with a mixture of visions: the President and the General optimistically stiff-upper-lipping it through another press conference; the Vietnamese decorating their ancestral graves and sitting in whispered conversation way into the night; Marines huddling in their bunkers through another rocket bombardment, trying to catch a quick smoke, opening another rations can, and writing a letter home. It was uneasy sleep. The hurricane was out there.

Somewhere in the middle of the night—I have no idea what time it was—a volcano of fire and screaming noise erupted and we were right in the middle of it. The normal confusion of disrupted sleep was magnified a thousand fold; it was like the end of time, and you were waking up in the middle of a jerking, tumbling fall into hell itself.

Rockets were falling with pinpoint accuracy, as if coordinates of fire had been plotted for days down to square inches. Barracks were going up all around screaming soldiers. People were running out of these barracks with nothing but their underwear on, throwing themselves on the ground, being knocked off their feet by the concussions of falling artillery, falling over and into each other— total chaos.

Our only salvation was the fact that we were so close to the prisoner of war compound that the incoming fire had carefully avoided that area. But those prisoners, long so still and quiet, were yelling with their own frantic glee. Their deliverance was at hand, and somehow their blood must have been running with that special adrenalin of release and turning the tables of war on their captors.

I jerked on my clothes and boots. The only thought in my mind was to get a weapon. All I had was a knife. When I ran out into the space in front of the barracks, it was clear what was happening. We were under all out attack. The perimeter, especially beyond the flight line was already a total fire zone. You could see in the distance one machine gun tower and then another crumpling to the ground under the pinpoint accuracy of rocket fire. The cracking rattle of small arms fire—like a million million fireworks going off all at once and never stopping—made it clear that this was not simply the attack of artillery and rocket fire from a distance. It sounded like a division of infantry, coming in a mad charge, was right out there at the perimeter aiming, with the full intensity of the bottled energy of a thousand years, to overrun us like one great tidal wave of death.

I was heading for the armory. If I could get an M-60 and begin to return fire—I'm not sure if at that moment I felt like it would do any good, but it was the only thing to do. I thought about the flight line and the ammunition dump. I thought about getting in the air with a chopper.

No one was ready to fight. Hardly anyone had ever been in a fight. People were running in every direction. No one was in charge. No one had weapons. God help us that too many of those South Vietnamese guards out there on the perimeter had not been sent home for the holiday. All of the psychological warfare tactics were working. The surprise, the noise, the total surrounding inferno—I had never felt fear like this in all of my time in Vietnam. To be unarmed in the midst of all that was coming apart all around made you feel like your very soul itself was naked.

It was no use. To get to the armory area at that moment would have been like walking through a wall of pure fire and exploding schrapnel. I was already far enough beyond my own bunker that there was no use thinking about going back. It was probably so full already that it would have been impossible to get into it. In retrospect, it is interesting—and a little ironic—that I had so carefully built the thing, but when the time came to really use it, I was out of the barracks and heading for a weapon. The thought had never crossed my mind to dive, just outside the door, for the carefully crafted protection. The old idea leaped through all of the confusion: get something, anything that would shoot, and move in the direction of fire. The only problem—fire was coming from every direction.

At this moment, there was no question that I had made a mistake. There was nothing but the rain of death out there right now. I spotted the tunneled entrance of another bunker and dove for it. It is a miracle that I was not shot by the two men inside as I crawled in; for all they knew I could have just as easily have been the Vietcong coming after them. Probably, the only thing that saved me was their knowing that any enemy would have thrown in a hand grenade first.

There were two sergeants huddled in the bunker, and somehow they had M-16s. They had the idea that there would be a time of artillery and rocket softening of our entire compound, and then the all-out human attack would come. As long as the heavy bombardment was continuing, there was no need to be outside.

The only thing you could be sure of was that the enemy invaders, under the cover of their own fire, were creeping in closer and closer to our perimeter.

It all made sense, I guess, but I felt like a hiding rat in a hole. Everything about me said that I should be out there returning fire and advancing on the fire. I had not been trained to hide, and in that hiding I was not used to the way that fear could grow and you could become aware of being afraid. Across the years, even though on some level I have known better, it has been a source of guilt and personal humiliation, to think of myself hiding in that hole. I guess it was the only thing to do. Maybe it even saved my life, but I was not made to hide in a hole. If anybody should be out there fighting, I should be out there fighting.

There are a lot of things I do not remember. It was so loud and the light of the pouring fire so bright that memories simply must not have registered. I do remember finally being compelled by the feeling that, incoming fire or not, I couldn't keep hiding. In the rain of rockets, you could not help but feel that, given enough drops, the next one or the next one was bound to fall on your head. The other men thought leaving was insane, but if I was going to die I was going to die fighting, not like a trapped rat. John Wayne wouldn't have stayed in that bunker.

Somehow I got out of the hole and headed back for the armory. I don't remember anyone being in charge, but surely someone was telling us something. Maybe it was all instinct. I got an M-16, and the idea came that they would be trying to get into the ammunition dump to get ammunition or try to blow it up. Several people had gravitated in that direction and I did, too. It was possible to fire out into the perimeter, but you couldn't see anything. It did not seem that there was as much going on back in this area as along the flight line. The full force of the attack was coming there, out of the jungle and through the swamp and sawbrush.

Again, I don't have any idea what the details were. Somehow I was back at the flight line, in the bunker on top of the conex container with an M-60. Another guy was with me, but I have no idea who he was, what we said, where the gun or the ammunition was coming from. In some respects, it was like we were the only ones out there fighting—like a cosmic isolation from the rest of existence altogether.   There had never been anything like this before.

All we could do was fire out across the flight line. You didn't see anything really. There were shadows bouncing in and out of the flashing lights from the continual fall of rockets in behind you. You shot at the shadows, but shadows don't die. Everything was point blank. You saw red points of light in front of you. Maybe it was the fire coming out of their weapons; maybe it was their eyes. I was sure that I was going to die.

Morning came. Usually, everything stopped at morning, and they were gone back into the jungle. On this morning it was still going on. Maybe the artillery and rocket attack had diminished, but they were still fifty yards away coming at the flight line.

That it was morning didn't help us all that much. There was now so much smoke that it was like firing in a cloud. For all you knew, you could have been surrounded, out there by yourself, or floating on a dream island in the sky. You fired at the sounds out before you.

Then the gunships came, from where I don't know. They made one pass after another right in front of us. Thick, unrelenting fire was laid down right along the far side of the flight line and all back toward the jungle. God, if they were that close, we could have almost reached out and touched them.

The helicopter passes went on for what seemed like half the morning. I have no idea where our ammunition was coming from, but we kept firing as well. And then it all stopped. Usually, after any kind of an attack I had ever been in, there was sporadic small arms fire for several hours in the distance. This time it was like turning off an alarm clock that had unexpectedly starting blaring in the middle of the night. It just stopped.

There has never been a Hollywood movie that could have captured what the compound and the surrounding area looked like as the sun finally got up into the sky and the breezes began to blow the smoke away. I'm not sure that I think hell itself could look any worse than this.

There were holes everywhere. You saw that on the battlefields, but what the base had looked like the day before had been so radically transformed that the contrast was even more greatly exaggerated. Everything was on fire. I'm don't think a single one of our helicopters ever got off the ground. The new Cobras were blown apart all around. Ironically, neither the ammunition dump nor the prison area had been significantly touched. The prisoners still sat there in stoned silence. Somewhere behind their rock hard exteriors they had to know that any hope of deliverance was dead out there in the smoke. All of the noise that they had made precisely on cue had fallen into a silent wake of defeat.

There were dead bodies everywhere, especially out toward the perimeter. It was interesting, after the loses began to be counted, how few people inside the compound had been killed or wounded. The real death was from the outside of the perimeter, which was now totally destroyed, in toward the flight line—the area where we had fired into the blank darkness all through the morning hours before dawn, the area sprayed with death from the gunships.

There were dozens of dead enemy bodies, and when you walked among them it was amazing to see the evidence of the determination that had pressed the attack. Most of the dead had been wounded several times. It was common to find dead bodies with fresh bandages from wounds that must have occurred early in the attack, but wounds that did not deter them from their mission. More times than not, there was evidence of wounds in arms and legs—sometimes several—and then a final wound that had torn into the chest or split the skull. It was clear that these people had pushed their attack after they had been severely wounded—they had pressed it until the head or chest wound had killed them in their tracks. Most were lying face down, with hands and arms and faces still stretching out toward us. At that moment I sensed that Johnson and Westmoreland didn't know what they were talking about. They saw events on some global scale that made sense to our way of thinking; they didn't see the look of unrelenting determination now rigormortised into the faces of these soldiers.

I would find out later about all that Tet meant: the carefully coordinated attacks that spread across the face of South Vietnam, the atrocities at Hue, the invasion of the U. S. Embassy grounds in Saigon. I would come to learn about how 8000 North Vietnamese had been counted as a necessary sacrifice to rid the countryside of the 2000 French soldiers who had stood their ground to the death at a place called Dienbienphu in 1954. I learned of the North Vietnamese military strategist, General Giap, saying what Ho Chi Minh had told the French: "You can kill ten of my men for every one I kill of yours. But even at those odds, you will lose and I will win." He had been about right: most of the invading units suffered in excess of 90 percent casualties. I later saw the photograph published world wide of the South Vietnamese police chief, Loan, blowing the brains out of a captured enemy suspect at point blank range on the streets of Saigon.

This was what Tet would mean to the outside world and, although we had been infinitely successful by all standards of battlefield logic, Tet was what ultimately broke the will of the American people to fight in Vietnam. That was Vietnam: you could win the battle, yet lose the war. Somehow we had assumed all along that life had to make sense and, since Vietnam was part of life, it had to make sense as well. Sense and Vietnam never walked the same ground, especially the torn ground of death that we walked around the next morning at Can Tho. Most people will finally change if they are confronted with enough pain. These Vietnamese were different; they had been living beyond pain before any of us had come. Pain was a given of their total existence. How could we fight against that?

My main worry was the present condition of our vulnerability. There was no perimeter left and, as far as I could see, no South Vietnamese protective forces left to guard it. The towers were all blown down. There were huge gaps in the concertina wires. The enemy had attached satchel charges to some of its troops, and these men had hurled themselves onto the wire and set off the charges. It seemed suicidal to us, but they had been fighting here on this land for 10,000 years. Suicide had become heroism.

We had no idea how badly they had been hurt. All we knew was that we were without defenses and they might come back as soon as night fell again. With chaos still reigning and no one knowing exactly what to do, everyone was pretty much on their own.

My new, still-unnamed partner and I were instructed to continue to man the conex bunker with the M-60. Somewhere along the way more ammunition was brought in, food was passed around, and we established cover while more fortifications were established along the flight line. Twenty-five yards out across from us, the line of dead bodies graphically showed how close the enemy had come the night before. We were literally yards away from being overrun.

You never know what you will do when you don't know what to do and death is all around. I felt sure that they would come back. We had to do something besides just wait. Every emotion in your minds shouted: "Do something. They'll be back. Do something!"

I'm not proud of what we did next. Part of me recalls it with great shame, but I have to tell it or something of what happened in the horror of Can Tho after Tet will be left out. In the back of my mind, somehow I feel that if it is left out it encourages the chance of it happening again.

This guy and I—still I have no earthly idea who he was and after that day I don't think I ever saw him again—walked out across the flight line in front of our position. It was mid-afternoon by now and a hard stiffness had established itself in pale gray on the enemy soldiers. We took the small, stiff bodies, held them upside down between us and rammed them into the ground. The swampy ground was so soft that it was like planting huge turnips. In a few minutes we were able to create a horrible fence maybe fifteen yards across. The idea was that if a charge came back through this area that the horror of it all would turn the enemy in some other direction, or make them take pause for just a second. In that second, we might find the advantage needed to survive.

I hate that I built that fence. I carry those people in my mind's eye almost every day that I live. The horror stands in greater contrast to me when I think of the great care of human decency I always showed to the bodies of the dead when I worked for the funeral home. There was never any show of disrespect to the dead; something of the person was still there in the body. And, here we "planted" these brave men like human stop signs, warning any others who would try to enter here to go away. Here was the most intimate face of battle.

But they didn't come back. Thank God they didn't come back. The next night, the next day, the week that followed. They didn't come back. Someone came and got the bodies, and we began to repair and reclaim. The jungle covered most of it all pretty quickly; the war would go on.

After Tet, everyone was scared and a lot more careful. My friends at Soc Trang had had it even worse. They had beat the enemy back at the very gate of the compound in hand-to-hand combat. The city of Soc Trang, a city of beautiful people who had received us with a great deal of kindness, got caught in the middle. There had been no choice but to turn fire on the city to kill the attacking enemy, and the fire from the base had also leaped over into the town. The town was all but destroyed, and I am sure that many Vietnamese civilians I had come to know had to be killed. Their only legacy, as far as America was concerned, was the body count that was under way as soon as the sun had come up.

In the midst of all of this, it is strange how simply it all ended, how matter-of-factly, how the Army processes rolled on without any noticeable interference from the events of war. My rotation date came up, and the system of out-processing began. There was one matter of paperwork and then another. Equipment was to be turned in, medical checkups were held, and one matter of last minute detail and then another took place. There were no significant moments of parting with friends; I had not been at Can Tho long enough for that. I was bombarded with directions and instructions, but I don't really remember much. There was simply the consuming feeling of "let me get on out."

I was flown with a few other men up to Bien Hua, and there were a few more days of waiting and out-processing. The emotions were all mixed: you were glad that you had served, you hated to leave your friends still fighting here, you could not wait to get away from it all, you would want to remember some things, you prayed to God to forget others. It was all like you were in a great crowd trying to exit through a small opening: lots of shoulders and feet and staggering half-steps all easing in the same direction, caught up in a movement beyond your control in which no one looked at anyone else's eyes.

When the plane lifted off and the air-conditioning began to blow away the smells of the ground, most of the people on board gave a loud, relieved yell. I guess I did, too. There may have been a sound, but I can't remember any real enthusiasm going along with it.

You might expect that faces would have been glued to the windows, trying to get one last look at this place that you were likely never to see again, one last look to let the whole, long moment somehow sink in and become sealed in memory. I don't know that anyone did this. Most just stared straight ahead into their own thoughts. It was almost like a tape on some kind of recording device was trying to erase, but somewhere deep inside you realized that this would be altogether impossible. You sank back into the seat as the plane stopped its climb and sank into its own cruising pattern. For the moment, it was over. For the moment.

Chapter XX

We flew back to Oakland by way of Alaska. I had looked forward to seeing what Alaska was like, but we didn't even get off the plane during the refueling process. I can't even remember seeing snow, so whether we got off or not, it wasn't going to be exactly what I would have expected. I would have expected myself to be excited about things that were new, but somehow it felt like whatever emotions spark excitement had been dulled into extinction. I guess I just wanted to go home or to step back enough spaces to a starting-over point in which these Vietnam years could simply be lost. I guess I knew this would be impossible; here was the source of the dullness of emotion, like a mark on a page, so deep and dark, that attempts at erasure only worsened.

There was a lot of talk in Vietnam about how we would be closely inspected for any kind of contraband when we arrived at our outprocessing base. There was talk of time in military prisons, and most of us had had all of the military that we wanted by that time. I had all kinds of knives and small pieces of gear that I wanted to keep, and—like almost everyone else it just seemed right that the military should let you take a weapon home; they had even done that in the Civil War. But, I was afraid of being caught, so I left it all behind. As we landed and were put on buses in Oakland, we kept waiting for a customs-like search to take place. It never happened. I still think sometimes about all I could have brought back. It would have probably been my luck, though, that that would have been the very day the most detailed search would have taken place.

Most of my thoughts at that first moment of returning—in fact, it had been a major topic of conversation on the plane—had to do with the war protest movement that was going on in America at that time. We didn't get a great deal of real news about all that was happening, so it was easy for us to form stereotypes and caricatures. I was looking for nasty, free-loving, long-haired hippies in the streets with burning American flags. I could not believe that there could be this kind of anti-patriotic expression in America. I reasoned that the Communists must be thick on the streets of my own country.

We had heard all kinds of rumors. Most prominent of these was the idea that our returning planes were being met by busloads of protesters. When we got off of the planes, I envisioned having to march through corridors of yelling, cursing protestors who—from information we were getting—expressed their disgust for what we had been doing by spitting on our uniforms. We should expect this upon our arrival and in any movement through public transportation facilities on our way back home.

My first response, and that of my returning compatriots, was simple. Let them spit, it would be their last spit—if anyone spit on this uniform, I would fucking kill them. We were all ready. At the first sign of spitting, they were dead in their tracks.

It has always been interesting to me, thinking back, how quickly your mind went straight to "fucking kill." There was no in-between in terms of the emotions you felt; no spit back, beat up, simply fight. It was all an immediate leap to an emotion that had only one expression—destruction. Vietnam had become an angry and frustrating tunnel with no light at the end, no matter what the President joyfully proclaimed. Most of us had just come through the hell and near-death of Tet, most of us had seen friends blown to pieces, and most of us had seen the fat cats in Saigon getting richer and richer at everyone's expense. It was clear that someone, somewhere wasn't going to let us really fight, and now the country was turning on us. Our parents had gone off to war and returned heroes; now we were returning as murdering sons-of-bitches. When I thought of all my mother had given me—the very base of my survival—the very sound of "son-of-a-bitch" burned at the core of my total existence. Just one sound of those words directed at me, and someone was getting ready to hurt like they had never hurt before in their whole lives.

I wasn't interested in defending myself or simply fighting for what I believed. I came off that plane ready for battle; let the first spit fly, and they could start calling for the hearses.

Somebody was going to die! No one was there at all. No military bands, no friends and family, and no protestors. Instead of being relieved by it all, there was more of a sense of disappointment. It was almost as if you thought, "Let's settle all of this right now before we do anything else, and then we can go on about the business of living." Sometimes to this day, it seems that there is still something looming out there unsettled. The lid never exactly closed on Vietnam, the door was never exactly sealed shut, and there are still times when simple anger or simple fighting seems not to be enough. It is almost as if something still needs to be destroyed, and there have been times when it required all of the discipline that could be mustered not to go straight to destruction. Had they let us win that war, maybe the feeling of something still left undone would have gone away.

We stood in lines for about a week. There was a great deal of clerical work that had to be done. It seemed like there were as many physical examinations going out as there had been coming in. People from various veterans organizations had set up booths to give advice about benefit programs of one kind or another, and the way that we needed immediately to begin to establish Veteran's Administration records if we had suffered battle wounds. They insisted that this would make a great deal of difference down the line, but by the time you had heard fifteen pieces of information in one day, you weren't interested in standing in another line waiting for something that was optional.

There was no debriefing at all that related to what we had experienced in Vietnam and the way that it might affect us in the future. When I think back on it, this was one of the biggest mistakes the military made. They spent long hours getting us ready for Vietnam, and then no time at all getting us ready to come back into normal life. I felt a little like somebody who had been given a boat and pushed away from the dock, but who had never been on a boat in his life. They should have spent whatever time was necessary—maybe even a six-week "de-boot" camp—to get us ready for some kind of integration into civilian life.

Instead, they gave us just enough money to buy a ticket for a plane trip home, took us to the airport, and let us out. I don't recall anyone along the way even saying "thank you." At the airport stop, the guy driving the bus opened the door, said "this is it," and halfway revved the engine as we were lining out as a kind of signal for us to hurry because we were holding him up. He was more concerned about facing freeway traffic back to the base in Oakland than he was about anything that was taking place in our lives. There should have been a general standing at that bus door saluting everyone of us as we stepped down.

Suddenly, you felt totally alone. You were still in military clothing, but all that got you were blank stares, looks of coldness or disgust, and sometimes even the quickened or distanced pace of fear. Nobody had to be afraid of me. Hey, I had just been over there fighting for these people. There was no doubt about it though, fear was what was written all across their faces. If there was any one of us who had a negative side that could be brought out, this would surely do it. Whatever they were expecting of us wasn't good, wasn't good at all.

There was a long layover in Dallas. There was none of this young girls coming on to soldiers in uniform I had always experienced before. Now, people tried to avoid you. And, the emotion you felt was one of avoidance, too. You either stayed by yourself or took up a conversation with someone else in uniform. It was almost you against them. A dark corner of an out-of-the-way bar seemed to be the best cover. You took a defensive corner and peered out like an animal in a cage. All of the feeling of pride that you had in the uniform was gone. Instead, you felt a sense of shame.

It didn't make sense. You hadn't done anything wrong. You had fought the enemy. Why were you feeling shame? Why were you filled with the vision of killing anyone who came at you with spit or the bags of shit that were being thrown at returning soldiers in some places. All in all, you had a feeling of being out of place, misplaced—misplaced in your own country, more intimately your own that anyone else's because you had bled over it. Why all of the shame? Why all of the avoidance? They didn't understand, but—by God—you didn't either.

When I got back home, there were all of the kinds of celebrations that might be expected. There was a quick circle of contacts with family and what friends that were around. For the most part, the sense of being misplaced carried over like a shroud on these events and I don't remember anything of any great distinction about them. It was almost as if I was unsure about a lot of things and those closest to me sensed it. They would give me some time to work things out and stay back out of my space to some extent, but they didn't know what to do to help and I didn't know what to tell them. We moved around each other like married couples after a huge argument. It was all awkward and uncomfortable. I got the feeling that somehow I had done something wrong, but I didn't know what.

Life had gone on for them and was going on now. It would have to go on for me as well. For the moment, maybe just a deep breath, a little rest, and Momma's home cooking would bring about all of the healing that I needed. To have time when someone was not telling you what to do, time removed from the habits of the better part of three years, was wonderful in some ways and strange in others. You depended on the discipline, structure, and order of the military to control your life; now, you had to learn again how to control it for yourself.

It was time for me to think about what I wanted to do with my life. It was true that there was a "standing reserve" requirement that could allow me to be called back for up to two years, but I had never heard of anyone who had to do that. I also had built some excellent educational funds, but I still was not officially out of high school. I knew I didn't want simply to spend the rest of my life doing what I had done before Vietnam.

The most appealing thought was to go back, but not as a part of the regular military. I had gotten that out of my system, but the same could not honestly be said for Vietnam in general. It had not been resolved for the nation, and I had not resolved it either. Maybe it was the way they dropped you in and then plucked you out. The lack of time for transition still made it all seem like a dream. How do you get rid of a fantasy?

I thought about trying to make my way back to at least something that was familiar with another group I had seen operating in and out of the delta during my last tour and which held a certain attraction for me. Air America was, on the surface of things, a civilian transport operation. Almost everyone knew, however, that it was actually a CIA operation. The money was supposed to be especially good and, of course, there was the adventure that I longed for. If so much of Vietnam was taking place behind the scenes, maybe this would be the avenue to really do something about winning the war. I could see myself as an Air America pilot, and the experience I had flying the choppers made me know that I would like to fly. Maybe, I thought, I could use some of the educational benefits to get some kind of flight training and go back to Vietnam that way.

It took a while to find out what options were available. In the meantime, I went back to Plantation Cold Storage, and they put me to work immediately. One of the managers had been a fighter pilot in Korea. He seemed to understand where I was coming from, and he had an interest in talking about war experiences. That was fine with me. It was almost as if we could communicate about some matters in a way that did not even require language. I still remember, more than anything else, the cold in the building where we worked and the way it irritated the metal that held parts of my abdomen together.

I also went back to the funeral home at night. It was like I was trying to get back something that had been lost. Maybe walking the same paths that I had walked before would bring back some of the same feelings and thoughts about the world, about others, and—more than anything else—about my own self. I was glad to renew old acquaintances, but I never seemed quite able to renew some kind of acquaintance with the person that I had known as my own self before Vietnam.

The work, and some of my Army pay that Momma had saved for me, allowed me to purchase a Pontiac convertible, and Angelo Mario and I hung out quite a bit together. Plantation didn't work out; the cold and dampness kept stirring up infections and there was one ache and pain after another. It was clear that it just would be my place to start over. I would just quit. But then, I never quit anything in my life. Not me. But I quit anyway.

The possibility came on the horizon to go to work for the Life of Georgia Insurance Company. Their employment representative was certain that I had exactly the kind of personal skills that they needed in their agents. He was sure I could sell. It all sounded good to me, and the money would be first rate. Maybe this would work while I made preparations for some kind of flight training. I went in and took the qualifying test. I failed it flat. I never failed. But I failed all the same. Everything seemed confused and out of focus.

I started getting advice from some of the people in my family. It was almost as if they had given me some adjustment time, but it was clear that satisfactory adjustment wasn't taking place. They could especially see how quitting at Plantation and failing the Life of Georgia test had hurt. Unlike a lot of advice, what they gave me made pretty much sense. I needed to get to the VA and see what kind of physical problems were carrying over from Vietnam. If there were problems, they should be exercising responsibility. Up until then, I had basically operated under the idea that whatever damage was done was mostly part of the whole experience and not a lot could be done about it. The thought of government responsibility had not really occurred to me.

Nonetheless I made the appropriate appointments, went in for the testing and examinations, saw my mass of records poured over again and again, and came out with the determinations that my war wounds had left me 50% "disabled." I didn't feel half disabled, but I was not going to argue, especially since that meant a regular monthly check. I don't think, at the time, that having someone judge me as "disabled" had a negative psychological effect; maybe it did and maybe it didn't. To tell the truth, I didn't think all that much about it. The older family members felt that what I had done was important "just in case," and that it might make a lot of difference in the future. I figured that they might just know what they were talking about, and there was no good reason not to go along. Disability or not, I felt that I still wasn't going to let anything hold me back.

An obstacle suddenly appeared: I could not get involved with any further education that would be assisted by veteran's benefits or the vocational rehabilitation act without first having the high school equivalency, GED, examination. I started a course at Lindsay-Hopkins Vocational School which was designed to prepare for that test, but the English part kept giving me a lot of trouble. I quickly passed all of the rest, but the English just would not come.

I hit on the idea that maybe someone else could do that part for me, and I found this guy who claimed to know English like the back of his hand who would take the test for $10. There wasn't the slightest hitch. He took the test without any questions being asked, and when my scores were posted I had achieved a level of 90% on the English. That I had "cheated" bothered me a little, but everyone in the entire system that I was working in seemed to act relieved that I had finally discovered the time-honored method of taking care of this kind of obstacle and we could go on to the next step.

The next step was actually two-fold; I had never been one to take things one step at a time when my mind was made up. I entered both Miami-Dade Community College and Burnside-Ott Aviation Training Center. I was in school most of the day and on weekends—at the government's expense—and working at night at the funeral home. Miami-Dade was hard, but I was managing it;

the flight school was exactly what I wanted, and no matter how complex the material or operations we were learning, I was always at the front of the class. This was especially good for me because of the way old doubts about my inability to learn were being erased. Maybe I wasn't such a bad "student" after all.

The success with the flying meant one thing: back to Vietnam with Air America. I was so convinced of this that, without anyone knowing about it—which seemed to befit anything that would relate to the CIA—I went to Miami and got a passport. As soon as I had all the certifications and clearances I could get at Burnside-Ott, I would follow that incessant magnetic pull that gravitated all of my thoughts back halfway around the world.

I was feeling more like a loner around home than I ever had before. Kay was working and dating, Joe was married, and Momma had started dating a man from church. What television I watched seemed to be all about Vietnam. Part of me was angry at the protestors, and part sensed that they simply did not understand. I wanted to explain to them with as much intensity as I had used trying to save the drunks in the bar, but I didn't really know how to explain. You couldn't put all that had happened into words, especially for anyone who had never been there. At times everything was fine, and then it would all come back. When I would jump at a sudden movement or a car backfiring, people would laugh; they didn't mean any harm, but I felt a little like a freak show.

Even the popular radio station, WAXY, contributed to the down mood that I was in. They started playing a lot of late 60s music, or maybe they simply discovered for themselves what we had first discovered in Vietnam two or three years before. Almost like smells bring back vivid memories for some, these songs carried me straight into the middle of events and people's faces that somehow, even mercifully, I had been able to forget. Everyone played WAXY; you couldn't get away from it. I tried church, just to please Momma, but it was no use; all I could think about were all the promises that had been made and never kept.

The funeral home work didn't help. We were beginning to get more and more bodies of young men who had been killed in the war. Every time I worked on them, the ghosts of old friends and the recollections of old events came flooding in. I could get rid of some of this by working with special sensitivity with the families.

They always seemed to appreciate contact with someone who had been where their loved ones had been. I started feeling lucky to be alive, to be one of the living, and this gave my overall attitude a much needed shot in the arm. I couldn't escape feeling that somehow I had to contribute, not only for myself but for those who didn't get to come back. Feeling good about being alive is a real starting place.

Everything fell into a pretty settled routine. There was almost unlimited flying. The aviation school loved people like me; the veteran's benefits paid for everything. Quickly, I got the private and commercial licenses, and passed a variety of instrument, night flying, and multi-engine ratings. The various FAA tests that at one time would have seemed incomprehensible were completed with great ease. The only break in the routine came with a new pizza place which opened across from the funeral home. In a world where everything was almost always about the same, a new place to go like this was a real addition.

I renewed my old friendship with a guy named Garrett Bowling, and we hung out a lot together. He loved pizza, and we started calling in orders and carrying them out to the funeral home. After a while, we would drop in to eat. The man who ran the Pizza Inn, as it was called, was a Mr. Mize. He was a big, strong-looking man whose personality attracted you to him. He was a retired, military lifer, and I felt like I could relate to him. He talked a great deal, and I began to feel that the Pizza Inn gave me a sense of place, a sense of belonging. There was something about the whole environment which was created around Mize that made me feel better than anything I had experienced since I had come back from Vietnam—maybe even since before I had left to join the Army—a time that seemed a million years away. It was almost as if there was something here, or somehow near, almost waiting for me—me, and no one else. It stopped being "Mr. Mize" and became "Pop"—a term that somewhere within me I felt I had been needing to use about someone for a long, long time.

Then it happened; Garrett and I came in, sat down, yelled at Pop, and waited for a waitress to come over to take our order. She walked out across the room toward us like she had been there all of the time, and I kept feeling like somehow I had missed something and didn't know how it would have been possible to have missed it. She had a poise about her—although I'm not sure I would have

284 A War Still Raging

even known what "poise" meant at that time—that would have made it hard to imagine that she was only fifteen years old. She was the most beautiful girl or woman, or person—at that point I could not have analyzed what I was experiencing—that I had ever seen in all of my life. If she thought I looked stupid as I halfway gawked and halfway tried to retain what "cool" I could muster, I'm sure she was right. This was the nearest thing to a religious experience I had had since I could not even remember when.

"Sandy" was Pop's daughter. I'm not even sure if it had ever come up that he had a daughter; if it had, it hadn't registered. I'm also not sure if it took two minutes or two months, but I was in love. I guess from the moment I saw Sandy, I was in love with her. There never would be anyone else.

Here was one emotion that I had never felt before, and my whole attitude and approach suddenly changed. This was one girl different from all the rest. There was no inclination to "put the make" on her; it would have been like coming on to an angel. This time there were feelings of respect and kindness and a sense of gratitude that were entirely new to me. To say that she was bringing out any "best" in me that might have ever been there would have been an understatement. She was causing me to experience a whole new and different view on life in general, and of myself in particular, that I simply had never had before. What can I say: this was the realest real, the only real real that I had experienced in this way in my whole life. Was I ever in love!

There was a problem. She was fifteen and still in high school, and I was a twenty-one year old, battle-scarred veteran. Pop liked me, for sure, but this was his daughter. Besides that, he had had more than his share of Army types. When it came to his daughter, there would be more caution than I ever felt possible. I might not have liked it all the time, but I could not help but respect him for it. From that first moment on, however, there was never any other woman for me. Sandy was the sun, and everything in my life orbited around her.

Pop wouldn't let her date yet. He would—and this was pretty smart on his part—let me hang out at the Inn about as much as I liked. It was always under his closest scrutiny, but I was there most of the time when I wasn't in school or working. I must have cleaned that place a thousand times and washed tens of thousands of dishes—anything to be around Sandy.

These were some of the best days of my life. Even though I was experiencing pretty strong pain from time to time in my left side, there was too much happening to give it the attention that it probably was demanding. I was young. It would go away.

Sandy's brother, Tommy, and I got pretty close. He was full of life, and we had a lot of good times kidding around together. The Mizes were becoming more like family than anything else, even though Sandy and I had never yet had a first date.

Tommy kept asking all of the regular questions about funeral homes, dead bodies, embalming, and all the rest. It was hard to withstand the temptation of using someone's curiosity against them in this kind of situation. Finally, one night real late we were about to close the Inn, and Dennis Stitely called from across the street that there had been a body discovered up on the edge of Lake Okeechobee that I needed to go after. Two kids had stolen a plane and crashed it in the lake; a week-long search had finally turned up the crash sight. Tommy had to go along. He begged his dad, and Pop finally gave his permission.

By the time we got up there, it was about as pitch dark as the swamp could get. We made our way into an eerie little, fog-bound town and found the small building that served as a funeral home. We got the body onto a stretcher and covered it with a sheet and blanket; the death had been hard and the whole picture was pretty grizzly. There were numerous cuts and abrasions, and the fish and elements had already begun to do their work. Tommy saw it all, but didn't have anything to say.

We put the body in the back of the funeral home station wagon, and it covered the whole length of the back area of the vehicle. The feet were right behind Tommy's back, a fact that he seemed painfully aware of. He looked straight ahead as we headed back out into the dark; still there wasn't much being said.

Every time I would put on the brakes, even slightly, the stretcher would slide, and the body would hit the seat right behind Tommy. He looked like he was ready to jump through the windshield, but he was brave about it all. I had a lot of trouble keeping my eye on the road for watching the pained expression on his face.

Bodies usually didn't slide around like this one was, so I finally figured out that there was some problem. The body had so many lacerations and the thawing process which occurs after a body is taken from a cold storage room had begun so that the blood and body fluids had begun to leak out. None of the fact of this made Tommy's ride any more comfortable.

Finally, we had to stop at a small truck stop out on "Alligator Alley" to wash the back of the wagon out so that the blood would not begin to dry and become almost impossible to get out. Just as we were flushing out the last of the blood, a highway patrolman pulled up along side of us. He had a drunk black man in the back seat of his car, and where he pulled up to a stop the man was staring straight into the running blood not three feet from his face. The patrolman, not seeing any identification on the station wagon, stepped out, loosened the strap holding his pistol in its holster, and asked us just exactly what was going on and what we had in the bag. As he asked the questions, I was looking almost directly into the black man's face.

The explanation was easy. Yes, it was blood that he thought he was seeing, and there was a dead body in the back. I explained the whole story, and he had no trouble with it. The black man was another story. He was sobering on the spot, and in the process all the color had long since drained out of his face. The ashen look gave every appearance in the dim light from the truck stop sign of a ghost or even of a white man suddenly sitting there in the car. Tommy was taking it all in. Needless to say, this was his one and only trip to pick up a dead body; all the questions about the funeral home had a way of stopping as well.

Finally, Pop began to let me take Sandy home after work. This involved Sandy in my car, sitting very much to her side of the front seat, and her parents directly behind us in their car. This was all right. I was making progress, and no matter what the obstacle or the wait, it was worth it.

Then he let us date. This meant that I could pick her up a few minutes before church, take her to church, and then be back within the carefully calculated span of time that Pop knew it would take to get from the church to their home. If Momma was praying that some kind of miracle would get me back in church, this must have been the answer. I might not go to church for lots of reasons, but I would go for Sandy.

The work at Burnside-Ott was coming to its conclusion. I was licensed to fly DC-3 transports, a main component of the Air America work in Vietnam, and finished all the instrument ratings.

On one instrument flight to Savannah, I had taken Momma and Sandy with me. They flew well, but about a hundred miles outside of Savannah we ran into a terrible storm and had to climb above it. There were no reference points anywhere, just the instruments. This may have unnerved them a little but they didn't show it. Finally, it came time to drop down through the storm to where the airport was supposed to be. For a couple of minutes the clouds were dark as night around us, and then we broke through. The first sight was the airport a half mile or so right out in front of us, exactly where it was supposed to be. Momma sometimes hides her feelings, but there was no doubt that she was proud of me at that moment.

They had kept me around long enough to get a seaplane rating, and I had a ball racing with the powerful, long-nosed racing boats called "Donzies." We would start out even on a long stretch of open water. At a predetermined signal we would throw the power at our engines. The Donzie would always get off the line first and pull ahead. Then, you would begin to feel your plane lift out of the water and skip along on its pontoons. In a moment you were by the Donzie, throwing water all over the yelling people riding in it, and off into the air. The Burnside-Ott people took me to the end of their schooling, the flight instructor's certification.

It was decision time. I was ready now to play my cards back toward Vietnam, but I can't exactly say that the passport and the information I had gotten about hitching up with Air America were really burning a hole in my pocket. In fact, with Sandy at the center of my life, Vietnam seemed farther and farther away and of less and less importance. She had been brought up in a military family and was more interested in settling. That was fine with me, as long as somehow that "settling" might involve me. There were a lot of ghosts back there, but she had chased them away.

Burnside-Ott had no trouble putting me to work as an instructor; in fact, they had been planning for it for several months. I had it made: a respectable, interesting job; a new Pontiac GTO; a sense of place with a new "family"; and, more than anything else, love.

Those first experiences as a flight instructor were right down my alley. We were extremely busy and there was a lot of work. There was an especially large number of Indian and African students that were coming in to learn how to be pilots. The differences in language and custom made for some interesting times.

I had gotten to know an older lady from the funeral home; I had embalmed both of her parents in years past. She came in to see me one night and explained that she was dying with cancer. She stopped me from expressing regrets with the idea that everyone had their time, and at least she knew hers was coming and she could make some plans. Part of those plans involved me; she would be cremated and wanted her remains sprinkled out on the ocean which she loved so much. She reasoned that I, being a pilot, could find opportunity to take care of her wishes. I agreed to the plan.

In only a couple of months the woman died and, in keeping with her wishes, Stitely saw to it that I got the ashes. I was taking out a young African student to do some flying along the coast and brought the small urn of remains along with me. I directed him to fly out over the ocean, and I got everything ready. He didn't know what I was doing, but he was giving his attention to the control of the plane.

When I opened the window and began to pour out the ashes, the prop wash began to throw most of them back into the cockpit. We were both covered before the urn was empty and I could get the window closed. He quickly questioned what was in the bottle and, not thinking, I answered "Mrs." whatever her name was. He, like the man at the truck stop with Tommy, turned deathly white and froze on the controls. We tilted over into a slight dive, and I couldn't get him loose. I found out later that it was taboo for people in his religion to be around a dead body, much less have one all over you. At this point, however, I was mostly concerned with what could be quickly a very serious situation. Still he wouldn't let go. I finally had to elbow him loose with all of my strength in order to regain the controls. To say the least, the moment we got back on the ground he was off to make arrangements for a new instructor.

I was staying busier than most of the instructors, even the older ones. Once word of mouth began to get around, people telling their friends about me, there was hardly enough time in the day to get all of the work in. Of course, I didn't know what it meant to pace myself, so I was cramming two week's work into one on a regular basis. The other instructors and I got along fine; in fact, after a while they began to pass on the hard cases to see what I could do with them.

On one occasion, I took over the responsibilities for a young Indian who had nearly 100 hours of instruction but who still had not soloed. You should be able to solo within about 20 hours, but one instructor after another had not been able to bring him to that point.

He was an excellent student, and I couldn't understand what the problem was. He followed every detail of procedure and responded immediately in the cockpit to any request that you made. The only problem I saw was his inability to retain from one day to the next what he had learned or done on the preceding day.

Finally, after about 10 hours with me, I was convinced that it was simply a confidence problem, and he would perform fine in the solo and thus gain the positive feelings necessary to go on and be a pilot. We went through the solo procedure a half-dozen times with him doing everything. I simply sat there beside him, and everything went perfectly. Just to be certain, I had two other instructors check him out. Their evaluation was as positive as mine.

I took him out to the flight line early in the morning on what was a very slow day in the area. There were a couple of other students getting in some time at touch-and-go landings, but besides that the sky was empty. We taxied out to the end of the runway, checked all of the pre-flight clearances, and waited for the plane in front to take off. When it was his turn, I got out, telling him he was ready with every ounce of encouragement that I could muster, and stood in the grass to the side of the runway.

He was supposed to take off, make a 90 degree turn to the left, go about half a mile, make another 90 degree turn to the left paralleling the runway, continue on this course about a mile, and then turn back on a similar course that would bring him back toward a landing. No problem. Essentially, all he had to do was follow the student out in front of him and land the plane.

All went well. He rolled off, gained speed, and rose into the air. On out ahead was the other plane, and he was rising in the same pattern nearly a half-mile behind. Then, I began to sense a problem. He should have settled into a slower or at least steady speed; instead, he was gaining speed. He was gaining on the front plane.

At first, I figured that the front plane would turn, which it did, and he would go a bit beyond that point and turn himself. No problem. Instead, he turned on the same point as the preceding plane and continued to gain on it. In a moment, it looked like he was in hot pursuit, like a fighter pilot on attack.

As he got closer and closer, I began to yell—as if it would do any good. I knew he could see the plane and that he was going to pull away or slow down at any second. God, would I kick his ass when I got him back down on the ground. But he never strayed from his path.

The planes collided in mid-air. If he had ever moved the throttle back from its initial place from takeoff, it would never have happened; he simply forgot!

The planes bounced away from each other as the sound of the collision cracked across the airfield. People's attention was turning from every direction to watch what should have been a disastrous crash. Instead, both planes miraculously stayed aloft. The front student turned straight down toward the runway and got his plane on the ground. My student flew straight ahead, just like he was supposed to do. He made his last two turns and descended for a near-perfect landing. His plane had lost about a foot of its wing; the other plane had lost maybe three feet. How it continued to fly was a miracle in itself.

I all but jerked him out of the plane. He thought it was all in celebration for the successful solo. Even when I showed him the three feet of wing missing from the other plane, he didn't understand. In his opinion, he had been minding his own business when the other plane "backed into him." This aeronautical impossibility never registered in his mind.

The FAA came in and did an extensive investigation, which would have been normal under these circumstances. That created no problems for me, as I had carefully had the two other instructors check the young Indian out before I had recommended the solo. Until the end, no matter how intense the questioning, he stuck to his story; the other plane had backed into him.

I'm not sure why the flight instructor's work began to lose some of its appeal. The pain in my left side was continuing to mount, and the close, cramped quarters of the small Cessnas that we trained in all day probably didn't help that much. I didn't want to tell anyone for fear of losing my job, but all the time I worried about the pain becoming so great while I was in the air with a student that I might pass out or something.

I kept going to the VA, and they kept giving me pain medicine. In my mind, this didn't make sense; they were treating the symptom and not the cause. I kept telling them that there was something in that side, but they kept thinking—or so it appeared to me—that it was all in my mind. Constant pain becomes a terrifying distraction. Had it not been for that, I have often wondered if aviation would not have been a direction that would have worked out fine.

Instead, the feeling of confusion began to return. Maybe some of this was the medicine, I don't know. Whatever it was, I began to try to think in terms of what else could be done. There was no sense of panic. Instead, there was the strong feeling that I could always find something that would work.

Throughout it all, there was Sandy. In a life that had never known very many constants, she was as solid as a rock. I may not have known what I wanted in some areas, but there was the one certainty that I wanted to be with her for the rest of my life. Certainty is a wonderful feeling, especially when life has been more vague than clear. As events, and now years, come and go, I believe that just one, singular certainty can be enough to sustain you—if there are more, fine, but one will do—one, singular certainty that can act as a ground or an anchor. Sandy was that, and somehow from the first, what I thought about her was the most crystal clear insight that my life has ever had.

With a sense of the highest celebration—a real happiness like I had never known—we were engaged.

Chapter XXI

I had an uncle and brother who were working for a transport company in Atlanta. The company was maybe twenty years old but had just relocated its main operation to Atlanta and was really beginning to grow. They had heard that the company was thinking about hiring a pilot for a new company plane and encouraged me to apply. That sounded pretty good, squiring executives around the United States, seeing new territory, and making a lot more money than I could ever make teaching people to fly. It was the kind of job a man could support a family with.

The people in Atlanta were as congenial as anyone could be. All the way up to the two main owners they welcomed me and treated me with an unusual amount of respect. There was a problem with the flying; although I had well over 1500 hours of flying time by then, it was easy for them to get someone coming out of Vietnam who had over 4500 or 5000 hours, and a lot of that in jets. There was, however, they assured me a place for someone with my personality and determination in their company. It all sounded like the red carpet was somewhere nearby and would be rolled out at any moment. They had been good to my uncle and brother, why not me, too?

I went back to Florida for a while and continued the flight instruction. Sandy and I talked about Atlanta. It seemed like the place to be. The success in flight school had convinced me that I was not stupid; I could learn as well as anyone. Whatever the trucking company had for me, I could handle. I called my uncle, he talked to the bosses again, and I was invited to come on up and start immediately.

As I came in for work the first day, it had not really crossed my mind very much what I would be doing. I anticipated an office with a name on the door, maybe some kind of title; some kind of responsible work. There is no way to describe the deflating feeling that came over me when I was assigned to the loading dock to unload trucks. I was back to where I was at Plantation years ago, even before Vietnam, and this hot, humid, nasty hellhole didn't even have the redeeming feature of Plantation's cool. I had left Sandy, Momma and the family, South Florida and my friends—for this?

What I found out was that this particular trucking company started almost everyone at the very bottom. Not only could a person learn the business from the bottom up, but it didn't take long to test the mettle of anyone who thought they wanted to work. I had had my mettle tested before; if this was the game, I could play it as well as anyone. It was a challenge to show them.

Several weeks later, the two main bosses came walking through. It may have all seemed very casual on the surface, but there was little question that they were checking on me. Finally, after a moment or two of friendly chatter, they asked straight out what my "intentions" were now concerning working for them. What did I want to do with their company?

I looked straight in the face of the company owner and, without batting an eye, responded: "I'm going to have your job someday." They weren't expecting that, but they weren't disappointed either. My uncle, who I was living with at the time, said he would never have answered that way; they could have fired me on the spot. I had a feeling that they were duly impressed and good things would come from that conversation.

It took three months, but it happened. They put me in charge of OS and D. This meant that I was responsible for dealing with over, short, and damaged freight. This required a great deal of attention to detail, and there was a constant juggling act to keep everything straight. It didn't seem unreasonable at all to start thinking about being a station supervisor or even a terminal manager. It was also reasonable to proceed full speed ahead with our wedding plans. Happy days were here again, and there were seldom any weekends that passed without me hitting the roads for Florida. I had never missed anyone before like I now missed Sandy when we were apart.

Our wedding took place on June 30, 1972. I'm not much for dates, but this is still the keystone that has held a lot together, maybe that has held it all together. Somehow, I can't help but believe in guardian angels or God finding a way to take care of people—for me, it was Sandy. She was beautiful, the day was beautiful, everyone was there—I didn't even look so bad myself.

We moved into a really nice apartment in a new development in Atlanta. I was promoted into sales and was going through the company's training programs. I was dedicated to my wife. I was dedicated to my company. Our goal was for me to work my way back to Florida. It would be hard, but I would do right by the company and they would do right by me.

Dedication is a two-edged sword. It can cut in your favor. There is no doubt that the dedication to detail which I took with me to Vietnam helped save my life. There is also no doubt the dedication of a husband and a father to a wife and children is positive and very necessary to make a family work as it should. You have to be careful though, because dedication can create corners that are not easy to get out of. That sword can cut you, too. I didn't know that at first; all I wanted to do was to prove to Sandy how much I loved her and to the company how committed I was to getting their—our—work done. The dedication and commitment worked quickly, and I was moved from the docks for a try at sales.

Several of our best sales people had been on a sales blitz over in South Carolina, trying to open up a new area. We were getting our share of new contracts, and I was telling Sandy every night with great enthusiasm of my—our—successes. We had just come in from dinner, and I had a message waiting; the president of the company had called and wanted me in Atlanta first thing the next morning.

I had time to stop by the apartment and clean up, and then be at his door waiting on him when he got there. That was what he would have expected of me, and I would not have expected any less of myself. Getting called in by the boss usually means trouble, but Sandy and I knew that this could be nothing but good news.

It was good, indeed. They wanted me to go to Cleveland, Ohio, immediately, to take over a new terminal operation that they were going to try to open. The opportunity had just come on the scene and timing was everything; we had to get in immediately and make a strong showing or we might not get in at all. Cleveland was a union town and we were not union; it would be hard.

Sandy and I didn't know exactly what to think. Neither of us knew much about the "North." It was like talking about a foreign land. But there was no time to think. We loaded up some clothes and headed out. Cleveland, Ohio, might just as well have been Russia.

We got into town after midnight and had no idea where to begin to look for a place to stay. Beyond that, it was snowing and neither of us had even seen snow—at least not for many years. It was nearly knee deep and all we had were street shoes and light jackets. After we tried all of the good places, we settled for the seedy leftovers. I carried Sandy on my back, and we fell, exhausted into a roach bug motel room. She cried over what in the world we were doing in this God-forsaken part of the world; I wanted to cry with her, but somehow I remained convinced that strong men didn't cry. I wondered if John Wayne had ever been in a rundown motel in Cleveland, Ohio, in knee-deep snow.

The whole idea was to expand the basically southeastern regional operation of the trucking line into the North and Midwest. Cleveland would be the test case. If we could make it here, we could probably make it almost anywhere. The problem was still that we were non-union.

I went to work and the company backed me with every help available. We had all new trucks and paid the drivers well, especially considering that there would be no dues for unions or other expenses. I was able to get all kinds of business by explaining that we were not a union shop and would not be governed by strikes. By giving us some of their business, a company could be certain of getting their freight moved in spite of what the unions might do. It made sense and our business grew. The only problem was that the better the business, the more notice we received, and the unions had quickly put the word out on the street that Cleveland was and would only be a union town; no one else was welcome.

Business grew so quickly that I was able to bring in others. Sandy's brother, Tommy, came up to work and that helped both of us to have him around. I was working all day—from terminal manager to loading on the docks when we were shorthanded—and wining and dining potential new accounts at night. I kept dock clothes and sales clothes at the office and sometimes changed four or five times a day depending on what work was required next. I was dedicated. I didn't owe my soul to the company store, but I was flat choosing to give my soul to the company store—it was my company, just like it had been my country.

It was inevitable: a big, black Cadillac pulled up to the dock late one afternoon and two huge, gorilla-like men unfolded out of it. They might not have been armed—though they probably were—but there was no question that they were dangerous. They asked for me, and they called for me precisely by my first and last name.

I was friendly and they weren't unfriendly. They were there to deliver a message; simply and short: "Don't mess around with Mr."___" and they called a man's name that I had never heard. I'm sure the idea was that I would find out who they were talking about, and any word I found out would probably be a frightened exaggeration from someone who had had trouble out of this guy.

My first response, and it was genuine enough, was diplomatic. At least, it would have been the diplomatic response in the South. I wasn't interested in being a problem to anyone. I was simply doing what I was paid to do. Why didn't everyone just let everyone else make a living. It was a big country with plenty to go around for everyone. In the South where minding your own business is an ingrained virtue, this would have worked. They left, but there was this lingering feeling that my diplomacy had not worked. I wasn't afraid or angry; we were too busy for that anyway.

Trouble started happening on every side, drivers were threatened, trucks were fired on, and damage was done around the terminal itself. Some of the drivers were refusing to come in with their loads, and most of the local drivers were scared and wanted to stop going out to pick up material for distribution to other parts of the country. They were generally ill at ease with the North and wanted to get back to Atlanta or South Georgia where they had come from. If we could not be depended on by the people we were establishing contracts with, they would quickly go elsewhere. We had to keep trucks rolling. In this business, you could go out as quickly as you came in.

I was on the job maybe 18 to 20 hours a day, seven days a week, trying to bridge every gap that appeared as fast as I could. We were at least keeping freight moving in and out. The petty violence and intimidation continued, and it was impossible to get any help from the local authorities. It was clear that we were in this battle by ourselves.

A couple of weeks passed, and still we were in business. The news seemed full of Vietnam, but there was no time to pay it any attention. A "negotiated peace" seemed to be in the works; Nixon went to China. Part of me couldn't think about Vietnam; another part was generating the same kind of resolve that I found in battle which would allow me to survive in the middle of what was becoming a very real battle on the Cleveland waterfront.

The black Cadillac returned with its two gorillas and their boss, a smaller but much meaner looking man. His face was pitted and scarred, as if he were the model for most of the Hollywood mob movies I had seen. He did all the talking. It would not be possible for him to "hold off" the tempers and strategies of those that wanted us out of town; he emphasized the word "those" but remained intentionally mysterious about who "those" might be. With a cold, steady stare, he then added his highest statement of intimidation: "Somebody could get shot." He wasn't talking about drivers or dock workers.

Somehow, I was just as cold. I reached down to my belt line and took hold of my shirt. I raised it with one long jerk and revealed a chest and stomach full of battle scars. They had not had this response before; the coldness of their stares changed to near timidity. The two gorillas visibly retreated a half step, almost like I was going for a gun. Looking the boss square in the face, holding the shirt up to my chin, I simply told him the fact, "I've been shot so damn many times—that it doesn't bother me." I didn't build on that, telling them to get out or go to hell or whatever. I couldn't even say I had any sense of personal hatred or anger for them, but they understood as I did— for better or for worse, I wasn't afraid of them. They left, I put my shirt back in place, and work continued.

When we came in the next morning, the terminal and trucks that were parked on the lot had been shot all to hell. Not a single truck was free of damage. It was the nearest thing to the appearance of fire fight remains that I had seen since Vietnam. But there was only one thing to do; "steal" working parts off of enough damaged trucks to get at least one in service. More than any other time, we had to pick up and deliver today; the whole town must be watching.

It took the better part of a morning to gerry-rig a working truck, but then there was the matter of who would drive it. All but one of the local drivers had simply left, and the one who remained had already given all his explanations about having a family and being afraid.

I climbed into the cab of the mismatched eighteen wheeler, grabbing the clipboard of delivery directions for the freight we had just loaded on the back. I had never driven a truck like this in my life. The gear system may have been vaguely similar to the trucks I had driven in the Army, but not enough to be of any real help.

The one remaining driver stared with sympathy; part of him was wanting to be in that truck cab, part of him was plenty happy not to be.

The engine roared to life and I slapped the shift lever into what I thought was the right gear. The whole front end reared, and the truck jumped out of the parking lot—straight for the river that ran through Cleveland and led to Lake Erie. I couldn't get it to stop, change gears, or anything. In a moment I would be in the river, and this would be the end—no one was interested in finding out that freight they were waiting on was resting on the bottom of the river.

Suddenly, that one remaining driver was running along beside me shouting directions about gearing and clutching. I stared straight out at the river growing larger before me all the time and tried to do what he said. It worked and I got going in the right direction. All along the way out to the main exit road, the guy ran beside me giving his shouted instructions. Not quite in five easy lessons, but more like five quick minutes I learned how to drive an eighteen wheeler. Without incident, deliveries and pickups were made throughout the day.

Whoever was responsible for all the damage must have viewed what they had done as their last stand. Immediate negotiations were initiated with the Cleveland Teamsters Union and our Atlanta office. In some sense, they got what they wanted; we started working through a Teamster cartage agent in Cleveland. But, what they really wanted was us out, and they didn't get that at all. Our trucks, with a growing amount of freight every day, came in and out of Cleveland at will. In the end, the success in Cleveland opened the company's operations throughout the North.

I have often wondered what would have happened if I had called Atlanta the morning when everything was shot up and told them we were shut down. I have often wondered what would have happened if I had driven that single load of freight off into the river. A large part of the company's eventual operations would have been stalled and perhaps stopped for good. But I was a "company man," just like I had been in that jungle which now seemed a million miles away. Instead, I had called Atlanta, told them what was going on, and that I was keeping trucks on the road somehow. I was their man. They could count on me. My plan had been approved, and the day took its course. At least one of our trucks, although with a somewhat less than skilled driver, rolled defiantly through the streets of Cleveland that day.

The local cartage agent who was eventually hired could now make the business work. He was of foreign descent and had connections to the union. The company decided that, all things being equal, this might be a more accommodating way to deal with any movement into the North. Without any complaint on my part, after about two months of training the new agent and setting up the new mechanism of operation, I was pulled back to Atlanta and, with Uncle Ben's advice, went to work in central dispatch at the main Atlanta terminal. It would be a perfect place to learn the overall operation and prepare myself for the possibility of a terminal of my own somewhere in the South.

The new work involved a lot of responsibility, but now I was in close contact with the higher organization in the Atlanta office. Sandy and I still wanted Florida and my own terminal, but this would do for the time being. We were settling in with the general kinds of ups and downs that most married couples face. On the high side we were able to buy a house near Conyers, Georgia, and three acres of land. I got Sandy a horse. We were happy. On the down side, she had experienced a miscarriage, but we were young and undeterred by this. The company gave her a job, and we had more money than we had ever had. Sandy became pregnant again, and our son, Doug, was born. It seemed like a lot was working out just like it needed to. Except for the reminders of pain in my old, wounded side, Vietnam was about gone.

The central dispatch job had its boring side, but word of new terminals kept my interest peaked. In the midst of one rather regular day, the president called a quick meeting of all the Atlanta management—there was a problem. We had about a dozen, loaded trucks pinned down by rifle fire at a large truck stop in Tiny Town, Kentucky. He was sure the unions were behind this, and that no local help was likely to get the situation resolved. A good deal of this freight was perishable, and all of it had guaranteed delivery dates. We had to do something.

He asked for volunteers to go up there right then and do whatever was necessary to break the siege. I was, of course, one of the first to step forward. Within an hour we had a convoy of cars and station wagons and headed north with probably 15 or 20 men—armed men. I had, for example, an AR-15 assault rifle and over 1000 rounds of ammunition. This beat central dispatch any day. We weren't necessarily going up there to start anything, but if anything happened we would be ready.

When we got up to Kentucky, everything was just as it had been described. There were our trucks, circled almost like a wagon train under Indian assault in an old west movie, and up along the steep hillside was the evidence of riflemen hiding behind rocks and trees, ready to fire on anybody that tried to put a truck on the road. The local police and the Kentucky State authorities were there, but no one was doing anything; truckers, union officials, and police create some unusual accommodations sometimes.

We pulled up along the roadside beneath the overlooking hill. The opposition was pretty much in full view, and we made little secret of what we had and what we had come for while we started unloading and our bosses walked on up to where the police and what must have been union officials were standing around.

There was not the slightest question in my mind what I was getting ready to do. I would have thought no more about charging that hillside than I would have thought about moving on fire in a Vietnamese battlefield. It all fell under the heading of fighting for what you believed in. I was amazed that the police made no move to stop us. In thinking back, had I been in their shoes I would have stood back as well.

I was loaded and ready. I would have deployed our "troops," given the directions, and led the charge if that had been necessary. Instead, the conversation between the police and our bosses broke up, and they walked back toward us. A deal had been cut: our trucks could go without harassment and head back to Atlanta. A signal of some sort went up to the hill, and you could see men climbing out from behind rocks and trees and leaving. We had been there maybe ten minutes, and it was all over.

As we unloaded our weapons, broke them down, and prepared to leave, there was a lot of bragging going on. People were expressing disappointment about not getting to fight: we would have kicked ass, shot the sons-of-bitches, and on and on. I mostly didn't say anything. I would have fought, but I was glad that we did not have to. Most of these other men had no idea about war and fighting. They should have been thankful to be going back home in one piece. I was glad that I had showed everyone there just how dedicated to the company I was. The looks of admiration that came from every direction made me feel ten feet tall.

We no more than got back to Atlanta than I was called in, thanked for all the help, and offered a new terminal manager's position in Fitzgerald, Georgia. It wasn't Florida, but it was on the way. Do a good job there and the new terminals planned for the deeper South could be mine.

With single-minded devotion—there is no better word—I took to the new task with every energy imaginable. I sold, drove, worked the dock—it didn't matter; this was going to be the best damn terminal in the entire system. It all worked. Not long after getting there, I landed the entire freight contract for a major battery producer in the area, one of the biggest single accounts in the entire company operation.

The sales were easy. People liked me and I liked people. It wasn't long until a matter of kickback came up with another company, and I called Atlanta to find out how to respond. The bosses were big family men with strong Christian ties, and the liquor-in-exchange-for-freight deal being asked for sounded pretty far-fetched to me. I was surprised by the instruction to go ahead, to do whatever to get the accounts. I got the freight; I supplied the liquor in return and hid it, just as I was told, in my expense account. The difficulty was handling all the business I was creating. I came early and stayed late, worked weekends, or anything else that was demanded. I found in Fitzgerald that the "speed" that was a regular part of the over-the-road driver's life could help me as well. It was all abusive, to be sure, but it might help get us to Florida.

The highlight of Fitzgerald was a hardware owner whose grandfather had been what he called a "great white hunter." On the entire top floor of one of the downtown buildings which he owned, he had stored every kind of stuffed animal imaginable. We got a lot of his business—without kickbacks—and he and I became friends.

One day he called me up with a special shipping problem. He was donating a huge, stuffed grizzly bear to a museum somewhere and wanted to know if we could ship it. I never said no, and went personally to get it. I was amazed by the size. It was almost exactly the height of a transfer trailer. It was standing erect on its back legs, with outstretched forelegs and the look of vengeful attack on its face. It was a ferocious sight.

I had it carefully placed near the back of a trailer and packed other odd freight in boxes around it to provide protection. It would be sent to Atlanta, repacked, and then sent on to its destination. I hadn't thought much about the unpacking process in Atlanta. The morning after we shipped, I got a call from the general operations manager. First, he ripped me up one side and down the other for all the trouble I had caused, and then he broke down laughing. The truck from Fitzgerald had arrived about three in the morning, and in the dim, sleepy light of the midnight shift the unloading had started. A large box was moved from the back of the truck and the bear was exposed. The docks had cleared in screaming chaos and men jumped and ran in every direction. It took over an hour to get all the workers back and, when they did, they could not wait to get other workers with what was now a grand practical joke. The joke went on the rest of the night and then passed throughout the day shift as they came to work the next morning. The operations manager explained how throughout the morning the air would be pierced by screams of fear. It must have been something to behold.

When the first terminal in Florida—Orlando—opened, it was given to me. All that we were hoping and working for had finally taken place. It was now only a short trip—at least compared to what we had been making—down the Florida Turnpike to home. I was running the entire state of Florida, which was no small source of pride, and business grew again. The idea was getting around that if you wanted a tough job taken care of, all you had to do was send Chuck Matherson. I kept hidden the feelings of being tired—feelings that were not simply fatigue from work, the growing pain in my side which the VA continued to treat with medication, and the pills that were keeping me going.

It was not long until word came that the terminal system in Florida would grow to Miami and, since I had already been managing that area anyway, it was mine. Home!

We moved in with Sandy's parents and it was a beautiful homecoming. Not like coming back from Vietnam; this time it was returning as a successful company man with the responsibility of an entire new operation. Everyone was impressed. Hard work did pay off. It was "my" company. I would make the Miami terminal the best in the entire system, and make a super good life for my family in the meantime.

Life's funny sometimes. You seem to be able to get rid of some pressures and new ones come. Doug, our son, was exhibiting developmental problems that were becoming pronounced enough that we knew he had to have some kind of help. We began to take him to doctors, and the conclusion was reached that he had some form of debilitating disease that he had had from birth. The first diagnosis was a minor form of spina-bifida and arrested hydrochephalus, and the doctors seemed to think this was not all.

The VA was giving me a new diagnosis as well. Since I kept coming back with the same complaints and their medicine was not working, they decided that the problems were mental rather than physical. They suggested that I start seeing VA psychiatrists. I resisted this and insisted that the pain was real. No, it was my mind, they stubbornly insisted, but I was equally as stubborn. I was not going to a psychiatrist, but having someone tell you that you needed to was enough to sow seeds of self-doubt.

Though my performance on the job and the success of the terminal were all but a foregone conclusions, there were new job pressures that I had not experienced before. The terminal we would use until a new terminal was built was in the heart of the roughest section of Miami; there had been rioting in this very area a couple of years before. There was a huge Cuban and black population, and trouble all of the time.

Atlanta was backing most of my requests. I got a little more money with the idea of paying a little better and getting better workers. I got everything cleaned up and began to train the new employees from the ground up in exactly the way I wanted things to be done. I was even able to hire Bobby as my assistant, and thus could be away and leave things with someone that I could completely trust. In addition to the work at the terminal, I had to oversee the building of the new terminal, and we were starting the construction of a new house. No one could tell me about trying to do too much at one time. Undoubtedly, some of the work created a distraction from worrying about Doug; there was also the need for a continual distraction from Vietnam which the pain and the suggestions of the VA doctors kept bringing back to mind. To top it all, Sandy was now pregnant again.

Theft was the major problem. Seldom a day passed without enough stealing to make a noticeable difference. It was important to me, but on much too small a scale to interest the police. We had, more or less, to be our own police. I hate a thief and, perhaps even more, the idea of being outdone by someone who was not good enough to work like everyone else. I took over a kind of self-imposed police duty in addition to all of the other responsibilities.

One morning I broke my typical arrival schedule by a half hour and was walking around checking to see if anything was out of place from the night before. As I came around a blind corner on the dock I confronted a man loaded down with CB radios. As he dropped the radios and started to run, I grabbed him. He fought back, and it took nearly ten minutes of fighting to subdue him. In the process, I broke my hand on his head. By the time the day was over, word circulated back to the men working on the docks that the captured thief was back on the streets again. It was not uncommon to repeat this process of catching, fighting, capturing, and release at least once every two weeks. No one was really afraid. It was too easy to get off.

Finally, I hit upon what I hoped would be a better idea. It was an idea borne of Vietnam: if I could convince the thugs and petty thieves in the neighborhood that we were crazy, maybe they would stay away. A large steel cage had been sent down from Atlanta to store drugs or especially valuable merchandise. The next thief I caught went straight in the box; the police were not even called. I let him sit there for most of the morning, returning on occasion to let him know we were planning something special for him. A little after noon, I had the steel cage loaded in the back of a truck and told the guy inside that we were sending him up to South Georgia and would let him out up there in a Klan town.

In actuality, we simply rode the guy around in the back of a truck for most of the afternoon and brought him back. You cannot imagine the look of relief that was on his face when we opened the steel cage and he realized he was still in Miami. We called the police and had him arrested. He was shivering with fear, or some drug withdrawal, when they arrived and told his whole story. I simply told the police he was crazy and didn't know what he was talking about. They didn't ask any questions, and word got back that this guy was sent back to prison.

Problems slowed a bit but we caught a third guy a couple of weeks later. I took this one into my office and shut the door. Bobby was there with me and a couple of men from the dock. I had an antique ice pick on my desk that I used as a letter opener. I held the captured thief back across the desk and eased the ice pick up into his nose. I explained very carefully that if he made the slightest movement that I would ram the ice pick into his brain. He hardly breathed.

I made the man talk. What was going on out there? When were they going to learn? What was it going to take to keep people away? He was only concerned that we not do with him what we had done with Willie—evidently the thief from the steel cage. On the street, people were convinced that we had taken Willie away and killed him. I let him think that. Maybe that would work.

One of the dock workers in the room was a black, Baptist preacher. He must have been scared by all that was happening, and asked me to let him talk to the man. I agreed and removed the ice pick. The preacher's compassionate advances got him smashed in the face, and the thief turned to run. Maybe he got two steps before Bobby caught him and beat him into submission. Again, we called the police and again the whole story was told. In like manner, we acted like it was all a lie. But somehow the tactic worked. The word got out that we were crazy, a bunch of deranged Vietnam vets. Maybe that was right. Now, the street people and the VA psychiatrists were in agreement. Whatever the truth might be, the stealing all but stopped.

The greatest pressures finally started coming from the drivers. I was having to run a tight ship to make everything work, and this kept them running constantly without the free time or down time that they had been used to. Of course, they complained—I would have complained, too. The only problem was that they could be in and out of all the other terminals and Atlanta. This gave their stories a chance to grow, and gave them an access that I didn't have at times. It also gave anyone who might have jealousies about the way I was running my operation a chance to put me down to their advantage.

The drivers almost revolted in a desire to have more pay. I had always worked for that, but still what I had done was not enough anymore. Atlanta got put in the middle; they could either lend their support to me and send a message to the drivers, or lean toward the drivers and put me in a position of having to scramble even more. Surprisingly and unpredictably, and in spite of all I had done, the support clearly moved in the direction of the drivers. I felt a great deal of anger, lack of understanding, and rejection. What was going on?

All of this was almost the straw that broke the camel's back. I felt the need to retreat, to follow the advice that some within the company had already been giving me to back off and take care of myself a little more, to spend more time with my family. The company would always be there, they said. It had gone against the grain of everything I believed in; didn't they know I would make it work, would do a job that they could be totally secure in and proud of. Hadn't I always done exactly that?

About a half dozen of us—me, Bobby, a black dock worker named George that we all admired, and three others—headed out for the Everglades for a weekend of fishing. This would get us away and we could clear the air a bit.

When we got there it was already late, but Bobby wanted to get fishing. His idea was to walk out into the shallow water so that he could cast out a greater distance. I told him not to, that there were alligators all over this place, but he thought he knew better. While we started to set up camp, he grabbed his fishing gear and waded out.

I finally got to the place of lighting the Coleman camp lantern and walked down toward where Bobby was fishing. When I held the lantern up to light the area around him, it looked like the red lights on a pinball machine lighting up—alligator eyes! Jesus Christ walking on the water would have had a hard time keeping up with Bobby coming out of that water. There must have been a dozen gators within ten feet of where he was standing.

We fished and drank beer for maybe two hours, and I began to get so sleepy that I couldn't stand it. I headed for the car to stretch out and sleep. They shouted obscenities about my being weak as I walked away; George decided to come with me, and we bedded down as best we could.

They gave us long enough to get off to a sound sleep and make their plans. In only a few minutes they had caught a small alligator—maybe four feet long, but still big enough to do plenty of damage. They slipped up to the car and dumped him in on top of us. He went wild and so did we. Fortunately, no one was bitten, but we all but tore the car apart getting out, while our four "friends" fell out in every direction wildly laughing at our sudden, startled fear. One thing was for sure: it broke the pressure about work—at least for a while.

When I got back to work on Monday morning, it was clear what needed to be done; I had to take some time off and get things back in perspective. I had weeks of untaken vacation time, so that was no problem. Just like Sandy and I had discussed, I called my division manager and told him I needed a couple of weeks; I wanted to go back up into North Carolina, make arrangements to put a tombstone on my father's grave, and simply get away from it all.

His flat, almost arrogant answer was no. In this division, one week at a time was all the vacation that could be taken. I wondered if he was kidding, and that was my first response. He was not, however, kidding. I knew that stupid rule, but I also knew it didn't apply on my level and was seldom enforced. We got into an argument but it didn't do any good. The very idea that I probably had taken less vacation time in the past eight years than almost anyone on my level in the company made the refusal of my request totally absurd.

All of the accumulating tension simply made the pain increase, and my desire to escape from it went through the top of the ceiling. I worked late a few days later, and as I left for home I stopped by a convenience market and picked up a couple of six packs of beer. I didn't drink much beer, but maybe it would help tonight. As I pulled in the driveway, it was clear that everyone at home was in bed asleep. That wasn't unusual, but on this night it heightened the frustration—look at all I was giving and still I couldn't get two weeks off.

Somewhere into the second six pack—it must have been two o'clock in the morning by then—I called the vice-president of the company. I cried through my beer to him about my father's tombstone, no time off, the troubles of running a terminal in Miami, the pain, Vietnam.

He listened patiently enough; in fact, we had gotten to be pretty good friends. There wasn't anything he was going to do at that hour in the morning though, and I was getting pretty unsatisfied with his continual suggestion that I go on to bed, get some rest, and call him in the morning. I began to insist on getting the president's home number, but he wouldn't give it. I pleaded and cajoled. He should have hung up on me, but instead he finally worked his way to a gentlemanly way of ending the conversation. I simply called Atlanta, said there was an emergency, and got the president's number without any hesitation.

I hung up on the man in Atlanta and called the president without any thought to what time it was. All the old story was repeated over and again. He, of course, had no trouble telling that I was drunk. He didn't like being awakened in the night, but more than that, he was greatly offended at the lack of control and self-discipline and especially the drinking. He told me, in no uncertain terms, to be in Atlanta the next day. The haunting feeling that I had gone too far began to set in—its sobering effect was almost immediate, and I began to get clothes ready for the trip to Atlanta even before nearly collapsing into a couple of hours of sleep before daybreak.

As the plane lifted off the runway and banked back over Ft. Lauderdale and to the north, I realized that I had screwed up. My first inclination was that if I was going down, there would be a whole lot of others go down with me. I quickly wrote off a ten page paper documenting kickbacks, cover ups, and one variety of screw up after another. It was easy; there had been plenty going on that I knew about. The hell with it all!!

Somewhere along the way, I decided that the ten pages—none of half-truth or lie—simply wasn't me. I could do a lot of things before I could become a rat. I tore the papers into small pieces and left them to be picked up on my breakfast tray. As soon as I arrived, I was ushered into the president's office; the vice-president and my division manager were already there. I made my apologies for the late-night calls. I began to offer whatever explanations I could. I just needed some time off. I was wrung out. They could see what it was doing to my nerves. Maybe they could put me in some small terminal in South Georgia until things settled down. I talked about Doug's illness and the operation that he was now needing. I talked about Vietnam.

As the conversation went on, I got even stronger. I reminded them of all I had done since I had come to the company. I reminded one of the bosses about how I had all but chaperoned and babysat for his son while he was at the University of Miami. He had a few hard times, and I had bailed him out. Now, I wanted them to bail me out. I finished by saying that I was not going to leave something that I had invested the better part of my life since Vietnam in; I told them what I was going to do.

The last part was a mistake. You don't tell people what you are going to do when they are the ones who are in control. You don't even tell people the truth sometimes, especially when they are not interested in dealing with the truth. People can take the business end; the personal end can get too close.

They ended the conversation with what for them was a delaying tactic. They told me to take all the time I needed. At first I thought everything was all right, but somewhere in the back of my mind there was something of a tone in their voices that made it seem like they were babying me or humoring me or putting me off for the moment. Part of that tone may have even had some uncertainty or fear in it—fear in their minds that I had caused, and people are always uncomfortable when they are made to feel fear.

I got back to Miami, assured Sandy that everything was fine, and we headed for North Carolina. For nearly two weeks, it was like we were a family again. Doug's sickness, my pain, all of the demands of the Miami terminal seemed like pages torn from an old book. The two weeks passed too quickly, but I felt like a new man. We stopped in Atlanta on our way back, just to show them what a new man looked like and that all was well. There was no indication that anything was changed. I was the old Chuck again; their interests were well in hand.

When I came in on Monday, all seemed fine. The district manager was there, but that was pretty much to be expected. I went on up to my office and began to check through the paperwork, but I kept noticing that instead of the manager leaving—which should have been his normal response to my return—he kept moving in and out like he was running things.

About noon, I started asking questions. Why was he still around? No one seemed to want to answer. Finally, I had him come in. What was going on? His answer was flat but unbending: they would give me a chance to resign or I would be fired. It would be up to me, but something had to be done by the end of the day.

I immediately called the president. He didn't try to avoid me. In fact, it was almost as if he had been expecting my call. I went back down my list of all that I had done. He kept saying, "That's right. That's right. That right." Then, he had to go. That was it.

No "thank yous" or "good byes," nothing; I said one more thing as he was obviously finished, there was a final "That's right," and he was off the line. The sense of finality was devastating.

I gave it up. There was no use doing anything else. It was almost as final as death on the battlefield. You could want to bring it back all you wanted to, but it did no good—no good at all.

The district manager volunteered to drive me home and bring the company car back to the terminal. I told him that I would much rather Old George take me. On that short-long drive, George didn't say a thing. For that moment, it was like something of his background and mine had a way of merging. He knew how I was hurting at that moment, and I somehow felt a world of hurt that he and his people must have known since the days of the slave ships. I was outside. I was minority. I was powerless and at the mercy of a two-faced system. I was used up and now they could let me go. It all went on for them; for me it had to start all over again. George wanted to know if he could do anything. I shook his hand and told him no—I was tired, I said, and just needed to rest.

Used up.

Chapter XXII

I sat around the next couple of weeks more or less in a state of disbelief. There was no way that I could have given any more to the business than I did. Somehow I had the idea that life was fair if you were honest and worked hard. Somehow I thought that you got back in kind what you had given. Here was my first real experience with the "System," and it was clear that it simply used you up and then spit you out; there was always someone else standing in line ready to take your place. Whether that person could do as good of a job as you didn't mean a thing; all that was really important was filling the place. If a note of skepticism and cynicism is being heard, there is at least a clear reflection of exactly what I was feeling. Rejection and disillusionment are powerful forces that can play havoc with human emotions.

Most people think of the military as the school of hard knocks, the place of unreasonable discipline, the place where you are depersonalized into non-being. That had not been the case with me at all. Sure it was hard, but hard is OK if it is fair. I had given my best and that had been acknowledged. It was in this nearly righteous fragment of the outside world that I had gotten screwed over most royally, and there wasn't a damn thing that I could do about it that made any sense. Sure, I could assault their terminals, shoot their trucks at a distance, or go into Atlanta and kill everyone in their holy administration office. In fact, those thoughts crossed my mind. They simply did not make any sense.

When I looked around, I couldn't believe all that I saw. Doug had been diagnosed as having arrested hydrocephelus, thyroid problems, and pituitary problems. He would need operations to correct circumstances that had existed since birth, and these would be hard on him and extremely expensive. We had a house worth well over a hundred thousand dollars, and now there was a new baby, Brad. It was hard to imagine how all of this could be handled.

Sandy was the rock through it all. She was able to put an entirely new face on everything. She hadn't liked the transport company anyway, and now she saw this as a chance to have me home more. She had felt all along that I was being used to some extent, but I had not been able to see it for myself. She encouraged me that something, even something better, would turn up soon. It was hard for me not to think that in some kind of greater contest that I had been beaten.

One advantage that I felt was sure to come from the time away from work was enough rest to start feeling less tired. I looked forward to the renewal of strength that rest and relaxation would bring. It really surprised me to find that the strength did not return. If anything, I was getting more tired all of the time. I thought maybe that I was just depressed, but that didn't make sense either because the main emotion that I was feeling was anger—along with a determination to continue to be the "provider" that my family needed. Depression always seemed to me to be more the result of a giving-up passivity, and I certainly wasn't feeling passive. The tiredness should have been going away but it wasn't.

Sandy was right about work finding me soon. I got a job working for Ryder Truck Lines as a dock supervisor; it wasn't on the level of work that I had been used to, but it was respectable and didn't have many of the old hassles. For some reason, I just didn't seem to be able to shake the tiredness. I couldn't get into the new work; I did my job, no question about that, but I wasn't dedicated. On top of that, I was in a position of having to almost continually come in contact with the old truck company. Every time I saw one of their rigs roll by, the hurt of all that had happened was reinforced.

Soon, a chance came along to go to a better job with Yellow Trucking Company. It went pretty well. Yellow was bigger than anything else I had worked for. It wasn't family oriented, so the ability to move up was less but at least it was fair. For about a year everything worked out pretty well. I was continuing to go to the VA for medicine, and they were continuing to feel sure that there was no physiological reason for the pain that I was feeling. The tiredness hung like the heaviness in the Vietnam air after a rain, after the relentless, continual rain.

One day a guy from Jacksonville walked in and introduced himself. He represented an express company and had been given my name by an old district manager from the first company in Atlanta. He was looking for a Terminal Manager for their operation at Miami International Airport. They were having all kinds of problems, and the word was out that I was a problem-solver. There was the possibility of prestige and responsibility;

there was the certainty of immediately having more money. Why wait on Yellow? His only negative—to me—came with a smile: "We are a family business. We'll treat you right!" I had had one family business too many, but I didn't say anything about that. I would think about it.

Sandy and I talked. That in itself was a new transition for me. In times in the past, I had felt that the "man of the house" made all of the decisions. The woman simply followed his leadership. I had operated like this in the past. But the past couple of years had taught me an important lesson; we were in this together—all the way. Sandy had strengths and insights that had to be heard.

On one side, Yellow was a known quantity. I could stay there, avoid a lot of pressure, and advance in their system as openings occurred. I didn't like the "family business" end of the proposal; it was just like asking for trouble.

On the other hand, we needed the money, and I was always craving for a challenge. It pleased me to no end to know that I had gotten a reputation as a problem-solver in difficult situations. There was a lot of action around Miami International and I could see myself going in there and whipping it into shape. We could not help but think it over.

While we were working through all of the possibilities and having no small number of misgivings, this new company invited us to a party on one of the privately owned islands in the northern part of the Keys. All of the top brass from Jacksonville would be there, along with several people from the movie industry. There would be no obligations; just come.

We talked about how all of this sounded like the same old runaround, but who was going to turn down a private party on a rich estate? We went and thoroughly enjoyed ourselves. This was the kind of living comparable to my ability as a manager and a potential company man. I could do exactly what they needed, and something like this might be some of the reward for a job well done. I hadn't seen many movie people hanging around Yellow lately. Driving back through Miami early the next morning, we decided to give it all a shot.

There were problems: 95% of the workers were Cuban, drivers were using trucks for their own activities, the manager who had been fired had been Cuban, there was low pay, and the day-to-day management system was non-existent. I, of course, hit the ground running at full speed. There would be no more sitting around reading the magazines that we were supposed to be delivering. Drivers were required to call in on a regular basis to report their whereabouts and the way that the day's work that I laid out was being completed. There would be no more stopping in at the movie theaters and watching movies on company time. And, more than anything, the terminal would be cleaned up; if you worked in a mediocre environment, you tended to become mediocre.

Of course, everyone was bitching and complaining, but discipline and structure can be good for people. They began to sense that I was in charge and, if they helped me, I would find ways to help them. We all worked hard, but it was successful. Within two months, it was like a different world.

I tried to do it all, just like before. The only difference was that this time I started—in spite of the enthusiasm of the challenge— tired. Many times I would go out and get the work underway or check on it to see if it was being done correctly, and then go to the office, shut the door, and literally collapse in sleep. It wasn't drinking—which really never was that much—or the drugs that I was getting at the VA. It was like a damn giant leech on my insides sapping all of my strength. I told them, I told them, I told them, but it didn't do any good. They kept on insisting, "It's all in your head!"

My idea was that if my workers could save money by working harder that I could get some of that money back for them in raises; money is always the best incentive for those who do not have it. If a man has any pride and is trying to help his family, he will work. At least, he will work if you come through for him with pay.

I promised but I could not deliver. Sure, the people in Jacksonville were delighted with all they saw on the surface. Shipments were going and coming on time, profits were up, and the word was getting around that the operation was now first-rate. They were picking up new accounts right and left. But it was all hanging on a thin strand. I could do it, but only if I could keep my promise. At that point they did not budge. There were plenty of workers. If they didn't like what they were paid, get some more. My argument that any workers were not necessarily good workers fell on deaf ears. I tried to explain in both Jacksonville and Atlanta but it didn't work.

It wasn't long until a good deal of unrest began to surface. There were threats of unionization and some union type organizing was started. Incidents of intentional sabotage heightened the tension in the environment, and the very word "union" sent panic attacks rippling all the way to the Florida-Georgia border. And, what did I do? Call for more money for my workers; what else? That would solve every problem in a hurry.

But the company wouldn't budge. Instead, they got angry with me. I had done exactly what they wanted, and the proof was on every side. I was telling them how to simply and efficiently solve their problems, but all they could see was unions on one side and me demanding higher wages on the other. I told them that I could manage the union initiatives, and I did. Ironically, on the same day that I called to inform them that the union organization activities had totally ceased, they were back on the line to me by close of business to let me know that my services would no longer be needed. I had never been so arbitrarily and categorically fired in my life. It was a long way from the party on the private key.

I crawled back into unemployment again, exhausted, and starting to personalize all that was happening to me. If something had not been pulling me down so badly, I don't think that it would have happened, but I couldn't see that it wasn't me that was the problem here. Both of those major operations in those Miami terminals had been run more professionally and efficiently by me than at any time in their entire history. They were a picture of organization, and that was the opinion of everyone involved. But I started feeling shame; shame for failing, not providing, causing Sandy worry, and not being able to hold a job. In my background and every orientation of my values, not being able to hold a job was about as low as a person could go. I had had three jobs in three years; I started looking at myself as if I were not worth a damn.

The VA didn't help. There was only more and stronger pain pills and their continual insistence that it was all mental. I was about convinced. Anything to help the pain and exhaustion!

I agreed to see the psychiatrists, and they were quick with their solutions: psychiatric drugs and dredging out the hidden remains of Vietnam. In retrospect, I'm sorry that the psychiatric process ever started. Most of the drugs were highly experimental and maybe they gave me Vietnam back more than they took it away. Maybe it is true that you have to flush some things out of your mind that get repressed, but maybe time and life had already done that to a large extent. If they had just taken care of the physical pains that I described over and over again until we were all sick of it, the mental can of worms might never have been opened.

Sometimes I think **they** created the way that I felt like I should respond to Vietnam. Sometimes I think **they** gouged out implications that never had really occurred to me. Between the drugs and their digging around for explanations, Vietnam came flooding back in like some dead monster digging its way out of its own grave and twisting at the door of your most private space. The drugs seemed almost like a glue that stuck Vietnam deeper and more irremovably in my brain than it had ever been.

The end effect of the drugs, the digging and gouging, the exhaustion, and the feelings of failure and shame was one thought and one thought alone: "Fuck it all!!" I let my hair and beard grow—something that never happened, even when we were in the field for days; I had never felt so totally overwhelmed in all of my existence.

I had to work, but the last place I was interested in was a trucking company; there were too many bad memories. Several people who knew me and saw the problems suggested going for some kind of disability related to the war. It made total sense to them and probably was too painfully obvious, but not to me. It seemed too much like a handout. I was not a freeloader or a bum. I could make my way. I had been a provider; I would be a provider!

One of my neighbors hung wallpaper. That sounds like near-minimum wage, day labor, but not the way my neighbor did it. Don't forget that this was a one hundred thousand plus neighborhood. He hung for the fanciest, most upscale design gallery in Miami, and his clientele consisted of multi-millionaires in the entertainment, sports, real estate, and banking industries. It was not unusual for him to hang ten thousand dollars worth of wallpaper in part of a day.

I started helping him and made enough to continue to maintain our lifestyle to some extent. It wasn't paying all of the bills, especially the medical ones that were mounting with Doug, but it kept some of the ends meeting.

The wallpapering was easy. I learned quickly and could begin to see myself learning enough to go out on my own. The hard part was the way the people looked at you and treated you. It was almost as if you were some kind of specially bred animal only capable of the function that they had hired you for. You were a nothing, a zero, a place holder.

Whatever my neighbor was feeling of this belittlement and abuse, he had times of passing it on to me. He would go through moods of unrelenting cursing and name calling. Some days you could do nothing right. You were a "hunk of dog shit," a "stupid son-of-a-bitch." And this was from my neighbor. His mood changes were amazing. I took it, though, for a couple of reasons: I didn't have a particularly violent response streak and, more than that, I was learning something that could mean a lot of money.

One day we were working in a luxury high rise overlooking Biscayne Bay. The apartment must have cost two or three million dollars. It was time for lunch and we were eating on a balcony fifteen stories up. The large, sliding glass door was open and air-conditioned coolness was pouring into the stirring breezes. Even though it wasn't yours, you sure could enjoy the view.

Easing along down below, a huge private yacht was coming along under us. My neighbor started watching it and cursing the rich people on board. They couldn't hear at this distance, but he was yelling every obscenity in the book. Finally, he reached into a large supply box that we carried and brought out a quart-sized bottle of the especially thick, oil paint that we used to touch up places on the wallpaper. He said, "Watch this," and hurled the bottle in front of the yacht. It struck the water maybe fifteen yards right in front of the boat and broke all to pieces. A large patch of bright yellow-red paint covered the surface of the water and the yacht moved right through it. He was beside himself in triumph; it would cost those rich bastards plenty to get all of that cleaned off.

I thought he was totally stupid, and he must have sensed that from the expression on my face. He turned on me with the arrogant command, "Well, you dumb son-of-a-bitch, get off your lazy ass and get back to work."

That was it. I had had all I could take. I grabbed him under the arms and had him up and over the railing of the balcony before he knew what was happening. I held him out at arms length with nothing but fifteen stories of air between him and parking lot pavement. He was too stunned to beg.

With a totally calm and fixed concentration of my face, I told him that I was going to drop him and laugh at him all the way to the ground. He was limp in resignation. This was it. Then, I told him he deserved to be dropped. He didn't say a word in reply or argument. Finally, I said that the only reason I would not drop him was because of his wife and kids, and my wife and kids. I lifted him back across the railing and set him down gently. He folded up like a deflating water float. From that moment on, he treated me with perfect decency.

The VA psychiatrists started hitting nerves now made raw and exposed by their digging. They concluded that Vietnam was all of my problem. I had simply hidden it with all of the work that I had done since I had returned. It had to come out and be dealt with— like a "shadow," they said, that had to come out and be destroyed by light.

They honed in on Rick's death which, when you think about it, was the only thing that made sense to hone in on about that first tour of duty. They honed in on the nuns and children in the sanpan, the bodies we planted during the Tet Offensive, and the American bodies that had been staked out along the river like something you would see in some kind of grotesque horror movie about inhumane torture which, when you think about it, were the only episodes that made sense to hone in on about the second tour. They picked out these few tragic moments and built my entire adult life around them. Instead of taking away shadows, the black darkness of guilt that I began to feel was smothering, like being caught in a lightless cave and drowning in a creeping, slow rise of dark, black, syrupy oil. The deeper they took me, the more dependent on their drugs I became. The deeper they took me, the more I felt like I had to talk. By creating an existence for me that probably was mostly gone, they created a circumstance that justified their own existence as psychiatrists. I felt like I was being sucked down the whirlpool black hole of a giant bathtub, and peering over the edge I could see them standing, talking, holding the plug high in their hands.

In the middle of all of this, Doug had to go back in the hospital for more surgery. No matter how hard you work, there is no way to keep up with general bills and medical bills at the same time. There were continual calls from collectors, and finally a couple even came to our house. The house itself was threatened, and we had to carefully watch due dates on every utility bill.

It nearly killed me to do it, but we had to go to Sandy's dad for help. His strong Mize hands—he was kin to the legendary Yankee pitcher Johnny Mize—were no bigger than his heart. There was no question of every help and support that Sandy's parents could give. They knew that I would do the same for them, and I would.

I'm sure that a lot of people had written me off as being crazy as hell. All of the Vietnam vet caricatures that were becoming too prominent in the media were in the minds, and then faces, of many people that I crossed paths with. I was probably drinking too much and that didn't help, although I never hurt anyone or became abusive to my family. It even made me sad to slap down a bug that might be flying around my face.

The drugs had to be something of the culprit; even in my confusion and pain, I realized that. I started swapping the drugs that the physicians were giving me for marijuana. I hate that now. The people that got the drugs didn't need them, and I know I hurt them. But pain will make you do lots of things that you would not normally do. Most of the people that I dealt with would have gotten the drugs somewhere anyway.

One thing that I want to make perfectly clear. The people that I was swapping out with were people that I had known for a long time, other Vietnam vets that I crossed paths with almost daily. In no way would I have ever, ever gotten involved in any kind of process that would have hurt or even been exposed to children or young people. I may not be perfect and those times were altogether less than perfect, but I had an insatiable morality about children and young people and drugs. I would have died before I crossed that line.

It was sickening to sit and watch them. The pain killing drugs would be put in an old, often dirty spoon and held over a source of heat—sometimes a cigarette lighter, sometimes a stove eye. The material in the medicine would smoke and melt, and then would be sucked up into a hypodermic needle. With the tip of the needle still steaming, the drug would then be mainlined right into the arm. That just compounded my guilt, but either the absence of the medication or the marijuana seemed to ease my overall pains. For a while the drugs and marijuana would allow us all to accept or not think about what we had done. When you came down, it all came back.

It seemed like I was leading two lives; like a fugitive I was continually running between two places. On one hand I was living in a nice, upper middle-class neighborhood in a $125,000 house, and still dressed and acted the part. On the other hand, I was dropping into a much less affluent area where I was an outsider, but a much needed outsider. They learned my doctors' schedules and were calling the house the day before to remind me to come as soon as I had medicine. I liked these people and still would. I might not like what they were doing, but I understood it to an extent and knew all too well that I didn't like everything that I had ever done either. Still, there was the outsider feeling—in their neighborhood, in my own—everywhere except the Everglades.

The physicians finally decided that I had to accept VA temporary disability. This would, they said, relieve some of the financial pressures of having to work, and give me a chance to fully concentrate on getting rid of the ghosts of Vietnam. I took it, although it was not really enough to allow our family finances to function. But, maybe they were right. I thought they weren't, but I was filling up more and more with every level of question and self-doubt. To be totally on the country's dole simply made me feel that I was losing it all.

I hadn't been in church for so long that I couldn't remember the last time. I'm not sure that Momma or Sandy had given up on me in this regard, but nothing much was ever said any more. Maybe it was the desperation or a total grasping for something—anything—that would help, but we decided to start going as a family again.

The Methodists had started a new congregation in a school about ten miles inland from Ft. Lauderdale at a place called Cooper City. It was small, but growing, and the people were friendly in the way that seemed real. The old feeling of church people being mostly hypocrites that the Atlanta situation had left me with didn't get in the way very much after a couple of weeks. We hit it off well with the people and began to develop some friendships.

The friendships were good for all of us, but a lot of the church situation added to my grief. It was almost as if an additional burden suddenly surfaced as I was forced by the environment to recall all of the old promises that I had made to God that were still going completely unkept.

I would go to church on Sunday, the perfect picture of human normalcy, and then head out to hide in the swamps and get away from it all the rest of the week. This pattern was repeated over months—church, the VA, the swamps—God, psychiatric drugs, isolation. And all the time there was the constant and increasing pain in my side. It got so bad that every time I coughed an almost unbearable pain would occur; I would then push my side back into place—whatever that meant—and the pain would subside. I told all of the doctors about it, but no one would believe me—it was all in my mind. Hell, I told them, I'm not pushing my mind to make the pain go away. Still, they wouldn't listen. It was always, "Chuck, we've tested all of that; there's nothing there."

In the course of the drug experimentation, they put me on Nardill, a MAO inhibiter—a psychological drug designed to put people in a more positive and pleasant frame of thought. It was amazing. I almost instantly had a sense of well-being. It seemed like I wanted to be real sweet to people all of the time. I wrote poetry—of all things! I kept going off into the deep trains of thought and was hypersensitive to everything that was happening around me.

In addition, it was like being on speed of some sort. There was a sudden unleashing of energy. I couldn't sleep at night and wanted to work all of the time. I even went so far as to rig lanterns so I could work in my yard at night. One time, I can remember Sandy coming out looking for me about three o'clock in the morning; she found me on my hands and knees pulling small weeds out of my grass. It was a real picking up of enthusiasm from where I had been, but it was also somehow phoney. I could feel the phoniness, but the good was so much better than what I had felt— it was like a strange feeling trap in which there was no good choice for getting out.

Finally, there was too much speed. I started reacting to situations in absurd ways. The house started leaking and, even with the help of the police, I couldn't get the contractor to come over and remove some pieces of the wall to find and repair the leak. I ended up going in and, with my bare hands, tearing off most of the wall coverings in the house down to the bare studs. It was an awful mess, and one which we didn't really have the money to fix. I stared at those walls that I had demolished and felt even more like a son-of-a-bitch. **But,** I hadn't been able to control it. That "but" didn't help me much or anyone else, and we all knew it.

A television that had just been "fixed" at no small cost by a local repairman went dead on us as we were sitting in the living room watching it. Without thinking I grabbed it up and threw it across the room smashing it into a million pieces. All the time, the front window and door were open and neighbors were out in the street. There is no question that they thought I was completely crazy. Even the minister asked Sandy how she could stay married to me.

The lawn mower wouldn't work and I tried for most of a day to get it started. Finally, thinking that it would go, I moved it into the front yard and began to crank away. Nothing happened. I cranked and cranked, and the more that I tried, the more frustrated I became. Nothing!

So I grabbed it up—it was a rather sizeable riding mower and threw it over into the middle of the street. A couple of men in the neighborhood rushed over as I was pouring gas all over it and getting ready to set it on fire. At first it was "Chuck, calm down, don't do it." Then, it went to "Chuck, don't be crazy" or "You are crazy." Finally, there was a warning about calling the police. With total calm, I turned to them and gave an invitation, "Damn you! Go ahead and call the police." And then my own warning, "Just remember, if you do, there's getting ready to be a bunch of dead policemen laying around here." I meant that, too. That's how high the desperation and drugs had taken me. Thank God, they backed off and disappeared. I never lighted the fire.

The worst thing that happened while I was on the high took place one afternoon when I was getting ready to go with a couple of old buddies to the swamp for a weekend of fishing. They were already outside waiting and in a big hurry while I was getting some equipment ready to go in the garage. As I lifted a load of gear back toward the truck we were going in, I rammed my arm into a frog gig that I had laid down in the way. The gig's sharp prongs sunk into the flesh of my left upper arm. The flanges held it there anchored in place.

My friends gasped in horror as I stepped back with the frog gig hanging from my arm. I didn't say a word but began to twist the gig back and forth in my arm, cutting the meat of the arm apart so that it could be pulled out. Finally, with blood pouring, I jerked the gig out. It pulled muscle and tendon out with it. One of the guys nearly passed out, but I simply stuffed what meat I could back in and found something to bandage the bleeding wound. Hell, it was on to the swamps. Nothing was stopping that.

Within two days the arm was swelling with infection to the point that it looked like it would burst. Even at that, it took every threat and plea that they could muster to get me in. The doctors that fixed me up were certain that in a matter of hours, it could have all gone too far and the whole arm could have been lost. In retrospect, I'm not even sure that I even felt any pain. The drugs were masking it all; I wasn't better, only covering up what was really there.

Just as the kind of situation that I was in had the potential for the tragic, it also had the potential for the ridiculous and the absurd. I got to know a military type in our church who I seemed to hit it off with right from the very first. He was a really nice fellow, and we had some things in common; he was a Captain in the National Guard and in charge of one of their infantry training units. We talked about military strategy and training on several occasions and got to be pretty close friends.

On one occasion he got to talking about a weekend bivouac that his unit was going to be holding in a back area of the swamps that I knew like the back of my hand. I offered the suggestion that I could mount a surprise attack and see how well his troops would respond. I was deadly serious but, although he did not really express any objection, I am sure he thought I was kidding. He probably forgot all about it; with hyped excitement I began to make my plans.

I began to collect all matter of "attack" devices; this included cherry bombs and a couple of tape recorders. The basic idea was to create a frightening diversion, give the impression that the woods were full of attackers, and then slip in and capture the command post. It sounded so exciting that Johnny Frazier, in one of his less-than-fully-alert moments agreed to help me.

When the night of the bivouac came, we gathered our materials including camouflage clothes and facial paint—and headed for the swamps. It was pouring one of those intolerable, Florida rains that was guaranteed to go on all night, but this probably made it even more realistic—even more like Vietnam. We had both had a few beers, even though I was supposed to stay away from alcohol with the medicine I was on.

We carefully parked our truck at a distance and loaded our gear. Somewhere in my mind I was thinking like a Viet Cong. That meant total camouflage, no shoes, and perfect quiet as I became one with the jungle. We slipped into where they were supposed to be camped. It was so dark that you couldn't see anything and nothing could be heard. I had the idea that my National Guard friend had taken me seriously and was waiting.

I left Frazier to "guard" and circled the entire encampment area. Carefully I rigged cherry bombs to cigarettes. By the time the cigarettes burned down, the blasting diversion would be on one side and I would be on the other. The tape recorders were set up with carefully timed blank spaces in the front to give me time to get in position. Everything worked perfectly.

When the cherry bombs and recorders began to blast, the silence of the swamp erupted like a fire fight. It could not have been more realistic. I carefully slipped down into the area of the encampment—they were not even there! Nothing was there but more darkness. Damn!

And Frazier had taken off running, believing that part of the explosions was return fire. When all of the sound stopped, I couldn't find Frazier. It took me the better part of an hour, feeling my way around in the dark, to finally locate Frazier and explain to him that there was some mistake.

We went straight back to my house and I started making midnight phone calls to anyone who knew my friend. This only added to the rumors of my insanity, but I did find out where the bivouac had been relocated. Without any supplies now, I headed immediately there with the charge of excitement still running high. Frazier's excitement had more than dwindled by now; he refused to go. The drugs spoke, that did not matter, I would carry out the "attack" by myself.

Maybe the best diversion was no diversion at all. I simply parked at a distance and went walking out the muddy roadway toward the encampment. It was still pouring rain; I was still barefoot and camouflaged.

Two sentries stepped out to meet me. All I did was say "hello" and kept right on walking. No attempt was made to stop me in any way. I came up on a sergeant and lieutenant at the immediate perimeter of the encampment. All it took was the word that I was looking for their captain and, not knowing any better than that it was all part of the training, they pointed out exactly what covered trailer was the command post. I melted into the "enter" part of the campsite.

Just as I slipped in behind and up to the opening that lead into where my friend was sleeping in the dry, and just as I was reaching to pull back the opening and step in, a young Black guy stuck his head out—maybe just to see if it had stopped raining. Our faces were no more than two inches apart.

He swallowed a half-scream and fell back into the trailer. There were several waking curses, but I could hear him saying in a startled voice, "There's something out there! There's something out there." The response came back, almost totally annoyed by now, "What?" He could only say, "Something."

By the time my friend got someone out to look around, I was completely hidden. A quick look by someone in the trailer brought back reassurances that the young soldier had been having a nightmare, and there was the near-order from my friend that everyone get back to sleep.

I gave them long enough to drift off, and simply climbed into the command post trailer. I crouched down next to my friend and whispered in his ear: "Captain, wake up. You're captured." There was some uproar, especially from the lieutenant and sergeant, who were embarrassed by their momentary incompetence more than anything else. The captain wasn't all that interested in having been awakened, but he seemed to get a kick out of the whole thing. I went around for days bragging about how I had single-handedly captured an entire company of the Florida National Guard.

On another occasion, I had gotten to know several of the Seminole Indians who lived in and around the swamps. In some ways, they seemed to respect me because I respected them and had come to learn about their environment. We fished, hunted, and talked a lot together.

One day the conversation turned to alligators, and I got the hair brained idea that I would like to have an alligator head; it could be some kind of good luck symbol or at least an unusual conversation piece. Killing the gators at that time was illegal, but no one watched too closely what was going on in the swamps. There would be times when the Indians would have to kill a gator for their own safety. The conversation turned to other matters, and I basically forgot all about it.

On one of the afternoons when I was at the VA, Sandy and her mother were at our house playing with the kids. A truck load of Indians pulled up in our driveway, looking for "Old Chuck," and acting like they had had more than their share of "fire water" that day. They had "something" for Chuck.

Sandy told them just to leave it in the garage, and the Indians proceeded to start to unload a twelve foot, thoroughly alive alligator. At that point, Sandy and her mother "attacked," and the Indians and their gator barely made it out of the yard with their skins in tact. I'm not exactly sure how much of my own was lost when I got back home, but there was no more talk of my wanting alligator heads. All that I could do when I saw my friends again was to share a moment of head shaking and laughter; there is no telling how they talked about me when I was not with them. At least, with them it was all in good fun and a certain relief from the shallow seriousness that I continually confronted at the VA where they still were convinced that it was all in my head.

More than anything else I wanted people to see me as I had seen myself at my best. I didn't want them to see a sick, out-of-work, and thoroughly depressed shell of the person that I had once been. I bought an entire combat uniform just like I had worn in the field in Vietnam—all they ever wanted to talk about was Vietnam. I painted on the camouflage and went to the swamps. It was better to stay there; on one occasion I went to my church friend's house in full dress just to show him and succeeded only in nearly causing his mother-in-law to have a heart attack when she answered the door. It was better to stay there among the Indians and alligators.

There was a game warden that I crossed paths with regularly. He seemed to somehow understand better than anyone. He never got in my space or asked too many questions. He simply said: "Do what you need to do; just don't hurt anyone." Hurting anyone never entered my mind by that time—even with the confused stimulation of the drugs. But he was right: I was doing exactly what I felt I needed to do. Nothing else was working and no one that could really help would listen.

Chapter XXIII

Everywhere I turned, I was met by guilt. It was all over the preacher's face, and it seemed like everything that he had to say was directed straight at me. I sat there and listened with a mind filled with all of the promises made to God that had not been kept. I tried to pray, but somehow it seemed that until the promises were kept the prayers would be of no effect. It was hard to look him in the face and know that he had told Sandy that he couldn't see how she stayed with me. But, in my desperation, I kept going back. The guilt was always there.

The psychiatrists were just as bad. Two times a week they dug back into Vietnam. I would sweat. I would cry. I could not find any explanation for why God had let me live. It would have been a lot better for everyone if it had been Rick who lived—or anyone else. Sometimes I would stop right in the middle of what I was doing and just stand there and cry. The drugs didn't help, so they just gave more.

I had started building small mirror boxes in the garage with the idea that some additional income might be provided. I would take large pieces of mirror, cut them down, and line the surfaces of small designs that I had cut out in wood. The mirror pieces were heavy, cumbersome, and easily broken.

As I was lifting a large piece out of the way, it snapped and fell all around me. One piece fell across my wrist and cut a deep gash. It had not struck an artery, but was bleeding pretty profusely. I quickly wrapped the cut with a rag to stop the bleeding and rushed upstairs to get Sandy. She could see the severity of the cut and immediately rushed me to the hospital.

While we were in the car on the way to get treatment, one thought settled in my mind: it would not matter what I claimed, they would simply assume that I had tried to commit suicide. With all of the questions that they had been asking, it was clear that they already were considering it a possibility. In everything— even the drugs—killing myself had not been on my list of possibilities. Disappearing in the swamps, maybe, but not taking my own life. God knows, though, as much as they brought it up, if there was anything to the power of suggestion, I was quickly becoming a good candidate. Maybe the thought did come to enter my mind, but only after they placed it there. I would fight against that thought, though, fight against it with all of my might. My boys—my wife—would simply not be without a father and a husband.

I got stitched up and we went back home. Besides feeling even more inept and unable to get anything done, everything was fine. It would not be difficult to imagine the immediate response written all over the faces of the psychiatrists when I went in for my regular session the next morning: suicide! They talked all around it, even to the point of my belligerently putting it out right on the table: "Look, dammit, I didn't try to kill myself! All right?" Their "all right, Chuck" clearly conveyed that they were sure that I was lying.

They had been talking occasionally about my committing myself for a period of in-patient psychiatric care. Following the accident with the mirror, it was a regular topic of conversation. The power of suggestion began to work again, and I was about ready to give it up and go.

Sandy was opposed totally and completely, and she had expressed that every time. She could begin to sense, however, that I was about to go along with their suggestions. She asked for one thing first; let her take me to Miami and see what it would be like in the psych ward of the VA hospital. Feeling that I could at least do this for her and then go on, I agreed.

The pitiful, helpless hell that we had unveiled before our eyes defied description. It was more like a prison than a hospital. People were sitting around with dazed, frightened stares on their faces. Since everyone's mood seemed identical to me, I was convinced that they were all being drugged just so they wouldn't be any problem. I began to remember the faces of the children that we pulled out of the fire zones; total confusion, no understanding, no control, horrible fear—the look of the absolute victim.

Thank God for Sandy. What she made me see awakened me to the abundance of sanity that was still there. I was not the guy who never looked up, who never spoke, who was deep into his three hundredth page of scribbled journal. I was not the guy racing down the hall with a broom stick to face the next Viet Cong attack. I was not the near animal-like sobbing, crying coming from behind one door and then another. Sandy simply said no—once you got into a place like this, you were in it for the rest of your life. We went home.

Life was better in the swamp. I would head for the grocery store and end up in the swamp; start to the post office and end up in the swamp; be scheduled for the VA and end up in the swamp. It was familiar in the swamp. The preachers and psychiatrists weren't there. The ghosts were not there. The pain was still there, but maybe not as bad. I planted marijuana seeds, but they never grew. I fought snakes as big as my leg, but always won. I felt a lot closer to God out there.

It might have been a strange indication of the sanity that I did have—and that Sandy undoubtedly saw, because she had no trouble with me taking Doug and Brad with me to the swamps. Other people sometimes warned her about it, but she had no hesitancy to respond that "their Dad will take care of them." I always did.

We had our close calls, none of which had to do with sanity, but I took care of them. On one occasion, we were towing an old World War II communications trailer that I had rebuilt. As we were moving through a residential neighborhood, one of the boys said, "Hey Daddy." I responded, "What is it?" The word came back: "There goes the trailer." Sure enough, it had come loose and was heading right for the front of a nearby house. Had it not been for a large tree, it would have gone right through a large picture window and into the living room.

On another occasion, Doug had not been able to wait for me to get set up before he got in the water. I was working on some rigging, and he began to yell—rather calmly—"Alligator, alligator." From the tone of his voice, I thought he was kidding, and I almost didn't even look. When I did look, there was a huge mother gator between Doug and her babies, bearing down on Doug. I grabbed the gig and, like something out of a movie, buried it into the gator's brain not five yards away from where Doug still was swimming. We cut off the huge tail and had all of the alligator meat that we could eat.

The boys told their mother that they had eaten alligator meat. That was all that she wanted to hear about it. It would not have done, given our interest in camping, for her to have known where that alligator meat had come from. If she had ever asked, I was hoping that she would buy the idea of crazy old Indian friends. She never asked.

On a more serious level, I was feeling the need to give the boys something of me that would stay with them. I was getting to the place where I couldn't see the pain going on much longer. There had to be something bad inside me. They had quit looking for it at the VA, but it was still there. If I could teach the boys to survive in this place, to survive off of the land, then they could make their own way if they had to. These were always good times, but we always had to come back in.

All of the feeling started going out of my left arm and leg. Since the feeling ebbed and flowed with the pain in my side, there was no question in my mind that there was a connection; something was wrong in the side. One "team"—this was their terminology— of VA doctors were assigned my case. An entirely new round of examinations took place, but they found nothing. There was little question that I was beginning to become a nuisance to them. The head doctor on the team made only one suggestion; he could get me more psychological help.

Finally, the pain became so great in the middle of one night, that I had to have help right then. There was no time to get to Miami, so Sandy took me to Hollywood Memorial—the first civilian hospital that I had been to. The doctor on duty was a Cuban who had seen war wounds as a surgeon during the Bay of Pigs invasion period. He didn't seem to have any problem at all in believing that something was still there from Vietnam.

He gave me something for the pain and did a series of basic, preliminary examinations. He listened to everything that I said, on into the early morning, with great interest and care. As the results of the tests started coming in, he said with real certainty that there was definitely something there, possibly some herniation in the old wound and probably scar tissue breaking loose and creating infections. When I told him about all of the problems with the VA, he made arrangements for me to see another private physician whom he described as the "best internal surgeon in South Florida."

When I walked out of Hollywood Memorial as the first light of day was breaking on the distant ocean horizon, it was like I was born again. Finally! Finally! Someone was confirming everything that I had said. It was more than just being right; it was being sane! I wanted to shout!

I got right in to see this "best surgeon," and he proceeded with all of the examinations. When he first saw me, he acted startled. Had he not seen anyone scarred like I was? Surely, he was not so easily put off.

When the examination was complete and he had finished the initial tests, we waited to get his final decision. I was certain that everything was on the brink of being solved. It had taken the better part of two years and a lot of pure hell, but now things would turn around.

He called us back into his office and asked us to be seated. After a long pause of looking me up and down one more time, he said it straight out: "Mr. Matherson, I'm sorry. I can't help you. I haven't been able to find anything." All that I can say is that I simply lost it. I broke down and started crying uncontrollably. He said we could use his office for a few minutes. He excused himself and left.

We got back home and I waited until after midnight. I knew that the Cuban had written his report down. I would get it and take it to the VA. I called but he was not there. At least, that's what the voice on the phone said. I could tell it was a lie.

I drove straight over to Hollywood Memorial, and the Cuban was there. I told him what had happened. Suddenly, he was very busy, although there were no other patients waiting. He kept muttering about how this guy was the best, how he would have to go along with what this best doctor had said.

"OK," I finally gave up, "Just give me a copy of the report that you wrote down last night." He looked me straight in the eye and said, "What report? I didn't write down anything about you." I started to argue. Under some circumstances, I would have had him by the neck. At this moment, all I did was break down and start crying again.

It was all too clear. The expert had evidently had his delicate sensibilities offended. Maybe he saw me as a no pay or low pay veteran. And the Cuban, trying to find a place for himself in a foreign system, was not going against that system in any way. I broke down again. The Cuban didn't leave. He was torn. He knew better than he was doing, but he couldn't jeopardize his own life for me. I talked to him between the crying, but it was really talking to the whole system that I could not seem to budge, "I don't understand why you are doing this to me. I have a wife and two little kids." All he would do was deny everything that he had found, said, and written. I continued, "I can live with myself, and I'll have to answer for everything that I have done. You have to live with yourself, too. If you can live with this lie, that's the way it will have to be." I got myself together and stood to leave. It looked like at any second that he would reconsider, but he did not. I kept trying to make a final, last hope, eye contact, but he never looked up from the meaningless paper he was flipping through.

Total desperation was setting in. Where was I to turn next? The pain was coming close to being unbearable, but no one would listen. I had been about everywhere that I could think of. For the first time, I could actually see myself dying from all of this. For the first time, I could genuinely say that I was afraid. The pain, the tiredness, the fear—all came together to envelope me in a dull spasm of confusion and despair.

A few nights later, we had to go again—somewhere, anywhere. Hollywood Memorial and the main VA facility were out. The only other possibility was a large emergency center in Miami across from the VA. Many of the younger doctors who worked there also worked at the VA.

It seemed to take no time at all for examinations to be run and a strong, tentative diagnosis to be offered. Just as the Cuban doctor had found, these emergency room physicians were convinced that—at minimum—there was severe herniation of some sort and probably dislodging of scar tissue. This time, though, I knew better than what I had done with the Cuban doctors; I got names of the examiners involved and written copies of the reports that they created for my file.

I was sitting at the front door of the VA facility when it opened the next morning with a fist full of documents and the conviction that now, finally, they would have to do something. The head doctor of the "team" that had dealt with me had to see me, but it took only about two seconds to see that he was totally irritated and simply pissed off that I was back again.

I made all of the new explanations and showed him the written reports. He seemed to take special notice of the names that had signed off on the examination; it was almost as if he would make sure and find them before that morning was over. The last thing he needed, in all of his self-glorified busyness, was me to have to deal with again. He would be sure that these particular young doctors would not be sending me his way again.

He looked up from the report, now becoming arrogant, "Listen, we can't find anything. I don't know what they thought they found, but there is nothing there. More tests won't do any good." Then, he paused and, tiring of any and all niceties, made his last pronouncement, "Matherson, you need help. You need help."

I made my last pronouncement as well, "Yeah, I need help. But not that fucking kind of help!" I was out of there. I was back to the swamps.

For the next two months, I decided to bear the pain—even if I died, I wasn't going back to that son-of-a-bitch and his arrogant attitude. I would also get myself off of all of the medicine that they were giving me. If I could get it cleaned out of my system, maybe I could think again. I felt like a prisoner of war in my own country.

At first I tried doing it cold turkey. Every medicine cabinet and drawer was cleaned out and the drugs flushed down the toilet. That moment of resolution was the strongest thing that I had done for myself in what seemed like years. I was determined.

Within two days, it was clear that cold turkey was not working. My brain felt like it was starting to burn. It was almost like the skin of my head was wrapped around a hot, searing coal. The process of coming off the drugs had to be managed in a more reasonable way, but by the end of maybe eight or ten weeks, I wasn't taking any of the "mind drugs." If anything, the pain had become worse, but I was compensating for that by knowing that I was controlling the other. Finally, I could think again.

Only one thing made sense: go to the top. I would put my case before the main administrator of the entire Miami VA facility. I took Doug with me and headed for Miami.

When I got to his office, of course I had no appointment—as if I could have gotten one anyway—and he simply had no time to see me today. Could I make an appointment and come back later? I simply took Doug's hand and barged straight into his office. He pushed back from his desk, with his glasses halfway falling off of his face. The secretary could hardly have thought of restraining me and stood behind me in the doorway with a kind of "it wasn't my fault, I couldn't do anything about it" look on her face.

I don't know what kind of images or experiences he had of Vietnam veterans, but it was clear that he was taking no chances.

Somehow he must have known that the best thing to do at that moment was to listen. If he could have read my face and my mind at that moment, he would have had every reason to be afraid. I was ready to blow something up, to kill someone. Anything to get some attention of the damned system that I was confronting. If I could have gotten my hands on the head of the "team" at that time, I would have choked him to death. The only real thing that was holding me back was my own family and what would happen to them; and a strong sense that it was not fair to do something that might hurt innocent people. I had already seen —and been a part of—too many innocent people getting hurt. At that point, what would have happened to me was of no consequence.

After a few half-hearted attempts to quiet me, the administrator knew that I was not playing around. Desperation filled ever corner of the room. He just flat asked what he could do. My first response was to listen, and he listened. He heard the whole story. I concluded it by saying—with Doug clutching at my side: "Do anything you want to with me. But this is my child. Why do you want to hurt him? Why are you doing this to my family?"

Somehow, and I don't think it was just to get himself off of the spot, he was touched, visibly touched. It was like all of the administrative, edgy busyness was gone. He may have still been aggravated by the interruption that he was having to deal with, but he showed no hesitancy in dealing with it right then. He personally called the head surgeon. This man was instructed to send me to someone else immediately. "Immediately" was underscored in no uncertain terms.

My first stop was an individual meeting with this head surgeon. He had evidently been briefed by the head of the team that had been dealing with me. He was pissed off, insisting that I was wasting everyone's time, and that I was "fooling." At that word, I was in his face. I was ready to kill him. No question about it; simply ready to kill him. Would he actually avoid so easily the instruction that his own administrator had just given him? Maybe so—doctors who operated thought that doctors who were administrators were somehow beneath them. I could not go on. I would just have to kill him.

Some animal instinct leaped in place and he started backing off. In retrospect, what took place in that moment—as far as the rest of both of our lives might be concerned—was miraculous. He quickly got me shuffled off to a whole new "team," "Alpha Team." In a very condescending manner, he said that maybe they could find something. It all seemed like a better option than killing him, so I went on.

This "Alpha Team" was new on the scene, so they had no reason to have their minds made up about me already. The head doctors were a man and woman from Sweden and, for the first time in my recent history at the VA, they sat and listened carefully while I gave my broken record account one more time.

Then, they commenced a long, detailed, totally unhurried, examination. There was no question, behind those metal sutures and mass of scars was some kind of major difficulty. I needed surgery to find out exactly what was there. If I did not get it quickly, I could die. There was no question.

While they wrote up detailed suggestions and findings, ideas that could not be swept under some administrative carpet, I began to cry. No hell of Vietnam had come close to what the last year of my life had been like. No jungle, even in the dark of night, could be so filled with destruction as a set of closed minds that would not listen. God must have heard my prayers, Sandy's prayers, Momma's prayers, and sent these people from Sweden.

I had a cross that I had worn around my neck for a very long time that had become special to me, a possession that I had held on to even when so many other things were sold to make ends meet. Sandy had given me the cross, and when Doug was a baby he had teethed on it sometimes. Sandy's having given it to me and his small, tooth marks made it a unique possession in my mind.

I took it off and handed it to the doctor. At first, he did not want to take it, but realizing how important that he took it was to me, he accepted the gift. It may have been a feeble gesture, but it was the nearest act of love and gratitude that I could put together at that moment.

Regulations made it impossible for them to do the surgery, which was my wish; I had to go back to "Bravo Team" for that. They were filled with near hate about my return, but this time they could not do anything about it. The head doctor spoke so everyone could hear, "I don't know who's the craziest—him or me—but I'm admitting Matherson for surgery. Take him on, take him away, to the surgery ward."

For the next week, every test and examination imaginable was performed. Two times a day, the doctors would come in to press and gouge at my side. The scar tissue on the outside of the upper trunk of my body became raw from their probing. I still am convinced that they wanted to create so much pain and trouble for me that I would call a halt to what they still perceived as a crazy man's hoax. Still, they said nothing. Still, the psychiatrists that came daily now said it was in my mind. I kept insisting that they would operate or I would sue their asses all the way to Washington and back. I made every threat and they pushed all the harder. I had almost absolute pain on my side by now; they could push all they wanted to—it couldn't hurt any worse. When you have gone to absolute pain, nothing else matters.

I'll have to describe the scene in the surgery room as it was described to me. The team assembled and the head doctor came in. He was cursing and filled with skepticism, bitching about the waste of time and the crazy son-of-a-bitch on the table. All of the procedures involved in the surgery were followed to the letter of the law, but there was no compassion in that room on anyone's part by the time he had finished his tirade. It was, more or less, let's get this over with, make our records that will demonstrate that we were right, and get the hell out of here. It's costing the government a bundle, but if it gets this crazy asshole off our backs, let's do it.

The first layer of skin came away in as normal of an incision as it could be. Then, it is not clear what happened exactly. It was almost as if my side exploded from the inside. Black, infected blood and dark green body fluids spewed out all over me, the doctors, and everything that was nearby. The dark, smelling fluids kept running in a stream off of the table and into a large puddle on the floor. Everyone's breath was taken. In one piece of a short second, the realization gripped the entire room that they were dead wrong, that this was intensely serious business, that this man—not "son-of-a-bitch" or "crazy asshole" anymore—was at the point of death.

Over the next three hours these doctors worked quickly and with every skill in their experience. They found an entire, upper left side filled with infections and fungus-like growths penetrating into all of my body lining from the inside and almost ready to attack all my vital organs in the area. There was infectious bacteria and even old debris that had been there ever since Vietnam. I was carrying slime from the jungle that had been growing inside me for over a decade. One large bag of the infected material that they removed was as large as a pineapple.

By the time that they had cleaned the side out, there was a hollowed out hole that you could put your hand so far up that the whole hand and wrist completed disappeared. The word got around that the mess in the operating room was the worst that any of the people involved had ever seen. They were literally walking around in it to complete the surgery. It took hours of disinfecting and cleaning until they were confident enough that the infectious material had been destroyed and the area could be used for surgery again.

The only explanation that was ever offered—and not much of one was—was that somehow my body had worked to save itself. It had sealed off the growing infection in a bag of thick scar tissue. The pain was coming from the bag swelling and trying to burst. Had it burst, the poison would have flowed into my body and I would have been dead in a very short period of time. The presence of the infection was creating the loss of energy and tiredness as my body's defense mechanisms were being called on to work overtime to keep me alive. There was no telling, they said, about how much pain I had come to be able to accommodate. I didn't know about that, but I knew plenty about the pain that I had not been able to accommodate.

My first waking moment came as they were bringing me from the recovery room to the surgical intensive care unit. I was in an elevator and the door was just opening. I could see Sandy down the hall, and she was talking on the phone. She held the phone down and looked at me. I could tell from the look on her face that what she saw was bad—real bad. What she saw was the covering of a hole in my side as big as a football filled with all kinds of packing and tubing. What she saw was the pain all over my face.

It felt like someone had taken a knife and split me open, but had not put me back together. That was exactly the case. Because of the great possibility that the fungus filled abscesses had not all been cut out and could come back, they had to keep me open. I would stay open for over two months and the packing was changed at least two times a day.

The pain was unbearable. I was screaming and cursing. I was wanting to die and wanting to kill whoever had hurt me. Had Sandy not been there and told me that she was talking to Momma, I guess that I would have tried to tear my way off of the gurney that they were transporting me on. I even talked to Momma—they would do anything to try to calm me down—but I don't remember anything about the conversation. All I remember was that Sandy was there. She was there through it all.

I cried for more morphine, but I had had my limit. Any more and it could stop my heart. All I could do was lay there in the pain.

That night, the head team doctor and his assistants came to check on me. He didn't say a word or never made eye contact, but from that time on he worked with the greatest care. He never apologized, said I had been right, or even really talked. I didn't either. We both knew.

The process that he initiated was repeated literally hundreds of times. They would shoot me up with the pain killers, wait for them to take some effect, and then begin to unpack me. I would put towels in my mouth to mask the screaming from the ripping, tearing pain that came when the packing and the flesh which merged with it were pulled loose. Then, with the hole in my side fully open, they would pour me full of Betadine solution. I would hold this in place for several minutes, letting it reach into all of the abscess cavities, and then roll over so it could drain out. New packing was then inserted. The doctors' hands would disappear and you could feel the sensation of them poking the packing into every crevice that they could feel.

As the head doctor left that first night, I heard him tell Sandy—my chances were 50-50 at best. There was no time to contemplate the possibilities; the dull of the drugs evaporated everything that was happening around me.

After a couple of weeks, I settled into the routine. In many ways I was able to take care of myself. I could change the dressings, pour in the Betadine, drain and repack myself. It helped to be self-determining, but there was no—even slight—indication of how long it would be before they could sew me up again. The wounds would have to heal from the inside out so that the bacteria would not be blocked in and begin to grow again.

On one day in particular, it seemed that I couldn't get any cooperation at all. My hair had not been washed in so long that it felt like it was beginning to mat. My personal hygiene habits made me hate that feeling, but I could not get anyone to help me wash it. When Sandy came, she helped. I hated to put her through this when I felt that it was someone else's job. Then, after she left, the wounds began to secrete fluids and dressings needed to be changed. I called a nurse, she looked at it, but only wanted to put clean pads over dirty ones as a temporary measure so that someone else would have to do the dirty work. We argued, I told her to get me the materials and I would do it myself, but she bitched, griped, and complained—she simply walked away and wouldn't come back. I lay there the rest of the night, unable to sleep, and mad as pure hell.

Finally, I couldn't stay in the bed any longer. I got up, was able to reach the stands that held the intravenous devices, and used them to steady myself as I walked down the main hallway of the hospital. I hadn't gotten ten yards—ten wonderful yards—until here came the head doctor and his team. They saw me and then had the look of a small child who had suddenly shit in his pants. They broke into a run, surrounded me, and all but lifted me back toward the bed. All of the time, the head doctor was bitching for all that he was worth about my carrying these strange Vietnamese infections all over the hospital. There was no telling what was still growing inside of me and I could spread it to others.

I fired back that that was all bullshit. If he was worried about infection being spread, he would do something about the cockroaches that came out at night. Huge Florida cockroaches that waded through inept attempts to mop the floors and had full run of the hospital at night. There wasn't much he could say, except that I stay in bed. He ordered me to do that, and I explained that I couldn't be ordered anymore. It was almost like, "Oh yeah, I forgot." So, he changed to, "Please, for Christ's sake, stay in bed."

On one weekend, an Air Force doctor had taken over rounds; there were not too many people around. He came by to remove and repack, and got the needle ready for the pain killer. He had a look on his face that indicated he had been deep into the pills that would help keep him awake. When he spoke, you could clearly hear the slur in his voice, "I'm going to give you a real rush tonight." I'm not sure I had ever heard the term "rush." He filled the needle, maybe a little more than normal, and stuck it into my arm. Then, he sucked some of the blood into the needle. You could see the fading red mixing with the more transparent fluid in the needle. Then, he inserted the needle full into my arm and rammed the plunger down, not in the slow, easy manner that was normal. In a moment, I knew what he meant by "rush." I also realized what he was doing and what he must have thought about me. I felt degraded.

I started bitching and griping about what had happened when the regular people came in after the weekend. They sent in the psychiatrist. I hadn't asked for a psychiatrist but I couldn't make him stay away. It was almost, in retrospect, like he was the one who could cover ass if nothing else worked. He started having some kind of medicine put in my IV. It worked; at least it worked for them. I got a kind of floating, happy feeling, and they could not shut me up from telling and retelling and retelling how wonderful I was, how wonderful they were, how wonderful the hospital was—wonderful, wonderful, wonderful.

Finally, in the last couple of weeks of the two-month stay, they moved me every morning over next to a window. I could watch the construction going on for Miami's new rapid transit system. That was wonderful, too.

One night a young, Cuban nurse came in to change the packing. She had many times. Every time she came, she half chanted, half sang some kind of little tune in Spanish. It was always the same. She was real gentle and never seemed to hurt like some of the others.

I asked her what it was that she was saying. She paused for a moment and in a broken English voice explained, "It's a prayer. I'm asking God to give you the same anesthetic that he gave Jesus when he was on the cross and they stuck the sword in his side."

It was one of the most overwhelming religious moments that I have ever experienced. Nothing else was said. It was almost like she was no longer a nurse, but now an angel. An angel sent from God to help me. For the first time in so long I could not remember, I had a keen awareness of the nearness of God. He had not given up on me. He had not turned his back. In spite of all, he was still with me. God felt as close as the air I was breathing, like an old friend, lost, and found again after many years.

Chapter XXIV

The hospital experience finally became one of as much isolation as I could create. It was not so much my side that was laying wide open as my entire soul. I felt vulnerable, too open; I didn't want anyone else to see me. They might see too much.

I broke off all relationships with everyone except Sandy and the kids. She had seen it all, and she was still there. In many respects she was all that was there that I was sure of, but by the same token, all that mattered anyway.

The doctors would do their work, but still there was not the integrity of an apology, still they sent the psychiatrist to cover their asses. The preacher would come and pray, but I was completely disillusioned by knowing what he had said about Sandy staying with me. Let him take his empty, judgmental attitude somewhere else. Sandy would bring the kids, and we were even able to go out onto the grounds and have picnics together. Part of me hated for the kids to see some of the things that they were being exposed to, but another part felt that at least they could see the results of war and the price of freedom.

After more than two months, I was released from the hospital. The car going home was an amazing sight to behold. Sandy driving, me sitting beside her wrapped and bandaged with the side still open and full of packing, and every square inch of the rest of the car crammed full of material that would still be used to change the dressings no less than twice a day. It looked like an ambulance on the way to a plane crash or terrorist raid.

Sandy's parents had stayed with the kids and were there to meet us. They were amazed. When Sandy's father saw my condition, it was like a light went off in his mind. He had come to like me as his daughter's husband and the father of his grandchildren. He could not have helped but had doubts about all that I had been saying about my pains and moods; his own patriotism kept him from being able to identify with my anger for the VA. In just one look, he knew that it was all true. From that moment on, he affirmed me and all that was happening. Like became love and respect. He cursed the VA and the very idea that they could even send me home in this shape. That look on his face went a long way in dispelling those "professional" opinions expressed in words and attitudes written all over faces that I had confronted over the past two years. Finally, someone else was believing me, believing in me.

Over the next few months I continued to daily care for the wounds. There were repeated trips to see the doctors and, with each trip, some degree of improvement. The wound was finally closed and, although there would be a continual need to monitor recurrences of the growth of the infections, I was on my way to "full recovery."

Recovery was easier said than done. It might be one thing to get beyond the physical damage that had been done; it would be quite another to get rid of the backwash of the massive drug therapy and pain-killing treatments that I had received. Beyond that, there was the erosion and destruction of self-image, esteem, confidence, and an ability to be fully self-determining that had taken place. I was hitting on forty years of age, didn't have a job, was on full government disability, and had an old war still raging all around me. Some wounds could be closed more easily than others.

They began to start to take me off of the medications. I began to have to face a reality that the medications had somehow masked. That "reality" included the regular notice of past-due accounts and the frequent appearance of bill collectors. That "reality" included a world in South Florida that had become a strange and unusual land open to little or no possibilities to reclaim the life that seemed to be deteriorating all around us. I kept falling into a deep depression and longing for a new beginning of some sort.

The musical group "Alabama" was rising toward its peak of popularity at that time. I would sit around and listen to the words of their songs and begin to envision a "real South," a place where there were mountains, fresh cool breezes, and down home people who treated each other with a sense of dignity. It seemed that somewhere out there in the "real South" that there was less pretentiousness, less phoniness, less complication; people were accepted for who they were—period.

Momma and Ted had moved to southeast Tennessee and two of my brothers and one sister lived in the same area. They seemed especially pleased with their surroundings and the people they were meeting. It was more like "home" in the Carolinas had been.

Maybe this was the answer that I was looking for. If we could get into a new environment, maybe I could get well and start over.

There is a difference between being unwilling to listen and being unable to listen. Sandy would do anything to help, but she kept telling me that I was running, not from South Florida and all of the supposed emptiness of possibility that was there, but from myself; it would be impossible to do that. Her father was more measured in his advise: the grass was not necessarily greener. I was unable to see it. In an ideal setting, I could have understood that you don't make life-changing decisions when you are still only months away from a surgery in which your life was in the balances. I was a million miles away from ideals. If I could just be around Momma and family, I might get things back to where they had been. I was unable to see it any other way.

We put our house on the market, but for weeks and weeks nothing happened at all. It was an expensive enough house that just about anyone who could afford it could afford to build themselves a new one exactly like they wanted. Real estate simply was not moving.

I worked around the house, building little boxes covered with mirrors that brought in some extra income. I had the disability check—the subsistence check. I spent a lot of time talking to God—or to myself; what did He want me to do? Since He had allowed me to live, what did He want me to do with what He had given? Why me live and not someone else? The questions were unrelenting, but there were no answers in sight anywhere. Except, maybe, in Tennessee.

I would sit outside at night and stare up into the sky. God must be up there somewhere. I would cry. I would plead. I would curse. I admitted to God that I had screwed up. But—but—but, I did not know that there were nuns and children on that sanpan. If He was God, He had to know that. If He was God, He had to know what was in my heart. Would He punish me to insanity and death over something that I didn't know. I was sorry! I didn't know! I didn't have anything that I could do about it now!

Desperation became so great on one evening as I sat looking into the heavens that I demanded some kind of "sign." I was going to sit there until something happened, until some "sign" was given. If it didn't come, I was contemplating suicide. It was only a half-hearted contemplation in some sense, because on some level I knew that I could not leave Sandy and my kids like Momma and her kids had been left. But the thought was there.

I was looking straight into a full moon and one, bright star was hanging off to the side. It was like that moon and star were the only objects in the entire sky. Suddenly, the star began to move. It moved behind and to the other side of the moon and stopped there. I was startled, shocked, shaking, and crying. Here was my "sign." There was a sense that God was still there, that everything would work out.

What was I to do about this? Maybe at some later time, I might be able to count it all off to imagination, seeing what I wanted to see, or coming off of drug therapy. In deep depression, I know that people are capable of hallucinations. But I can never get away from saying "maybe." I'm not honestly sure what happened out there that night. Maybe it was a simple figment of my imagination; maybe a star moved.

I had to tell someone. But I was afraid to. They would think that I was crazy. I told Sandy—I could tell her anything—but with great caution I added, "Whatever you do, don't ever tell anyone about this."

It must have been ten o'clock at night by then or nearly eleven. The phone rang. It was the real estate agent, filled with apology for the unorthodox hour of her call, but with a family that wanted to see the house right then. They came, saw the house, and bought it for essentially our asking price. Maybe the star had moved.

In many circumstances, a young family moving to a new place with new possibility would have some positive feelings associated with it. In spite of leaving friends and family, moving can have some good side.

But the timing could not have been worse. The new family was wanting to move right in, and it was Christmas. They even wanted to buy the house with our Christmas tree in place. That was too much. It began to dawn on me—on us all—what we were losing. This was a big, nice house—now a home; what we would be able to find was open to question and filled with uncertainly. Above all, this was "Sandy's house," and a real bonding of her life to it had taken place. She was willing to move for my sake, but I felt that I was taking something precious away from her. I felt selfish.

We moved out two days before Christmas, spent the holidays with Sandy's parents and headed for Tennessee. Part of me felt that what we were doing was the only thing that we could do, the best thing for us to do. Another part felt that I was taking Sandy away from her family and letting everyone down again. It was a pattern and feeling that I could hardly stand. Nothing was clear cut; it was always "one part made sense, one part made no sense at all." One thing was certain, however; we would have to fight twice as hard to get back to where we had been.

We were planning to stay with Momma for the short time that it would take to find a new house. When we got to her house, it was cold and snowing. It was almost like a repeat performance of the time of despair when Sandy and I had moved to Cleveland. Suddenly, Tennessee seemed a million miles from South Florida.

There was no utopia here. The very first thing to happen was two of the "real people" that were supposed to be so "down home" and respectful of everyone stood at a distance and almost suspiciously watched me struggle with the trailer that had carried some of our belongings and never offered to help at all. Was I mistaken? Were people the same everywhere? Had I wanted to see it so differently, needed to see it so differently, that my own illusions had blinded my common sense?

Getting settled was not nearly as easy as I had assumed either. We wanted a place on flat land. I had nightmares about the kids riding bikes on some of the hills. There seemed to be no flat land to be had. We looked and looked without success, and all of the time, though Momma and Ted gave their total hospitality, there was no privacy, and we must have been crowding their space.

Finding schools was an even greater problem. The school system wanted to place Doug in a situation with kids that were severely retarded. Doug simply was not that way, but it seemed impossible to convince anyone. That situation finally worked out, but it wasn't simple. Nothing was simple.

With no luck in finding a house to buy, we ended up renting for $400 a month—a little, nothing house that wouldn't even hold our furniture. I looked around at this place of new possibility and prosperity, this place where we could start over, and it was like the very walls were pushing in on me. My God, what had I done to my family?!? There was even a new baby on the way. What had I done?!?

A whole new cycle commenced: depression, sleep, crying depression, sleep, crying—depression, sleep, crying. What had I done? Tennessee.

Chapter XXV

Tennessee provided a lot of mixed emotions; maybe it wasn't Tennessee, just life. The whole idea of "Southern hospitality" was proving itself to be a myth. Although we did make friends, it wasn't like the Alabama songs. Family was also important, and I loved my family, but I came to realize that once you marry and have kids that your own family becomes the only real "family" that matters. There was a kind of "double lack" in everything that we were doing; on one side, we could no longer go back to the way that life had been at any time in the past—on the other side, it was not yet clear what life might offer that would make some measure of sense. Maybe life always has that "double lack" and I was just now finally awakening to that fact.

There must have been a hundred times when the only answer that made any sense was to load up and head back to South Florida. But that didn't make any sense either. The schools for Doug in Tennessee were much better; the VA system was much more humane in every sense, and I knew that the VA and I were probably in the beginnings of a long term relationship. Even the housing in Florida wouldn't really work; $85,000 would get you a pretty decent place in Tennessee, but in South Florida living in a "rough" neighborhood would probably cost more than that. If we were "stuck," at least we could be stuck in a much worse place. It finally begin to make sense for us—Sandy, Doug, Brad, Justin, and me—not our extended families, to make Tennessee our home. Florida might continue to be a part of our minds, but Tennessee could be home —a better place to raise our kids.

We were finally able to find a place to buy. The house was fine—maybe not as fine as the home we had built in Florida—but it would work well for the time being. In addition, it had a whole acre of land, something unheard of in Florida. For now, that acre was almost like the wide open spaces of some frontier. You could walk around, get off by yourself, have plenty of room for play, and enough yard work to give plenty of distraction, if that happened to be what you needed.

The VA provided its next round of examinations and helped keep the variety of recurring infections under control. They also provided the predictable visits to the psychiatrists. This meant bringing Vietnam up again. Maybe the idea in the end was to finally exhaust the topic rather than understand it and sort it all out; if it were exhausted, maybe something else could get underway.

That may have been what eventually began to happen. Between one more return to Vietnam in my mind as it was being stripped bare by another set of psychiatrists and the time that I was spending by myself exploring the Tennessee woods and river banks in search of the Indian arrowheads and artifacts which had always fascinated me, a couple of realizations began to dawn: I had indeed lost most of my personal pride and confidence. Most of the "getting by" that had occurred had been gut instinct, the pressure of necessity, and Sandy's strength. Maybe I could get that pride and confidence back but, if I did, it was going to have to have some specific starting points. It would not simply happen. If I waited around for it to happen on its own, I knew that all that I had before me were endless cycles of passive depression.

I also knew beyond any doubt that no matter what I did, I was going to have to go back to school. That probably wasn't absolutely true, but somewhere deep inside school was an area where I knew I lacked something, and it was a very specific lack that I could work on in a definite way. If I could do school, I could train or prepare for something—God knows what—and I might also get some of my pride and confidence back.

There was now a definite course spreading out before me. There was at least something that I could put my hands on and do! At least, I wasn't being a victim any more. All things being equal, though there were matters that would remain up in the air of uncertainty, this had to be progress. One very positive note that signaled a new and better direction was the birth of our fourth son, Joshua, that occurred about this time. It was a happy distraction for all of us.

At the first of the summer of 1987, I got all of the information and paperwork ready to begin work at the local community college in the fall. In some respects, it was like this was the first thing that I had done in a long time that moved in a direction—some direction, any direction. That was not exactly accurate: we had bought a home, settled in it, started attending church and found some measure of acceptance, our kids were making friends and in school—on the outside we were managing a typical American suburban existence pretty well. What I am saying is that this was the first thing that I had done on the deep inside of our lives—of my life—that had direction.

I knew (which is the third time now that I have used a word that had become all but absent from my existence) that before I could give the attention to school that it would require that I had to clear some of the bases that remained. I wanted to see if I could find out for sure what had happened to the men of my airborne company when we got shot apart out in that field where Rick died. I wanted to get the matter of my record and my medals straightened out; it wasn't that I needed the medals, but that something was left hanging that needed to be closed. If a chapter could be closed, a new chapter could begin. Maybe there was a way to say "Goodbye" in an appropriate manner to those friends left over from Vietnam. MacArthur was right about soldiers fading away, but that "fading" left an empty, incomplete feeling that yearned to have something done about it.

It seemed that this important stage of sorting out could perhaps be accomplished by going back to Fort Campbell and making contact with my old company again. In retrospect, I'm not sure why I had not thought about that before. It all makes sense now: at Fort Campbell I had found my highest moment of pride, confidence, and accomplishment—maybe it was exactly the place that rediscovery of that pride could occur.

I imagine that all kinds of receptions could have been possible for what was now being called a "Vietnam Era Veteran" showing up unannounced on the door step of a busy army post. I've often wondered what might have happened to me if the first person I made contact with had been too busy to fool with me.

In fact, just the opposite occurred. Across three full days, it was almost like I was an honored guest; almost like the returning hero status that hadn't happened twenty years before was finally happening. Beginning with a Captain and working all the way up to a full Colonel, the people that I met could not have been more helpful or more cordial. They treated me like I was someone who was important and like what I had done had been important. Almost within moments, I was feeling better about myself than the grand total of hundreds of hours with psychiatrists. There was a sense of place here, a sense of belonging and of acceptance.

A Captain West, a Major Havilak and Major Cannon, and a Colonel Leigh helped locate all of the information that they had on the old company movements and what had happened to us that day. They were able to push through the paperwork of the system to verify and rectify the problems about the missing medals. More than that, they gave me a detailed exposure to all that was happening on the base with the new soldiers that were coming on in their training as I had years before. As we went from one place to the next, it was like I was some kind of visiting dignitary.

It became clear that the snap of the salute, the posture of the march, the crispness of the cadence, the shine of the boots, the pride of person, of accomplishment, of country—was still there. As I rubbed shoulders with that pride, I felt something coming back that had been lost. It was almost like an empty desert low place beginning to be filled—first by a trickle and then a flood—by waters that had pushed a track across a dry, stubborn wasteland from some distant refreshing rain. Like the damning, incessant rains of that Vietnam jungle had finally pushed themselves to a place that even they could restore life again. I was the man dying of thirst who could take that distant water in the midst of that wasteland and drink again.

Colonel Leigh moved away his busy schedule and spent part of an afternoon talking to me; almost the father-son talk that I had never had. He had been in Vietnam as well and across twenty years had had his own sorting out to do. He shared how he had known about killing. Killing was no matter of pride now, but he had sorted it all out in his own mind and now believed that talk about killing was really talk about survival.

He had come to understand that every virtue taught by civilization got set aside in war, and that dealing with that setting aside when normalcy is restored is the burden carried by most combat infantrymen who had to face battle at its worst. War reversed everything normal; you laughed when you should be crying; you cried when you should be laughing. Because all of the emotions got so severely jumbled up, it was hard to get them sorted out again. Maybe I had been told that before, but for the first time it made sense. I understood.

Colonel Leigh also knew about the flashback of reminders that could come at the most unpredictable times. He had had all kinds of negative recollections, but he was not interested in talking about them. He was, rather, interested in describing for me the flashback that had finally sorted all of the others out and made them go away; that had, at least, abolished their power over him.

He had been on assignment in South Korea in the middle 1970s, and it was the type of assignment that his family was able to accompany him. While he was out in the field on a training mission, word came that his son had gotten suddenly very ill and was going to have to be helicoptered out to a larger medical facility than was immediately available on the base where they were stationed.

He had quickly made arrangements to get back to his family, but by the time that he was helicoptered back and found out where his son was, he got to the flight line just as his son's helicopter was lifting off. At a distance he caught a glimpse of his son in the chopper just as his son caught a glimpse of him. Their eyes met across the distance and in that split second the son flashed his father the thumb's up signal and smiled.

Leigh said that it took his breath away and nearly caused his knees to buckle. He had never seen his son do that; it was not an expression that they used in their family. He did not know if it was a kind of universal expression that just happened or if his son had seen it somewhere else. He did know, however, exactly where he had seen it—Vietnam! It all came flooding back to him in that moment. The countless number of GIs he had seen, many wounded or ill and being helicoptered out like his son, many on their way to help, and others so severely wounded that death was imminent. But, in the midst of it all, the thumbs up was still flashed.

In the end, for Leigh, the way that this image came at this particular moment, became his way out of all that Vietnam had come to mean in his life. Sure it was a bad war, maybe the worst war that the United States ever participated in. Sure, it was a loss. Sure, it was fought more for the rich fat cats and the politicians.

But when it was reduced to the most basic element, the essential element—to the soldier in the field doing his job—it was possible still to flash a thumbs up. If that soldier, grinding through the mire, caught up in death and injury, could still rise out with the thumb triumphantly jammed into the face of all of the stupidity, the absurdity, the politicians and their system—if that soldier, probably hurting and scared, could still back that thumb with an heroic smile—then it would be possible to give a "thumbs up" to life in spite of Vietnam's after effects, in spite of all of the voices of analysis and criticism that had risen around Vietnam, in spite of all of those other flashbacks of the inhumane side of existence that is inevitable in war.

There seemed to be a choice; it could either be the middle finger of cynical defiance and even desperation crying out "fuck it all," or there could be the much less bitter and even heroically conquering thumbs up. There was the essential image of Vietnam: the muddy, tired, bloodied foot soldier, suddenly surrounded by a world of hurt, flashing the smile—flashing the thumbs up. Leigh had found a way of riding that realization into an understanding that allowed his life to make sense and find stability; I must do the same.

When I was ready to leave, Captain West asked me to come by his office. I had no special expectations. I had gotten what I had come for and probably even more. I assumed that it was simply a goodbye and a way of letting him know that any responsibilities that he might have toward me were complete. He wanted me to go with him to Major Havilak's office; he gave no explanation.

As I walked in, three of the officers that I had met were there. They had something for me. In what took on the feeling of the most formal of awards presentations, they explained a very important medallion of the 101st Airborne, a medallion presented to men when they came to a place of leadership as officers in the Division. They had gone together and purchased a medallion and wanted to present it to me as a way of letting me know that I would always be a part of the Division—that I belonged. The medallion was presented. They saluted me.

It was the most profound moment of a new life that was beginning to strain to assert itself. It wasn't just the medallion that they were giving me, but they were giving me back my sense of self-respect. They were giving me back the stirring of my pride and confidence that had been suppressed into near non-existence. They were giving me back what I had lost.

It was all that I could do to hold together. Part of me wanted to burst into tears, to cry out with release. Something of what I was rediscovering make me stand erect, accept their salute, and hold myself up to a height and straightness that was all but forgotten. In a moment I got turned toward the corner and slapped away the tear that had formed, and it was back to the group shaking their hands, embracing, getting invitations to return at any time. As long as there was a 101st, I had a place that was my place. I had fought for it. I left that room with a determination to fight back, to get back into the mainstream of life, to never be a shameful bum.

I hadn't done anything wrong. I understood that I was not in this boat of guilt by myself. I understood that I was OK in spite of Vietnam and all that had happened there. Others were ridding themselves of guilt. Others were finding new determination to fight back. Others were making it. I could, too!

The trip back from Fort Campbell to where I lived near Chattanooga took maybe five hours. It was a time for a lot of emotions of the previous three days to sink in. It was a time for reflection about what my life had come to at this particular juncture. The clarity of thinking that occurred in that period of contemplation was amazing; almost like the first really clear thinking that I had done in twenty years. The thoughts came like the rush of a swollen river or spinning tornado. In that rush, it was like the debris of my mind was being swept away and something clear and fresh was being left in its place. If it had been the proverbial dark tunnel, I guess that some kind of light was appearing in the distance. It was, in fact, more like a fresh, cool Carolina morning with the sun peaking over the distant mountains ready to burn away the morning haze.

There was no logical pattern, but all kinds of thoughts began to appear like shafts of light in a forest clearing.

People, the general public, many of those of my own age who were my peers didn't understand Vietnam; they didn't understand the Vietnam vet and the rejection that he felt from the land that he loved, the land that he had fought for. They couldn't understand because they were not there. All that most of them saw came second and third hand through a television set, through statistical graphs published in newspapers that kept score of kills, through commentators. All they understood was what was asserted in the anti-war trend at the end of the war. What they didn't know was that I was more anti-war than they would ever hope to be. For the first time, I was beginning to be able to think about forgiveness for their lack of understanding. Maybe, somewhere out there in the country, they were also beginning to look again at the war and me and others like me, and understand what we were about, and understand that we were not baby killers, and understand what we faced. Maybe, somewhere out there, they were beginning to retool their impressions and give us the acceptance and affirmation that was our just due. We were not the politicians; we were simply soldiers.

God did not put on people more than they could stand, but He continually was with people to help them cope and live their lives. It would be nice if the "valley of the shadow of death" would go away, but it won't. What the Bible says is enough though: He will walk with us through the valley.

When you saw those peasants in their shanty huts, with children in next to no clothes and with no real food to eat—when you saw pleading eyes out of proportion to the rest of their faces— you wanted to help. That was what I wanted to do more than anything else—I wanted to help. It was military propaganda. John Wayne may have gotten me there, but when I got there I didn't want to hurt anyone. I just wanted to help.

The idea about being a baby killer was almost more than I could stand. I didn't know there were nuns and children on that sanpan! I didn't know!

There was too much brutality to be exposed to and keep your sanity in tact. The contrast from the Burger King in Hollywood was too great; it ripped at whatever was holding your mind together. A teenager still capable of watching cartoons on Saturday mornings should not have seen human ears that were dried and carried on dogtags as trophies. He should not have seen fellow Americans who had been tied to a turning log and roasted alive over a fire. He should not have seen officers who would present their elite companies with hatchets to take enemy scalps and heads. He should not have seen an old man staked out with bamboo rammed up his insides, his severed testicles crammed in his mouth, and his wife and children standing helplessly by watching him die in miserable pain. He should not have seen nuns and children floating face down in the yellow Mekong River, its dirtiness being streaked by their innocent blood. He should not have seen his best friend's head blown off, a bullet scaring the friend's brain with ripping divots of death and his own brain with memories that he would never be able to completely erase. A teenager—no human being—should have seen all that or—God forbid—participated in it. That you had to match the enemy horror for horror didn't have to make sense then, defies sense now, and can never be allowed to make sense ever again.

The extreme contrasts frayed and jerked emotions in a way that all but destroyed them; sometimes it was impossible to think and feel like a normal human being. You lost all contact with the reference point of "normal." One day you would be covered with blood from the people, and pieces of people, that you were pulling from fire zones. The next day you would be lounging beside the base pool, the most important concern being the latest status of the tan that you were working on. One hour you would be watching a John Wayne movie in a makeshift base theater, all the time knowing that the bullets were blanks and the actors would walk away when it was all over. The next hour you would be dropping soldiers into a raging inferno of real bullets spraying death indiscriminately—theirs and yours. There were no actors here and the dead didn't get up and walk away. All the same, it didn't seem any more real sometimes than what you were seeing on the movies.

If you let yourself think about all that you were seeing, you couldn't stand it. You would get keyed higher than you would think that it was possible. In the heat of a gun run, every sensation was intent on giving the enemy as much burning hell as you could throw out. Then, there was the frantic dragging of wounded and near-dead—and dead—into the chopper to pull them out to safety. Then, you lifted out with dreadful slowness, knowing that you were a perfect target, knowing that the next bullet could rip your head off. You got back and cleaned up all of the blood—all of the blood. Then, at about the same moment, the adrenalin flow exhausted and the realization of all that you had seen set in. It was a dark, deep pit, more hollow and infinitely deeper than any grave—a grave that was really an angry, devouring mouth pulling you down and sucking you in.

Maybe part of the difficulty was the way in which the war was too close to the civilian populations. The way I understand it, that had not happened in most of the country's other wars. You had to see the hurt and pain too much. You had to look at the people in their faces. You had to burn their houses and destroy their rice while they stood there, helpless, and watched you. And they were so much smaller than us.

A lot happens when you have your own children and become a parent. You realize that you didn't just kill soldiers. You killed parents and children and brothers and sisters. Not just soldiers. The guilt grows.

Here you would be, walking along fat, dumb, and happy. Then you would push back some brush or undergrowth covering a path and an American head, cut off and jabbed down on a stick would be there in the middle of the path staring you straight in the face. You freaked out. You had a distraction placed in your mind. All the time you knew that this was the enemy's strategy; your moment of distraction would be their advantage over you. When I dug those holes and stuck, planted, those dead Viet Cong in them like a human fence in front of my bunker at Can Tho, I didn't do it to be cruel or inhumane; I did it because I was scared and wanted to live. I was on short time. I wanted to live. I wish that I could go to those people's families and tell them that I was sorry, help them dig a fitting grave, and mourn their loss—and mourn my loss.

It hurt to have to find out, after a lot of denial to the contrary, that the war kept on and on—not because our soldiers could not win—but because of what the politicians hoped that it would do for the economy. It is ironic the way that it almost destroyed the economy of the nation in a way that it is still not over. The debts of Vietnam and all of its implications may never be paid. If they had just let us do our jobs like we knew how to do them, we could have won quickly and come home in positive roles. Why didn't they let us do it right? Why can't we put politicians in office who can make strong, right decisions? If you have to fight like animals, do it, get it done, and get it over with.

When I had come home, I allowed my pride to be taken away from me by people who had no idea what they were really protesting against. If someone like Jane Fonda could have seen the cruelty that the Viet Cong and North Vietnamese inflicted on their own countrymen, she would have at least had a two-sided view. It was not enough to simply see what our bombs had done in Hanoi.

I hope that the feelings of the general public will begin to change; not toward the war, but toward the soldier. If it doesn't, what will my own children think about me?

I respect those resisters who had the intelligence to see the subtle, political dimensions of the war. I wish I had. I respect anyone's right to stand up for what they believe. I just want that same respect accorded me. Had that respect come, I don't think that I would have been haunted by Vietnam for twenty years. Why have I and others like me become the whipping boys? Maybe guilt can be so deep for a nation that it will beat a dead horse; that's all right, unless you are the dead horse who is really not dead but filled with feelings and emotions that still are crying out.

I allowed beliefs of others to bring me down and to break the belief that I had in myself. I feel degraded that I allowed a system to get me down, to bring me to the place that I would do something like smoking pot. That was not the person who went to Vietnam; this was not what I had been trained to do. I allowed the feelings of others to eat at me—maybe, more than anything else, that was what was really eating at my insides—and put questions in my mind. Was I really as they depicted me? Am I really a baby killer?

I don't want a party. I don't want a parade. I don't want a comforting pat on the back. I simply want the respect that somewhere deep inside of me I think is coming because I put my life on the line. When I saw those people, I knew that they needed help. On the most basic human level—which as a young, naive man in the middle of war was the only level I could relate to—they simply needed help. Helping them was the only thing besides just basic survival—that really mattered. In fact, time and again, I saw people—I saw myself—put basic survival aside for a moment and help anyway.

People do have a right to freedom from oppression. It is never enough to let some have it and others not. The ones that do have freedom must make the same available to others that do not. Nobody told me that. That's all on my own. That's the one thing I believe after twenty years. I doubt that I could have articulated it twenty years ago, but somewhere deep inside I know that it is how I felt. That's not exactly Rambo. I'm not sure I ever plugged along hot and wet and scared through a rice paddy or a black, jungle night with a Rambo. What it is, I think, is what this country is about at its best. Not always, but at its best. That best is still something that a person can be willing to give to sacrificially. I believe that!

All the movies showing the dope—as far as my own experience was concerned—were sensationalized all out of proportion. My first time through, I saw absolutely none. And I was in the right places to see it. The second time, it was only slight, at the most a

little pot to ease the pain of the awfulness of the circumstances.
Why would anyone want to sensationalize the dope? Is it a way of
writing off and giving an easy explanation for all that went wrong?
They were just a bunch of dopeheads. Everyone was on dope. No
wonder we lost the war. All of those explanations are too easy. I
never, even one time, saw a soldier's performance lessened by
some kind of dope. Not one single time.

I kept seeing the picture that Major Havilak had shown me on
the first day at Fort Campbell: First Lieutenant James A. Gardner,
O5321930, United State Army. A determined, young face like my
own had been twenty years before—intently staring out through an
army photograph, proudly wearing his single silver bar and the
emblems of the 101st Airborne and the Ranger chevron. Gardner
had led a platoon in February of 1966 in those same highlands we
had trudged through and in which Rick Crossland had died. His
platoon had come to the rescue of men pinned down by superior
enemy fire just as we had been —maybe it was us precisely.

His courage turned the tide of battle for a whole field full of
dying American soldiers. His courage won him the Congressional
Medal of Honor. It also cost him his life. Havilak had me sit there,
look at the picture, study the face, and read the commendation:

> The enemy occupied a series of strongly fortified
> bunker positions which were mutually supporting and
> expertly concealed. Approaches to the position were
> well covered by an integrated pattern of fire including
> automatic weapons, machine guns, and mortars. Air
> strikes and artillery placed on the fortifications had
> little effect. Lieutenant Gardner's platoon was to
> relieve the friendly company by encircling and
> destroying the enemy force. Even as it moved to begin
> the attack, the platoon was under heavy enemy fire.

Suddenly, I was there. Back in the jungle. I had been there.
Not just at that particular moment, but in that moment time and
time again. I was taken back more powerfully than in any dream
that I have ever had.

> During the attack, the enemy fire intensified. Leading
> the assault and disregarding his own safety, Lieutenant

Gardner charged through a withering hail of fire across an open rice paddy. On reaching the first bunker he destroyed it with a grenade and without hesitation dashed to the second bunker and eliminated it by tossing a grenade inside. Then, crawling swiftly along the dike of a rice paddy, he reached the third bunker.

I could see it all as plain as day. I had seen it all, not just with Gardner but with dozens of Gardners, unnamed and undecorated heroes who knew one command—move in the direction of opposing fire.

Before he could arm a grenade, the enemy gunner leaped forth, firing at him. Lieutenant Gardner instantly returned the fire and killed the enemy gunner at a distance of six feet. Following the seizure of the main enemy position, he reorganized the platoon to continue the attack. Advancing to the new assault position, the platoon was pinned down by an enemy machine gun emplaced in a fortified bunker. Lieutenant Gardner immediately collected several grenades and charged the enemy position, firing his rifle as he advanced to neutralize the defenders.

Somewhere deep inside me a feeling began to rise that I had not experienced in years. I know now that this was why Havilak was showing me the picture, making me look at the face, making me read the lines of the commendation. I wonder now how many others he had done this for. It was more powerful than anything that the psychiatrists had ever done.

He dropped a grenade into a bunker and vaulted on. As the bunker blew up, he came under fire again. Rolling into a ditch to gain cover, he moved toward the new source of fire. Nearing the position, he leaped from the ditch and advanced with a grenade in one hand and his rifle in the other. He was gravely wounded just before he reached the bunker, but with a last valiant effort he staggered forward and destroyed the bunker and its defenders with a grenade.

Although he fell dead on the rim of the bunker, his extraordinary actions so inspired the men of his platoon that they resumed the attack and completely routed the enemy.

It was men like James Gardner and Rick Crossland—and me at my best—that needed to be my ideal. I didn't need to look through the lens of the stereotypes and caricatures of Vietnam veterans being constructed in movies and on television. Gardner and Crossland—and me as well—were not baby killers. We were not part of a wild bunch of crazy, doped-up people running wild in Vietnam and now on the streets of the United States.

These were people of pride and love of country. I wanted to get back to being like them, to being like I was. The way that I was letting everything get me down did little more than reinforce the general public's view of the Vietnam veteran. I owed it to the Gardners and Crosslands—I owed it to myself and my wife and my sons—to convey an image that would honor them and their sacrifice.

In reality, there were many Gardners and Crosslands. I took great pride in my life's having touched lives like theirs. They may be dead, but in some special level of truth they are still alive today. They still inspire me today. They help me to reach back down and regain my pride and renew the feeling that I can get back. Their deaths are meaningless only if I allow myself to die. They fought and died for this country, for the people of Vietnam—in a way, now, they fought and died for me. I can, through my living again at my best repay them. It is a big order, but no bigger than the imperative that drove them in that jungle.

All along the way, back home—home—the thoughts came. In some ways they exhausted me. In others, it was like my life was being given back, like someone had drained all of my blood out and had been holding it, and now in some kind of gigantic, spiritual transfusion, they were pumping my own blood back into my life.

At forty-two years of age, I was starting all over again. I didn't know what I was going to do, and in some respects still don't. I know what I am going to do next—finish school. Maybe for now, maybe for the rest of my life, knowing what I am going to do next—today, tomorrow—is enough.

There are good days and bad days. That is not just me or Vietnam though—that's for everyone. On some days I feel that I can conquer any problem that I have. On others, I know what it is like to want to string myself up to the flagpole that stands in front of the VA center and leave a note that reads "now, I won't be any more trouble to anyone." No day is going to be bad enough to bring that thought to fruition, especially because of Sandy and the boys.

You're damn right that I know about bitterness. But that bitterness that has ranged far and wide and found one target and then another is, at least now, an accurately aimed bitterness. I have quit being bitter at the resisters and war protesters. I was as inaccurate in my first assessments of them as they were inaccurate in their assessments of me. I have quit being bitter toward the politicians. What do I matter to them? What good would that bitterness do? Most of them are dead or run out of office now anyway.

I can't complain all that much about how the system that took me to war was set up. After all, I volunteered. It is the way that that system has worked out that is unfair. I am bitter about the way that people hurt most deeply by that war are continually confronted by mountainous walls of red tape, red tape so imposing that it is easier to walk away from it than it is to get lost in it and continually be trying to find your way out. People that sacrifice for their country deserve to be treated better. It's time that a movie was made, not about the horrors of war, but the horrors of needing help and not being able to get it. But, who's going to watch that movie; there's very little to sensationalize about once strong and decent men who have been broken down so far that they don't know where to start to try to get up again? It goes against everything I was taught, everything my mother told me from the very beginning, everything that I wanted to go and fight for.

In it all, I know one thing; if it hadn't been for Sandy. . . . If it hadn't been for Sandy, what? I don't know. I don't know how to complete that sentence. Maybe I don't want to complete the sentence because on some deep level, I'm afraid that I know the answer. There is not enough that can be said for women of Vietnam veterans who have stuck by their husbands. Some could not, I'm sure, and I can completely understand. Sometimes I know that that minister was probably right; how could she have stayed

with me? The answer could only be love—tried, tested, real love.
I thank God for that every day. I believe that it was His answer to
all of my cries and pleas for help. It is not possible for an award to
be created sufficient to show adequate praise for women like Sandy.
But then, she isn't out looking for an award. All she wants is me,
back at my best. And that's what I'll give her. That is the one,
clear, certain goal.

More than anything else, I want my boys to understand me. I
want them to realize that I am not a bad person and that what I did
in Vietnam did not make me a bad person. Boys should not have
to think that their dad was a bad person.

I want my boys to know that Rambo and John Wayne and
playing army in camouflage are a million miles from the horrible
suffering and ugly battle face of war. I, more than anything, don't
want them to walk into what I walked into like an unsuspecting
virgin.

I want them to realize that the life which they enjoy has cost
dearly. It cost Rick Crossland, it cost those nuns and children in
that sanpan, it cost the little girl that I pulled out of hell at the last
second with the burning jet fuel streaming down her back, and it
cost me and who knows how many others like me. It still costs us.
I don't want them to think about these costs and get sad or morose.
I want them to think about the costs, and then live every moment
to its deepest and fullest. I need to think that thought, too—if I
don't, then it wasn't worth Rick and the nuns and the children
and everyone else dying. I can only redeem their lives and purge
the guilt of my own by living to the very fullest possible.

I want my boys to learn about forgiveness, but not just learn
about it—even more to be able to come to the place of accepting it.
In my traditions there is a lot of talk about the saving blood of Jesus
Christ. Most of me thinks that I do not deserve one tiny drop of
that blood. Vietnam makes me think that. The forgiveness that I
want my boys to know about isn't concerned with what we think
we deserve. It involves the love of a God, given to us as a gift,
regardless of what we deserve. It doesn't make sense and I am
trying to accept it. That is the hard part. If I can, maybe it will be
easier for my sons, too. I have felt the presence of what I am
convinced with all of my heart is a living, caring God who walks
with people in their deepest time of need. I want my boys to be
able to experience that for themselves.

Boys need, somehow, to know that their father was—is—a good man.

huck (with ball) and Joe

Patsy, Ellen, Kay, Chuck
March 20, 1949
Laurinburg, NC

bby, Chuck, Joe

School Days

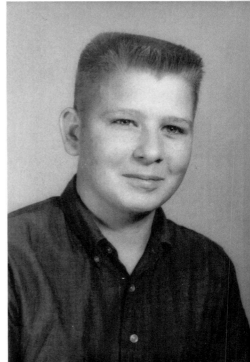

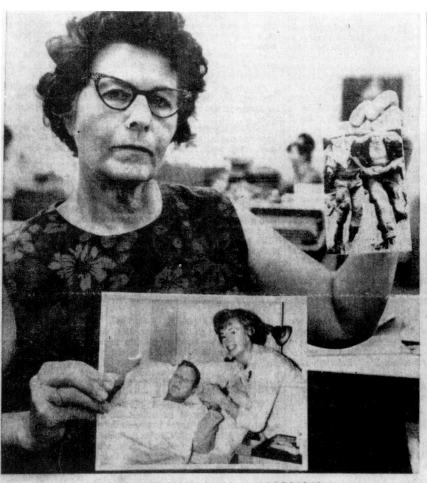

MRS. MATHERSON HOLDS PHOTOGRAPHS
Wounded GI (Right), Recuperating, Bottom Photo

Mom Hopes News Photo
Isn't Of Son In Vietnam

A mother's horror.

A short-timer's bunker at Can Tho.

My "fortress" on the Can Tho runway before the Tet offensive.